The Qur'ān

The Qur'ān: An Introduction

ANNA M. GADE

ONEWORLD
OXFORD

A Oneworld Book

Published by Oneworld Publications 2010

A CIP record for this title is available
from the British Library

ISBN 978–1–85168–704–6 (Hbk)
ISBN 978–1–85168–694–0 (Pbk)

Typeset by Jayvee, Trivandrum, India
Cover design by Design Deluxe
Printed and bound in India for Imprint Digital

Oneworld Publications
UK: 185 Banbury Road, Oxford, OX2 7AR, England
USA: 38 Greene Street, 4th Floor, New York, NY 10013, USA
www.oneworld-publications.com

CONTENTS

Foreword vii

Acknowledgments viii

Illustrations ix

Notes on the Text x

Introduction xii

1. The Written Qur'ān 1
2. The Multifaceted Qur'ān 7
3. Readings of the Qur'ān 56
4. The Qur'ān's Guidance 109
5. The Present Qur'ān 160
6. Space, Time, and the Boundaries of Knowledge 217

Conclusion 268

Glossary 271

Bibliography 277

List of Verses Cited 293

Index 297

FOREWORD

The Qur'ān stands at the very heart of the Islamic tradition. It is both scripture and the direct means of access to the Divine for Muslims. Yet far too often, many readers have had a hard time approaching the Qur'ān, or grasping its real significance for Muslims. This is not so much because of the Qur'ān itself, but rather due to the perplexing ways in which the Qur'ān is introduced to wide audiences. Many "introduction to the Qur'ān" textbooks have fallen into the trap of presenting the Qur'ān as a fossil, a relic, a dead text mired in a medieval world of debates, and thus rendering the Qur'ān incomprehensible to a contemporary age. The present work avoids that trap, and conveys the vitality and freshness of the Divine text in a highly engaging format.

A scripture is never a scripture in a vacuum. Every scripture is scripture to some community. In fact, aside from the question of Divine inspiration or revelation, what makes a text scripture is the way in which a community comes to interact with that text. And this is the crux of how Professor Anna M. Gade approaches the Qur'ān, by examining Muslims' interaction with the sacred text.

Anna Gade breaks new ground by approaching the Qur'ān in light of contemporary insights of religious studies. She probes the myriad ways in which Muslims have engaged the Qur'ān to present a living and dynamic text that is read, embodied, ritualized, memorized, internalized, and yes, contested by Muslims. The Qur'ān here is one that is not a dead fossil, but rather the living subject of calligraphy, memorization rituals, interpretative debates, and the inspiration of Muslim feminists.

Gade's valuable contribution is the third volume in the *Foundations of Islam* series, alongside Mohammad Hashim Kamali's *Shari'ah Law: An Introduction*, and Jonathan Brown's *Hadith: Muhammad's Legacy in the Medieval and Modern World*.

Omid Safi
Series Editor for Foundations of Islam

ACKNOWLEDGMENTS

Thanks to Paul R. Powers for discussion related to Chapter 4. I would also like to express my gratitude to my teacher, Leila Adam, and also to Rehanna Ali, Robin Aronson, H. Hasan Basri, Farid Esack, R. Michael Feener, Kenneth M. George, Sadia Hameed, Marcia Hermansen, Marion Katz, Michael Kodysz for graphic design, Susan Lloyd McGarry and the Harvard Image Bank, Ira Putuhena, Nur Saktiningrum, Kristin Zahra Sands, Laury Silvers, an anonymous reader for extremely helpful comments on the first draft of the manuscript, and the Series Editor of *Foundations of Islam*, Omid Safi. I am grateful to Professor Emeritus A. D. Pirous for his kind permission to print the reproduction of his painting of Sūrat Al-Ikhlāṣ. I would like to say thank you to Arthur Buehler, Paul Morris, and the rest of faculty and staff in Religious Studies at Victoria University of Wellington, New Zealand, for warm support. I am always grateful to my teachers from the Divinity School and Near Eastern Studies at the University of Chicago, including Frederick Denny, Fred Donner, and Wadad Kadi. I would like to thank Jill Morris, the manuscript's expert editor, and also the outstanding team at Oneworld Publications, for all their generous help and assistance. Finally, thanks go to former students who were at Oberlin around September 2001, like Aaliyah, Alison, Avi, Barya, Charlie, Dan, Evan, Guy, Jena, Jesse, Kate/Catherine, Kyla, Laura, Lina, Mariko, Sarah, Shahana, and Zainab.

Original material on contemporary memorization handbooks analyzed in Chapter 5 was obtained in Makassar, Indonesia, in 2009 under a faculty research grant from Victoria University of Wellington. Some material that appears in Chapter 5 is also adapted from the book *Perfection Makes Practice: Learning, Emotion and the Recited Qur'ān in Indonesia* (Honolulu: University of Hawai'i Press, 2004).

ILLUSTRATIONS AND TABLES

Figure 1	Al-Fātihah in "*ta'liq*" calligraphic style. Rendered after practice example in the textbook, *Kaidah Menulis dan Karya-Karya Master Kaligraphi Islam* by Ali Akbar (Jakarta, Pustaka Firdaus, 1995), p. 111. Rendering assisted by Michael Kodysz.	69
Figure 2	The Ka'bah in Mecca. Photo by S. M. Amin/Saudi Aramco World/SAWDIA. Used with permission.	192
Figure 3	Embroidering the *Kiswah* for the Ka'bah in Mecca. Photo by S. M. Amin/Saudi Aramco World/SAWDIA. Used with permission.	192
Figure 4	"Ayat Al-Kursi" (37.5 × 24.5 cm, 1996, glitter and glue on velveteen), Java, Indonesia. Photographic image design by Michael Kodysz. Photo by author.	194
Figure 5	Illuminated Qur'ān manuscript (showing Al-Fātiḥah, 19th–20th century), Aceh, Sumatra, Indonesia. Photo by author.	194
Figure 6	A.D. Pirous, "Al-Ikhlas '89 / Surah 112, Al-Ikhlas" (55 × 60 cm, 1989, marble paste, acrylic on canvas). Presented with permission of the artist. Photo courtesy of Kenneth M. George; image has been enhanced for contrast. Used with permission.	196
Figure 7	Competition in Calligraphy ("Khatt Al-Qur'an"), National Competition for the Recitation of the Qur'an, Sumatra, Indonesia, 1996. Photo by author.	212
Table 1	"Abbreviated Letters" in the Qur'ān	85
Table 2	Ninety-nine "Most Beautiful Names" of God	204–205

NOTES ON THE TEXT

The English meanings of Qur'ānic verses cited here are taken from Majid Fakhry's translation, *An Interpretation of the Qur'an: English Translation of the Meanings, A Bilingual Edition* (New York: New York University Press, 2002). This text has been selected from among many good available translations for reasons that are pedagogical. At the time of this writing, this affordable edition is readily available. It is also one of the few that includes the Arabic text clearly and legibly, paired with a straightforward presentation of English meanings that are easy to scan visually verse by verse. At points, I have adapted Fakhry's original English wording slightly for the sake of readability, such as to make a more standard word choice or spelling for North American readers, and I have also changed language in order to be gender inclusive; in addition, I have also reduced instances of the capitalization of nouns. The publishers Ithaca Press and Garnet Publishing have granted kind permission for the quotation of all of the Qur'ānic material that is based on this source to appear throughout the present work.

Throughout this book, I have tried to quote textual excerpts as complete verses (*āyah*s) rather than only partial verses. In citing Qur'ānic statements, I have also attempted to give as much information on verses' textual context as possible, as well as to indicate connections among the various examples that are provided. Following convention, dates are according to the Christian calendar, or the "Common Era" (C.E.). In order to give introductory academic students what I have found to be the most straightforward format for reference with respect to learning to become familiar with using the text, Qur'ān citations are made first by *sūrah* number, then chapter name in transliterated Arabic, followed by *āyah* number(s).

INTRODUCTION

This book introduces the study of the Qur'ān. It presents to readers, Muslim and non-Muslim, many sorts of authoritative Muslim approaches to reading the Qur'ān. These are all applied to the same "multifaceted" text, through standard Islamic religious principles and methods. The Qur'ān itself is the shared basis of this diversity, the kernel of a stunning depth and breadth for Muslim religious lifeworlds across space and time. The book's examples provide a groundwork in order to consider how the Qur'ān may be understood by plural and global Muslim communities, past and present. This represents an effort of "translation," intended to relate diverse Qur'ānic worlds to one another, and also to explain these in terms of the academic frameworks that are appropriate for a university classroom.

The book's main objectives are three. The first is to support students' familiarity and confidence in reading the text. Many English-speaking students who wish to "read the Qur'ān" as an academic or personal project are confounded as to how first to approach the book. Each chapter in this Introduction considers case studies and passages of text with some depth, allowing the reader to work in a manageable way with actual Qur'ānic material. Textual examples have been chosen with consistency in order to develop an appreciation the Qur'ān's uniquely refracting structure and style. This can equip students to recognize the interrelation of types of rhetoric and content in the Qur'ān; these are precisely the relationships that Muslims have long held as unique and affecting features of Qur'ānic structure and style. The book attempts to guide readers to appreciate how law, narrative, description, parables, and other content weave together throughout the Qur'ān.

A second objective of the present work is to encourage students to understand Muslims' questions, and answers, about the Qur'ān. This means apprehending shared assumptions and ideals from Muslim conversations and practices, cast in terms of the many forms that are encountered in any setting that Islam has touched. To this end, this introductory work presents an overview of the mainstream traditions of Qur'ānic study and practice that are integrated into Qur'ānic traditions. This includes some of the key terms and concepts that are basic to the varied traditional Muslim approaches to the text, including spirituality and law. Absorbing some of the technical terminology of Qur'ānic study and piety allows readers to move forward with a conceptual foundation for understanding global Muslim viewpoints.

Third, significant sections of this work are shaped in expectation of the questions most often posed by students in the religious studies classroom. These questions naturally are framed outside traditional Qur'ānic assumptions and approaches to the text; the questions themselves in fact represent the learner's effort to bridge a gap of difference. Addressing this educative process has been the greatest challenge in writing the book. As an author, I have tried to anticipate themes that are common to such questions (such as gender and conflict), and to present relevant Qur'ānic material. At the same time, it has been crucial to avoid distorting an overall translation of the sense of the Qur'ānic message within the actual readings of Muslim traditions. Following this pedagogical rationale, an entire chapter of this book is dedicated to themes of cosmology and eschatology. This is also often difficult material for students in Muslim-minority contexts to understand, while it also represents one of the Qur'ān's primary themes.

The book is based on over ten years of experience teaching a course on the Qur'ān, first offered in the Near Eastern Studies and Religious Studies Programs at Cornell University in 1998, and then as an annual "core" course in the Religion Department of Oberlin College in Ohio, U.S.A., for many years after that. Its writing reflects many past trials, and errors, standing at the front of an undergraduate class. It is based on the original academic syllabus, developed at a time when courses on the Qur'ān were still rare, if not absent, from the religious studies classrooms of North America.

The structure of the book is as follows: introduction to the material text and its themes, including principles of historicity; social and intellectual receptions, representations and "readings" of the Qur'ān; traditions of law, ethics, and Qur'ānic responses to social change in the past and the present; aesthetics, practice, and piety; and expressions of divinity, the created world and worlds to come. The final chapter of the book guides readers to read actively rather lengthy sections of actual *sūrah*s (chapters) of the Qur'ān, highlighting Sūrat Al-Kahf, the *sūrah* of "The Cave." I hope that this may serve as an invitation to some readers who have not had the opportunity actually to read any portion of the text of the Qur'ān now to begin.

Secondary material and non-Qur'ānic examples have been selected with the past experience of teaching in the English-language classroom in mind. Many of these materials are readily available in North America, such as the work of Michael Sells that presents the shortest *sūrah*s of the Qur'ān along with an accompanying compact disc sound recording. I have tried as much as possible to cite from primary texts that may be accessed at the present time in affordable English-language translations, such as the *Risālah* of Al-Shāfi'ī, so that interested students may begin to deepen their study right away. In an academic setting, materials like these could even be used as study companions to this book, and I have included a short list of suggested reading for each of this book's chapters. The other books in the series by Oneworld Publications, *Foundations of Islam*, are natural complements to the present introduction as well.

I am sincerely grateful for the privilege of this authorship. For my own limitations as an author, I ask for readers' understanding in advance. My academic field is the history of religions (religious studies) and, more specifically, the study of lived worlds of religion in Muslim Southeast Asia (especially Indonesia, Malaysia, and Cambodia, which is a Buddhist-majority country). Asia is the region in which the vast majority of the world's Muslims reside today. In writing Chapters 5 and 6, which consider the impact of the Qur'ān in lived religious experience, I have self-consciously selected examples from Indonesia, which is the world's most populous Muslim-majority nation. This is in order to provide a coherent cluster of material from a single global setting, and to give depth to the description of Muslim lifeworlds. In addition, material on Muslim social and cultural experience in Indonesia is comparatively accessible in the English language for further study, starting with the foundational works in cultural anthropology by Clifford Geertz.

My intentions in attempting the task of presenting this Introduction have been, first, to support global learning and appreciation of human diversities, Muslim and otherwise; and, second, to try to convey insight into the power, beauty, and scholarly tradition of a text that, as the Qur'ān itself claims, moves people to laugh, weep, reflect, and to change. I hope that for these ends it may have some benefit. At key points in writing this book I have highlighted a question that is only now beginning to be put forward as the urgent theological problem of our time. Personally, I believe that the Qur'ān offers profound guidance on this question from a perspective that is Islamically "green": how may human communities take responsibility for sustaining the resources of Allāh's creation under conditions of environmental and ecological degradation? And God knows best.

1

THE WRITTEN QUR'ĀN

To begin to read the Qur'ān actively means first to encounter the book as a material or visual object. An edition of a printed Qur'ān, always in Arabic, is called a *muṣḥaf.* A book of which more than half is not the Arabic Qur'ān (a "translation," for example) is not considered by Muslims to be an actual *muṣḥaf* of the Qur'ān. (Electronic media are not considered under this framework, which is traditional.) The Qur'ān contains 114 chapters, each called a *sūrah*. Editions of the Qur'ān provide standard information about a *sūrah* within its printed heading. This includes the name of the *sūrah*, a term which is usually derived from a key word that appears in the first few lines of the chapter. These Arabic names may differ for the very same *sūrah*. For example, *sūrah* number 96 is sometimes called "Sūrat Al-'Alaq" ("The Clot," from an Arabic word at the end of the first verse) or, alternatively, "Sūrat Iqrā'" ("Read!," from the first word in the first verse after the opening formula). The titles of *sūrah*s do not indicate what is the thematic content of the chapter to follow; for example, reading Sūrah 4, Al-Nisā' ("The Women"), would not yield everything that the Qur'ān has to say on the topic of women and gender. The entire book contains over 6,230 verses, each called an *āyah* (singular) or *āyāt* (plural). *Āyah* endings are marked in the written text with the corresponding verse number.

In traditional Islamic education, the numbers of the *sūrah*s are generally not used for identification. Nevertheless, a numerical ordering may still be the best reference for readers new to the Qur'ān in academic settings. This is for at least two reasons. First, non-Arabic designations are not used, nor often even known, in Muslim religious contexts, whether English speaking or not. Second, students who are not at all familiar with the original Arabic titles often find it difficult to use translated names for the *sūrah*s without the aid of some indexical system. This is because translations of the names of *sūrah*s can differ a great deal, even just in one language such as English, with no one designation clearly more accurate or precise than another.

For example, variant English translations of the title of Sūrah 90, Al-Balad, convey different primary meanings, and with them different moods. A number of contemporary renderings of the Qur'ān yield a possible range of titles for this chapter: "The City" (this is the most common translation), "The Countryside," "The Earth," "The Ground," "The Land," "The Soil," and "The Town." This wide semantic range reflects varying translations of the word "*balad*." It also reveals differing assumptions about the generality of specificity of the term in its textual context. Is "the city" a generic or even a universal space? Or, alternatively, is it to be understood specifically to be the city of Mecca (from which the Prophet Muḥammad originated)? Understanding such "multifaceted" dimensions of Qur'ānic words and expressions presents a challenge to anyone who engages an interpretation of the meanings of the Qur'ān into another language system. It may become a practical consideration for new students who might not even realize at the very start that the *sūrah* named "The Countryside" in one edition is in fact exactly the same as "The City" in the next edition. Both are English-language renditions of the same Arabic *sūrah* that is called "Al-Balad."

Underneath the Arabic name of the *sūrah*, but still within the chapter's heading, copies of the printed Qur'ān usually designate the number of *āyah*s, or verses, that are included within that particular chapter. With this there is also usually an indication of whether most of the content was understood to have been revealed at the time when the Prophet Muḥammad was in his home city of Mecca (this material is called *Makkī*, "Meccan") or later, after he had emigrated to the city known as Medina (verses said to be *Madanī*, "Medinan"). A flexible rule of thumb is that there are eighty-eight Meccan and twenty-six Medinan *sūrah*s in the Qur'ān. The "Basmalah," that is, the formula "In the name of God the Beneficent the Merciful" (*Bismillāh Al-Raḥmān Al-Raḥīm*) starts every *sūrah* except for one (9, Al-Tawbah).[1] The Basmalah is also recited at the start of any act of recitation of the Qur'ān, no matter where one begins in the text. It is also and commonly uttered before beginning everyday acts like eating, drinking, or boarding any means of transport.

The written text of the Qur'ān is comprised not only of its words, which are grouped as *āyah*s and *sūrah*s (verses and chapters). Written copies of the text also include cues and direction about its reading and recitation. Some markings indicate how to pronounce the Arabic sounds according to accepted variant "readings" or vocalizations. Other signs direct recitation in terms of desirable and permissible stops and starts in phrasing. These guidelines assist readers and reciters with the choices they need constantly to make in voicing the Qur'ān aloud and, by extension, in hearing and interpreting the voiced text. There are no marks for melody types in cantillation, however; pitch change is always improvised.

Such markings indicate how closely Qur'ānic text and voice are linked. Performance is a primary mode by which the Qur'ān impacts its readers and listeners in any immediate present. For example, at over ten points in the Qur'ān, when reading comes to the point in the text at which it is mentioned that God's servants bow down before their Lord, it is considered obligatory to perform a prostration (in the condition of ritual purity) when reciting the text or hearing it recited. An example of this is the verse 41 Fuṣṣilat 37. This *sūrah*, Fuṣṣilat, is also known as "*Ḥā Mīm* Al-Sajdah." The alternative title connotes the chapter's beginning with the unexplained "abbreviated" letters, "*Ḥā Mīm*," and also the act of prostration to be performed during its recitation (the "*sajdah*"). The verse reads: "Of His signs [*wamin āyātihi*] are the night and the day, the sun and the moon. Do not prostrate yourselves to the sun or to the moon, but prostrate yourselves to Allāh Who created them, if it is He you truly worship."

Along with the standard numbering of the *sūrah*s from one to one hundred and fourteen, there are other traditional systems of sectioning the text of the Qur'ān that relate directly to its recitation and performance. The Qur'ān itself refers to its own sectioning for the purpose of reading, for example, in 17 Al-Isrā' 106, "It is a Qur'ān which We [God] have divided into parts that you may recite it with deliberation, and We revealed it in stages." Of the standard partitions of the text into equal parts for reading, the one most often used for study and practice is the division of the text into thirty equal sections, each called a "*juz'*." Each *juz'* is further divided into two halves, each of these called a *ḥizb*. Notation in the margins of printed Qur'āns indicates the beginning of a new *juz'* section. The final *juz'* of the Qur'ān is called "*Juz' 'Ammā*" because the first word of the *juz'* is "*'ammā*", which happens to be the first word of a rhetorical question that opens the section. It appears at the beginning of a *sūrah*, 78 Al-Nabā':

Bismillāh Al-Raḥmān Al-Raḥīm

1. What [*'ammā*] are they asking each other about?
2. About the great tidings [*al-nabā'i al-'aẓīm*]
3. Concerning which they are disputing. (78 Al-Nabā' 1–3)

Material from the final thirtieth of the Qur'ān, "*Juz' 'Ammā*," is commonly selected by Muslims to be recited during daily required prayers. It contains the first *sūrah*s Muslim girls and boys tend to memorize as children, and largely for this purpose, since some recitation of the Qur'ān is required in every enactment of daily canonical prayer (*ṣalāt*).

The division of the entire Qur'ān into thirty parts allows for the sectioning of the text for the purpose of completing a full reading over the course of a month, such as during the holy month of Ramaḍān. This is the month in which Muslims observe extra prayers at night, called "*tarwiḥ*." During these prayers, which are punctuated by prostration, lengthy sections of the Qur'ān are read aloud by the *imām* (prayer leader). This is so that the entire Qur'ān is read over the course of the lunar month before its final days. A basic meaning of the word "*tarwīḥ*" connotes being "winded" or out of breath, as an *imām* would be when reciting an entire *juz'* aloud for a congregation during a night's prayer during Ramaḍān. In addition, the division of the text into thirty *juz'* also aids rehearsal among memorizers of the text, who can practice and repeat the Qur'ān over the course of every month. For this same purpose, memorizers may also use a division of the Qur'ān into seven equal parts for repetition of the entire text over the course of one week.

After the "opening" *sūrah*, which is called the "Fātiḥah," the chapters of the Qur'ān are arranged in roughly descending order of length; there are exceptions, however, to this general rule. The shorter Meccan *sūrah*s of *Juz' 'Ammā* thus appear at the end of the text, consistent with their generally shorter length. Although the arrangement of the Qur'ān does not follow the accepted chronology of the revelation of its verses to the Prophet Muḥammad, the "occasions of revelation" of particular verses and chapters do have an important place in the Islamic "religious sciences" of the Qur'ān. The standard interpretation of "*al-balad*" in Sūrah 90 as the city of Mecca, for example, rests on information preserved in tradition about the history of the revelation of the Qur'ān to the Prophet Muḥammad. Classical approaches teach Muslims to learn to read and interpret the Qur'ān with this specific history in mind. It is key information for determining what it is to which Muslims consider verses of the Qur'ān to refer, as well as their scope and application. This material is found the form of "*ḥadīth* reports."[2] These "traditions" about the Prophet Muḥammad became the basis for Islamic understandings of the model of the exemplary comportment of the Prophet Muḥammad (*sunnah*), an idea which became vital to traditions of Islamic law and piety.

In the Qur'ān, there is no topical organization of material that has bearing on a particular theme or subject. Nor is the Qur'ān arranged in terms of a narrative or story, as is much of the Pentateuch of the Hebrew Bible or the Gospels of the New Testament. (Only two *sūrah*s within the Qur'ān represent a single sustained narrative, 12 Yūsuf, the "most beautiful of stories" of the Prophet Joseph [Yūsuf], and 71 Nūḥ, the story of Noah.) Muslim scholars consider the unique organization of themes and content in the Qur'ān to render the presentation of material within the text, whether its stories or its law, especially powerful and persuasive. For generations, they have studied how the juxtaposition of content grabs the attention of readers and listeners, even as recursive combinations across the text continually suggest ever deeper levels of meaning.

Arrangement of material in the Qur'ān makes the impression of fractal-like, nonlinear patterns of shifting structure and style. Such principles of organization and coherence of the received text have been recognized by Muslims to support the theological claim of the Qur'ān's miraculous "inimitability." They have also led Muslims to reflect profoundly on the interrelation of parts of the text. That the "Qur'ān explains itself" has been said by classical scholars such as the influential Abū Ḥāmid Al-Ghazālī (d. 1111) to be a first rule of Qur'ānic interpretation across many sorts of Muslim religious study, and it is considered by some to be even more significant today. In traditions of pious reading, any one particular expression in the Qur'ān is also understood potentially to open up uncountable dimensions of "multifaceted" significance.

NOTES

1. Historically, it has been debated whether the formula of the Basmalah is actually the first numbered verse (*āyah*) of the Fātiḥah, which is the first, or "opening," *sūrah* (as today's editions do show it to be).
2. A *ḥadīth* report or "tradition" came to be defined in Islamic tradition as an authoritative account of the sayings, actions, or tacit approvals or disapprovals of the Prophet Muḥammad. A "sound" *ḥadīth* is "supported" by an unbroken and reliable chain of oral transmission traced back to the generation of the companions of the Prophet Muḥammad.

2

THE MULTIFACETED QUR'ĀN

Qur'ānic expression is said to be *dhū wujūh*, an Arabic phrase that means "multifaceted" (literally, "having faces"). In classical sources, this expression refers to the multivalent meanings of particular words and phrases in the Qur'ān. An example of this would be the ways in which the morphology (structure) of the Arabic language allows for many different words to be derived from a single "root" form. The very title for the text, "Qur'ān," is itself an example of a multifaceted expression.

Many names for the Qur'ān appear within the Qur'ān. These include the actual word "Qur'ān." The Arabic word "*qur'ān*" is usually said to be a derived form of the Arabic root "*q, r, '*", where the final character is the Arabic letter *hamzah*. This three-part root denotes "reading" or "recitation," as in the word, "*iqrā',*" the command to "read" that opens *sūrah* 96. There are many self-references to "the Qur'ān" within the book itself, which is a highly self-referential text overall. The Qur'ān, for example, calls itself a form of scripture or writing as a "*Kitāb*" or "Book." This latter term is a material counterpart to the oral and aural medium of its "recitation." The scriptural concept connects the Qur'ān to the idea of previous revelations that were sent to former prophets, which the Qur'ān also calls "books." Other terms for the Qur'ān within the Qur'ān, such as "guidance," "reminder," and "light," emphasize differing facets of the "meaning" of the term and experience "Qur'ān." In addition, the Qur'ān refers to itself by many other terms as well, including a "revelation" (*tanzīl*) and a "reminder" (*dhikr*). Other common self-references are "light" (*nūr*), "proof" (*burhān*), and "criterion" (*furqān*), and longer expressions such as "fairest discourse" (*aḥsan al-ḥadīth*). In 10 Yūnus 57, the Qur'ān offers several terms for itself within one single utterance: "O humankind, there has come to you from your Lord an admonition [*mu'iẓah*], a healing [*shifā'*] for what is in the hearts, and a guidance [*hudā*] and mercy [*raḥmah*] for the believers."[1]

The Qur'ān identifies itself explicitly as an "Arabic" reading many times. Arabic, a Semitic language, is related to Hebrew. Qur'ānic Arabic is not exactly the same as the everyday vernacular dialects that are heard in most parts of the Arabic-speaking world today. However, Qur'ānic Arabic, or *fuṣḥā*, is much like "modern standard" Arabic, the more formal register that is heard in broadcast and public communication across the Arabic-speaking world. Mastery of *fuṣḥā* has long been the mark of education and "eloquence" in Arabic language systems, the latter being a basic meaning of the Arabic term itself. This is the form of the Arabic language that four out of five Muslims, as non-native Arabic speakers, would study from the very basics for religious purposes. Qur'ānic Arabic is understood to be the dialect that was used by the Prophet Muḥammad, one of several that was said to have been spoken on the Arabian peninsula in his era (of the early seventh century C.E.).

The very notion of its "Arabic" expression is a facet of the Qur'ān's own self-presentation. In the Qur'ān, the mention of the Arabic language is linked to the text's clarity and, somewhat paradoxically (given, for example, that at the time of its revelation its dialect was one of many), its universality. In many instances in the text itself, the idea that the Qur'ān is an Arabic discourse conveys its lucidity, accessibility, and comprehensibility. An example is the following verse (*āyah*), emphasizing the "clarity" of Qur'ānic Arabic:

> And We [Allāh] surely know what they say: "Surely a mortal teaches him [the Prophet Muḥammad]." The tongue of him to whom they allude is foreign, whereas this is a clear Arabic tongue. (16 Al-Naḥl 103)

Other verses of the Qur'ān relate the idea of Arabic to "understanding," such as 43 Al-Zukhruf 3, "We have made it an Arabic Qur'ān that perchance you may understand." The introduction to another *sūrah*, 12 Yūsuf 1–2, expresses a similar idea:

> *Bismillāh Al-Raḥmān Al-Raḥīm*
> 1. *Ālif Lām Rā*. These are the verses of the clear Book [*al-kitāb al-mubīn*].
> 2. We have revealed it as an Arabic Qur'ān [*qur'ānan 'arabiyyan*], that perchance you may understand." (12 Yūsuf 1–2)

The idea of the "Arabic" Qur'ān also relates to the text's presentation of the specificity and generality of the very message which is to be "understood":

> Had We made it a foreign Qur'ān [*qur'ānan a'jamiyan*], they would have said: "If only its verses were well expounded!" What, whether foreign or Arabic, say: "It is for the believers a guidance and a healing; but for those who do not believe, it is a heaviness in their ears, and for them it is a blindness. It is as if, those were called from a distant place." (41 Fuṣṣilat 44)

In this verse, the Qur'ān has provided a rationale for its own language, expressed in terms of a hypothetical alternative ("a foreign Qur'ān"). The statement then affirms both the Qur'ān's Arabic nature and also the universal accessibility of the message overall. Here, religious truth is claimed either to be accepted or not based primarily on the listener's inner capacity to affirm it, rather than its intelligible expression within a particular language system.

As the "speech of God" (*kalām Allāh*), all of the Qur'ān is understood from a religious perspective to be the narration of God's voice, even as it is expressed audibly by the voices of believers during its recitation. The actual "words" (*kalimāt*) of the Qur'ān itself, however, are rendered by many textual voices, by myriad figures and in various forms of speech. The "voice" depicted within the Qur'ān is God's, but the rhetorical style of the Qur'ān, expressed through its many internal speakers and forms of speech, is not stable. Expression constantly shifts in structure, style, and in deictic category. That is to say, even when a statement is rendered in Allāh's own voice, the first person plural of divine locution ("We") may shift unexpectedly into a more intimate voice of the deity in the first person ("I"). Such instances of shifts in register often occur at dramatic instants, in a poetics of rupture and surprise that is formally recognized and analyzed in classical Muslim tradition.

The form of some types of Qur'ānic "voices" signal the kind of message they themselves express. For example, a direct address to the Prophet Muḥammad or believers begins many verses of the Qur'ān. This indicates that theological or instructional content follows. For example, some verses begin with the command "Say:" (*Qul*); these cases represent a divine command that is dictated for repetition by the voice of the Prophet, and also by those who follow him. In many cases, figures and in fact entire classes of beings in the Qur'ān are described not primarily by what they think or what do, but rather by what they say and how they talk. Syntactic voices of believers, unbelievers, and hypocrites may illustrate the speakers' characters in this way, and it follows that in such cases, first-person statement may function as a moral identification. These and many other rhetorical modes in the Qur'ān are all considered aspects of "God's speech" in the text within the classical fields of Qur'ānic study.

Multivocal expression characterizes Qur'ānic locution overall. When Qur'ānic structure and style is considered as a complete phenomenon, as most religious sciences attempt to see it to be, its mathematical aesthetics is "*dhū wujūh*." Kaleidoscopic arrangement branches into exquisite referential structures that extend in new directions even as they continually mirror one another. These patterns are recursive, not iterative; they are dynamic, not static; they are not "one-to-one" but instead they are "multifaceted." Over time and under many repetitions, such correspondences form expectations and connections that in turn will come to shape each and every hearing of the Qur'ān. Many Muslims have developed an elaborate, habitual, intimate sense of the text that comes not from formal study but rather from the depth of the experience of having heard and read the Qur'ān many times and in many contexts.

Muslims accept the Qur'ān to be revelation from God that was "sent down" to the Prophet Muḥammad over a period of twenty-two solar years (610–632), which corresponds to a period of approximately twenty-three years by the Islamic lunar calendar. According to Muslim history of the Qur'ān, these revelations were fragmentary at first, and were later compiled after the Prophet had passed away. Some verses are viewed to have specific content addressing the Muslim community at the time of the Prophet Muḥammad, while others are recognized to have more general scope. Muslims understand the Qur'ān to be "multifaceted" in the modes by which it speaks simultaneously to the specific experience of the Prophet Muḥammad and his historical community; and, by extension, it speaks to all Muslims who follow them; and, more universally, it is believed to provide a message for humanity and other classes of created beings in the phenomenal world, seen and unseen. These Qur'ānic frameworks, and the analogical relation between them on "general and specific" levels, are essential principles of religious sciences from textual interpretation (*tafsīr*) to jurisprudence (*fiqh*) to theology (*kalām*).

This chapter presents two principal facets of the overall message of the Qur'ān. The first dimension relates to accepted understandings of the historicity of the text. The presentation of this material loosely follows an Islamic classical genre called *sīrah* (the biography of the Prophet Muḥammad). For the purposes of this Introduction, this functions also as a "historical background" for the reader who would otherwise be unfamiliar with Muslim accounts of the context of the revelation of the Qur'ān. However, with the rigorous Islamic study of the Qur'ān, "historical background" is more than a fixed scene; it is also an active hermeneutical principle. Religious readers of the Qur'ān value Muslim knowledge of the history of the revelation of the text as a key to its ongoing reading, and for the application of its guidance to ever-changing circumstances.

Second, an overview of some Qur'ānic "themes" follows as the second part of this chapter. These represent what Muslims view to be universal facets of the text's meanings. Muslim scholars have developed many frameworks for analyzing various types of thematic and theological content in the Qur'ān. What are said to be canonical "beliefs" of Islam in this book inspire a presentation of the Qur'ān's "major themes." The Qur'ān's content is therefore grouped here in terms of main fields of topical material, such as: God and His divinity; beings He created, such as angels, *jinn* and humankind, with the latter including the prophets who received revelation; eschatology, or the "last things"; and legal and theological elements, such as the question, do people determine their actions and/or does God? Any careful reader of the Qur'ān, no matter what is his or her attitude or faith orientation, will perceive these themes in overlapping patterns of ever-shifting, "multifaceted" meaning and experience.

FORMATIVE HISTORIOGRAPHY

Reports concerning the historical conditions and particular circumstances of the revelation of verses of the Qur'ān are a foundation for

Muslims' readings of the text. They also provide information for students who begin to read the Qur'ān academically with which to start to appreciate how the same text may be read authoritatively by Muslims in diverse ways. The context of revelation, as Muslims understand it, is integral to the meanings of the text, even though this key contextualizing information is not actually narrated as a part of the text. In other words, Muslim religious history is a presumed framework that determines the reception of the meaning of the Qur'ān's verses and its many oblique references. Developing awareness of this temporal system is a crucial first step for any student who is new to the academic study of the Qur'ān and its intellectual systems.

The principle of time shapes how Muslims, and others, have received and interpreted the Qur'ān. An example is the foundational categories "Meccan and Medinan." These designations, while overtly pertaining to place (the cities Mecca and Medina), in the Muslim "Qur'ānic sciences" instead refer principally to the time of revelation. In particular, they indicate whether a verse or chapter in question was understood to have been revealed before or after the event of the Hijrah, or "Emigration" of the Prophet and the Muslim community from Mecca to Medina in 622 C.E. Beyond this, these temporal labels may also be used to discern properties of Qur'ānic language and style, in both classical Islamic religious sciences as well as in more recent European academic tradition. For example, verses that begin with the formula addressing listeners "O you who believe" (*yā ayyūha alladhīna āmanū*) are taken to be "Medinan" because verses in that style are all reckoned to date to a later period in the history of the first Muslim community. Ideationally, some modern Muslim approaches have constructed "Meccan" and "Medinan" as hermeneutical principles in order to analyze what are considered to be the "universal" and "contextual" dimensions of ethical and theological injunction. Understanding temporal categories of the Muslim Qur'ānic sciences, whether as idea types, rhetorical styles, legal categories, or historical times and places, requires knowledge of how Muslims have understood the Qur'ānic text to relate to its accepted chronology of revelation in the course of the historical experience of the Prophet Muḥammad.

The intertextual relation of the history of the first Muslim community (and, specifically, the biography of the Prophet Muḥammad) to the actual text of the Qur'ān occurs through at least three modes in Muslim religious thought. First, historical experience is understood to be a context for the Qur'ān's revelation from the perspective of universal Muslim sacred history. Muslim religious historiography starts with creation of the first person, the prophet Ādam. The event of the revelation of the Qur'ān is part of one of the stories of the prophets who came after him, namely Muḥammad, the last Prophet. Second, much Qur'ānic content is understood to refer directly to the specific historical experience of the community of the Prophet Muḥammad. For example, there are figures who are not named in the Qur'ān but whose specific identities are nevertheless said to be known to Muslims through the history of the first Muslim community. Third, history, context, and change are in themselves all fundamental principles for interpreting the text. This is especially relevant for matters of law, such as with the accepted "abrogation" of the application of legal rulings that nevertheless still remain preserved within the revealed text. (This final, critical point can be missed initially by students who first approach the Qur'ān with questions about its legal directives and their significance in Muslim lives.) Within each of these modes for understanding the Muslim sacred past, the "historical background" of the revelation of the Qur'ān determines how the meanings of the text are received and understood within the religious present.

Historians working within the European academic tradition have asked related, but at times also fundamentally different, sorts of questions about the Qur'ānic text and its historical contexts. The historians and philologists of the Qur'ān generally known as "orientalists" include the German scholar Theodor Nöldeke (1836–1930) and others who came after him. One of their primary interests relating to the Qur'ān was to determine the chronology and dating of manuscripts. In general, these documentary historians of Europe were less interested in learning about the ways in which intertextuality is applied and experienced within robust traditions of Islamic intellectual and religious sciences. Many in the "orientalist" tradition of the colonial era, and even after, were also unappreciative of the Qur'ān as a heartfelt, pious, and performative human tradition.

Since the heyday of this circle of scholars, who enjoyed great global influence, modern historical questions about the origins of the Qur'ān have been approached with rigor by those with religious as well as non-religious inclinations, in European and other global languages. Since these historians may be Muslim or non-Muslim, and may reside anywhere in the world, methodological matters related to history should be viewed primarily as matters of academic discipline and approach. It is now considered an outdated framework to correlate them with named faith communities or to the now-hybrid frameworks, "east" and "west."

The approach taken in this chapter is not restricted to a documentary approach to the origins of the Qur'ān as represented by the tradition of Nöldeke. Instead, it follows more widely the streams of what have become the mainstream Muslim accounts for presenting the history of the Qur'ān. The reasons for this are formally disciplinary and methodological; academically, they do not reflect a preference for Muslim truth claims as such over any others' claim to the "truth." Material is framed here in terms of widespread Muslim sources because this book's approach follows the discipline of religious studies (rather than history, theology, or another academic field).[2] The "history of religions," a field of study open to anyone irrespective of faith commitment or lack thereof, describes the phenomena of lived religious communities in order to explain, often through comparison, their human diversity. This requires studying voices found in Muslim traditions in order to understand Muslim systems. For this academic purpose, even the work of secular historians themselves could be considered primary data, insofar as they occasionally provide a contrast or context for Muslim truth claims within wider discourses of "orientalism" (that imagines the Muslim "East") and its counterpart, "occidentalism" (an imaginary that presumes to know the non-Muslim "West"). In addition, and secondarily to this, in most cases there is in fact sound historical basis for accepting the historiographical accounts that have originated in Muslim traditions.[3]

Following the methodological and disciplinary approach established in the history of religions, this text refers to the Qur'ān as "revelation," as attested by Muslims. This is not put forward as either a historical or theological assertion. Instead, it is an attempt to be descriptively accurate in terms of the perspectives of Islamic tradition and the statements Muslims make about the Qur'ān itself, which are here the principal objects of academic study. The method and approach of the history of religions reports such claims, while at the same time it performs a phenomenological "*epoché*" or "bracketing" of their truth value for the sake of analyzing their presentation and reception in living religious traditions. To adopt this sort of approach academically actually means neither affirming unverifiable truth claims nor denying them; it simply means that the facts of the "phenomenon" are reported accurately and with attribution.[4] *Everyone* agrees that *Muslims* consider the Qur'ān to be revelation from God; thus, generalizing statements that appear in the form "Muslims accept the Qur'ān to be the Word of God" are necessary information for contextual analysis and explanation of the diverse ideas Muslims have held. Outside the classroom, or any other setting for the study of religions, the deeper knowledge about human religious difference gained through this academic project may further be applied in any way, whether principled or not.

One must know the standard account of the early community as Muslims know it in order to understand Muslim conversations about the Qur'ān. It is difficult even to carry out a first casual reading of an English-language interpretation without having some prior awareness of the religious hermeneutics (interpretation) of the text as accepted by Muslims. For example, while documentary historians would not accept the "night journey and ascent" of the Prophet as an actual event, understanding the significance and impact of this "true story" within religious systems would be basic to an understanding of Muslim readings of the text. In addition, the account of this important episode is foundational to Islamic ideas of prophecy in general and the traditions of the veneration of the Prophet Muḥammad in specific.

The genre of material that is known as *sīrah al-nabī* (pronounced *sīrat an-nabī*) is comprised of the standard biographies of the Prophet Muḥammad. In its skeletal form it is accepted by Muslim communities worldwide. The genre became known in the beginning of the second century of Islam, and influential versions circulated under the names Ibn Isḥāq (d. ca. 765) and Ibn Hishām (d. 833), and later Ibn Kathīr (d. 1373), all of which relied on known accounts about the Prophet Muḥammad (from *ḥadīth* "traditions") as well as material from the Qur'ān. *Sīrah* texts also shaped the development of a devotional tradition centered around the Prophet Muḥammad, which remains a core aspect of Islamic piety up to the present day.

A brief sketch of the standard religious account of the revelation of the Qur'ān follows, drawing on Muslim accounts about the life of the Prophet that are known from *sīrah*. The basic narrative below would be taught to children across the Muslim world, and would hardly be restricted to being the knowledge of the religious expert. That is to say, one could assume any Muslim who had been schooled in religion would know the story to follow.[5] This contrasts with specialist knowledge, such as the "occasions of revelation" of specific verses, which is used to carry out an advanced exercise such as the determination of principles of law from the text. In the presentation to follow, I have also included some verses of the Qur'ān in the context in which they are understood by Muslims to have been revealed, in order to offer a sense of the genre of the "occasion of revelation" of Qur'ānic verses (which is a topic for a later chapter).

THE QUR'ĀN AND THE FIRST MUSLIM COMMUNITY

According to Muslim sources, the Prophet Muḥammad came from a center of commerce and pilgrimage in Arabia that was called Mecca (Makkah). The region around the city was known for trade in goods such as leather and dates. The Prophet came from the tribe known as the Quraysh, belonging to one of its clans called the "Banū Hāshim." There was contact and mutual influence among communities of Jews, Christians, Zoroastrians, as well as pastoral nomadic Arab tribes across the region at that time. However, Arabia was also reckoned to be something of a cultural and political backwater of the wider Mediterranean and Persian worlds. Regional politics were dominated by the power of two empires, Byzantine (Greek) and Sassanian (Persian), both of which were experiencing economic upheaval at the time of the rise of Islam.

Mecca was the focus of an annual pilgrimage undertaken by the Arabian tribes of the region; it was the area of the Ka'bah, a structure for which, tradition reports, the family of the Prophet was responsible for upkeep. The Prophet Muḥammad's own grandfather, 'Abd Al-Muṭṭalib, is said to have rediscovered the well of Zamzam on the site; in other accounts of religious history that extend even further back in sacred time, this is the same source of water that was revealed to Hagar (Ḥajar) as she searched for water for her child, the prophet Ishmael (Ismā'īl) after they had been left alone in the desert by Ismā'īl's father, Abraham (Ibrāhīm). The Ka'bah itself, the great structure that is also called the "House of God" (*bait Allāh*), is said to have been rebuilt by Muḥammad himself, after having been first constructed on the site by the prophet Abraham (Ibrāhīm), according to the Qur'ān. Islamic traditions further hold that the original people,

Ādam and his spouse, were expelled from the Garden to this very same location at the time of the beginning of the world. Today, it is a central ritual focus of Muslim pilgrimage and prayer (Figure 2, p. 192).

Reference to the "Year of the Elephant" in Muslim sources would date the birth of the Prophet Muḥammad to approximately 570 C.E., reckoned to be the year of a failed military attack by a Yemeni ruler to the south. Muslim tradition recounts events in the childhood of Muḥammad, including happenings that foretold his future destiny as a prophet. The Prophet Muḥammad was said to have been orphaned when his mother, Āminah, passed away at the time that he was a boy of about six years. He then came under the care and protection of his uncle, Abū Ṭālib. Muḥammad's cousin 'Alī, the son of Abū Ṭālib, later was to become the Prophet's own son-in-law when he married the Prophet's daughter, Fāṭimah. 'Alī is the first *imām* in every Shi'ite Muslim tradition. At the age of about twenty-five, Muḥammad married a widow of means, Khadījah (mother of Fāṭimah), who was about forty years of age, according to the sources. Also at about that time, Muḥammad began to undertake a kind of meditative retreat, called *taḥannuth*, a practice which reports suggest could have had some popularity in the Arabian peninsula at the time. According to tradition, he would go up to a cave on Mount Ḥīrā' near Mecca for this purpose.

In Mecca in the year 610, according to religious history, revelation began to come down from God to the Prophet Muḥammad in the form of the first *sūrah*s of the Qur'ān, such as 96 Iqrā'. Shortly after this, according to most Muslim accounts, there was the conversion of 'Alī and Khadījah, and a follower of the Prophet named Zaid. The conversion of Abū Bakr, a figure who would be known as the first "caliph" in Sunni tradition after the Prophet Muḥammad had passed away, also occurred at the same time. In 613, as the story goes, the Prophet Muḥammad began public preaching of the Qur'ān. There was immediate opposition on the part of the established Meccans, by figures given nicknames in tradition such as "Abū Jahl" ("Father of Ignorance"). The Prophet's message in the form of the first Meccan revelations, following the standard Muslim account, would indeed have threatened the center's pilgrimage trade with a call to monotheism.

Many historical figures to whom the Qur'ān is understood to refer are not actually mentioned by name in the text. They are only identified in commentaries. A Qur'ānic exception to this referential style is the curse on "Abū Lahab" (a nickname meaning "Father of the Flame," 'Abd Al-'Uzza), an uncle of the Prophet and a notorious enemy of his cause. This reference occurs in 111 Al-Masad, an "early Meccan" *sūrah*. The words of the complete *sūrah* read as follows in translation:

Bismillāh Al-Raḥmān Al-Raḥīm

1. Perish the hands of Abū Lahab, and may he perish too
2. Neither his wealth nor what he has earned will avail him anything.
3. He will roast in a flaming fire,
4. And his wife will be a carrier of fire-wood,
5. She shall have rope of fibre around her neck. (111 Al-Masad)

According to the Muslim *sīrah* literature, during the time of the early persecution of the Muslims in Mecca, the Prophet Muḥammad still had the protection of his uncle, Abū Ṭālib. It is debated whether Abū Ṭālib ever converted to Islam, but standard accounts hold that he did not. It was also at about this time that a former enemy of Islam and the Muslims, 'Umar bin Al-Khaṭṭāb, accepted Islam. As the story goes, he embraced the faith when he heard the Qur'ān recited. Later he would be the second caliph recognized in Sunni Islam, under whose leadership there was a great geographic expansion of Muslim rule.

Those Muslims who were in the weakest social position would have been the most adversely affected in terms of treatment by the Meccans in this period. And Islam, according to accounts, had attracted many who had a low social status. Among these, for example, was Bilāl, an African slave freed by the Prophet's companion Abū Bakr; both of these men were said to be among the very first Muslims. According to the story, in about 615 there was an emigration of some Muslims to Abyssinia, a kingdom in present-day Ethiopia. In the flight to Abyssinia, Muslims without protection left Arabia to travel across the Red Sea. There are accounts (although related on a less reliable basis according to tradition) that the reigning Christian king received them warmly. According to legend, the Muslims read the "*sūrah* of Mary" (19 Maryam) to the ruler, and he wept in sympathy with his own faith and pledged his protection to them.

Times were hard for the Muslims in Mecca in this period. In 616, according to Muslim sources, there was a general boycott of the

Prophet's clan of the Banū Hāshim. Some returned from Abyssinia on a false report that the situation in Mecca had improved for the Muslims. It had not and in 619 tradition records that the conditions of the believers in Mecca had become dire. According to Muslim historiography, both Khadījah and Abū Ṭālib passed away in that year, and with them the Prophet would have lost much personal and social support. This was also a period in which it is believed that revelation stopped coming down to the Prophet for a time. Some Meccan *sūrah*s of the Qur'ān are understood to reflect the experience of this period of trial for the Prophet Muḥammad, offering him consolation and encouragement, such as the *sūrah* 94 Al-Sharḥ, which is said to be "early Meccan." Like 111 Al-Masad, it is found in the very last part of the Qur'ān, *Juz' 'Ammā*. The full *sūrah* reads as follows:

Bismilllāh Al-Raḥmān Al-Raḥīm

1. Did we not dilate your breast;
2. And lift from you your burden;
3. Which had weighed down your back?
4. Did we not exalt your name?
5. Surely, along with hardship is ease.
6. Surely, along with hardship is ease.
7. So when you have finished, toil on;
8. And unto your Lord, incline. (94 Al-Sharḥ)

This *sūrah* has a personal tone, reinforced by its probing rhetorical questions in the second person singular, understood to be addressing the Prophet directly. It also carries a poetic and emphatic repetition of phrase (verses 5 and 6), which is a characteristic feature of Meccan style. Tradition pairs this *sūrah* with the one that precedes it, 93 Al-Ḍuḥā, which is also associated with the same period in which revelation allegedly stopped coming down to the Prophet for a time, grieving him. By extension, this Qur'ānic material would speak to any human being reading the Qur'ān in a condition needing consolation.

Next in the story of the *sīrah*, Muḥammad looked outside Mecca as he sought protection and support. He approached a tribe in a neighboring settlement, but when he was rebuffed he returned to Mecca. Around 620, however, fortunes turned for the Muslims. Members of tribes from nearby Yathrib, a trading center that lay about 250 miles to the north, had come to Mecca for the annual pilgrimage. According to Muslim historiography, Yathrib was a town with a sizeable Jewish population. Also within the population of Yathrib, leaders of the tribes known as Aws and Khazrāj might have been seeking mediation of a dispute. Such circumstances would explain the roots of the conflict that accounts record later ensued among these communities and the Muslims. At a place called 'Aqabah, representatives from Yathrib accepted Islam and pledged to follow Muḥammad's authority. An arrangement was reached that allowed the Prophet to emigrate from Mecca to Yathrib.

In 622 came the decisive "Hijrah" or emigration to Yathrib. Henceforth, that city was known as *Medīnat Al-Nabī*, or "The City of the Prophet." This name was shortened to "Medīna," which is the name for the same city in Saudi Arabia today. The Muslim lunar calendar begins from this year, which marks the break between the "Meccan" and "Medinan" period. According to the *sīrah*, the Prophet Muḥammad and Abū Bakr followed behind the main group of Muslims who made the trip. At one point, according to the story, Muḥammad and Abū Bakr slept in a cave as they were fleeing from the pursuing Meccans across the desert. That night a spider came and spun a web at the mouth of the cave, diverting the pursuing Meccans from their path.

Those who made the Hijrah were known as the "*Muhājirūn*" ("those who made Hijrah"); and those already in Medina who were there to receive them were called the "*Anṣār*" ("the helpers"). The Qur'ān itself draws this distinction, making reference to the "Emigrants," although the historical connotations of the term are not clarified in the text. An instance of this is found in 9 Al-Tawbah, a *sūrah* which is understood to date mostly to the later Medinan period. The following verses that mention the "Emigrants" and the "Helpers" signal temporal context more than do some other Qur'ānic verses that also use the same terms:

> 100. The early emigrants [*al-muhājirīn*] and the helpers [*al-anṣār*] and those who followed them up in beneficence – Allāh is well-pleased with them, and they are well-pleased with Him, and He has prepared for them gardens beneath which rivers flow [*tajrī taḥtihā al-anhār*], abiding therein forever. That is their great triumph [*al-fauzu al-'aẓīm*].
>
> 101. And some of the desert Arabs around you are hypocrites [*al-munāfiqūn*], and some of the people of Medina persist in hypocrisy. You do not know them, but We know them. We shall punish them twice, then they will be afflicted with a terrible punishment. (9 Al-Tawbah 100–101)

These designations ("*Muhājirūn*," "*Anṣār*") would remain significant for the identity of those who were among the generations of the descendants of the first community of Muslims, many of whom wished to trace their own Muslim ancestry in a prestigious lineage back to this time. The verses above also introduce the idea of the "hypocrites," a class of person which the Qur'ān disparages as much as, and perhaps even more than, the "unbelievers" (*kāfirūn*). The designation, "hypocrites" (*munāfiq*), while fundamentally a moral category, in Muslim tradition also carries a direct historical reference to those in Mecca, Medina, and outlying areas who obstructed the work of Prophet and the cause of Islam in this period.

After the Hijrah, the Prophet Muḥammad established residence in Medina. He married 'Ā'ishah, the daughter of Abū Bakr. 'Ā'ishah would become an important named source for the transmission of information about the Prophet, and was a key figure in the development of both pious and political tradition after Muḥammad had passed away. She is said to appear as an unnamed subject in the Qur'ān in the fourth verse of 24 Al-Nūr; here, a prohibition is made against slanderous accusation, of which 'Ā'ishah was allegedly the target in one reported incident. Among the Prophet's other wives was Ḥafṣah, the daughter of 'Umar, according to religious tradition; her codex of the Qur'ān was the basis for later redactions of the text. The Prophet would conduct many marriages in the years that followed this, and many of these formed alliances were said to have provided support and protection to women who had lost spouses to war.

Because of the Prophet's unique status, he would marry more than the number, four wives, that is the maximum sanctioned in the Qur'ān for other men. As an example of material in the Qur'ān addressing such issues, 66 Al-Taḥrīm pertains to the unique social circumstances that surrounded the family and marriages of the Prophet. It contains a great deal of content that addresses specifically the conduct of the Prophet's wives, beginning with an incident of dispute among them that is known in tradition to have been about "Mary the Copt," the mother of the Prophet's son (and a legitimate concubine). In later times, Muslims and others have questioned how to understand what norms, if any, come out of this sort of gendered information that seems historically specific to the context of the house of the Prophet on the one hand, and which also comprises the most excellent religious model for personal conduct for Muslims for all time.

Another *sūrah*, 33 Al-Aḥzāb, also offers a great deal of information to Muslims about the Prophet's special domestic situation; many of its verses are said to date to a time after the Muslims' arrival in Medina, to around 626–627. Its language and content renders it a highly gendered *sūrah* overall. For example, it contains verses that specify the gender of its listeners, such as 33 Al-Aḥzāb 35:

> Men [*muslimūn*] and women [*muslimāt*], [men and women] who have submitted, [men and women who have] believed, [men and women who have] obeyed, [men and women who] are truthful, [men and women who are] steadfast, [men and women who are] reverent, [men and women who are] giving in charity, [men and women who are] fasting, [men and women who are] guarding their private parts and remembering Allāh often, Allāh has prepared for them a forgiveness and a reward. (33 Al-Aḥzāb 35)

There is a similarly gendered reference that also appears later in 33 Al-Aḥzāb 58, the same *sūrah.*

Elsewhere in the Qur'ān, the ideas of gender, gender relations, and gender parity are addressed across many levels of specificity and abstraction. For example, part of a verse, 2 Al-Baqarah 187 (which pertains mostly to practices during the month of Ramaḍān), expresses the idea that male and female spouses are "garments for one another." Overall, the Qur'ān presents principles of creation's gender-balanced and even its partnered nature, as in the meanings of the following verse (which is also quoted within a longer excerpt in Chapter 6):

> And of His signs is that He created from you, from yourselves, spouses [*azwājan*] to settle down with and He established friendship and mercy between you. There are in all that signs for people who reflect. (30 Al-Rūm 21)

In the case above, "spouses" is a mixed-gender term. Elsewhere in the Qur'ān, however, it may be questioned what is the range of meanings of a Qur'ānic expression that indicates that men have a "degree" over women (2 Al-Baqarah 228), or that they "stand above them" (as "*qawwāmūn*" in 4 Al-Nisā' 34, a verse that is considered in more depth in Chapter 4).

In the *sūrah* 33 Al-Aḥzāb (which was mentioned above), there is also further treatment of the role and position of the Prophet Muḥammad relating to a matter of a marriage. There is reference to the woman, Zainab bint Jahsh, who wed the Prophet after she had been married to his companion, Zaid bin Harithah (33 Al-Aḥzāb 36–38). Elsewhere in the *sūrah* there is a consideration of the matter of divorce also in more general terms, stipulating the required "waiting period" for remarriage after a divorce (33 Al-Aḥzāb 49) as well as answers to the question, between and among whom may a marriage be legally contracted? This *sūrah* also presents such material in a textual context that affirms the Prophet's unique authority. This is put forward, for example, in verse 40, in the famous phrase that the Prophet Muḥammad is the "seal of the prophets," as well as within a general command found in verse 66 to "obey God and His Messenger." Finally, verse 56 of this *sūrah* instructs Muslims of the past and the present to "bless" the Prophet:

> Allāh and His angels bless the Prophet. O believers, bless him and greet him graciously, too. (33 Al-Aḥzāb 56)

This is a scriptural basis for a widespread practice of venerating the Prophet through recitation that calls down peace, blessings, and prayers on him. Formulas that greet and bless the Prophet may be uttered during canonical worship, and it is an everyday Muslim practice to state "God's peace and blessings be upon him" whenever one has spoken or written the name of the Prophet Muḥammad.[6]

According to the *sīrah* narrative, in the early Medinan period, new domestic alliances came into the house of the Prophet Muḥammad, related to the new political alliances that were forming for the Muslims. To this period there dates a document, "The Constitution of Medina," which casts local community identities according to the status of "peoples of the Book" (Jews and Christians). For the Medinan period there are also recorded ongoing conflicts between the Muslims and the three major Jewish tribes. Over time, these tribes were eliminated from the scope of the agreement, and ultimately they disappeared from Medina itself. These tribes were the Banū Al-Naḍīr (its people were banished), the Banū Qaynuqā' (the tribe came under a siege), and the Banū Qurayza (male members of this tribe were killed or underwent arbitration). The Qur'ān is understood to reflect these historical circumstances of local conflict, particularly in its statements about "hypocrites," indicating those who went back on their professed support for the Muslims during this time.

In the historiographical literature of Islam, more prominent than historical confrontation with Jewish and other tribal communities in the Medinan period is the Muslims' continued conflict with the polytheistic Meccans. The Qur'ān presents material that relates to all of these conflicts simultaneously, and in fact shifts seamlessly from one reference to another, even eliding them into other and more universal time frames in sacred history. Muslim sources recount three important battles with the Meccans, all of which are said to be "occasions" or context for verses of the Qur'ān that pertain to conditions and conduct during conflict. The first was the battle at the Badr wells in 624 (the year 2 of the Islamic calendar). At Badr, a Muslim raid attacked a large Meccan caravan, and there was a great deal of booty taken as a result. The clash ended in a victory for the Muslims, although many Muslims also died. The Qur'ān states that angels came to the aid of the outnumbered Muslim forces during the fighting, in the following verses:

> And when you called upon your Lord for help, He answered you: "I will reinforce you with a thousand angels following one another." (8 Al-Anfāl 9)

And,

> It was not you [plural] who slew them, but Allāh; and when you [singular, Muḥammad?] threw it was actually Allāh who threw, so that He might generously reward the believers. Allāh is All-Hearing, All-Knowing [*samī'un 'alīm*]. (8 Al-Anfāl 17)

Many verses in this same *sūrah*, 8 Al-Anfāl, are read in the context of the Muslims' victory at the Badr wells. The name of the *sūrah* refers to the "spoils" (of Badr), a term found in a statement that appears in the opening *āyah* about the division of these caravan goods (quoted in Chapter 3), which comes along with another command to "Obey Allāh and His messenger." Without knowing the history of the Muslim community, however, one might not even be aware that these verses were understood to refer specifically to Badr. Knowing this background becomes all the more significant when Muslim textual references themselves are approached in tradition in terms of being self-consciously multilayered; for example, the latter verse about who it was who "threw" the Prophet's weapon at Badr has often been quoted by mystics.

This Medinan *sūrah* (all verses of 8 Al-Anfāl are considered to be Medinan except for two) also offers many examples of the sorts of theological content that are typical of what are said to be the later

Qur'ānic revelations, including a verse for which mystics have also found a special affinity:

> O believers [*ya āyyuhā alladhīna āmanū*] respond to Allāh and to the messenger [Muḥammad] if he calls you to that which will give you life, and know that Allāh stands between a person and his or her heart, and that unto Him you shall be gathered. (8 Al-Anfāl 24)

An entity that may occupy the space between a person and his or her very own heart is close indeed. 8 Al-Anfāl also contains a verse that is well known in the context of the vexed intellectual issue of "free will" and God's "predestination," here suggesting the role of human choice in God's determination:

> That is because Allāh never changes a favor He confers on a people unless they change what is in their hearts, and because Allāh is All-Hearing, All-Knowing [*samī'un 'alīm*]. (8 Al-Anfāl 53)

This verse appears in the *sūrah* in the context of the "people of Pharaoh" and the Qur'ānic proof that at the time of the Prophet Moses (Mūsā) the Egyptians deserved the punishment they received in the past; in addition, they will also be deserving of their punishment in the world to come. This content, typical of sacred narrative of the Qur'ān (see Chapter 6), shifts the moral frame of revealed truth across past, present, and future within a single *sūrah* (here 8 Al-Anfāl).

According to Muslim historiography, in 626 there was another major clash at 'Uḥud, whose outcome was a major setback for the Muslims. In 627, or the year 5, there followed the "battle" of the "Trench" or the "Ditch" (Al-Khandaq). This was a siege by the Meccan forces (who are elsewhere known as the "confederated forces," or "Al-Aḥzāb," in the Qur'ān). In this period, most of the verses of the *sūrah* 33 Al-Aḥzāb were said to have been sent down, some of which have been discussed above. According to accounts, the tactics that led to the Muslims' victory in this standoff included a brilliant idea on the part of "Salman," famous as the first Persian convert to Islam, which was to dig a trench around the city to protect against threatened attack.

Verses on the theme of conflict that appear in the Qur'ān pertain to the context of the clashes with the Meccans, the conflict with the tribes of Medina, or events in sacred history such as the experience of Moses, Lot, or other prophets. For example, the *sūrah* 47 Muḥammad contains material about the issue of conduct in warfare, and addresses especially the problem of the reluctance among some Muslims to sacrifice for the sake of the cause of the time. 59 Al-Ḥashr pertains to the banishment of the tribe of Banū Naḍīr in 624/625, which is said to have occurred after the battle of 'Uḥud. 9 Al-Tawbah (which is said textually to be a continuation of the *sūrah* 8 Al-Anfāl, although in tradition these chapters carry differing "occasions" of revelation), also contains material addressing the difficulty of gaining military support for campaigns against the Meccans in the later Medinan period; its references reflect conditions of an all-out war.

This *sūrah* contains the famous "sword verse" (9 Al-Tawbah 5), which at the time of its revelation, so it is said, "abrogated" or canceled previous stipulation to resist such open battles (see Chapter 4). These verses urge the Muslim forces to overcome any reluctance they might have had to fight in the ongoing war of the day, and also at the same time to accept Meccans (who would be the Emigrants' kin and former neighbors) who would turn toward their cause and to Islam:

> 5. Then, when the Sacred Months are over, kill the idolaters wherever you find them, take them [as captives], besiege them, and lie in wait for them at every point of observation. If they repent afterwards, perform the prayer and pay the alms, then release them. Allāh is truly All-Forgiving, Merciful [*ghufūrun raḥīm*].
> 6. And if any one of the idolaters should seek refuge with you, give him refuge, so that he may hear the Word of Allāh, then convey him to his place of security. This is because they are a people who do not know. (9 Al-Tawbah 5–6)

Addressing the painful personal difficulty of carrying out civil war against former close Meccan friends, relatives, and associates in this period, the same *sūrah* contains the following verses:

> 113. It is not for the Prophet and those who believe to ask for forgiveness for the polytheists even if they are near relatives, after it becomes clear to [the believers] that they are the people of the fire.
> 114. Abraham asked forgiveness for his father, only because of a promise he had made to him; but when it became clear to him that he was an enemy of Allāh, he disowned him. Indeed Abraham was compassionate, forbearing. (9 Al-Tawbah 113–114)

Islamic legal perspectives on conflict and war are mediated by jurisprudential tradition. Such legal opinions are not determined directly by Qur'ānic verses such as those above, nor immediately by other material in the Qur'ān that pertains to various conflicts at the time of the establishment of the Prophet's community within the context of its changing circumstances (i.e. peacetime to war to peace again). In addition, legal rulings on *jihād* (in just the restricted sense of armed conflict), being the academic views of scholars, have historically rarely affected real Muslim leaders' political and military decisions of the past or the present.[7] On the other hand, the universal human problem of loving someone who cannot be helped is addressed directly and often by the Qur'ān in its multiple textual frames, including through the experiences of prophets such as Muḥammad, Noah, Moses, and (in the case above from 9 Al-Tawbah) Abraham.

After this time, as the story continues, fortunes turned for the Muslims once again. There was a successful campaign to an oasis to the north, which marked the beginning of an expansion of Muslim political and military influence that would continue across Arabia, and was soon to spread across West Asia and North Africa. According to the *sīrah*, in 628 the Prophet announced that he would undertake the Ḥajj, the annual pilgrimage, which would require entrance into the sacred precinct in Mecca. He set out on the journey, but reached only as far as a site called Ḥudaibiyya before he encountered the Meccan forces. There was a negotiation at that point, and the following year the Prophet performed a lesser pilgrimage at the site of the Ka'bah. The *sūrah* 48 Al-Fatḥ is understood to have been revealed at this time; it opens with the verse, "We have indeed given you a manifest victory."

There are some events disputed in Muslim historiography that relate to varied interpretation of the context of a few Qur'ānic verses. An extra-Qur'ānic report of the words spoken by the Prophet at the pool at "Ghadīr Al-Khumm" as he returned from his pilgrimage has been said by some among Shi'ite groups, for example, to have included the designation of 'Alī as his successor; in Sunni accounts, the report is interpreted only to mean that the Prophet spoke publicly in defense of the cause of 'Alī at this time. These controversies affect historicized Muslim readings of some Qur'ānic content. For example, references such as those in *sūrah* 33 Al-Aḥzāb to the "People of the House [of the Prophet Muḥammad]," the *ahl al-bait* (33 Al-Aḥzāb 33),[8] and, in the same *sūrah*, a reference to the bonds of direct kinship (33 Al-Aḥzāb 6) support the committed Shi'ite view that the family of the Prophet (that is, Fāṭimah, 'Alī, and their sons) has a privileged status in tradition.

In 630, there was the "Campaign of Mecca," according to Muslim historiography, when the Prophet re-entered this city accompanied by the Muslims at last. According to tradition, Bilāl, the first Muslim Black person, offered the call to prayer at that time. It is at this point that, according to accounts, Muḥammad destroyed the idols in the Ka'bah except for a picture of Mary (Maryam), mother of the Prophet Jesus ('Isā). It is said that Muḥammad now fulfilled the full Ḥajj, now as an Islamic pilgrimage. His ritual actions at that time are believed to be the direct model for Islamic pilgrimage today. Soon after this, the Muslims saw victories over a tribe called the Hawāzīn at Ḥunayn. The year that followed became known as the "Year of Deputations," as tribes from throughout Arabia pledged allegiance to the Muslim political order and the leadership of the Prophet Muḥammad.

The *sūrah* 49 Al-Ḥujurāt is said to have been revealed in this period. Its mention of "allegiance under a tree" in verse 18 is taken to be a reference to the agreement made with the Meccans at Ḥudaibiyya. Like 33 Al-Aḥzāb, it addresses the domestic situation of the Prophet's house, but now reflects wider concern for protocol with respect to his new role in regional diplomacy. The *sūrah* opens with an affirmation of the Prophet's authority, offering instruction on conduct around the house of the Prophet, along with other courtesy and conventions. In the context of verses that mention contemporary conditions (such as its reference to the "desert Arabs," who were joining Islam at this time), the Qur'ān also comments on a universal principle:

> 13. O humankind [*yā āyyuhā al-nās*], We have created you male and female and made you nations and tribes, so that you might come to know one another [*lita'ārafū*]. Surely the noblest of you in Allāh's sight is the most pious. Allāh indeed is All-Knowing, All-Informed [*'alīmun khabīr*]. (49 Al-Ḥujurāt 13)

The meanings of the verse imply that difference is a natural and intended aspect of God's design for humanity. Perhaps this is so that people may ponder difference itself as a reflection of the multifaceted greatness of the Creator. (This interpretation would be consistent with the meanings of other Qur'ānic verses about the multiplicity of the natural world.) 49 Al-Hujurāt is also compatible with other verses in the Qur'ān that imply that differences among faith communities are part of an ultimate divine "test." The meaning of the verse 5 Al-Mā'idah 48, for example, exhorts believers to "compete in good works," appearing along with other material relating to Christian tradition that is found in this *sūrah*. Another verse in the Qur'ān expressing similar ideas is:

> To everyone there is a direction towards which he turns. So compete to do good works [*fastabiqū al-khairāt*]. Wherever you are, Allāh will bring you all together. Surely Allāh has power over all things. (2 Al-Baqarah 148)

Ideals of communal and human solidarity would hold strong throughout the history of Islam, even while in reality the alliances that are documented to have formed at the end of the Medinan period, which apparently were based largely on the personalized authority of the Prophet Muḥammad, soon fragmented after Prophet Muḥammad passed away. After the Prophet's death, the allegiance of Arabian tribes was reconsolidated under the leadership of Abū Bakr. At that time, supporters of the cause of 'Alī were also already developing an alternative model for the legacy of Muḥammad's leadership.

The Prophet Muḥammad passed away in the year 632, according to the *sīrah*, after undertaking what became known in tradition as his final "farewell pilgrimage." It is understood that at this time the final verse of the Qur'ān was revealed (5 Al-Mā'idah 3), which includes words that convey the following meaning: "On this day I [God] have perfected your religion [*dīnakum*] for you, completed My favor upon you, and chosen for you Islam as a religion."

QUR'ĀNIC BELIEFS

Some of the most common questions that students bring initially to the study of named religious systems in the classroom, Islam and otherwise, are about "beliefs." When considering matters of creedal or doctrinal "belief" (*'aqīdah*), the Qur'ān in fact lays the foundation for many sophisticated and diverse Muslim theological understandings. Underlying all of these is a single teaching of the Qur'ān and its prophets, that is, the unity of God (*tawḥīd*).

The monotheistic message is emphatic and, in Qur'ānic terms, indisputable.[9] The Qur'ān casts and recasts this central truth-claim into exquisite patterns of meaning and sound, persuasion and power.

In the Qur'ān, the word "Islām" has connotations both of submitting to the will of God as well as belonging as a member of a Muslim community. It is not just persons who may be "Muslim," but the Qur'ān actually describes all of creation in terms of this natural state. The Arabic term, "*islām*," can be found several times in the text; for example, it appears in the verse that is sometimes claimed to be the last to have been revealed to the Prophet Muḥammad (quoted above), as in "… Islam as a religion for you" (5 Al-Mā'idah 3). This verse is located in the context of other textual information regarding the law prohibiting the eating of forbidden meat (such as carrion, blood, and pork). 5 Al-Mā'idah 3, then, accentuates a facet of "Islam"'s meaning that relates to groups and their practices.[10] Although the Qur'ān often designates "Muslims" as a faith community in such a social or ritual sense, the Qur'ānic terms "Islām" and "Muslim" are not restricted to such meanings, however.

Religious commitment also transcends named faith communities in the Qur'ān, as suggested by the following verse describing the religion of the prophet Abraham (Ibrāhīm), who is elsewhere called the "friend of God":

> Abraham was neither a Jew not a Christian but a *ḥanīf* and a Muslim. And he was not one of the polytheists. (3 Āl Imrān 67)

The Arabic term *ḥanīf* denotes a "monotheist." In many episodes recounted in the Qur'ān, Ibrāhīm vigorously demonstrates and defends his monotheistic faith. For example, in 6 Al-An'ām 74, he testifies to his father and his people that he will not worship a star, the moon, or the sun, but that he will worship only Allāh; at the end of a section in 19 Maryam, verses 41 to 49, Abraham breaks with his father and prays to "his Lord," an event which is depicted more than once in the Qur'ān. In 21 Al-Anbiyā' 51–70, Ibrāhīm smashes the idols of his father's people, leaving one large one untouched and then claiming to its devotees that "the big one did it." This absurd irony, an instance of Qur'ānic humor which is not unique to Islam, drives the point home that idols possess no existential reality and thus have no power to act at all.

The Qur'ān's own terms for "belief" are, not surprisingly, *dhū wujūh*. For example, consider a verse in 49 Al-Ḥujurāt; it comes directly after the verse that was cited previously about human diversity. The context of this verse's revelation is said in tradition to be the "Year of Deputations," when Arabian tribes were accepting the Prophet's authority after the "opening" of Mecca to the Muslims. The verse is richly theological, apparently distinguishing a concept of "belief" (*imān*) from the term "Islām" ("submission"):

> The bedouins [desert Arabs] say: "We believe [*amannā*]." Say [*qul*]: "You do not believe, but say: 'We Submit' [*aslamnā*] for belief [*al-imān*] has not entered your hearts." If you obey Allāh and his messenger, He will not stint you any of your works. Allāh is surely All-Forgiving, All-Merciful [*ghufūrun raḥīm*]. (49 Al-Ḥujurāt 14)

The Qur'ān connects consistently the meaning of Qur'ānic concepts such as "faith" and "Islam" (as above) to action like good deeds (*ṣaliḥāt*), and attitudes and moral sentiments like sincerity (*ikhlāṣ*) and gratitude (*shukr*). Further, the Qur'ān often expresses such ideals in intellectual as well as affective terms.

In just a few contexts of the Qur'ān, there is found a suggestion that, in this world and in the world to come, there may even be a spiritual ranking among the believers determined by moral actions and characteristics such as these. For example, there is a verse found in the description of paradise in 56 Al-Wāqi'ah that has perplexed and intrigued many generations of Muslims:

> *Bismillāh Al-Raḥmān Al-Raḥīm*
>
> 1. When the "happening" [*al-wāqi'ah*, i.e. judgment] comes to pass [*waqa'at*]
> 2. Of its occurrence there is no denial;
> 3. Abasing some, exalting others.
> 4. When the earth shall be shaken violently
> 5. And the mountains shall be reduced to rubble,
> 6. So that they become scattered dust.
> 7. And you shall be three categories:
> 8. The companions of the right – behold the companions of the right?
> 9. And the companions of the left – behold the companions of the left?
> 10. And the outstrippers [*al-sābiqūn*], the outstrippers [*al-sābiqūn*];

11. Those are the favored ones;
12. In the gardens of bliss;
13. A throng of the ancients
14. And a small band of the latecomers. (56 Al-Wāqi'ah 1–14)

This section is typical of Qur'ānic locution that introduces a term (here, *al-wāqi'ah*), and then immediately elaborates upon it in subsequent verses. However, in this case there is also a repeated word found in verse 10, *al-sābiqūn* ("outstrippers"), which is clarified only ambiguously in the Qur'ān, whether within these verses, elsewhere in this chapter (such as verses 88–94, discussed in Chapter 6), or at any other point in the text. As a consequence of this open semantic range, a concept like that of the "outstrippers" can offer a rich and productive area for the pious to imagine and even to seek to attain such a privileged status. For example, formulations like these have been important among Sufis, followers of systems of esoteric piety, who have wished to claim that within their hierarchical spiritual lineages there are or have been special persons who could be said to be "outstrippers" in their virtuosic capacity to realize divine unity.

Qur'ānic faith is understood, first and foremost, to be the recognition of the absolute unity of God (*tawḥīd*). The root of the word *tawḥīd* also forms the Arabic expression for the cardinal number "one" (*wāḥid*). Esoteric thinkers and others have studied derivatives of this root as aspects of understanding the unity of divinity, such as the term "*al-aḥad*" ("The First"), a Name of God. "*Tawḥīd*," as a noun, is derived from a verbal form which means actively or purposefully to create oneness. The Qur'ānic doctrine of the unity of God is expressed in the following *sūrah*, 112 Al-Ikhlāṣ (Figure 6, p. 196; transliteration of the Arabic words is given in Chapter 3):

Bismilllāh Al-Raḥmān Al-Raḥīm

1. Say: "He is Allāh, the only One [*Allāhu aḥad*],
2. "Allāh, the Everlasting [*Allāhu al-ṣamad*],
3. "He did not beget and He is not begotten,
4. "And none is His equal."

3 Āl 'Imrān 64 is another case of the expression of the monotheistic commitment, here linking this fundamental Qur'ānic tenet to the faith communities of Muslims, and others: "Say: 'O People of the Book [*yā ahl al-kitāb*], come to an equitable word [*kalimatin sawā'i*] between you and us [Muslims], that we worship none but Allāh, do

not associate anything with Him and do not set up each other as lords besides Allāh.' If they turn their backs, say: 'Bear witness that we are Muslims.'" *Tawḥīd* is the message brought by the prophets, including the Prophet Muḥammad, as affirmed in the Qur'ān.

The statement that begins the Islamic profession of faith (*shahādah*), "There is no god but God," is found several times in the Qur'ān. A form of the statement is found, for example, at the beginning of the famous "verse of the throne" (2 Al-Baqarah 255, discussed in Chapter 3), which affirms God's omniscient awareness and omnipotent power over all things. In Islam, any and all belief (*imān*) originates with such affirmation. A required action, *shahādah* is also a validation of faith embedded within other religious acts such as canonical worship (the daily prayers called *ṣalāt*) and joining the faith community of Islam as a convert. As the first "pillar" of the practice of the Islamic religion, the full statement of the *shahādah* rendered into English is, "There is no god but God and Muḥammad is the messenger of God."[11]

After the fundamental message of *tawḥīd*, "There is no god but God," Qur'ānic themes extend out toward many horizons. These reflect mutually within the text's multilayered expression, making it an arbitrary exercise to frame the Qur'ān's "themes" decisively. In order to introduce the Qur'ān with a framework that translates naturally into Islamic systems, here I draw on a standard paradigm known as the "five beliefs." The idea that there are "five beliefs," and what they may be said to be, is based on a report of an encounter between Muḥammad and the Angel Gabriel (Jibrīl) in which they are conveyed. As with the legal obligations of worship that are known as the "five pillars" of Islam, while each of these beliefs has a basis in the Qur'ānic text, they are all also inflected by tradition. In the Qur'ān, the "beliefs" are suggested together as a grouping in 2 Al-Baqarah 177 (in a passage that is quoted in Chapter 3), and also in the following verse, which is located in the same *sūrah*:

> The messenger [i.e. the Prophet Muḥammad] believes in what has been revealed to him by his Lord, and so do the believers too. All believe in Allāh, His angels, His books and His messengers. We make no distinction between any of His Messengers. And they say: "We hear and obey. Grant us Your forgiveness, our Lord. And to You is our return." (2 Al-Baqarah 285)

According to tradition, the five beliefs are said to be: God, angels, prophets and scriptures, final judgment, and "divine decree and determination." These tenets comprise the basis of *imān*, or "faith," in a tutored sense. These "beliefs" here inspire a framework for apprehending Qur'ānic "themes" according to three main groupings of material: 1. Creator, created beings, and their responsibility (which would also include a consideration of the fifth belief, the foreordination of events known as "divine decree"); 2. prophecy, prophets, and their missions and messages; and finally, 3. the last things.

First, the characteristics and attributes of the One God are elaborated outside the Qur'ān in Islam, such as in traditions of the Most Beautiful Names of God (*Al-Asmā' Al-Ḥusnā*), which are presented in Chapter 5, and have their basis in the Qur'ānic text. In the Qur'ān, God is the Creator who sustains the world He has made. He has filled it with "signs" (*āyāt*) that point to His nature and existence (see Chapter 6). Rephrasing the monotheistic commitment, Allāh is the only divinity, the only source of reality that can be said to exist. The Qur'ān states such an idea many times, often in the form of declarations that are made by prophets, such as the following Qur'ānic utterance of the prophet Joseph (Yūsuf) in 12 Yūsuf 40: "You do not worship, besides Him, [anything] except names you have named, you and your fathers, for which Allāh has not sent down any authority." Abraham, Moses, other Qur'ānic prophets, and the Prophet Muḥammad after them, all challenged or destroyed false idols. The greatest transgression is said by Muslims to be idolatrous "*shirk*," or the confused association of something that has been created with the being of the Creator Himself.

The Qur'ān vigorously denies the claims of polytheists in terms like these, in prophetic voices of the sacred past and the textual present, and even the future. The Qur'ān also issues challenges that are apparently directed to claims of specific groups or faith communities that might have been well known in Arabia at the time of the Qur'ān's reported revelation (for example, the divine nature of Jesus Christ as *Logos*), as well as what appear to be Arabian polytheistic beliefs that might take "*jinn*," angels, or other figures as gods. For example, at the end of time in the Qur'ān, the Prophet Jesus ('Isā) denies that he ever urged his community (of Christians) to view his nature as divine (5 Al-Mā'idah 116): "And when Allāh said: 'O Jesus, son of Mary, did you say to the people, "Take me and my mother as gods, apart from Allāh?"' He [Jesus] said: 'Glory be to You. It is not given me to say what is untrue. If I said it, You would have known it; You know what is in my soul, but I do not know what is in Thine. You are indeed the Knower of the unseen.'" It is part of the Qur'ānic responsibility of the prophets to witness on judgment day that they delivered the fundamental message of God's unity to their people, whether or not it was ever heeded or later even remembered.

God the Creator is transcendent in the Qur'ān, and there are expressions in the text that hint at the possible immanence of God as well. This is a highly productive theological tension in Islamic traditions. The Qur'ān affirms God's transcendence in statements such as that He is "Mighty," "Exalted," or that He "does not beget" (as in the example from 112 Al-Ikhlāṣ, above). Such absolute transcendence cannot be within human comprehension, and God's unity is therefore ineffable and ultimately "unseen." For example, human vision may not apprehend Him, as attested in the following Qur'ānic passage, which has also been the basis of sophisticated philosophical study by Muslim scholars:

> 102. That is Allāh, your Lord; there is no god but He, Creator of all things. Worship Him then; He is the Guardian of all things.
> 103. Vision does not attain Him, but He attains the vision, and He is the Kind, the All-Knowing [*al-laṭīfu al-khabīr*]. (6 Al-An'ām 102–103)

These verses have led to nuanced theosophy regarding the "unity of witness" with God, a goal of some forms of esoteric piety that seek experiential knowledge of the unity of God.

At the same time that the Qur'ān affirms the absolute transcendence of Allāh, there are verses in the Qur'ān that also suggest His immanence, such as *āyah*s that imply that faces "gaze on God" at judgment (75 Al-Qiyāmah 22–23). The expression of God's immanence that may be the best known in Muslim tradition is the verse:

> We have indeed created a person, and We know what his soul insinuates to him or her. We are to him closer than the jugular vein. (50 Qāf 16)

This echoes the meaning of 8 Al-Anfal 24, a verse cited above, in which God is said to "slip in between a person and his/her heart."

Everywhere one turns, as the Qur'ān reminds its readers in many of its verses, there is the "face of God."

God is both omnipotent and omniscient in the Qur'ān, and found both in the Qur'ān as well as in wider tradition there are many Names of God that convey aspects of these two attributes of God's essence. His omnipotence is expressed in the Qur'ānic fact that He needs only to state "Be" for a situation to manifest, as in the cosmogonic act of creation itself. One example of this, selected from many, is the verse 2 Al-Baqarah 117, "Creator of the heavens and the earth [*badī'u al-samāwāti wa'l-arḍ*]. When He decrees a thing, He only says to it: 'Be,' and there it is." (Similar examples, each with a differing tone and emphasis, are 6 Al-An'ām 73, 16 Al-Naḥl 40, and 40 Ghāfir 68.) God's ability to raise the dead, just as He makes the dry earth come to life with falling rain, is another typical expression of His power in the Qur'ān. The Qur'ān affirms that Allāh is the King (Al-Mālik) with dominion (*al-mulk*) over all things. God is also All-Knowing, depicted as knowing the "unseen," whether this is understood as His knowing what is concealed in people's hearts, or as His knowledge of unforeseen or unknowable events. His omniscience is stressed in verses such as 6 Al-An'ām 59: "With Him are the keys of the unseen; only He knows them, and He knows what is on land and in the sea. Not a leaf falls but He knows it; and there is no grain in the dark depths of the earth, nor anything green or dry, but it is [recorded] in a clear book."

Within Islamic theological reconciliations of the question of God's power in relation to human choice ("predestination" versus "free will"), theories of causation tend to link closely divine attributes of omnipotence and omniscience. Such doctrines, discussed further below, had become mainstream Sunni "orthodoxy" and a matter of creed (the "fifth belief") by the latter part of the formative period of Islamic religious science in about the twelfth century. These points were accepted even as some religious thinkers still struggled to understand Qur'ānic verses such as those in which Allāh sets forth life as a "test," "seeking to know" who are the believers. Such a verse appears in 18 Al-Kahf 12, where the sleepers of the cave are awoken so that "We" may know who among them could reckon the amount of time they had been asleep. (The entire story is treated in detail in Chapter 6.) According to what became the accepted view, God already would also have known the very result of that which He is also "seeking to know," such as what choices humans will make when they are "tested." The Qur'ān's verses offer rich grounds for such reflections.

Belief in God and His unique role as Creator has a counterpart in the Muslim belief in the created beings that the Qur'ān mentions, both seen and unseen. In the Qur'ān there are found three classes of sentient beings: *jinn*, angels, humans; belief in angels is one of the canonical "five beliefs." All of these types of beings may be identified Qur'ānically by the primary substance from which God originally created them. *Jinn* are a type of being made of "smokeless fire" (for example, in 55 Al-Raḥmān 15; the Qur'ān states that humanity comes from clay and *jinn* come from fire in 15 Al-Ḥijr 26–27). The Qur'ān presents them as being much like humans, only they inhabit an unseen world. There are good *jinn* and bad *jinn* in the Qur'ān, Muslim and non-Muslim *jinn*. Ambivalently presented in the Qur'ān, *jinn* are often said in global Muslim traditions to be mischievous and bothersome; at the same time, in the Qur'ān it is they who come to the aid of the prophet Solomon (Sulaimān), such as in 34 Sabā' 12–13 and 27 Al-Naml 17 and 39. *Jinn* listen to the Qur'ān in the Qur'ān (72 Al-Jinn 1); and, responsible for witnessing the revealed message, *jinn*s too are judged at the end of time. *Jinn* were known in pre-Islamic times as desert spirits, and the Qur'ān states that they are not to be confused with deities, implying that some non-Muslims could have considered them to be powerful beings. In Arabia, *jinn* were understood to have the power to possess people, making them inspired or *majnūn* (this is also an Arabic word meaning "insane").

Angels (*malā'ika*) are made of light. They are the messengers and helpers of God. Among the angels is Jibrīl or Gabriel, understood in tradition to be the entity who is also called "Our spirit" or the "holy spirit" in the Qur'ān. The Qur'ān also mentions others angels by name, such as Mikā'il in 2 Al-Baqarah 98. Angels are always good, circling the "throne" of God and singing His praises (for example, in 40 Ghāfir 7). Some of God's angels even guard hell (such as 74 Al-Muddathir 30–31, with another mention of their presence there appearing in 96 Iqrā' 18).

There is one fallen and rebellious angel or *jinn* in the Qur'ān: Iblīs. (The Qur'ān identifies him as being a *jinn* in 18 Al-Kahf 50.) Iblīs is the devil in Muslim tradition. There are also "satans" mentioned in the Qur'ān, *shāyāṭīn*, which seem to be a class of troublesome spirits (such as in 2 Al-Baqarah 14, quoted in Chapter 3, where they are shown to be nasty allies of the "hypocrites"). It is understood that when the Qur'ān refers to "satan" (*shaiṭān*) in the singular, which it does with some frequency, this is the same figure known elsewhere in the Qur'ān by the proper name, Iblīs. His primary mediums in the Qur'ān for interfering with humans appear to be forgetfulness and pride, and in the final *sūrah* of the Qur'ān, 114 Al-Nās, it would seem to be he who is said to be the "whisperer" who "whispers in the hearts of people." The *sūrah* reads in its entirety:

Bismillāh Al-Raḥmān Al-Raḥīm

1. Say [*qul*]: "I seek refuge with the Lord of the people;
2. "The King of the people [*maliki al-nās*];
3. "The God of the people [*ilāhi al-nās*],
4. "From the evil of the slinking whisperer [*al-waswāsi al-khannās*]
5. "Who whispers [*yūswisu*] in the breasts of people,
6. "Both *jinn* and people." (114 Al-Nās)

Satan's lurking presence can even affect the missions of Qur'ānic prophets, as in the story of the prophet Moses (Mūsā) in 18 Al-Kahf, verse 63, when the servant of Moses claims it was "*shaiṭān*" who made him "forget the fish" on a journey to the place of the meeting of the seas. In 22 Al-Ḥajj 52, the Qur'ān makes a statement that is understood to have bearing on an event in the experience of the Prophet Muḥammad, "We have not sent a Messenger or Prophet before you but when he recited the devil would intrude into his recitation." In tradition, this verse is said to carry a reference to the episode of the "satanic verses" (discussed further below and also in Chapter 4). In other parts of the Qur'ān, its readers are instructed to take refuge in Allāh from the "accursed" (literally, "stoned") satan, such as 7 Al-A'rāf 200 and 41 Fuṣṣilat 36. This same idea appears in the form of an explicit command for Qur'ān recitation in 16 Al-Naḥl 98: "When you recite the Qur'ān, seek refuge with Allāh from the accursed devil [*al-shaiṭāni al-rajīm*]." Following this guidance, any recitation of the Qur'ān begins with a formula seeking this protection.

Stories of Iblīs in the Qur'ān, of which there are several re-tellings, recount a moment after creation in which all the angels bowed to Ādam on God's command – "except Iblīs." This disobedience is, in almost all Qur'ānic instances of the narrative, attributed to his rebellious pride. However, Iblīs also then comes to an agreement with God that he may be permitted to interfere with humans, just as he interfered with Ādam and his spouse by tempting their disobedience in the heavenly garden, until the end of time. The primary accounts of Iblīs that narrate this story are: 2 Al-Baqarah 30–39; 7 Al-A'rāf 11–25; 15 Al-Ḥijr 26–44; and 17 Al-Isrā' 61–65. Shorter versions are to be found in 18 Al-Kahf (one single, long *āyah*, number 50); 20 Ṭa Ha 115–123; and 38 Ṣād 71–85. The version of the account that appears in 38 Ṣād 71–85 reads as follows:

71. When your Lord said to the angels: "I am going to create a mortal out of clay.
72. "When I have fashioned him and breathed into him of My Spirit, fall prostrate before him."
73. Then the angels prostrated themselves entirely
74. Except for Iblīs; he waxed proud and was one of the unbelievers.
75. He [God] said: "O Iblīs, what prevented you from prostrating yourself before what I created with My Own hands [*biyad-dayya*]? Have you waxed proud or were you one of the exalted?"
76. He [Iblīs] said: "I am better than he; You created me from fire and You created him from clay."
77. [Allāh] said: "Get out of here; you are truly accursed."
78. "And my curse shall pursue you until the day of judgment."
79. He said: "Lord, give me respite till the day they shall be resurrected."
80. [Allāh] said: "You are one of those respited,
81. "Until the day of the well-known time [*al-yawm al-ma'lūm*]."
82. He said: "By Your glory, I will seduce them all,
83. "Except for your sincere servants among them."
84. [Allāh] said: "Truly, and I say the truth;
85. "I will fill hell with you and those of them who follow you, all together." (38 Ṣād 71–85)

At this point in the narrative, satan has become the "avowed enemy" of humanity, "whispering" to lead them astray. At the end of the account of the same story given in 7 Al-A'rāf 16–17, satan pledges to God, "16. Because You have misled me, I will lie in wait for them on Your straight path. 17. Then I will come from before them and behind them, from their right and their left; and You will not find most of them thankful." This episode begins at a cosmogonic moment a scenario that will culminate at final judgment. From this time on, created beings are henceforth to be tempted and "tested." In many versions of these Qur'ānic accounts, Iblīs next whispers to Ādam and his spouse (who is not named) that they should disobey God's command, leading to their banishment from the Garden and the beginning of the human moral drama on earth.

These narrated events set up one structure of Qur'ānic theodicy: all good is from God, but evil comes from human choice as influenced by satan, to the degree that persons are susceptible to his whispering, also as directed by God. Humans are judged by their choices, and in the mainstream theological view God has already "determined" these choices as well. Issues of God's determination, comprising the fifth of the "five beliefs," were central to the development of early traditions of theology, in which groups of Muslim thinkers upheld both sides of the issue of "free will" and "predestination." According to the position that was *not* accepted in the mainstream (but which nevertheless has some Qur'ānic support), humans should be said to have free will on the rationale that God is good and just; since all good is from God, and only good may come from God, any evil act must therefore have originated with humans. Further, so the reasoning goes, the Qur'ānic promise of reward for good and threat of punishment for evil must be true; and, for this judgment to be just (that is, for it to be possible for persons to be punished for their bad actions by a just God), there must have been free choice and responsibility all along.

In what became an "orthodox" challenge to this perspective, the point was made that any claim to human "free will" compromises the omnipotence of God. The mainstream view holds that with God are *al-qaḍā' wa al-qadr*, "the power and the determination." This theology was clarified by the twelfth century by figures such as Abū'l Ḥasan Al-Ash'arī (d. 935). The arguments were supported by a theory of atomistic causality and human "acquisition" of actions (*iktisāb*) that were previously authored by the omnipotent God with His omniscient foreknowledge. Thus, it may be said that God authors actions for persons, and then these persons "acquire" their responsibility for them according to their own actions in chronological time, and just as God had known they would do.

The Qur'ān's statements appear ambivalent on this theological point, and there are verses that Muslims historically have read in support of either view. For example, in early theological and political history the "Qadarites" opposed the idea of God's foreordination of all events, including the ascendancy of the 'Umayyad Dynasty. An early pietist and preacher (later remembered as a mystic), Ḥasan of Baṣra (d. 728), supported these positions with Qur'ānic verses. For example, 18 Al-Kahf 29 begins with the words, "And say: 'Truth is from your Lord. Whoever wishes, let him believe; and whoever wishes, let him disbelieve.'"[12] On the other hand, balancing this perspective, for example, is 6 Al-An'ām 149: "Say: 'To Allah belongs the decisive argument [*al-ḥujjatu al-bālighah*]. Had He pleased He would have guided you all.'" The sense of meaning of the latter verse is consistent with the articulation of what came to be the "fifth belief" in Muslim tradition. In general, the Qur'ān's comments on the topic, when taken all together, would appear to clarify the idea concepts along the following lines. Once a person is established with a certain moral proclivity, God enhances that tendency, such as by "setting a seal on the hearts" of those who already disbelieve, or by rewarding those who righteously follow the straight path and by opening or "softening" their hearts to further reception of the message.

The Qur'ānic position on ultimate moral responsibility was argued by early Muslim theologians on other issues as well. A related point that was also a subject of dispute in early *kalām* (theology) is the notion conveyed by the Qur'ān that "no one carries the burden of another" (6 Al-An'ām 164). Intercession (by prophets, holy persons, or even the Qur'ān itself) has been a vexed issue in the history of Islamic thought and practices. In addition, the question of ascribing moral status to someone in this life (who is still yet to be judged in the next) was another key issue in early *kalām* that was debated on a Qur'ānic basis. While there is material to support the view that a "grave sinner" could not be considered a Muslim, the position on this point that came to dominate in the social and intellectual history of Islam was that which was upheld by a group who claimed that only God would or could know what was to be the fates of His beings at the end of time. Thus, determination should be "postponed" until that time. Consistent with this attitude, it has remained relatively rare right up until the modern period for any Muslims to accuse other Muslims of outright "*takfīr*," or utter non-belief.

Humanity, the final category of God's creatures considered here, is made out of clay, just as Ādam was fashioned as the first person. One of the "five beliefs" pertains to a special class of humans, namely prophets like Ādam himself, who received revelation or divine inspiration. Humans, including prophets, maintain horizontal human relationships with others as well as the vertical relation with respect to their Creator, and both dimensions are treated in the Qur'ān. The Qur'ān typically presents people as ethical beings, and in many cases it will identify persons solely in terms of what is their moral character. The Qur'ān instructs that humans will be brought to life again with a "second creation" at the end-time. Then, they will be judged individually and collectively, both as persons and as peoples simultaneously.

It is typical of the Qur'ān to present people as being members of groups or communities. The faithful and uniting bond among persons may even in itself have a religious quality, as in the following famous *āyah* about the "rope of God":

> And hold fast to Allāh's bond [*biḥabli Allāhi*], all of you, and do not let go. And remember Allāh's grace [*ni'mata Allāh*] upon you; how you were enemies, then He united your heart so that you have become, by His grace, brethren. You were on the brink of the pit of fire, but He saved you from it. Thus Allāh manifests to you His revelations [*āyātihi*] so that perchance you might be rightly guided. (3 Āl 'Imrān 103)

The Qur'ān also demonstrates that humanity bears a responsibility for communal action, social justice, and for care of the non-sentient creation of Allāh on a collective level. All of these may be alternative interpretations of the idea of the "trust" (*amānah*, 33 Al-Aḥzāb 72) that humanity has accepted according to the Qur'ān. The Qur'ānic command to believers to "stand up for justice" (discussed in Chapter 4) could be interpreted as consideration for those who are at the margins of the social order or who otherwise need support (the Qur'ān often mentions widows and orphans in this regard). Humans additionally bear the burden to maintain the "balance" (55 Al-Raḥmān 8) and not to be "oppressors" or to "corrupt the earth," spiritually and physically, ideas that are all discussed at more length in Chapter 4. Prophets remind people and groups of these duties and obligations, warning of the consequences if, as careless and forgetful as human nature is shown to be in the Qur'ān, they go unheeded.

The Qur'ān mentions some twenty-eight prophets, and clearly names twenty-five. Stories of these messengers and their communities appear in extended form in the *sūrah*s 7 Al-A'rāf, 11 Hūd, 21 Al-Anbiyā', and 26 Al-Shu'arā' (discussed further in Chapter 6).

There are Qur'ānic prophets who were also known from the Jewish and Christian scriptures: Adam, Moses, Aaron, Lot, Abraham, Isaac, Ishmael, Jacob, Joseph, Jonah, David, Elijah, Solomon, Jesus, and John the Baptist. In addition, there are Qur'ānic figures identified speculatively in Muslim tradition as Elijah, Elisha, Enoch, or Ezekiel, who correspond to Qur'ānic prophets such as Idrīs, Ilyasā' and Dhū'l Kifli. The Qur'ān's prophets also include Arabian figures, Hūd, Ṣāliḥ, and Shu'aib (the latter has occasionally been said to correspond to the biblical figure Jethro). The usual list of twenty-five prophets, rendered in the same form that is often memorized by young children, is the following:

> Ādam, Idrīs, Nūḥ, Hūd, Ṣāliḥ, Ibrāhīm, Lūṭ, Ismā'īl, Isḥāq, Ya'qūb, Yūsuf, Ayyūb, Shu'aib, Mūsā, Hārūn, Dhū'l Kifli, Dawud, Sulaimān, Ilyas, Ilyasā', Yūnus, Zakariyyā, Yaḥya, 'Isā, and Muḥammad.[13]

In addition, there are the figures: Dhū'l Qarnain (mentioned in 18 Al-Kahf, and in tradition associated with Alexander the Great); Luqmān (who appears in the *sūrah* that bears his name, 31 Luqmān 12, and is said to be a figure of wise sayings and prophet to the Arabs); and 'Uzair (who some say is Ezra; 9 Al-Tawbah 30 mentions that some regarded him to be the "son of God"). Finally, in 18 Al-Kahf there appears a mysterious "servant of God," who in tradition is called "Al-Khiḍr" or "Al-Khāḍir" ("the green-colored one"?). Khiḍr is usually not considered a Qur'ānic prophet, even though he appears to instruct the prophet Moses (see Chapter 6).[14] The Prophet Muḥammad is said in the Qur'ān itself to be the "seal of the prophets" (33 Al-Aḥzāb 40), bringing the final and complete revelation from a chain of revelation in sacred history since its beginning with Ādam. Belief in "prophets" and their "books" is among Muslims' five canonical "beliefs."

A genre of religious narrative called "stories of the prophets" (*qiṣāṣ al-anbiyā'*) developed relatively early in the Islamic tradition. This narrates the stories of each of the Qur'ān's prophets serially, rendering the various and disparate accounts of the prophets throughout the Qur'ān into a single, smooth, coherent story (which the Qur'ān does not do). This also includes some information that is not found in the Qur'ān, such as material drawn from other religious traditions about figures also known in Hebrew, Hellenic, and Christian religious literatures. A classical work of this type is by Ibn

Kathīr (d. 1373), and an edition by Al-Kisā'ī (ca. 1200) is readily available in English.[15]

Muslims have discussed whether Mary (Maryam), the mother of the Prophet Jesus, could be considered a prophet, even though she is never called one in the Qur'ān.[16] Mary is also an especially gendered figure in the Qur'ān because she is depicted giving birth, an act for which males lack capacity. Further, Mary is shown to conceive, give birth to, and nurture her baby without any human partner or other community assistance, only God's. The Qur'ān emphasizes the support, such as food, she receives from a divine source before pregnancy (3 Āl 'Imrān 37). The depiction in 19 Maryam details her birthing her child in isolation from others. At this time, needs which would otherwise be provided by family members or a midwife are fulfilled from a supranatural source; dates fall from a tree when she shakes it, water appears to cool her down, and Mary even hears a voice to soothe her pain (19 Maryam 24–26). Mary's greatest achievement in the Qur'ān, that is having her child, is underscored by her community members' shocked reaction when she appears with her newborn infant in her arms and, it is implied, no reasonable account for the child's appearance (19 Maryam 27–29). The Prophet Jesus, a rational and speaking newborn, in the verses that follow immediately after this announces publicly that he is a prophet and that he supports his mother, Mary; and further, and also by the will of Allāh, he will not be a fussy baby or difficult to look after (19 Maryam 32).

Considering the exemplary figures in the Qur'ān now in female and male terms, Mary is among the female figures depicted in the Qur'ān and prophetic tradition who provide models of autonomous leadership (such as, for example, the mother of Ismā'il, Ḥajar, according to extra-Qur'ānic tradition). In the Qur'ānic case, Mary heads her own nuclear family (the Prophet Jesus is called "son of Mary" in the Qur'ān).[17] The Qur'ān also gives an example of a woman who is a head of state, the Queen of Sheba (named Bilqīs), who comes to accept the prophetic message of Solomon (Sulaimān) in 27 Al-Naml 22–44. Across the text of the Qur'ān, Bilqīs appears to be like a female, believing counterpart to the figure of the male, unbelieving ruler, Pharaoh of Egypt, who hears the message of the Prophet Moses but rejects it. The Qur'ān also depicts women who possess social power who are not good, such as the woman householder (elsewhere called Zulaikha) who fabricates a slanderous accusation against her servant and the object of her affections, the Prophet Joseph, in 12 Yūsuf. In general, the portrayal of non-autonomous women in the Qur'ān (such as wives of kings and prophets) either reflects or contrasts the prophetic message within their own milieu, such as the disobedient partner of Lot. The same also holds true for males who are members of prophets' families, such as Qur'ānic fathers and their sons, since in general prophets polarize their mix-gendered audiences into those men and women who accept the message and affirm the warning on the one hand, and those who do not on the other.

The Qur'ān gives two primary Arabic terms for prophets in the Qur'ān: *nabī* and *rasūl*. The latter term, *rasūl*, is the designation for Muḥammad that is heard in the words of the *shahādah*, the profession of faith. The Qur'ān depicts prophets as being exemplary persons chosen by God, sent to bring warning (*nadhīr*) to their communities to deliver a message about inevitable and impending judgment. They all receive inspiration from God as they bear His message. Typically, their mission divides their communities into those who accept the message, and those who reject it. In many instances the Qur'ān presents the personal experiences of prophets in emotive registers, such as when they break with family and community, as did the Prophet Muḥammad, as well as the figure Ibrāhīm (Abraham) who disowned his own father, and also Nūḥ (Noah) who witnessed his own son, who would not listen to him, drown. The structure and style of the presentation of the prophets who preceded Muḥammad in the Qur'ān corresponds to the Qur'ān's unique textual logic, discussed further in Chapter 6.

In Muslim tradition, prophets are studied academically in terms of their particular or even unique qualities. For example, the Qur'ānic Prophet Jesus ('Isā) is known for healing and miracles, and the Prophet Solomon (Sulaimān) is revered for supranatural knowledge, such as his mastery of the speech of animals, especially birds like the *hudhud* (hoopoe). It is often said that the Prophet Muḥammad's "miracle" is not one outstanding personal capability such as these, but rather the Qur'ān itself. In Muslim tradition, the coincidence of the alleged illiteracy of the Prophet Muḥammad, that is, his incapacity to read or write, and his subsequent bearing of the Qur'ān is itself recognized to be miraculous, and this is considered even more remarkable given the Prophet's own recorded statements that he did not come to bring "miracles." Esoteric and devotional formulations imagine transcendent ideal prophetic "realities" based on observations such as these, while religious philosophers have investigated more categorical topics intellectually, such as what could be the nature of prophetic knowledge with respect to other kinds of knowing (divine, angelic, and human). The "reality" of the Prophet Muḥammad spans Islamic traditions of piety, from esotericism to popular practices of veneration. All prophets in the Qur'ān are human and mortal (although, according to Islamic tradition, Jesus did not die at his crucifixion).

Prophets are shown in the Qur'ān at times to be challenged personally by aspects of their very own human characters. An example is the unsure speech of the Prophet Moses. Occasionally, under the influence of their human natures, they may even appear vulnerable to making mistakes. For example, it is possible to read a verse in 18 Al-Kahf to suggest that it was Moses (and not his servant) who was the one who "forgot the fish" that was meant for lunch under some sort of satanic influence (discussed in Chapter 6); Joseph acknowledges his struggle with his own "nature that is prone to misbehaving" (*al-nafsa la'ammāratun bi'l-sū'*, in 12 Yūsuf 53); Abraham is actually telling a lie when he claims that it was the big idol that smashed up all the little ones (in 21 Al-Anbiyā' 51–70); and finally, although not a "prophet," Mary calls out in labor pains (with words that mean "Would that I had died before this!" in 19 Maryam 23), as if she would resist the will of God that she would have her baby, the Prophet Jesus.

Many, although certainly not all, of the prophets mentioned in the Qur'ān bring scriptural revelation in the form of a "book." These revelations are variously named, such as, among others, the Ṭaurat (Torah, received by Moses), the Zabūr (Psalms of David), and the Injīl (teachings of Jesus, considered to have been lost in their original form; in tradition, these are not the Gospels, which are instead biographical accounts of the life of Jesus). The reality of these original scriptures is one of the tenets of the "five beliefs." All prophets are understood to have been inspired by God to bring a moral message of monotheism, and the promise and warning of the consequences of actions. The concept of prophecy is supported in the Qur'ān by numerous direct statements, including the first part of 14 Ibrāhīm 4, "We have sent forth no messenger except in tongue of his people so that he may expound to them clearly." Verses in 4 Al-Nisā' relate that soteriological accountability is a natural counterpart to prophetic revelation:

163. We have revealed to you, as We revealed to Noah and the prophets after him. And We revealed to Abraham, Ishmael, Isaac, Jacob and the tribes; and to Jesus, Job, Jonah, Aaron and Solomon; and We gave David a book.
164. And [We sent forth] some messengers we have already told you about, and some We have not told you about. And Allāh spoke to Moses directly.
165. Messengers, who were bearers of good news [*mubasharīna*] and warners [*mundhirīna*], so that humankind will have no plea against Allāh after the messengers' coming. Allāh is Mighty and Wise [*azīzan ḥakīm*]." (4 Al-Nisā' 163–165)

Once beings have heard the prophetic message, they are responsible for acting in accord with it.

In its presentation of the delivery and reception of their messages, the Qur'ān offers different names for prophets' "inspiration." These include *waḥy*, apparently a divine inspiration, and *ilhām*, which appears to be more human centered. In the Qur'ān, these terms describe the process of revelation coming down to the prophets, such as in part of 42 Al-Shūrā 51, in which the Qur'ān states, "It is not given to any mortal that Allāh should speak to him, except by Revelation [*waḥyan*] or from behind a veil [*ḥijābin*]. Otherwise, He sends forth a messenger who reveals by His permission whatever He wishes." Based on Qur'ānic verses like these, Muslims have wondered about the human experience of inspiration, most of all the experience of the Prophet Muḥammad as he received revelation from the Angel Gabriel. For example, in considering such matters, Muslims note that verse 164 of Sūrat Al-Nisā' (above) also states that Allāh once spoke to Moses "directly."

As the prophet of Islam, the figure of the Prophet Muḥammad is at the intersection of at least two kinds of sacred narrative: one is specific, relating to his own community and circumstances, as was presented previously in this chapter. Some of the Qur'ān's verses that relate to this specific historical context could be interpreted to have general application as well, and the Qur'ān rapidly shifts among such narrative frames of reference, as is shown further in Chapter 6. Muḥammad is also simultaneously a part of a universal narrative in the Qur'ān, in terms of his location within sacred history of a succession of prophets that have appeared between the start and the end of human time. The Qur'ān depicts Muḥammad's prophecy in both of these senses, contextualized historically as well as encompassingly universal, and also further expresses it in terms that are both personally psychological as well as those that are socially shared. Muḥammad's challenges, victories, and experiences are highlighted in the text within these superimposed frames, and naturally these are viewed by Muslims to have bearing on their own religious experience in the present.

The Qur'ānic depiction of the Prophet Muḥammad is "multifaceted" in its overlapping dimensions. In an article on the Prophet's experience, the scholar of Islam Alfred Welch divides Qur'ānic material on the presentation of the Prophet Muḥammad according to categories which may be loosely given as: 1. his personal experiences; for example, how he is comforted, urged patience, and how conflict and solidarity with others invokes his humanity; 2. his own prophetic experience, such as receiving revelation, dreams and visions, and other experiential knowledge; 3. the social power and responsibility of the Prophet; 4. Muḥammad's roles as warner, messenger, and bearer of the prophetic message; and 5. the universality of the mission.[18] The historical sketch given above has presented more than one of these aspects as it is known from the text of the Qur'ān, such as the consolation provided to the Prophet in times of trouble and the Qur'ānic assertion of his unique leadership and authority.

As the conveyor of revelation, the Prophet Muḥammad himself is not divine. Qur'ānic statements further emphasize the point that the Qur'ān is revelation from Allāh and not in any way the product of Muḥammad's human imagination or creativity (for example, by stressing many times that the Prophet is not a "poet"). Nevertheless, the exemplary model of the Prophet (*sunnah*) came relatively early in mainstream Islamic religious sciences to have a status like that of revelation for the purpose of jurisprudential argument in legal discourse (see Chapter 4). In addition, some extra-Qur'ānic statements are said to have been uttered while the Prophet Muḥammad was in a state of divine inspiration; these reports are known as "*ḥadīth qudsī*." Their status and authenticity have been debated in Islamic tradition, but they have nevertheless been profoundly influential in traditions of Muslim piety.[19]

According to the Qur'ān itself, the revelation of the Qur'ān occurred through a prophetic experience of contact with a wholly "other" and divine source. The first verses of 74 Al-Muddathir allude to the difficulty for a human to receive revelation (some scholars have claimed that these were the first verses that the Prophet Muḥammad ever received), in which the Prophet is said to be "wrapped in his mantle." (Tradition preserves an account that his wife, Khadījah, reported that Muḥammad covered himself under a blanket after experiencing the strain.) In the same verse of this *sūrah*, he is instructed to "rise up and warn." In tradition it is the angel Jibrīl who conveys the Qur'ān to the Prophet from God, and the actual name "Jibrīl" ("Gabriel") is also mentioned in three separate *sūrah*s. In the Qur'ān, there many references to the Prophet's direct encounter with this entity, such as with the idea of *rūḥ* ("spirit"), as in 97 Al-Qadr (quoted in Chapter 3), and also in the following verse:

> 102. Say [*qul*]: "The holy spirit [*rūḥ al-qudus*] has brought it [the Qur'ān] down from your Lord in truth, in order to reassure the believers, and as a guidance [*wahudā*] and good news [*wabushrā*] to those who submit [*lilmuslimīn*, 'to Muslims']". (16 Al-Naḥl 102)

With its context in the *sūrah*, 16 Al-Naḥl, this verse follows directly after a verse that mentions the possibility of God "replacing one verse with another," a phenomenon known as "abrogation" (discussed in Chapter 4).

At at least two points, in the Qur'ān the text suggests that the Prophet Muḥammad had an even more inexplicable, close encounter with Jibrīl. One of these passages is 81 Al-Takwīr 19–29. Here are the concluding verses of the *sūrah* (the beginning verses of this *sūrah* are considered in Chapter 6):

> 19. It [the Qur'ān] is truly the discourse of a noble messenger;
> 20. Who has power, with the lord of the throne [*dhī al-'arsh*] and is highly placed;
> 21. Obeyed, then trustworthy.
> 22. He saw him [Gabriel?] on the luminous horizon.
> 24. He is not, regarding the unseen, withholding;
> 25. And it is not the discourse of a devil, accursed [*shaiṭānin rajīm*]
> 26. Where, then, will you go?
> 27. It is only a Reminder [*dhikr*, (i.e. the Qur'ān)] to all humankind;
> 28. To whomever of you wishes to change your ways.
> 29. But you will not wish [this] unless Allāh, the Lord of Worlds [*rabbu al-'ālamīn*], wishes. (81 Al-Takwīr 19–29)

The event to which verse 22 refers is understood in tradition to be a vision of the angel Gabriel, whom the Prophet "saw on the luminous horizon." This passage also contains a typical, rupturing rhetorical sentence that leaps out of its own context: "Where, then, will you go?" (verse 26), and also a statement that seems to support the accepted theological view on "free will," namely that God ultimately determines human choices within the moral order (verse 29).

Some Muslims have related the experience of a vision "on the horizon" documented in 81 Al-Takwīr 22 to the event of the "Night Journey and Ascent" of the Prophet (discussed below), and have further also connected it to the depiction found in the first verses of 53 Al-Najm, which read as follows:

Bismillāh Al-Raḥmān Al-Raḥīm

1. By the star [*wal-najmi*] when it goes down,
2. Your companion has not gone astray or erred,
3. And he does not speak capriciously
4. It [the Qur'ān] is only a revelation [*waḥyun*] being revealed.
5. Taught him by a mighty one [Gabriel?]
6. Possessed of steadfastness. And so he arose,
7. While he was on the highest horizon;
8. Then, he came closer and hovered around;
9. Coming thus within two bows' length or closer.
10. Then [Allāh] revealed to His servant what he revealed
11. The heart did not deny what it saw.
12. Do you, then, dispute with him [Muḥammad?] concerning what he saw?
13. He has indeed seen him [Gabriel?] a second time;
14. By the Lote Tree of the outermost limit.
15. Close by it is the garden of refuge.
16. As the Lote Tree was covered by that which covers it;
17. His gaze did not shift nor exceed the bound.
18. He saw some of the great signs of his Lord [*āyāti rabbihi al-kubrā*]. (53 Al-Najm 1–18)

These verses relate a personal proximity of the Prophet Muḥammad with the source delivering revelation to him. The passage has provided rich material for traditions of esoteric, aesthetic, and mystical piety. (According to tradition, following just after this was the textual instance of the so-called "satanic verses," discussed in Chapter 4.)

Finally, among the themes of this cluster of Qur'ānic passages that relate to the Prophet's revelatory encounters is one episode that has been highly elaborated in the hagiographical tradition of the Prophet Muḥammad. It is known as the "Night Journey and Ascent." In the traditional telling of this event, the Prophet was first transported to Jerusalem, from where he then ascended up to heaven on a celestial creature, Burāq, encountering several previous Qur'ānic prophets along the way. The first verse of 17 Al-Isrā' or "Banī Isrā'il" (it is also sometimes just known as the "The Subḥān," from the *sūrah*'s first word) is taken by Muslims to refer to this event:

> *Bismillāh Al-Raḥmān Al-Raḥīm*
> Glory be to Him [*subḥāna alladhī*] Who caused His servant to travel by night from the Sacred Mosque [*al-masid al-ḥarām*] to the Farthest Mosque [*al-masjid al-aqsā*], whose precincts We have blessed, in order to show him some of Our signs [*āyātinā*]. He is indeed the All-Hearing, the All-Seeing [*al-samī'u al-baṣīr*]. (17 Al-Isrā' 1)

The "Isrā'" ("night journey") and "Mi'rāj" ("ascent" to heaven), an event in the *sīrah* of the Prophet, remains a key model of ascent for mystics, called "Sufis," in Muslim tradition.

The Qur'ān continually underscores the Prophet's humanity, even and especially in reference to supranatural experiences. In tradition, the very humanity of the Prophet contrasts with the divine nature of the Qur'ān itself. The Qur'ān emphasizes, sometimes in the language of unbelievers' retorts, that the Prophet bears no "signs," brings no "bands of angels" to surround him. For example, 29 Al-'Ankabūt 50 states: "They said: 'If only signs from his Lord were sent down to him.' Say: 'Signs are only with Allāh, and I am only a manifest warner.'" Or, in another example, the Qur'ān puts the idea in stronger terms:

> 7. And they say: "What is the matter with the Messenger? He eats food and strolls in the markets. If only an angel had been sent to him to be a warner with him;
> 8. "Or a treasure had been cast upon him, or he was given a garden from which he could eat." And the wrongdoers say: "You only follow a man bewitched [*mashūr*]."
> 9. See how they invent similes for you, and so they err, and then cannot find their way.
> 10. Blessed be He [*tabārak alladhi*] Who, if He wishes, will accord you better than that – gardens underneath which rivers flow [*tajrī min taḥtihā al-anhār*], and we will build palaces for you. (25 Al-Furqān 7–10)

These verses begin with unbelievers' snide comments about the Prophet's everyday behavior when he is observed out on the street. Immediately, the Qur'ān next explodes these insults rhetorically to the level of the trivially absurd (as in his not being given "treasure" or a "garden" in the town markets). Next, in verse 10, the Qur'ān inverts the entire idea of heavenly presence (angels, treasure) ironically into a cosmological affirmation of the reality of paradise. This is typical Qur'ānic rhetoric, whose persuasion often utilizes principles of surprise. Elsewhere, the Qur'ān describes other prophets who also endure similar taunts from their people, such as their harassing the Prophet Noah, interrogating him why there were no angels to accompany him, and claiming that he is possessed (23 Al-Mu'minūn 24–25).

As if anticipating resistance inside and outside its own textual frame, the Qur'ān continually asserts that it is not the product of a soothsayer, "madman," and especially not the work of a poet since the Qur'ān itself is not "poetry" (for example, in 69 Al-Ḥaqqah 40–41 and 36 Yā Sīn 69; see also Chapter 5). In positive terms, the Qur'ān states that Muḥammad is a human warner, charged with a teaching just as had been the prophets who came before him (for example, in 3 Āl 'Imrān 144 and 7 Al-A'rāf 188). While some prophets did enact convincing "miracles" by the will of God, such as when Jesus and even Abraham revive living things from the dead, or with Moses' proofs to Pharaoh and his magicians, the Prophet Muḥammad's one and only miracle (*mu'jizah*) is the Qur'ān.

Within the Qur'ān, the textual relationship of prophets in the past, present, and future is a rhetorical frame on which Qur'ānic themes have a shifting, "multifaceted" presentation. For example, there is a close thematic relationship and textual proximity of material about the Prophet Muḥammad with Qur'ānic narratives about Mūsā (the latter comprise approximately one-fifth of the Qur'ān's verses overall). Major accounts of the Prophet Moses are found in the *sūrah*s 20 Tā Hā; 27 Al-Naml; 29 Al-'Ankabūt; and 40 Ghāfir. In 28 Al-Qaṣaṣ, the comparison between Mūsā and Muḥammad is actually made explicitly more than once.[20] Thematically, the correspondence of these two Qur'ānic figures underscores prophetic experience that relates to tensions of self-doubt and self-confidence, ideals and realities of leadership and community, and others' acceptance and rejection of a prophetic call.

Finally, there is the theme of eschatology, or the "last things," which is one of the canonical "five beliefs." Students new to reading the Qur'ān are sometimes surprised by the relative amount of material that they find in the text that is about judgment day, that is, the future consequences of present action. About as much material, twenty percent of the Qur'ān, is dedicated to accounts of the Prophet Moses (Mūsā) as there are verses pertaining to judgment. The Qur'ān states clearly that there is an impending judgment, or an "hour," that is inevitable, although no one knows except God when it will come. And when it does come, it will come suddenly, according to the Qur'ān itself.

There are many names for this impending event in the Qur'ān, such as "*yawm al-dīn*" ("day of reckoning") in the first *sūrah* (the Fātiḥah), also "*yawm al-qiyāmah*" ("day of resurrection"), and "*al-yawm al-ākhir*" ("the final day"), or just "the hour" (*al-sā'ah*). At this moment in time, all will answer for their actions. Past events have all been recorded. Good deeds will weigh heavy on scales, while bad deeds (which apparently will have no substance in an enduring reality) count for nothing. When that time comes, people will be consigned either down to "the fire" (*al-nār*, hell) or up to "the garden" (*al-jannah*, heaven). Numerous statements in the Qur'ān about bodily resurrection imply that the Qur'ān anticipates a non-Muslim audience in an Arabian context to have had difficulty accepting the reality of these inevitable events. In the text of the Qur'ān, future judgment is portrayed in a vivid, dynamic, and dialogical style. This can present some of the most difficult content for English-speaking students who are new to reading the Qur'ān to apprehend, whether they profess to be Muslim or non-Muslim.

The depiction of the last things offers some of the most multivalent images and "multifaceted" concepts in the Qur'ān, due to the evocative ambiguity and striking language. In addition, the text often pivots and then reorients its key themes precisely at instances of the expression of the end-time; these eschatological events may reference a present, a past, or a primordiality within the Qur'ān's own textual metaphysics of space and time. Not merely rhetorical in the Qur'ān, multifaceted soteriology is also foundational to Islamic religious thought and practice. For example, it is required that all Muslims "stand" together at least once with a community of other believers on the Plain of 'Arafat (the term means "knowing") during Ḥajj (Islamic pilgrimage, which is required once in a lifetime as the fifth "pillar" of Islam). At this place and time, every man and woman is to reflect on the "knowing" of the prophet Abraham (Ibrāhīm) at what is said to be the same physical spot in the sacred past. This is performed all day long with the Qur'ānic knowledge of the inevitable standing together before God that is yet to come. Discussion returns to the theme of the "last things," Qur'ānic scenarios and depiction of the end-time, and their relation to the religious moment of the human present at the end of this book.

NOTES

1. For more examples like these, see Johns, "The Qur'an on the Qur'an."
2. Martin, ed., *Approaches to Islam in Religious Studies*.
3. Burton, *Collection of the Qur'an*; Crone, *Meccan Trade and the Rise of Islam*; Crone and Cook, *Hagarism*; Wansbrough, *Qur'anic Studies*. Compare this to Patricia Crone's more recent thoughts on the historical validity of Muslim sources in "What do We Actually Know about Mohammed?"
4. The study of Islam actually arrived relatively late into formal discipline of the academic study of religion, having previously tended to be located within the area of the study of the region of Europe's "Near East" (i.e. West Asia). A groundbreaking work from the 1980s, for example, is Martin, ed. *Approaches to Islam in Religious Studies*.
5. One way to learn the basic story of the life of the Prophet Muḥammad, for those who do not know it already, is to watch the feature-length English-language film *The Message*, which follows the standard sequence of episodes found in the *sīrah*.
6. On the tradition of venerating the Prophet, see Safi, *Memories of Muhammad*, and Schimmel, *And Muhammad is His Messenger*.
7. Three good surveys of the theory and practice of "*jihād*" are: Bonner, *Jihad in Islamic History*; Cook, *Understanding Jihad*; and Firestone, *Jihad*. See also Donner, "The Sources of Islamic Conceptions of War," and see Al-Miṣrī (trans. Keller) for standard jurisprudential rulings, *Reliance of the Traveler*, pp. 599–606.
8. There is another Qur'ānic instance of this phrase in 11 Hūd 73, here understood to refer to the "house" of Abraham.
9. For discussion of Muslim development of the Qur'ānic doctrine, see Welch, "Allah and Other Supernatural Beings"; and a perspective informed by the field of documentary history is offered in Hawting, *The Idea of Idolatry and the Emergence of Islam*.
10. For further discussion, see Donner, "From Believers to Muslims: Patterns of Communal Identity in Early Islam."
11. The "five pillars" or fundamental acts of Islam are: witnessing, *shahādah*; daily canonical worship, *ṣalāt*; annual legal almsgiving, *zakāt*; fasting during the month of Ramaḍān, *ṣawm*; and the pilgrimage to Mecca, called Ḥajj, to be performed at least once in a lifetime. These are all discussed at greater length in Chapter 4.

12. For example, see a letter by Hasan Basri that is translated in Rippin and Knappert, ed., *Textual Sources for the Study of Islam*, pp. 115–120.
13. Here is an English version of the same list of names: Adam, Idris, Noah, Hud, Salih, Abraham, Lot, Ishmael, Isaac, Jacob, Joseph, Jonah, Shu'aib, Moses, Aaron, Dhu'l Kifli, David, Solomon, Elijah, Ilyasa, Jonah, Zachariah, John the Baptist, Jesus, and Muḥammad.
14. "Al-Khiḍr" is sometimes said to be the same as the Qur'ānic figure Idrīs, or another esoteric figure like Hermes. Information that is provided here about traditional speculation on the identity of prophets comes from materials developed by Stephen Shwartz, which were kindly provided by R. Michael Feener.
15. Al-Kisā'ī, *Tales of the Prophets*.
16. Smith and Haddad, "The Virgin Mary and Islamic Tradition and Commentary."
17. This model would seem to have had special resonance with Muslim women in the early community who had lost spouses to conflict, according to Muslim sources. The disappearance of the community's men is also one of the standard explanations given in tradition for the Prophet's marriage to more than four spouses (Chapter 4), as well as the reason given in tradition for the attempt to compile and standardize the text of the Qur'ān itself in the first years of Islam (Chapter 3).
18. Welch, "Muḥammad's Understanding of Himself."
19. Graham, *Divine Word and Prophetic Word in Early Islam*.
20. Wheeler, *Moses in the Qur'ān and Islamic Exegesis*.

3

READINGS OF THE QUR'ĀN

In a Qur'ānic context, the idea of a "reading" may carry any one of several possible primary meanings. It may mean the act of reading aloud, whether from the text or from memory. There may be a "reading" for the meaning conveyed by the words of the text, including the sense of "reading" as an interpretation (*tafsīr*) or "translation." The term may relate just to a portion of selected text, as in an excerpted "reading" (*maqrā'*). In Qur'ānic sciences, a word for "reading" can also have a technical meaning as a "variant reading" (*qirā'ah*), one of several accepted vocalizations of the standard text. The broader religious "sciences of reading" treat the practice of recitation of the Arabic Qur'ān, or voicing the text aloud (*tilāwah*), according to established rules and guidelines (*tajwīd*). Most of the formal and informal guidelines relating to Qur'ānic reading determine flexible parameters that can support a diversity of modes of practice and understanding, all of which groups of Muslims may consider to be acceptable and authoritative. Although Muslims attest that the Qur'ān never changes, the circumstances of "reading in context" that relate to all of these practices do change. Further, contexts for reading the Qur'ān and for understanding and applying its meanings have been changing dramatically in the modern period. This has come along with new technologies and spaces for teaching, study and engagement of the Qur'ān. This chapter presents a constellation of approaches to the text through its "reading," constructed through terms and concepts that draw on the Muslim classical sciences for the reception, recitation, and rendering of the Qur'ānic message.

Established fields of the "sciences of the Qur'ān" (*'Ulūm Al-Qur'ān*) guide Muslims in reading and study of the text. Sub-fields such as *tafsīr* (interpretation) and *qirā'āt* and *tajwīd* (modes of reading aloud), for example, coalesced in about the thirteenth century as branches of "Qur'ānic sciences." These areas overlapped with other emerging disciplines of religious knowledge and learning, especially Arabic grammar. Just as was the case with legal questions and answers within Muslim jurisprudential tradition, the flexible frameworks for Qur'ānic sciences have remained relatively stable since the formative period, while Muslim social experience and its historical circumstances, naturally, have changed. As new avenues and opportunities form today for developing Muslim religious theory and practice, such as with new media, approaches to reading the Qur'ān are still accepted as legitimate through the perceived continuity and authority of classic study and learning.

The "Qur'ānic sciences" are treated formally in classical sources such as Jalāluddīn Al-Sūyūṭī's (d. ca. 1505) *Al-Itqān fī 'Ulūm Al-Qur'ān* and Badr Al-Dīn Al-Zarkāshī's (d. ca. 1392) *Burhān fī 'Ulūm Al-Qur'ān*. The major subject areas of these compendia include the history and compilation of the text; categories of Qur'ānic expression and rhetoric (such as parables and oaths); *tajwīd* and *qirā'āt* (sciences of textual vocalization and accepted variant "readings," respectively); grammar and *gharīb* (a designation for "strange and difficult" Qur'ānic words and expressions, of which early Muslims recognized many); exegesis (*tafsīr*), including differences among various perspectives; and intellectual questions about the nature of the Qur'ān such as *i'jāz* ("inimitability"), which may also bring to bear some consideration of the semantic and stylistic aspects of the revealed text.[1] All of these topics are to be treated in this chapter or in subsequent ones. They could all be considered to be aspects of the general idea, "readings" of the Qur'ān. In addition to this, the major written works on *'Ulūm Al-Qur'ān* treat topics that are discussed elsewhere in the chapters of this book, such as *naskh* (abrogation); *asbāb al-nuzūl* (occasions of revelation), found in Chapter 4; writing and calligraphic arts, considered further in Chapter 5; established systems of piety that underlie all religious facets of Qur'ānic learning and practice, also treated in Chapter 5; and *qiṣāṣ al-anbiyā'* ("stories of the prophets"), some of which are treated in Chapter 6.

The present chapter begins with standard religious accounts of early compilation of the text, comparing them to other rigorous paradigms for Qur'ānic study. Focus then turns to some of the classical categories of Qur'ānic study, including *tafsīr* (exegesis). The chapter concludes with some consideration of contemporary approaches to the "reading" of the text as shaped by new media. The latter considerations, while departing from material given in the classical sources, may still be seen as adaptations and extensions of material established a millennium ago and, for many Muslims, half a world away. As Frederick Denny writes in the conclusion to his article on the development of Islamic sciences of exegesis and recitation, the Qur'ān had already been the "master of the Muslims" for generations even as the methods and approaches were developed to "read" and interpret the text in Islamic religious tradition.[2] The Qur'ān was by its own account "easy to understand" and not in a "foreign tongue," yet at the same time the (mainly Persian-speaking) scholars who first developed the Qur'ānic sciences spent much effort in the formative period trying to comprehend it. Muslims worldwide who read the Qur'ān still grapple with the limits to claiming knowledge of "reading" the text.

READING THE QUR'ĀN AS A RECITATION

One of the most effective first approaches to the Qur'ān, at least for those who are not already familiar with it, is first to engage the Qur'ān on, and in, its own terms. Instead of opening an English-language "translation" to the first page, then reading in isolated silence, one would instead put all the books aside, including this one, and including even the book of the Qur'ān itself. By listening to the actual sounds of Arabic, one encounters the Qur'ān as practicing Muslims engage and embody it daily: in voice and sound, as a "recitation." For readers who may actually wish to do this now, there are many performances of reading available for appreciation on the Internet; for example, one can readily search for sound recordings and recorded live performances by one greatest reciters of the twentieth century, the late 'Abd Al-Bāsiṭ 'Abd Al-Ṣamad, who was from Egypt. Another excellent source is the Qur'ānic material presented by Michael Sells in *Approaching the Qur'ān*, which offers English-language interpretations of the meanings of *sūrah*s in *Juz' 'Ammā*, accompanied by an audio recording for study of differing kinds of recitations by men and women readers, who perform variants of five selected *sūrah*s.[3]

Listeners who would need to study Arabic in order to be able to discern the semantic meaning of all the words voiced in the recited Qur'ān will be sharing an experience with about four-fifths of the world's Muslims, none of whom is a native speaker of Arabic. First-time listeners, as learners, would probably also have an experience that differs a great deal from what most of the world's Muslims would expect, however. This is because most religious Muslims, no matter what their native language, have gained some familiarity with the Qur'ānic text through years of exposure through hearing it, and quite likely also reciting, reading, and actively listening to it. The claims that are made in Qur'ānic tradition (and which are also found in the text itself), that the Qur'ān is miraculous, transcendent, and divine in origin, are not at all inconsistent with Muslim traditions that describe it as being like an old friend with whom one has spent many nights up awake. The primary media for such experienced knowledge are time and rhythm, breath and pitch, and shapes sounded in human voice.

In Muslim tradition, among the very first material that is said to have been revealed to the Prophet Muḥammad was the ninety-sixth chapter of the Qur'ān, titled "Iqrā'" (or "Al-'Alaq"). The standard name of the *sūrah* comes from the command to "Read!" that appears in the first verse:

> *Bismillāh Al-Raḥmān Al-Raḥīm*
> 1. Read [*iqrā'*], in the Name of your Lord, who created:
> 2. He created humanity from a clot [*'alaq*].
> 3. Read, by your Most Generous Lord [*warabbuka al-ākram*],
> 4. Who taught by the pen.
> 5. He taught humanity what it did not know. (96 Al-'Alaq 1–5)

According to Islamic tradition, the circumstance of the revelation of the preceding verses was a gripping scenario in which the angel delivering God's revelation, Jibrīl, physically took hold of the body of the Prophet Muḥammad. The angel exhorted him to "read," even though the Prophet protested that he did not know how, or (depending on how one interprets the Arabic account) did not know what, to read.

As a "reading," the Qur'ān is as much a verb as it is a noun, as much a performance as it is a textual object.[4] Since the earliest period, the Qur'ān's authoritative preservation and transmission is aural and oral, not primarily written and textual.[5] Among Qur'ānic self-descriptions are its portrayals of the effect of hearing its own verses recited as well as self-referential, practical instruction on recitation. For example, the following verses merge ideas of God's word and human speech, the act of reading the Qur'ān aloud, and the possibility of "following" its content:

> 16. Do not wag your tongue with it [the Qur'ān] to hurry on with it
> 17. It is incumbent on Us [God] to put it together and to recite it [*waqur'ānahu*]
> 18. Then, when We recite it, follow its recitation [*fa'idha qar'anāhu fa'attabi' qur'ānahu*]
> 19. Then, it is incumbent upon Us to expound it clearly [*bayānahu*] (75 Al-Qiyāmah 16–19)

Another word used in the Qur'ān for recitation, "*tilāwah*," also carries a primary meaning of "following" the Arabic words according to both their sound and their meaning.

Ideally, reading the Qur'ān occupies the complete concentration of its reader. Reciters and listeners are instructed by the Qur'ān to "remember" and "preserve" it when reading and hearing. These activities are always in the awareness of omniscient Allāh, as suggested by the following verse:

> You do not go about any affair, nor do you recite [*wamā tatlū*] any portion of the Qur'ān, nor do you do anything, but We [God] are witnesses thereof, as you press on with it. And not a speck's weight in the earth or in the heavens escapes Allāh; and nothing smaller or bigger than that, but is in a manifest book. (10 Yūnus 61)

This verse also relates the book that is being read (that this, the Qur'ān) to the "recording" of all events in an indelible record, an accounting for the day of judgment.

The Qur'ān refers to itself often as a "revelation" that was "sent down." Multivalent Arabic words in the Qur'ān derived from the root "*n, z, l*" convey meanings such as: *nuzūl*, "revealed"; *tanzīl*, "revelation"; and *inzāl*, the act of "revealing." In statements found within the Qur'ān that relate the event of its very own revelation, the Qur'ān also suggests more than one dimension of the reality of its revelation. That is to say, it claims, simultaneously, to have come down in at least three nested temporal dimensions.[6]

First, according to the Qur'ān, it was revealed all at once, on a "night of power" or "determination" (*lailat al-qadr*), said to fall during the month of Ramaḍān. There are several verses from the Qur'ān that may be combined to support this point. Muslims interpret the entire *sūrah* 97 Al-Qadr in terms of the event of the Qur'ān's revelation, for example.[7] The verses of this *sūrah* are read in terms of the revelation of the Qur'ān by way of the "spirit" (Angel Gabriel, Jibrīl), as discussed in the previous chapter. The poetics of 97 Al-Qadr are typical of the Qur'ānic material that is said to be among the first that was revealed to the Prophet Muḥammad, "Meccan" material. Stylistically, the *sūrah* sets forward an idea (i.e. "night of power") and then poses rhetorical questions that expand the concept in verses of increasing length. The entire *sūrah* reads as follows:

Bismillāh Al-Raḥmān Al-Raḥīm

1. We have sent it [the Qur'ān] down on the "night of power" [*lailat al-qadr*]
2. If only you knew what is the night of power
3. The night of power is better than a thousand months
4. The angels and the spirit [*al-rūḥ*] descend thereon by the leave of their Lord with every command
5. It is peace [*salāmun*], until the break of dawn. (97 Al-Qadr)

The first verses of 44 Al-Dukhān are also said to refer to this same happening, a revelation taking place on a single "night":

Bismillāh Al-Raḥmān Al-Raḥīm

1. *Ḥā Mīm*
2. By the manifest book [*al-kitāb al-mubīn*, the Qur'ān]
3. We have sent it down on a blessed night. We were then admonishing.
4. Therein, every wise matter is determined. (44 Al-Dukhān 1–4)

Another passage, 2 Al-Baqarah 185, a verse which expounds legal matters about daily fasting during the month of Ramaḍān, also names Ramaḍān as the month in which the Qur'ān was sent down:

> The month of Ramaḍān is the month in which the Qur'ān was revealed, providing guidance for humanity, with clear verses to guide and to distinguish right from wrong. He or she who witnesses that month should fast it. But if anyone is sick or on a journey, [he ought to fast] a number of other days. Allāh desires ease and does not desire hardship for you, that you may complete the total number; glorify Allāh for His Guidance, that you may be thankful. (2 Al-Baqarah 185)

Based on the above verse, Muslims observe the night of "the sending down of the Qur'ān" (*Nuzūl Al-Qur'ān*) in the last week of the month of Ramaḍān, on an odd-numbered day of the lunar month such as the 21st, 23rd (this is common), 25th, or 27th (see Chapter 5). Revelation in a single night, as commemorated once each year, is only one aspect of the understanding of "*nuzūl*," however, which is a concept and experience that has more than one Qur'ānic facet.

Second, the Qur'ān states that it was revealed "piecemeal," or "in stages," just as Muslim tradition holds the Prophet Muḥammad received revelation over a period of years. The proof verse for this, 17 Al-Isrā' 106, which also contains instruction on "following" recitation, was previously cited in Chapter 1. Another verse that appears in a different *sūrah* provides a rationale for revelation having said to occur in this manner:

> The unbelievers say: "If only the Qur'ān had been sent down all at once." That is how We wanted to strengthen your heart with it and We have revealed it in stages. (25 Al-Furqān 32)

This verse is typical of the ways in which the Qur'ān appears to anticipate and address the objections of non-believers; in this case, the text confirms the idea that the Qur'ān came down to the Prophet, historically, "in stages."

Third and finally, the Qur'ān affirms the religious idea that it exists preserved eternally on a "tablet." The final verses of 85 Al-Burūj, the source of this Qur'ānic concept, are:

> 21. Yet, it is a glorious Qur'ān [*qur'ānun majīd*]
> 22. In a well-preserved tablet [*lauḥin maḥfūẓ*] (85 Al-Burūj 21–22)

Unlike "*lailat al-qadr*," for which the Qur'ān provides some explanation, there is no further apparent specification of the term "*lauḥ maḥfūẓ*." This makes it a highly productive site for the religious and scholarly imagination. The idea in tradition that the location of the revelation is celestial (as in a "heavenly tablet") is supported by other Qur'ānic verses, such as those that appear at the beginning of 43 Al-Zukhruf.

Both 43 Al-Zukhruf and 44 Al-Dukhān (mentioned above) belong to a consecutive series of chapters numbering in the forties, known as the "*ḥawāmīm sūrah*s," which tend to express themes that are heavily eschatological. (They carry this name in tradition because they all begin with the unexplained letters, "*Ḥā Mīm*.") The verses that begin 43 Al-Zukhruf are:

Bismillāh Al-Raḥmān Al-Raḥīm
1. *Ḥā Mīm*
2. By the manifest book [*wa'l-kitābi al-mubīn*]
3. We have made it an Arabic Qur'ān [*qur'ānan 'arabiyya*] that perchance you may understand
4. And, indeed, it is the mother of the book [*ummi al-kitāb*], with Us, lofty and wise (43 Al-Zukhruf 1–4)

After the opening letters, "*Ḥā Mīm*," the oath that follows in the second verse, and then the reference to the Qur'ān's Arabic nature, the fourth verse gives the phrase, the "mother of the book." Muslims have read this expression to mean the divine source of the Qur'ān, or as scriptural proof that the Qur'ān confirms the revelations that preceded it. This third, final aspect of the Qur'ān's self-presentation of its revelation is universal in its scope.

Elsewhere, the Qur'ān indicates the unlimited nature of its expression and potential to exceed even the bounds of textuality itself. Its own words and expression, as the "speech of God," the Qur'ān reminds listeners, are not finite, but extend ever-widening horizons of experience and recognition:

> Were all the trees on earth so many pens and the sea, coupled by seven other seas, supplying them with ink, Allāh's words [*kalimāt Allāh*] would not be exhausted. Allāh is, indeed, All-Mighty and Wise [*'azīzun ḥakīm*]. (31 Luqmān 27)

The revealed Qur'ān, the verse implies, expands beyond human cognition. The verse above connects the words of the Qur'ān with God's creation; in the Qur'ān, natural "signs" like trees and the seas are evidence of divinity, and represent a reminder to created beings to respond appropriately to the Creator. In another metaphor of an encounter with the natural world, the Qur'ān elsewhere describes its own impact to be inestimable, immediate, and overwhelming:

> Had We sent down this Qur'ān upon a mountain, you would have seen it bowing down and rent asunder out of the fear of Allāh. Those are the parables which We recite to humankind, that perchance they might reflect. (59 Al-Ḥashr 21)

In Chapters 5 and 6, more attention is given to the Qur'ānic message and the textual witness to its earth-shattering power. Discussion now turns to the history of this text and its readings as they have been presented by classical Muslim "sciences of the Qur'ān" along with other traditions of Qur'ānic study.

HISTORY OF THE QUR'ĀN

In Chapter 1, there was consideration of history as it is seen to be presented *in* the text of the Qur'ān. The focus is now on traditions of the history *of* the written text, which correspond closely to the history of its authoritative oral/aural transmission in the form of "readings." These are standard topics in the "Qur'ānic sciences." Muslim accounts of the transmission of the Qur'ān record some differences among those in the generation following the Prophet Muḥammad regarding both the collection of the text as well as the designation of authoritative "readings." These were resolved through a project of standardizing of the text that was said to have occurred not long after that. Another, rare matter that has been reported in tradition over the compilation of the written Qur'ān relates to "pro-'Alid" claims that parts of the Qur'ān validating the leadership of 'Alī, and subsequently the political and spiritual role of the "*imām*," were deliberately suppressed. Not surprisingly, among Sunnis there is little recorded debate over such issues. In any case, it can be said that the written form of the text that was established in the first generations was accepted remarkably uniformly by Muslims of many orientations, including Shi'ites. Divergences of view have tended to focus on differing readings of the same written text. It was not until the imposition of colonial orders and the regimes of knowledge and power they propagated that the Islamic claim to "unbroken" aural transmission of the Qur'ān from the time of the Prophet was ever seriously questioned by persons claiming authoritative knowledge with regard to Islamic religious systems.

There is enough diversity to be found just within Islamic religious history alone for it not to be necessary to leave the bounds of Muslim traditions in order to consider diverse views on the text of the Qur'ān and its reading. However, when it comes to the case of the historical narrative of the Qur'ān's compilation, juxtaposition of a religious and a non-religious view have become part of an internal discourse of Muslims worldwide. The contrast has been charged by the historical and ideological power and intensity of colonial subjugation. Echoes of this encounter may still be heard today when the term "orientalist" is heard used pejoratively within global Qur'ānic and Muslim religious contexts to refer to non-Muslim, European study of the Qur'ān.[8]

The European academic tradition shares with traditional Muslim sciences a great value placed on the exercise of exactitude and rigor.

Muslim historical accounts intersect vigorously with "Qur'ānic study" in European tradition on the point of the compilation of the text of the Qur'ān. These matters have been the primary subject of a "textual-critical" approach that was first developed in European biblical study. A defining issue for documentary historians has been the accurate identification and dating of the components of the compiled text. Gustav Flügel, for example, published an early concordance of the Qur'ān along with an edition that reordered the *sūrah*s according to his own understanding of their chronology. Many later authors used Flügel's edition instead of the standard Muslim arrangement of the text, among them the excellent translator of the Qur'ān into English, A. J. Arberry. The prevalence of the "Flügel edition" suggests the degree to which some orientalists did not have as their intellectual priority the appreciation of the received structure and style of the Qur'ān. In European-language scholarship of this historical era, more linear sensibilities tended to prevail over the approaches to dynamic intertextuality that had long been established across fields of Muslim religious readership.

An influential example of the reimagination of the ordering of Qur'ānic material in the colonial era is Richard Bell's *Introduction to the Qur'ān*, a book which was edited by W. Montgomery Watt after Bell's death. Like the works by scholars such as Theodor Nöldecke, it includes much standard material that is also covered in the traditional Muslim "Qur'ānic Sciences." However, Bell's work also puts forward its own original hypothesis of the Qur'ān's redaction, based on a theory of "duplications" in the text. In Muslim traditions, repetition is evidence of the many facets of Qur'ānic persuasion and experience. Bell, on the other hand, saw redundancy as a problem that he ought to try to solve.[9]

Such approaches dampen out the dynamic structure of the text, and thus may often contradict the very understandings necessary to have in place in order to appreciate the religious claims of Islamic scholarship. Classical Muslim approaches to these issues could be described as being methodologically "phenenomenological," in the sense that they take the multifaceted structure and style of the Qur'ān first to be a given before studying its unique rhetorical semantic properties. More recent non-confessional academic scholarship in English and other European languages has shifted toward the latter approach as well, such as with Rosalind Gwynne's *Argument in the Qur'ān*, which considers the presentation of Qur'ānic reasoning across the text in terms of its content and context.[10] Philosophers of religion such as Toshihiko Izutsu have also modeled approaches to the study of thematic elements of the Qur'ān that appear across the text, in this case by working with a philological focus on key terms and their relationality.

Orientalists and classical Muslim scholars of the Qur'ān also together have shared some key approaches in considering the Qur'ān's textual history. First, both kinds of approaches demonstrate an interest in Arabic language, philology, and the meanings of specific terms, as well as their connectedness over the Qur'ān. Second, they both consider the religious history of the Qur'ānic text to include a human component. According to accounts in the Islamic Qur'ānic sciences, for example, the Prophet Muḥammad rehearsed the Qur'ān with the Angel Gabriel prior to his passing away. It is also understood in religious formulations that the arrangement of the Qur'ānic text in the form it exists today was the result of the work of a historical committee making choices in redaction, as guided by God, and their efforts rendered the written text into the same form as the Prophet Muḥammad himself had learned. As part of the Qur'ānic sciences Islamic tradition preserves accounts of the work of this group and the textual sources that they used.

Third, both traditions of study, "religiously Muslim" and secular–"academic," have been concerned with dating the textual revelations as accurately and precisely as possible. Both systems have also linked matters of chronology and compilation to style (such as "Meccan and Medinan"). While often working from contrasting perspectives on the compilation of the text, both share a basic concern with chronology of "revealed" verses; this was in fact the guiding principle behind Flügel's reordering. For this, both may also accept historicized frameworks such as "Meccan" and "Medinan." Muslims developed frameworks for the study and attribution of the context of revelation in the form of a rigorous science of the "occasions of revelation" of verses, or *asbab al-nuzūl* (which is a form of *ḥadīth* report). In more recent Muslim religious thought, there has been a productive revitalization of the overlap of documentary and pious perspectives. Many modern and progressive interpretations by global scholars in fact rely on principles of contextualization and historicization (see Chapter 4 for discussion). A key example is the approach of Fazlur Rahman, a scholar from Pakistan who worked in the United States, as well as a group of

Indonesian scholars who, many having been influenced by Rahman himself, have developed sophisticated hermeneutical approaches based on contextualization or "*contextualisasi*."[11]

Here is the standard account of the history of the text of the Qur'ān, as it is documented in standard Muslim sources. According to these reports, the shaping of the arranged Qur'ān took place in three stages: first, there was the shaping of the form of the Qur'ān during the time of the Prophet Muḥammad; second, it was assembled with an attempted redaction at the time of the leadership of Abū Bakr soon after the Prophet passed away; and, finally, an authoritative version of the text was produced in the time of the third Sunni caliph, 'Uthmān bin 'Affān. This latter text is the version that Muslims read today. Throughout the entire era of the first generations of Muslims, however, the most authoritative mode of reading, transmitting, preserving, and studying the Qur'ān remained oral and aural.

Following the Muslim accounts, in the first stage there were "scribes" taking dictation at the time of the Prophet Muḥammad, such as Zaid bin Thābit. However, there was no complete written "book" produced at this time. After the Prophet had passed away, these "pages" (*ṣuḥuf*) remained, and they would later be the basis for a scriptural "collection" or codex (*muṣḥaf*). The Qur'ān was also being transmitted continually to the companions of the Prophet through recitation, even during the time while it was still being revealed. This represents the beginning of the authoritative "*muṭawātīr*" (unbroken) transmission of the Qur'ān. During the period that the Qur'ān was being revealed, therefore, there was early shaping of the ordered text simultaneously through both oral and written modes. At the time that the Prophet passed away, however, there was still not yet any standard written "text."

By as early as 633 (one year after the Prophet Muḥammad had passed away), many companions of the Prophet who had memorized the Qur'ān were lost in battles, according to the Muslim sources. There was at this time a first official attempt made at compiling a standard text of the Qur'ān. This was done under the leadership of Abū Bakr, with the direction of Zaid bin Thābit, the same scribe tradition records as having worked previously under the direction of the Prophet himself. Tradition reports Muslims' pious ambivalences about this undertaking, including Zaid's own reluctance to take upon himself such a weighty responsibility. There had already been various Qur'ānic codices compiled by that time, which were in the possession of various companions of the Prophet. Among these there were some minor differences; for example, some material, such as "Sūrat Khal" and "Sūrat Al-Hafd," did not appear in all of these collections (and they are also not found in the standard text today).[12] There were other slight discrepancies among them in recorded content. For example, some versions of 112 Al-Ikhlāṣ did not begin with the word "*qul*" (or, "say"), as it does in the standard edition; and there were also minor variants within the opening *sūrah*, Al-Fātiḥah. Within a year or two after the Prophet's death, as the result of this first attempt at rendering uniformity for the written text, the entire Qur'ān had been copied on to sheets, based on authoritative written sources as well as oral material. These pages were said to have stayed with 'Umar (successor to Abū Bakr), and were later passed on to his own daughter, Hafṣah bint 'Umar.

The second attempt at the redaction of the Qur'ān happened under the third Sunni caliph, 'Uthmān bin 'Affān, in 644. According to the story, this occurred when significant differences had arisen within the community about the correct recitation of the Qur'ān. By this time, according to Muslim historiography, there would have been more Muslims who had been among the original companions of the Prophet Muḥammad killed in war in places such as Armenia and Azerbaijan. As Islam expanded rapidly in terms of its geographic range (from Spain to the Indus River within a century), it became ever more important to have a standardized Qur'ān for teaching, learning, and study. 'Uthmān once again called upon Zaid bin Thābit for help. Zaid, along with others who had been among the original companions of the Prophet Muḥammad, prepared copies of the Qur'ān using the codex of Hafṣah as a guide. Copies of these manuscripts were then conveyed to various geographic regions, and this "'Uthmānic" text is the same as the one that is read by Muslims today. It is at this point in time, as very rarely a few Muslims later claimed, material about 'Alī and his designated authority was overlooked.[13] Already by that time there had been dissension (*fitnah*) within the generation following the Prophet about political authority and leadership, turning on contested claims about the status of the genealogical lineage of the Prophet Muḥammad through the family of the Prophet's cousin 'Alī and 'Alī's wife, the Prophet's own daughter, Fātimah.

As the Qur'ān was written down during the time of the Prophet Muḥammad, according to the reports in Muslim sources, the script that was used was probably derived from Syriac.[14] Later, by the third

Islamic century, markings for short vowels came to be written in the text. By that time, the text had also come to be rendered in an angular and vertical style known as "Kufic." It was written on parchment, often with embellishment in gold. By the fourth century of Islam, calligraphic arts began to flourish, just as also did many other religious sciences and practices that came to be known as defined and systematic fields at that time. In this period, standard "Kufic" script gave way to many variant forms of writing and calligraphy. Established conventions for rendering the Qur'ān with separations between *sūrah*s, along with the inclusion of written *sūrah* titles and markers for verse endings, occurred around this time as well.[15] This coincided naturally with the development of the sciences of "*qirā'āt*," or variant readings of the Qur'ān, since the sectioning of text depended on heard meanings and their vocalization.

According to the survey by Solange Ory, paper first began to be used during the period of the 'Abbasid caliphate, in Bahgdad. With this, a more rounded, cursive script also began to appear in texts of the Qur'ān. Writing in these new styles was defined by ratios rendered in proportions defined by the width of the pen nib. Definitive masters of developing circular style were Ibn Muqlah (d. 940) and 'Alī bin Ḥilāl, or "Ibn Al-Bawwāb" (d. 1022), to whom is attributed a script known as *naskhī*. *Naskhī* script was the one most commonly used in the classical period of Islam, and later. Derivatives of *naskhī* script, known as *rayḥānī* and *muḥaqqaq*, are similar to one another. Another style, called *thuluth*, also resembles these styles but it rarely has been used for rendering the entire Qur'ān. *Thuluth* is more typically of the decorative rendition of verses or for *sūrah* titles. Some distinctive styles also emerged regionally, such as in Islamic Spain (Al-Andalus) and North Africa, and such styles combined characteristics of orthogonal and cursive forms. All of these styles, whether Kufic, cursive, or *thuluth*, can be seen in many kinds of media, including carving, ornamentation, and inscription in art and architecture.[16] Figure 1 is an example of the Fātiḥah, the first *sūrah* of the Qur'ān, rendered in a Persianiate style called "*nasta'līq*" (see also Chapter 5).

Figure 1 Al-Fātihah in "*ta'līq*" calligraphic style. Rendered after practice example in the textbook, *Kaidah Menulis dan Karya-Karya Master Kaligraphi Islam* by Ali Akbar (Jakarta, Pustaka Firdaus, 1995), p. 111. Rendering assisted by Michael Kodysz.

VOICED READINGS

As arts and technologies of rendering the written Qur'ānic text emerged in the formative period of Muslim religious sciences, a rigorous tradition of sounded "readings" was developing as well. As Frederick Denny demonstrates in his article "Recitation and Exegesis," the Qur'ānic sciences of grammar, exegesis, and recitation (including variant "readings" or vocalizations of the standard text) developed simultaneously.[17] They were all responses to similar needs, circumstances, and conditions. Like the standardization of the 'Uthmānic text, the guidelines for *tilāwah* (recitation) and "readings" of the Qur'ān were formalized as a response to the potential variability of Muslim practices of recitation. Beginners learn a system called *tajwīd* in order to vocalize Arabic in the distinctive Qur'ānic style, which differs from ordinary Arabic speech and singing. *Tajwīd* covers proper voicing of the phonemes as well as rules such as the assimilation of adjacent consonants and the prolongation of certain long vowels. It also sets important guidelines for pausing for a breath and for emphasis, which affects heard meanings. Like the arts of calligraphy, *tilāwah* (recitation) regulates flexibility and artistry in vocalizing the speech and message of the Qur'ān, embracing components of formalism as well as improvisational expression.

The Qur'ānic sciences of recitation also include an advanced technical area called "*qirā'āt*," a term usually denoting the variant accepted "readings" of the Qur'ān. These "readings" do not relate to pitch variation, nor to any alternate texts. Rather, they are relatively minor differences in the vocalization of the same 'Uthmānic text; all of these deploy the same system of guidelines for recitation, *tajwīd*. In order to understand the many layers of the English word "readings" that may apply to the Qur'ān even just in this single technical sense (*qirā'āt*) there are several ideas to master. The first is the concept of "mode/reading" (a concept which is based on *ḥadīth*, a report said to date from the time of the Prophet Muḥammad); the second is the idea of "seven readings" of the text, which is what the word "*qirā'āt*" is usually said to refer; finally, there are aspects of reading that pertain to actual practice and performance, which are not a part of the formal science of *qirā'āt*.

The idea of a "mode," a concept that extends to "reading" (*qirā'ah*), appears in the important phrase "*al-aḥrūf al-sabā'*" ("the seven modes"). The expression appears in a standard *ḥadīth* report that has many accepted variants. One form of it is the following: "Narrated 'Abdullāh bin 'Abbās: Allāh's Apostle [Muḥammad] said: Gabriel recited the Qur'ān to me in one way. Then I requested him (to read it another way), and continued to ask him to recite it in other ways, and he recited it in several ways until he ultimately recited it in seven different ways." In a more well-known version, which, like the one above, is also found in major compilations of standard *ḥadīth*, 'Umar bin Al-Khaṭṭāb, the second Sunni caliph, complained to the Prophet Muḥammad that he heard a companion reciting 25 Al-Furqān in a way different from how he had heard it from the Prophet Muḥammad himself. According to the report, the Prophet replied to 'Umar, "The Qur'ān has been revealed in seven different ways [*aḥrūf*], so recite of it whichever is easiest for you."[18]

Muslim scholars have tried to consider what, exactly, could be meant by the word "*aḥrūf*," the word meaning "mode" or "manner" that appears in the *ḥadīth* reports cited above. Interpretation of this term has several alternatives. Some have claimed that the idea of the "seven modes" should be said to relate to different languages or dialects of the Arabs at the time of the revelation of the Qur'ān, for example. According to others, it could also mean use of words originally deriving from different languages that are found in the Qur'ān itself. Others have asserted that this could be a comment on Qur'ānic expression: perhaps these are different words that express the same idea or concept; or the "seven modes" could denote slightly different wordings of the same phrase that appear multiple times in the Qur'ān. Some have offered more abstract interpretations, for example, claiming that the "*aḥrūf*" are meant to be different kinds of Qur'ānic content, such as its promises, threats, stories, and so on. And these are not the only theories Muslims have put forward for this highly productive concept within Qur'ānic sciences.[19]

Usually, however, scholars have assumed that the term refers to a technical science of "seven readings." The root of the word for the accepted variant readings, "*qirā'ah*," actually means "reading," the same as the noun "*qur'ān*" itself. This view is the most common, and the *ḥadīth*s that were cited above are used to support interpretation of the idea, "*aḥrūf*," according to this aspect of the term. Reasons given for the very existence of more than one of these accepted "readings" within Islamic tradition include the notion that they make the reception of the Qur'ān easier for diverse learners, and also that they enhance the multifaceted layers of Qur'ānic meanings, including its legal rulings. There are generally said to be seven readings, coinciding with the number given in the *hadīth* above. These originally represented the actual practices of reading that prevailed in prominent schools in five centers of Muslim transmission of learning in the first centuries of Islam: Medina, Mecca, Damascus, Basra, and Kufa. The rationale for this selection was to follow independent lines of transmission from scholars who were spread over a relatively large geographic area.

A list corresponding to this selection includes the names of the following seven readers: Ibn Kathīr (Mecca, d. 737), Nāfi' (Medina, d. 785), Ibn 'Āmir (Damascus, d. 736), Abū 'Amr (Basra, d. 770), 'Āṣim (Kufa, d. 744), Ḥamza (Kufa, d. 772), and Al-Kisā'ī (Kufa, d. 804). Some have said there are as many as ten or even fourteen readings. Ibn Mujāhid, who died in 936, was among those who asserted there were seven readings and also designated a list of which seven they were. His views became accepted in tradition. Today, the most popular readings are those transmitted from the readers listed above by Hafṣ (d. 796, the reading of 'Aṣim) and Warsh (d. 812, the reading of Nāfi'). In practice, once a reader begins in the modes of one "reading," he or she must continue in that mode until the reading concludes. Knowledge and study of the different "variant readings" (*qirā'āt*) is becoming ever more popular among advanced reciters of the Qur'ān worldwide.

An example of variation among the readings is the following: a word in the third verse from the opening *sūrah* (Al-Fātiḥah) may be rendered either as "*Maliki*" or "*Māliki*," but both convey the same sense of meaning, which is God's dominion over the day of judgment (Arabic and English appear Chapter 4; see also Figure 1, p. 69). In another example, one that has led to differences of legal opinion on ritual law for ablution, 5 Al-Mā'idah 6 (quoted in Chapter 4) may carry two meanings depending on its vocalization: "wash" (*arjulakum*, according to Nāfi' and Ḥafṣ) as opposed to "wipe" (*arjulikum*, according to Ibn Kathīr and Abū 'Amr).[20] It is crucial not to confuse the *qirā'ah* with another dimension of Qur'ānic reading and expression, however, which are the unbound, individual choices made by reciters as they vocalize the text. This includes pitch variation, which is required to be improvised so that melodic human artistry is not confused with the revealed Qur'ān. This practice, considered in more depth in Chapter 5, improvises aesthetically upon a text that seems already to be arranged structurally and stylistically in compositional patterns of themes and their variations.

LANGUAGE AND STYLE

Muslim scholars have approached the language and style of the Qur'ān with a number of systematic questions. Some of these have been about the derivation of legal norms and principles, for example, while others have been connected to other kinds of classification, including the lexigraphic attempt to understand the semantic meanings of the text. The study of features such as Qur'ānic poetics, oaths, and repetitions is part of the Islamic sciences of rhetoric (*balāghah*), represented by classical works such as that of Ibn Qutaibah (d. 889). This field developed in large part as analysis of the unique expression of the Qur'ān; the theological doctrine of the text's miraculous *i'jāz* ("inimitability") has as one of its supports the unparalleled "eloquence" of Qur'ānic expression (see Chapter 5 for discussion). The scholar Al-Rummānī (d. 996) cites the following as some examples of the "proofs" of the inimitable expression of the Qur'ān: concision, similes, metaphors, harmony, puns, alteration of structures, mutual inclusion and interconnection among meanings, hyperbole, "pleasing expressions," and more.[21]

In the Qur'ānic sciences, including rhetoric, the study of formal stylistic elements is related closely to the analysis of the relevant content the Qur'ān conveys. The great scholar Abū Ḥāmid Al-Ghazālī (d. 1111), in his work *Jewels of the Qur'ān*, classifies the style of all Qur'ānic expression in terms of ten types of content. He further groups these in terms of types of verses, and summarizes these categories as follows:

> The divine essence, divine attributes, divine works, the life to come, the straight path, i.e., the purification and beautification [of the soul], the conditions of the saints, the conditions of God's enemies, [His] argument with the infidels, and [finally] the bounds of legal judgments.[22]

In this work, for example, Al-Ghazālī parses the seven verses of the opening *sūrah*, the Fātiḥah, with respect to six categories of content.

For many sorts of Muslim study of Qur'ānic language and meaning, the distinction between "Meccan and Medinan" revelation (that is, verses understood to have been revealed before or after the Hijrah in 622 C.E.) functions both descriptive and analytically. These categories have been discussed previously in terms of the history of revelation that itself is understood to be embedded in the text (Chapter 2). Muslim scholars long ago also developed lists of names of types of rhetoric and expression in the Qur'ān which link to the same designations, "Meccan and Medinan." For example, the appearance of abbreviated letters at the beginnings of *sūrah*s (see Chapter 5) is almost always considered to be an indication of Meccan revelation. "Meccan and Medinan" are also recognized as stylistic descriptions in studies of the Qur'ān originally in European languages. In the modern period, the designation has been used by some Muslim social thinkers as part of a sophisticated hermeneutic that distinguishes matters that are said to be general principles from explicit and specific commands.

Features of "Meccan" style found in *Juz' 'Ammā* include poetic meter, rhyme, and oaths. These *sūrah*s are beautifully introduced for English-language readers by Michael Sells in *Approaching the Qur'ān*, rendered into English in a way that accents features of their meter and rhyme in Arabic. *Saj'* is the Arabic word for "poetical meter," and Meccan expression in the Qur'ān often follows the meters of pre-Islamic poetry. Pre-Islamic poetry was preserved in Qur'ānic sciences so that exegetes and others would know what was said to be the spoken dialect of the Prophet, and this has been an important source for orientalist philology as well in the study of Qur'ānic meanings and expression.

Michael Sells gives an introduction to some pre-Islamic odes in another book, *Desert Tracings*. The subject matter of these poems pertains a great deal to boasting, drinking wine, appreciation of beasts of burden and travel, and the theme of the forlorn poet trailing after the caravan of a lost beloved. Here is an example of the latter, the first verses of the *Mu'allaqa* ("Hanging Ode") of 'Imru'l Qays, in which the poet visits a ruined campsite of a beloved who has traveled on:

Qafā tabki min dhikrā ḥabībibin wa manzili
Bi siqṭi'l-lūā baīna'ldakhūli fa ḥūmil
Stopping to weep in remembrance of my beloved and her encampment
On the winding sand track between the path and the stream[23]

As Michael Sells has pointed out elsewhere (for example, in *Early Islamic Mysticism*), the tropes of the separated beloved, the intoxicated lover, and the visitation of "stations" along the way of a journey and its path of experience are typical of high art poetical expression in many Islamicate languages. This is especially the case since traditionally these were viewed to be metaphors for mystical knowledge and sentiment along the spiritual "path."

The Qur'ān is not considered to be "poetry," as the Qur'ān itself emphatically states, and its themes differ radically from those of the genre of the pre-Islamic ode (*qaṣīdah*). However, the Qur'ān does present cadences of meter and rhyme, particularly in the Meccan revelations. For example, 112 Al-Ikhlāṣ has irregular rhythm coupled with an end-rhyme (English-language meanings are given in Chapter 2; see also Figure 6, p. 196):

Qul huwa Allāhu aḥad
Allāhu al-ṣamad
Lam yalid wa lam yūlad
Wa lam yakul[n]-lahu kufūan aḥad

This short *sūrah* is typical of the Meccan revelations in its suspension of the resolution of the rhyme with the increasing length of lines as the *sūrah* progresses. Other *sūrah*s in *Juz' 'Ammā* that deploy rhyme and a similar poetics of suspension and resolution are: 97 Al-Qadr (with rhyme on the consonant, *-r*), treated in Sells, *Approaching the Qur'ān*; 103 Al-'Asr (carrying another end-rhyme on *-r*); and 105 Al-Fīl (with end-rhyme on *-l*). The phonemes "*n*" and "*m*" are understood to rhyme on the same vowel shape, as in the endings of the verses of Al-Fātiḥah (transliterated from Arabic and translated in Chapter 4).

The rhyme formed by the consonants at the end of words, found in both Meccan and Medinan *sūrah*s, is sometimes generated by grammatical form. This often occurs in the presence of the accusative indefinite case ending ("*-an*"), which appears on indefinite nouns that are the object of a verb; an example is the ending of the oaths that comprise the first five *āyāt* of 100 Al-'Ādiyāt. The sound "*-ān*" (with an open long vowel) also characterizes the "dual" form of nouns and verbs, typical of Sūrat 55 Al-Raḥmān (part of which is transliterated, translated, and analyzed in Chapter 6). In addition, plural human verbal forms and human adjectives may produce rhymes on "*-ūn*" and "*-īn*." Pronominal suffixes may also further generate grammatical rhyme, as in the feminine ending for "hers" or "its," "*-ha*"; an example of this rhyme scheme is all fifteen *āyāt* of 91 Al-Shams (these verses are also treated in detail in Sells, *Approaching the Qur'ān*). Finally, there may also be internal rhyme within a given *āyah*.[24]

In addition to poetic meters and rhyme, oaths (pl. *aqsām*) are characteristic of the Meccan *sūrah*s, such as those found in *Juz' 'Ammā*. Oaths enhance and intensify meaning by adding emphatic affirmation. Seventy-four verses of the Qur'ān are entirely oaths, and seven more are partially oaths. Oaths are of various types, often opened by the Arabic connective participles "*wa*" or "*fa*," or the cue "*lā uqsimu*." These several different Arabic forms are usually rendered into English as "By this *x*," or "I swear by *y*." Two examples of extended oaths are the beginning of the *sūrah*s 51 Al-Dhāriyāt and 79 Al-Nāzi'āt. 51 Al-Dhrāriyāt begins:

Bismillāh Al-Raḥmān Al-Raḥīm

1. By the scattering winds as they scatter [*wa'l-dhāriyāti dharwa*]
2. And the clouds, bearing their burden;
3. And the smoothly cruising ships;
4. And the angels which apportion the command
5. Surely, what you are promised is true;
6. And the judgment shall come to pass [*al-dīna lawāqi'*]. (51 Al-Dhāriyāt 1–6)

Oaths in both the forms "*wa*" and "*fa*" also appear in the first verses of another *sūrah*, 79 Al-Nāzi'āt, which alliterates noun and verb forms:

Bismillāh Al-Raḥmān Al-Raḥīm

1. By those who snatch violently [*wa'l-nāzi'āti gharqa*]
2. And those who draw out lightly [*wa'l-nāshiṭāti nashṭan*]
3. And those who glide smoothly [*wa'l-sābiḥāti sabḥan*]
4. And those who outstrip suddenly [*fa'l-sābiqāti sabqan*]
5. And those who conduct an affair
6. On that day the fire blast shall reverberate
7. Followed by the succeeding blast. (79 Al-Nāzi'āt 1–7)

One can compare the rhyming sound and structure found in these oaths above to other Qur'ānic examples, such as the openings of 100 Al-'Ādiyāt and 77 Al-Mursalāt, which also demonstrate oath-rhymes, generated through adverbs (ending in "*-an*").

Sometimes the objects sworn upon in Qur'ānic oaths seem to appear in context like a coherent collection or logical progression, as in 91 Al-Shams, in which consecutive verses 1–7 contain oaths sworn on the sun, the moon, the day and the night, the heaven and the earth, and the soul and its Creator. At other points in the Qur'ān, however, a cluster of sworn-upon objects may not appear to be so consistent or even so intelligible, especially when the verse's content is heavily eschatological, as in the example of 79 Al-Nāzi'āt (whose meanings are given above). At several points in the Qur'ān an oath is made on the Lord or by Allāh himself, as in 4 Al-Nisā' 65 (*warabbika*, "and by your Lord"). The Qur'ān also swears by the Qur'ān itself in more than one instance, such as 36 Yā Sīn 2 and 38 Ṣād 1.

An example of the difficulties of "reading" Qur'ānic oaths in English is the beginning of the *sūrah* 90 Al-Balad. The first line of the *sūrah* conveys an oath that is ambiguous both in terms of its syntax and its semantics, making the Arabic difficult to translate. This "oath" contains the particle of negation, "*lā*" (in "*lā uqsimu*"), allowing it to be possible to render the "multifaceted" single expression into English in one of two ways, either positive or negative:

Bismillāh Al-Raḥmān Al-Raḥīm

1. No; I swear by this city [or, "Verily I do swear by this city"]
2. And you are a resident of this city. (90 Al-Balad 1–2)

As discussed in Chapter 1, translators into English must also make a choice about the word "*balad*" in the name of this *sūrah*, a term which is a "multifaceted" term in Arabic and in Qur'ānic context. In addition, these first lines may be seen to refer to the experience of the Prophet Muḥammad in his "city" (Mecca), or to a more generic human experience of belonging in any place. The two forms of English-language translations of the oath in the first verse seem relatively equally common.

Meccan *sūrah*s, like those in *Juz' 'Ammā*, are also characterized by repetition of various kinds (such as duplicated words or *āyah*s), as well as repeated refrains. Stylized phrases appear in the Qur'ān in sections of many kinds of material, such as the formulae that are typical of narrations of previous communities (see Chapter 6). Another example of a refrain comes in 55 Al-Raḥmān, which alternates a formulaic rhetorical question, "Which of your Lord's favors do you deny?" (*fa bi'ayyi 'alā'i rabbikumā tukādhibān*), with other substantive *āyahs*. In the ending verses of 77 Al-Mursalāt, there is another alternating refrain, in which *āyahs* 45, 47, and 49 all read, "Woe betide, on that day, those who denounce" (*wailun yawm'idhin lilmukadhdhibīn*). In addition, Meccan *sūrahs* also show a tendency to repeat lines with an emphatic effect, which evokes textually the same kind of emotional affect that trained Qur'ān reciters may produce when they read the text aloud and repeat lines for improvisational emphasis. Two examples of *āyahs* repeated consecutively, separated only by the conjunction "*fa*" ("and again"), are: 75 Al-Qiyamah 34–35, "Woe be to you and woe" (*awlā laka fa'awlā*); and 82 Al-Infiṭār 17–18, "If you only knew what is the day of reckoning" (*wamā adrāka mā yawm al-dīn*).

The Qur'ān continually establishes rhetorical expectation through formulaic structure and repetition only to rupture it in a poetics of surprise and attention, a phenomenon that has long been recognized by Muslim rhetoriticians. An example is the unexpected line in Sūrat 55, Al-Raḥmān (verse 60), which intervenes just at the point that the reader expects another repetition of the standard refrain (above); but instead, the Qur'ān interjects here – "Is the reward for goodness anything but goodness?" In terms of overall structure and style, different "voices" in the Qur'ān appear within an improvisatory structure on which then reciters actually would improvise with their own voices. "Voice" is not a classical category in the study of Qur'ānic rhetoric, as is "poetic meter" or "oath," but it helps the reader here to understand the dynamics of the structure, sound, and impact of the Qur'ān. Some of these modes include the vocative and imperative registers; dialogical modes; other address to the reader in the form of rhetorical questions; and voices of narration.[25]

Vocative and imperative voices are commonly introduced by the word *qul* ("say"), indicating a statement to be repeated by the Prophet, and, by extension, by believers. In this mode, the Qur'ān responds to questions and confrontation, and clarifies its message and meaning. An example, one of many, is the first *āyah* of 8 Al-Anfāl. This verse concerns the spoils of war acquired by Muslims after the Battle of Badr (in the year 624; see also Chapter 2). It reads: "They ask you about the spoils (*al-anfāl*), say (*qul*): 'The spoils belong to Allāh and the messenger. So fear Allah and settle your differences. Obey Allāh and His messenger if you are true believers.'" Another form of address with a similar function is *Yā ayyuha alladhīna āmanū*, "O you who believe," which usually introduces legal or theological material. In the vocative mode, there are also curses, such as 111 Al-Masad (the curse on Abū Lahab was presented in Chapter 2), and petitions and prayers. Besides the Fātiḥah, Qur'ānic expressions in the form of prayer come in, for example, 2 Al-Baqarah 136 (cited in Chapter 5) and at the end of 3 Āl 'Imrān, in verses 26–27. The latter reads:

> 26. Say [*qul*]: "O Allāh, Master of the Kingdom [*mālik al-mulk*], You give the kingship [*al-mulk*] to whom You please and take away the kingship from whom You please. You exalt whom You please and humble whom You please. In Your hand [*biyaddika*] is all the good, and You have power over everything!
> 27. "You cause the night to pass into the day, and the day to pass into the night. You bring forth the living from the dead and You bring forth the dead from the living, and You provide for whomever You please without measure." (3 Āl 'Imrān 26–27)

Prophets' own words also provide several instances of prayer in the Qur'ān, particularly in the case of Ibrāhīm. The last two *sūrah*s of the Qur'ān, 113 Al-Falaq and 114 Al-Nās, represent instances of supplication.

Dialogical voices in the Qur'ān often convey types of moral orientation through vivid characterization and speech. An example is the depiction of the "hypocrites" (*munāfiqūn*) in 2 Al-Baqarah 8–15. The passage shows the character of "hypocrites" through their sarcastic and insincere speech. The *sūrah* first introduces them in verse 8 in terms of a speech act:

> 8. There are some who say: "We believe in Allāh and the last day," but they are not real believers. (2 Al-Baqarah 8)

They try to deceive others, but, the Qur'ān then states, they are really only fooling themselves; their hearts are sick, and Allāh makes their moral ailment worse. Verses 11–14 next illustrate how hypocrites lie through their speech:

> 11. And when they are told: "Do not sow mischief on the land [*lā tufsidū fī al-arḍ*]," they say, "we are only doing good."
> 12. It is they who make mischief, but they are unaware of that.
> 13. And when they are told: "Believe as the others have believed," they say: "Shall we believe as the fools have believed?" It is they who are the fools, though they do not know it.
> 14. And when they meet the believers, they say: "We believe," but

> when they are alone with their little devils [*shaiāṭīnihim*] they say: "We are with you; we were only mocking." (2 Al-Baqarah 11–14)

Then the Qur'ān turns the terms of their speech back onto the hypocrites in the next verse, stating that Allāh will "hurl their own joke back on them," and will mock them instead. The following verses, 16–20, which further describe the state of the unbelievers, are an example of a simile in the Qur'ān. Now they are said to be like those whose fire has gone out, as they are cast into darkness. These "disbelievers" are as if they are lost in a raging storm, clasping their hands to their ears, only able to see or move during intermittent flashes of lightning. And Allāh, the Qur'ān warns, could take away their very faculties of hearing and sight at any time if He so wished.

Dialog is a primary feature of the Qur'ān's judgment scenarios, which is shown further in the depiction of scenarios of judgment in Chapter 6. God may also be an explicit speaker in the book of "God's speech," particularly on judgment day. In these contexts, a divine voice may interrupt a scene suddenly, or shift unexpectedly from plural to singular. Address and dialogical principle can seem like a confrontation that leaps out of the text, especially in such instances. Classical examples of such speech in the Qur'ān are the *taḥaddī* ("challenge") verses, which confirm the text's own divine nature and origin, and which are further considered in Chapter 5 in terms of the Qur'ān's claim to its own "inimitability."

There are frequent rhetorical questions in the Qur'ān, which may appear in many contexts. At some points, the Qur'ān deploys a persuasive rhetoric of surprise in its questions, especially (as in the case of 55 Al-Raḥmān, mentioned above) relating to the reality of responsibility and the consequences of actions at judgment. For example, a section of Qur'ānic text that begins in 68 Al-Qalam 35–37 shifts between exposition and direct challenge:

> 35. Shall We consider those who submit like those who are criminals?
> 36. What is the matter with you; how do you judge?
> 37. Or do you have a book with which you study? (68 Al-Qalam 35–37)

Out of just the Meccan *sūrahs*, 97 Al-Qadr exemplifies a typical structure of the Qur'ān's rhetorical questions, posed after introduction of a key idea: "Verily We revealed it on *lailat al-qadr*. And do you know what is *lailat al-qadr*?" (This may also be rendered, in English "And you do not know what is *lailat al-qadr*," depending on an alternate interpretation of the question participle, "*mā*," as a negative particle.) Or, consider the first verses of 101 Al-Qāri'ah, "*Al-qāri'ah*. What is the *qāri'ah*? And do you know what is the *qāri'ah*?"[26] Besides providing rhyme through repetition, and tension by way of increasing line length, these questions draw the listener into the recitation as its very reading interprets the Qur'ān within the text itself.

An example of the potential rhetorical power of the Qur'ān's direct questions is the opening verses of 67 Al-Mulk. (Sūrat Al-Mulk is said to have been revealed after 52 Al-Ṭūr and before 6 Al-An'ām.) Here, the Qur'ān presents an exhaustive string of rhetorical questions to its listeners, conveying the theme that Allāh's creation is perfect: there are no cracks between the tiers of heaven, not even if you look closely – and even after you look again and again. (Go ahead, look! Can you see cracks?) The idea that the perfection and diversity of creation point to the characteristics of the Creator were familiar in theological reasoning that was prevalent in the region in which the Qur'ān appeared, found also in the works of contemplative ascent in early Greek Christian texts, for example. 67 Al-Mulk begins:

> *Bismillāh Al-Raḥmān Al-Raḥīm*
>
> 1. Blessed be He in Whose hands [*biyadihi*] is the sovereignity [*al-mulk*] and He has power over everything.
> 2. He Who created death and life so as to test you as to whoever of you is fairer in action. He is the All-Mighty, the All-Forgiving [*al-'azīzu al-ghafūr*].
> 3. He Who has created seven stratified heavens. You do not see any discrepancy in the creation of the Compassionate [*al-raḥmān*]. So fix your gaze, do you see any cracks?
> 4. Then, fix your gaze again and again, and your gaze will recoil back to you discomfited and weary.
> 5. We have adorned the lower heaven with lamps, and We turned them into missiles launched against the devils [*lil-shaiyāṭīn*]; and We have prepared for them the punishment of the fire. (67 Al-Mulk 1–5)

The vivid description of heaven ends with the image of little devils (*shaiyāṭīn*) whose ascent is cast back down as if by comets and meteors hurled at them whenever they try to climb to the firmament. The *sūrah* then shifts to a dialogical mode, as its description next descends deep down into hell:

> 6. And to those who have disbelieved in their Lord, the punishment of hell is reserved; and what an evil resort!
> 7. When they are cast into it, they hear its heavy breathing, as it boils over.
> 8. It almost bursts with rage. Every time a new throng is cast into it, its keepers ask them: "Has no warner come to you?"
> 9. They will say: "Yes indeed; a warner came to us but we disbelieved and said: 'Allah did not send down anything; you are simply in grave error.'"
> 10. And they will also say: "Had we listened or reasoned, we would not be among the companions of the fire." (67 Al-Mulk 6–10)

The persuasive style of direct challenge and engagement depicted in these verses complements other modes of the Qur'ān's descriptive persuasion. Rhetorical questions, such as the one found in the last line of the same *sūrah*, 67 Al-Mulk (see Conclusion), can resolve rhetorical and stylistic tension with an even more personalized and lingering moral suspense.

INTERPRETATION AND ITS LIMITS

Even though the Qur'ān presents itself as a book that is "clear," this has not always meant that the meanings of the Arabic Qur'ān were always immediately evident, even to its most learned historical readers. In fact, many of those who developed the fields of the Islamic religious sciences, including Qur'ānic sciences, were, like the great scholar Al-Ghazālī, native speakers of Persian (Farsī) who resided on a periphery of the Muslim world of their time. These scholars developed the dictionaries and lectionaries of the dialects believed to have been present in Arabia at the time of the Prophet Muḥammad. They used sources such as pre-Islamic poetry as well as the sorts of handbooks, study guides, and reference works that were developed in order to allow the Arabic of the Qur'ān to be understood.

There are many established genres of interpretation for many types of "readings" of the Qur'ān, just as there are many classical categories of Qur'ānic themes and style. Typically, interpreters followed a verse-by-verse analysis, treating each *āyah* as a discrete unit; this is similar to the approach that was also taken in classical tradition to the scriptural "rulings" of law. There were some (like Al-Ghazālī) who interpreted verses according to conceptual classes, relating them, for example, to theological principles of divinity. Other forms of exegesis also developed based on rhetorical style and genre. For example, there was narrative explanation of the text, which resulted in the creation of an extra-Qur'ānic narrative incorporating all the relevant material, such as "stories of the prophets."

The formal fields of Islamic religious sciences shaped the formation of specialized disciplines of Qur'ānic exegesis. For example, legal interpretation developed in connection to jurisprudential tradition; arrangement of this Qur'ānic material was according to topics that represented legal categories that corresponded to classic headings in jurisprudential manuals. (These would be matters of worship such as the "five pillars" and topics in social interaction such as marriage, divorce, inheritance, contracts, criteria for "just war," etc.) Other forms of textual interpretation, such as those that focused on language, poetics, rhetoric, and style, differed yet again from this. Other modes of allegorical interpretation, which would include several types of esoteric and philosophical interpretation, sought the *bāṭin* ("inner") meanings that correspond to the "outer" (*ẓāhir*) meaning of the text. These perspectives are typical of the mystical piety of the Sufis as well as Isma'īlī and other Shi'ite interpretation. These approaches are often applied to isolated passages, such as the Sufis' favorite, the beloved "verse of light" (*āyat al-nūr*, 24 Al-Nūr 35), discussed below. Finally, in the modern period, Muslims have brought to the religious reading of the Qur'ān a new spectrum of concerns, such as contemporary questions of Muslim social ethics or the expression of Islamic identity with respect to the postcolonial state. Ever since the era of colonialism, the Muslim-majority and Muslim-minority worlds have also seen an enormous increase in the amount of exegetical works on the Qur'ān produced globally overall.

Any and all interpretation of the Qur'ān must implicitly address the question, what is the scope of material to be interpreted, and what are the limits of exegesis? Muslims have traditionally framed boundaries of knowledge for "reading" the Qur'ān for meaning in terms of categories apparently established by the Qur'ān itself. These terms, along with more than one kind of answer to the question of what can be interpreted, and by whom, are all found within a single passage in the Qur'ān, 3 Āl 'Imrān 7. Meanings of this verse may be rendered as follows:

> It is He who has revealed to you the book [i.e. the Qur'ān] in which are clear verses [*muḥkamāt*] that are the essence of the book [*umm al-kitāb*] and others that are unclear [*mutashābihāt*]. As for those in whose hearts there is a perversion, they follow the unclear part, desiring dissension and desiring its interpretation [*ta'wīl*]. But no one knows its interpretation [*ta'wīl*] except God … and those firm in knowledge (who) say, "We believe in it; all is from our Lord." Yet none remember except people who understand. (3 Āl 'Imrān 7)[27]

The meanings of the passage given above, 3 Āl 'Imrān 7, establish at least two points.[28] One relates to textual typologization; another pertains to the human authority to carry out the very task of interpretation in the first place.

First, 3 Āl 'Imrān 7 offers a way to label Qur'ānic content with respect to the bipartite categories, "*muḥkamāt*" and "*mutashābihāt*," based on some understanding of verses' "clarity." The Qur'ān, however, offers these as open terms. Knowledge within the various Islamic religious sciences would strive to understand and apply these terms with precision; their definitive application would also shape what the interpreter would, ultimately, consider to be the limits of this sort of human understanding. Although the terms are used in many ways across the religious sciences, there has been a general consensus within the Islamic traditions that "*muḥkamāt*" denotes a Qur'ānic expression with just one dimension; in other words, it would need no further explanation in order to be understood in Arabic. Many have liked to think that these expressions so designated could be said at least to comprise Qur'ānic legal rulings. "*Mutashābihāt*," on the other hand, are usually said to be expressions in the Qur'ān whose definitive meanings can be known only to God; they are terms with more than one dimension of meaning, and to ascertain these multifaceted meanings requires further explanation beyond the plain Arabic words.

What could be said to be "unclear" in a book that itself claims it has no lack of clarity, in a discourse that is "easy to understand?" There is one Qur'ānic case on which those in Muslim traditions have all agreed that there would be an appropriate application of the term "*mutashābihāt*": these are the "abbreviated letters." Some have said that this ought to represent the only case of "*mutashābihāt*" verses that exists in the Qur'ān at all. The "abbreviated letters" (*muqaṭṭ'āt*) are letters that begin twenty-nine *sūrah*s of the Qur'ān, always appearing immediately after the formula that invokes the Name of God, the Basmalah. The *sūrah*s containing these letters are all considered to be late Meccan or early Medinan. The "abbreviated letters" are not connected as one word when they are read aloud, but instead they are voiced as the Arabic names of the separate written letters. In the Qur'ān, there are three cases of one letter of this type; four cases of two letters and also four cases of three letters; two cases of four letters; and, there is one case of five letters (19 Maryam). Table 1 gives instances of the abbreviated letters in the Qur'ān.

Commentators all affirm that these letters are part of the revelation to the Prophet Muḥammad, but there has been little agreement about what they might mean. Some scholars have suggested they might be abbreviations for the name or words of the chapter in which

Table 1 "Abbreviated Letters" in the Qur'ān

Twenty-nine *sūrah*s have "abbreviated letters." They are all considered Meccan except for four Medinan *sūrah*s, which are: 2 Al-Baqarah; 3 Āl 'Imrān; 13 Al-Ra'd; 68 Al-Qalam. The following list of "abbreviated letters" is arranged by the ascending numbers corresponding to the *sūrah*s in which the letters appear.

2 ĀLIF LĀM MĪM	29 ĀLIF LĀM MĪM
3 ĀLIF LĀM MĪM	30 ĀLIF LĀM MĪM
7 ĀLIF LĀM MĪM SĀD	31 ĀLIF LĀM MĪM
10 ĀLIF LĀM RĀ	32 ĀLIF LĀM MĪM
11 ĀLIF LĀM RĀ	36 YĀ SĪN
12 ĀLIF LĀM RĀ	38 ṢĀD
13 ĀLIF LĀM MĪM RĀ	40 ḤĀ MĪM
14 ĀLIF LĀM RĀ	41 ḤĀ MĪM
15 ĀLIF LĀM RĀ	42 ḤĀ MĪM / 'AYN SĪN QĀF
19 KĀF HĀ YĀ 'AYN ṢĀD	43 ḤĀ MĪM
20 ṬĀ HĀ	44 ḤĀ MĪM
26 ṬĀ SĪN MĪM	45 ḤĀ MĪM
27 ṬĀ SĪN	46 ḤĀ MĪM
28 ṬĀ SĪN MĪM	50 QĀF
	68 NŪN

they appear (for example, "*Ālif Lām Rā*" for "Al-Raḥmān"), while others have wondered whether the letters could relate to revealed content in some manner (such as with the mention of a fish, or a snake, and so on). Other classical theories propose that they might be initials that relate to the project of ordering and arranging the complete collection of the Qur'ān; for example, what are called the "*ḥawāmīm*" *sūrah*s (numbered in the forties) appear as a consecutive grouping of chapters that all begin with the same unexplained letters, "*Ḥā Mīm*." There are other cases in which *sūrah*s containing the same or similar abbreviated letters also come in a block, such as "*Alif Lām Rā*" opening *sūrah*s numbered 10–15, and "*Ṭā Sīn*" and "*Ṭā Sīn Mīm*" appearing in *sūrah*s 26–28. The majority of the *sūrah*s that open with "abbreviated letters" do have some mention of the "book" (in fact, only three have no such reference, namely 19 Maryam, 29 Al-'Ankabūt, and 30 Al-Rūm). In his canonical work on the Qur'ānic Sciences, the scholar Al-Sūyūṭī states that the meaning of the letters is known only to God. However, even an authoritative statement such as this has not prevented Muslims from speculating further for generations. Orientalists have also been fascinated by the problem as well. (For example, scholars including Bell considered the "abbreviated letters" to be clues to the logic of compilation and the ordering of the Qur'ān's *sūrah*s.)

Some philosophers have considered a wider question than the matter of *what* in the Qur'ān could be said not to be *muḥkamāt* (i.e. "clear"). They also ask, *how* could there ever be said to be anything in the Qur'ān that is not "*muḥkamāt*?" Put another way, why would the Qur'ān seem to demand the exercise of reason, speculation, or faith on the part of its readers in this way? The rationalist exegete Al-Zamakhshārī (d. 1144) reasons as follows about the pious and intellectual utility of the existence of Qur'ānic material that is deemed "*mutashābihāt*." If meaning were too fixedly determined, he begins, then people would come to rely too much on this clarity and they would cease to reflect. "Reflection" is continually urged by the Qur'ān as a way to apprehend God and His unity. According to Al-Zamakhshārī, ambiguous verses may thus be considered to be a "test" that distinguishes between those who are firm in faith on the one hand (a group to which the verse itself refers explicitly), and those who are uncertain on the other. If a believer holds that there is no contradiction in the Qur'ān, but then thinks that he or she sees one, he or she must resolve the tension intellectually. If such reflection subsequently results in a successful harmonization of meanings with logical depth and rigor, and according to accepted religious principles that have been applied uniformly, then that reflection would have led to greater insight about divinity. Zamakhsharī writes that, with God's guidance, when the seeker finds harmony between such verses, with that harmony "certainty grows and conviction increases."[29] The intellectual task of harmonizing clear and unclear is thus, to Zamakhsharī, a rational project of piety. In the classical tradition, Shi'ite academic approaches have been known for preserving the productive spiritual and scholarly value of doubt and debate for the sake of establishing faith and certainty.

The second matter brought up by this verse (3 Āl 'Imrān 7), just who is it who could be said to be "firm in knowledge," is also a matter of dispute. Such debates would imply variable authority for specific interpreters and interpretations. (Zamakhsharī himself, for example, was deemed by many to have an unsound exegetical perspective because of his theological orientation.) Attitudes in this matter were also determined by differing "readings" of the same Qur'ānic verse, 3 Āl 'Imrān 7. Depending on how the verse is vocalized (specifically, whether or not there is a pause at the point where the ellipse appears above), a reading may convey the sense either that the Qur'ān's meanings are known "only to God" (on the one hand, long pause) or that they are known "only to God … *and* those firm in knowledge [who are then identified by their statement of a profession of faith]" (on the other hand, if no pause is taken in reading). Besides providing the productive words "*muḥkamāt*" and "*mutashābihāt*," the same passage has in this way also been rich in meanings for Muslims considering the boundaries of the pious task of the interpretation of the Qur'ān.

FORMAL EXEGESIS (*TAFSĪR*)

The earliest explanation of the Qur'ān and that which carries the most authority in Muslim tradition is said to have been made by the Prophet Muḥammad himself. This material is found in *ḥadīth* reports in which the Prophet explained the meaning of certain verses. Those in the generation of the companions of the Prophet, such as 'Abdullāh bin 'Abbās (d. 687), also contributed to tradition a great deal of material on the meaning of certain verses, including information on the "occasion of revelation" of *āyāt*. "*Tafsīr*" is the classical term for the exegesis of the Qur'ān, and as such it represents a primary "Qur'ānic Science." The word means "making meaning clear." This is not just a theoretical exercise, but may also represent a practical and applied undertaking, as in the case of adducing the law. The word "*tafsīr*" occurs only once in the Qur'ān (25 Al-Furqān 33), where it means "interpretation." After the eleventh century C.E., this term, "*tafsīr*," came widely into use; this corresponded to the development of the formal sciences of interpretation. The term for exegesis that had been used before the third Islamic century was the term read in the verse 3 Āl 'Imrān 7 above, "*ta'wīl*."

The word *ta'wīl* appears many times in the Qur'ān, where it refers not only to interpreting Qur'ānic meanings but also to interpretation in other contexts, such as the prophet Joseph's "interpretation" of dreams in 12 Yūsuf. In Islamic scholarly traditions as well as in the far more recent academic field of Islamic Studies, there has been much discussion of the shifting historical differences between the two terms *tafsīr* and *ta'wīl*. Both terms, for example, were used by Muslims for the Arabic-language exegesis of the Bible in both Judaic and Christian traditions. In general, "*ta'wīl*" has come to denote textual hermeneutics based on some sort of independent reason, or personally authoritative opinion. This has often been the case, for example, when an interpretive apparatus has been said to point to otherwise "concealed" or esoteric points of doctrine. Over time, "*tafsīr*" in the formal sense came to mean exegesis based on what was assessed to be the sound authority of *ḥadīth*. This has never been a clear-cut distinction in Muslim traditions of religious study, however. Application of the two relative terms, historically, has also reflected sectarian affiliations and polemics.

By the fourth century, the classical works on *tafsīr* had emerged. The great historian and exegete Muḥammad bin Jarīr Al-Ṭabarī (d. 923) established influential parameters for this project. The *tafsīr* that was produced by this encyclopedic author, titled *Jamī' Al-Bayān 'an Ta'wīl Al-Qur'ān*, was used by many later scholars who also adapted it to their own interests and sensibilities, including content now available electronically and refreshed globally on the Internet every day. Almost all of these later works were also shorter than Ṭabarī's own voluminous *Tafsīr*.[30] His work effectively became the model for how to cite from sources that had been handed down from other traditions, and it also indicated implicitly how much "opinion" was to be exercised by one who interprets by way of established "tradition." His work is thus considered a touchstone for considering what became the classical categories of exegesis in terms of method and systematicity: *tafsīr bi'l-ma'thūr* and *tafsīr bi'l-ra'y*. The first is "*tafsīr* by tradition" (e.g. *ḥadīth*s), and the second is "*tafsīr* by opinion." Ṭabarī's own work is considered to be a paradigmatic example of the first type.

Texts from the period of the development of the Islamic religious sciences in which Ṭabarī was active reflect an early scholarly confidence in the growing Muslim tradition. Identifying transmitters by name in his verse-by-verse analysis, Ṭabarī himself includes all sorts of material, even material he himself considers erroneous. In this way, Ṭabarī's work shows how the meaning of the academic distinction made in Muslim tradition between *tafsīr bi'l-ma'thūr* ("tradition") as opposed to *tafsīr bi'l ra'y* ("opinion") can depend on context to some degree. Within a "traditional" *tafsīr*, Ṭabarī nevertheless includes his own "opinion" a great deal, such as by the way in which he structures the "traditions" that have been transmitted by others. A great deal of "opinion" can be offered in this manner and within the bounds of methodology accepted within tradition. For example, when Ṭabarī comments on the reliability of the information he includes, he expresses freely his own personal assessment of it. A "traditional" work like Ṭabarī's also shows that even "sound" opinions were not accepted by all on controversial topics. Consider the example of Ṭabarī's interpretation of the Basmalah, the opening formula, "In the name of God, the Compassionate the Merciful," relying on a translation by J. Cooper. How much of his own "opinion" does Ṭabarī really include? The answer is, directly, some, and indirectly, he intervenes to a significant extent.

In interpreting the Basmalah, Ṭabarī considers both the prepositional expression "in the name of" and also the actual Name of God, "Allāh." Then he turns to the appositional Names, "*Al-Raḥmān Al-Raḥīm*." Ṭabarī begins by discussing these two proper nouns that are both derived from the same root (*r-ḥ-m*), explaining how they carry slightly different meanings based on their morphology. Next, he offers four separate opinions on how to understand the expression:

- First, Ṭabarī contrasts two views on the comparative meaning of the terms. One scholarly opinion he cites is that: "*al-raḥmān* denotes mercy to all creatures … and *al-raḥīm* denotes mercy to the believers." Another view of scholars, he says, has been that "*al-raḥmān* is the Merciful in the next world as well as this world; *al-raḥīm* is the Merciful in the next world." Ṭabarī determines that, "There is no reason to suppose that one of these interpretations is more correct than the other …" and then elaborates further.
- Second, he offers an opinion on the authority of the companion of the Prophet, 'Abdullāh bin 'Abbās, about the meaning of the same two terms. This is also an authoritative statement on the variant terms *raḥmān* and *raḥīm*, and Ṭabarī may treat it apart from the first set of points above simply because of the authority of the famous figure who is said to be the transmitter of the information, Ibn 'Abbās himself. Ṭabarī summarizes, "This interpretation resembles the previous one, in that *al-raḥmān* has a different meaning and interpretation from *al-raḥīm*."
- Third, Ṭabarī offers a view that comes under the name of a far more obscure figure, named 'Aṭā Al-Khirāsānī, which reads as follows in translation: "Originally there was *al-raḥmān*, but when *al-raḥmān* was cut off from His name it became *al-raḥmān al-raḥīm*." At first this explanation seems less than clear. How could a Name of God become "cut off"? And, "cut off" from what, exactly? Ṭabarī speculates about the historical origin of this report. He interprets the statement in terms of figure Musailama (whom Ṭabarī calls "the liar Musailama"), who was known to have been in Arabia around the time of the Prophet Muḥammad and to have claimed also to have received revelation from a divinity called "*al-raḥmān*." About this interpretation, Ṭabarī concludes, "This is not an unsound opinion …"
- Fourth and finally, Ṭabarī offers positions with which he actually disagrees, the views of purportedly "ignorant people." He writes: "Some ignorant people have claimed that the Arabs did not formerly know of the name *al-raḥmān*, that it was not in their language." He then proves this to be false by citing lines from pre-Islamic poetry that would have been familiar to scholars, evidencing that this Name would indeed have been well known. Finally, Ṭabarī mentions one interpreter who claimed that "*al-raḥmān*" and "*al-raḥīm*" were intended only figuratively to mean

> "he who possesses mercy" and "he who dispenses mercy," in an allegorical but not a literal sense. Ṭabarī quips, there is no sound basis for such an opinion whatsoever. (Nevertheless, he has still included it.)[31]

Ṭabarī has here presented a hierarchy of opinions in his analysis of the meanings of the Basmalah. Some opinions appeared to be more sound or more favorable to him than others, even though they are all to have been found in some form within "tradition."

In the centuries after the time of Al-Ṭabarī, there appeared sophisticated scholarly works of Qur'ānic exegesis, including interpretations that were labeled "*tafsīr bi'l-ra'y*." While many works that were considered to fall into this category built on the material and approach originally established by Ṭabarī, theological considerations were also coming to be more influential. For example, in the twelfth century there appeared the foundational philosophical exegesis by Muḥammad bin Zakariyā' Al-Rāzī (b. 1149), as well as the work of the famous grammarian and Mu'tazilite rationalist Abū'l-Qāsim Maḥmūd bin 'Umar Al- Zamakhsharī (1075–1144), who was mentioned above. Zamakhsharī's analysis was adopted by many, but key doctrinal conclusions of his were revised by the Sunni traditionalist 'Abd Allāh bin 'Umar Al-Bayḍāwi (d. 1260), in order to conform more closely to points of the Sunni mainstream of religious thought that was emerging at the time. Zamakhsharī's exegesis was appreciated outside his own elite philosophical circles especially for its sophisticated and subtle understanding of Arabic language and grammar. A work such as Zamakhsharī's was controversial for its speculative material, however, which is the usual (and at times perjorative) connotation conveyed by the term *tafsīr b'il-ra'y*.

In Islamic religious sciences, "*kalām*" is the formal field of theology. It developed according to conversations some of whose voices are now lost, such as the "Kharijites," a political and intellectual movement that began in the first generation of Islam, and the "Mu'tazilites," who achieved social prominence some two centuries later. By the second Islamic century, *tafsīr* began to reflect doctrinal disputes that relate to dialectical theology, or *kalām*, such as the following: free will and predestination (presented in terms of God's omnipotence, justice, and mercy, discussed previously in Chapter 2); the scope and application of law (Chapter 4), including the question of the worldly or postponed judgment of a "grave sinner" (mentioned in Chapter 2); whether the attributes of God are understood to be literal or allegorical (see below and also Chapter 5); the very nature of the Qur'ān itself (as "created" or "uncreated" in time, a topic further considered in Chapter 5); and the human experience of the divine and the hereafter (material that relates to the presentation in Chapter 6).

Responsible for provoking many discussions were a group of rationalists known as the Mu'tazilites. They were influenced by Greek learning, including Aristotelian logic and argumentation. This circle was well known for promoting "five points" that affirmed the principles of the transcendent unity and justice of God. The Mu'tazilites were in political favor through part of the early 'Abbasid period (750–1258). Several formative intellectual disputes over the nature of the Qur'ān and its expression in tradition involved various positions held by the Mu'tazilites. These included, for example, the description of the transcendent deity in the Qur'ān, which is now presented below as an example of a "classical" theological controversy in Qur'ānic interpretation.

An anthropomorphic (i.e. embodied) representation of divinity is a feature the Qur'ān. The text clearly refers to the body of God, as in the mention of God's hands (for example, 36 Yā Sīn 71, 48 Al-Fatḥ 10) and His eyes (11 Hūd 37). There are also many references to the "face of God" in the Qur'ān (for example, 2 Al-Baqarah 115). There are occasions in which the Qur'ān mentions God's own verbal actions, such as His speaking, hearing, and seeing. In 41 Fuṣṣilat 11, Allāh is said to carry Himself up to heaven during the act of creation: "Then He arose to heaven while it was smoke, and He said to it and to the earth 'Come over, willingly or unwillingly.' They said: 'We come willingly.'" According to Mu'tazilite views, such statements must be read allegorically, since any palpable representation of divinity compromises His transcendence and possibly also His unity. Mu'tazilites came to see such passages as figurative or metaphorical in meaning, with their literal interpretation appropriate just for those with a limited capacity for disciplined imagination with respect to understanding the scripture that was sent to guide them. The counterargument to this position was formulated along the lines: any "allegorized" reading of the Qur'ān could imply that its words are not true. Further, literalists challenged the authority of those who would presume to be able to determine what of the Qur'ān is metaphorical and what is not. The latter perspective became the mainstream view, put forward through careful textual readings and arguments.

In traditional and mainstream Qur'ānic sciences, there exists a classical division of Qur'ānic meanings according to contrasting categories, the "literal" (*ḥaqīqī*) and the "metaphorical" (*majāzī*). For example, in his text on Islamic jurisprudence, Kamali explains that the term "*ṭalaq*" literally means "set free" but has a metaphorical meaning which is usually applied in law, "divorce."[32] Determining what Qur'ānic meanings were palpable and what were metaphorical or allegorical was the basis of early disputes over the interpretation of the Qur'ān. These disputes often began, as in the case of "anthropomorphic" representation of the deity here, when philosophers and mystics claimed allegorical interpretation, such as the Qur'ān's mention of a "vision of God" at end-time. Interpretation of the "throne verse" is another such example.

The throne verse is called *āyat al-kursī* (literally, "the verse of the throne," 2 Al-Baqarah 255). It is a well known, often recited, and highly visible verse. It commonly adorns the walls of homes (an example of this is discussed in Chapter 5). Among its themes, the *āyah* evokes the idea that God is ever-watchful and protective:

> Allāh! There is no God but He [*Allāhu lā ilāha illā huwa*], the Living, the Everlasting [*al-ḥayyu al-qayyūm*]. Neither slumber nor sleep overtakes Him. His is what is in the heavens and on the earth. Who shall intercede with Him except with His leave? He knows what is before them and what is behind them. And they do not comprehend of His knowledge except what He wills. His throne [*kursiyuhu*] encompasses the heavens and the earth, and their preservation does not burden Him. He is the Exalted the Great [*al-'alī al-'aẓīm*]. (2 Al-Baqarah 255)

Rationalists like Zamakhsharī and Rāzī considered the verse to express the greatness and exaltation of God, for which the "throne" (*kursī*) was a metaphor. Others who strove for "subtle" religious meanings, like the later mystic Ibn 'Arabī (d. 1240), also interpreted the "*kursī*" mentioned in this verse to be an allegory, this time for knowledge.[33]

Opposing perspectives such as these, and specifically that of the Mu'tazilites, the great theologian of Sunni orthodoxy Al-Ash'arī (d. 936) puts forward the argument against the allegorical interpretation of the "throne verse" in this abridged excerpt (quoted from a translation by William McNeill and Marilyn Waldman):

> Some … have said that God's words, "The Merciful is seated on the Throne" mean that He has mastery and reigns and exercises power, and that God is in every place, and they deny that God is on His throne … and hold the opinion … that it [i.e. the throne] is God's power. But … God's being seated on the Throne cannot mean His having the mastery that is common to all things … [They] think that God is in every place; and so they are compelled to admit that He is in the womb of Mary and in gardens and the waste; and this is contrary to the Religion. May God be exalted above their belief! … It may be said to them: If He is not seated on the Throne … but is in every place, then He is under the earth, over which heaven is; and if He is under the earth and the earth above Him and the heaven above the earth, then this compels you to believe that God is under the depth, and created things are above Him, and that He is above the height, and created thing are below Him; and if this is true He must be under that above which He is above and that under which He is, and this is impossible and self-contradictory. May God be very far above your [i.e. the disputant's] calumny against Him![34]

The reasoning of this retort follows a typical strategy of dialectical theology, whose aim in a two-sided ("dialectical") debate is to catch an opponent on the horns of a logical dilemma of reasoning. Ash'arī was also known for the theological slogan "*bi lā kayfa*" ("without asking how"), which means not to complicate unnecessarily a plain logic of piety. Supporting further such a view, which came to be considered "orthodox," there are numerous accounts in formative exegesis such as Ṭabarī's that document traditions relating to the physical description and location of the throne, including its materials and size dimensions.[35]

When Al-Ghazālī interprets the same verse, which he does in more than one of his voluminous works, Martin Wittingham states that he presents not so much an exegesis of *āyat al-kursī* as a "series of references to some of his favorite theological views." Al-Ghazālī (d. 1111) had come to be a proponent of Ash'arite theology (as represented above by the writing of Al-Ash'arī himself). Wittingham explains that when Al-Ghazālī writes about the "throne verse," he "touches on the issues of God's uncaused and therefore necessary existence, freedom from the attributes of accidents, God's origination of all actions, and a statement to the effect that the understanding of

God's Throne must remain a mystery."[36] Similarly, pious tradition following that of Al-Ash'arī holds that the "anthropomorphic" verses should be taken as having a palpable reality, "without asking why."

However, despite warning against "interpreting the Qur'ān by one's own opinion," the authoritative scholar Al-Ghazālī himself also did accept many "opinions," as long as they were grounded in learning or, in other words, as long as they could be said to be, in Al-Ghazālī's own opinion, sound opinions. In a mode that was more pious than philosophical, Ghazālī often accepted the authority of "opinion" in the form of experiential knowledge.[37] He was sympathetic to the spreading movement of esoteric piety in his day, while remaining more critical of purely rationalist arguments, and also utterly rejecting Shī'ī esotericism.[38] Ghazālī in fact distinguished sharply the doctrinal approaches of Shi'ites (whose allegorical hermeneutics were methodologically actually similar to those of the "Sufi" mystics), against whom Al-Ghazālī was commissioned professionally to polemicize. For esoteric and allegorical interpretation such as that carried out by Shi'ites and Sufis, the term that was in use by the time of Al-Ghazālī in the twelfth century was the same expression that is used in the Qur'ān for "interpretation," *ta'wīl.*

Sufism was a revolution in Muslim thought and practice that occurred in about the fourth Islamic century, as pious religious adherents sought experiential knowledge of divinity. The tradition was influenced by: a mode of world-rejecting asceticism that had many models, such as those in the first generations of Muslim pietists and Qur'ān readers like Ḥasan of Baṣra (b. 642, d. ca. 737); the practices of Christians who were active along the border with the Byzantine empire, who propagated prevalent notions of spiritual brotherhood and martial "chivalry"; "neo-Platonic" or "gnostic" ideas of divine emanation of perceptible reality from a monad, and dualist symbolic systems of light and dark as influenced by Persian traditions that came to be associated with this; and the teachings of particular masters. These latter lineages were known as *ṭarīqa*s or the "ways" of various figures following progressive paths and practices leading to the recognition of God's unity. The term "Sufism" applies to doctrine and practices as well as the global lineages that carry the names of such authorities, such as "Qadiriyya" after the twelfth-century figure 'Abd Al-Qādir Al-Jilānī (d. 1166).[39]

Key intellectual structures began to be systematized by the eleventh and twelfth centuries in teachings, treatises, and handbooks that theorized the way of the "*ṣūfī*," presenting alternative "paths" of experiential knowledge that could lead to recognizing divine unity. There were always key questions about what such a recognition might mean, and, further, how it could be acceptably expressed. Abū Al-Qāsim bin Muḥammad Al-Junaid (d. 910), for example, became famous in a "Baghdad circle" of the tenth century for his "sober" expression. According to his formulation, through the knowledge and practice of the *ṣūfī*, attributes of the self would be replaced by those that were divine. Esoteric theoreticians would later idealize the "complete person" in terms of an experiential consciousness (or manifested "grades of being") whose perception could encompass concepts of unity and divine unity. Devotion to the Prophet Muḥammad also featured strongly in the development of these traditions, as did some key concepts of Shi'ite esotericism that were being disseminated during the height of missionary activity under the Fāṭimid Dynasty in the tenth and eleventh centuries.

In Islamic tradition, *ta'wīl* is esoteric or speculative Qur'ān commentary. In Sufi systems, such works often took the form of reflections on key words or concepts. As such, they would apply the principle of multilayered textual meaning as a core hermeneutical principle. This approach views key terms and concepts (such as "power" or "knowledge") along a spectrum of meanings, from exoteric to esoteric. The capacity of interpreters themselves is also said to range across a hierarchical classification, from the crudest grasp of the contours of an idea at one extreme to the exercise of the most subtle philosophical or experiential intellect at the other. In both Shi'ite and Sufi systems, much material is attributed to two figures, 'Alī, the central figure of Shi'ite Islam, and Ja'far Al-Ṣādiq (d. 765), the fifth or sixth *imām*, depending on the Shi'ite lineage. In Shi'ite systems, both persons carry the special authority of *imāms*, living interpreters for community.

Shi'ite traditions are the heritage of about one-tenth of Muslims in the world today. Beginning as movements that opposed established rule by the Umayyads (to 750), pro-'Alid trends developed into Shi'ite intellectual systems with theories of the imamate. It is difficult to generalize doctrine across Fiver (Zaidī), Sevener (Ismā'īlī), and Twelver (Ithnā' 'Asharī) systems. Common concepts are ideas of authority such as its "designation," "power," and "proof." As in Sufi traditions, Shi'ite thought developed the metaphor of "light" as guidance and the experience of prophecy and knowledge. Some

Shi'ite systems have also come to include millenarian ideas and tendencies, focusing on the restoration of justice at the end-time. The idea that the *imām* is "hidden" or in "occultation" and will return in the future supports this perspective.[40]

The writings attributed to Ja'far Al-Ṣādiq provide an example of Shi'ite interpretive principles. He posits, as did traditions of Islamic philosophical inquiry more widely, including Sufism, different levels or capabilities of human understanding.[41] He is in fact known for this "hierarchical principle," which was typical of Muslim philosophical and esoteric traditions overall. He claimed that there were different layers or grades of interpretation that were appropriate for persons depending on their own differing capabilities: 1. expression for common people; 2. allusion for a privileged and elite few; 3. grace for a "saint"; and 4. "realities" for a prophet. In *Early Islamic Mysticism*, Michael Sells presents Al-Ṣādiq's interpretation of letter symbolism in the Basmalah on the basis of allusion (*ishārah*). For example, he writes the following about the written word "*Bismi*" ("in the name of"):

> It is said of Ja'far ibn Muḥammad that he said: The *B* is enduring (*baqā'*) and the *S* is his names (*asmā'*) and the *M* is dominion (*mulk*). The faith of the believer – his remembrance is through his enduring. The service of the seeker – his remembrance is through his names. The knower passes from the kingdom to its king.[42]

Comparing this to the interpretation of the Basmalah given by Ṭabarī (above) suggests how those performing *ta'wīl* could claim to offer an entirely different level of scriptural interpretation than that which relied on reports from "tradition."

Usually, esoteric *ta'wīl* tends not to be a sequential *tafsīr* of the verses of the text, but instead it focuses on key meanings that are said to have both an "inner" as well as an "outer" component. Qur'ānic material especially open to this sort of allegorized explanation includes metaphors, which come in the rhetorical forms both of parables and similes. Some parables in the Qur'ān are like drawn-out similes. For example, there is the tree of a "good word" in 14 Ibrāhīm 24–26, which would have been an image familiar to readers of the Christian Gospels at the time of the rise of Islam:

> 24. Do you not see how Allāh sets forth as a parable that a good word is like a tree, whose root is firm and its branches are in the sky

25. It brings forth fruit all the time, by its Lord's leave. Allāh gives parables to humankind that perchance people may be mindful.
26. And a foul word is like a foul tree which has been uprooted from the surface of the earth, having no stable base. (14 Ibrāhīm 24–26)

A recurring theme of parables that appear in the Qur'ān is that of the "blighted garden." For example, in 68 Al-Qalam 17–34, those planning the next day's harvest are shocked to find that God has punished them. Elsewhere, in 18 Al-Kahf 32–44, there is a parable of two gardens, in which a complacent cultivator also finds his crops suddenly destroyed.

Similes also often describe the state of hypocrites, polytheists, and unbelievers, as in the previous example of the "hypocrites" running deaf and dumb in a storm in 2 Al-Baqarah 8–20. In another example, 29 Al-'Ankabūt 41, the Qur'ān suggests that the worldview of non-believers is as flimsy as a spider's web:

> The case of those who took up other protectors, apart from Allāh, is like that of the spider who built a house. Truly, the most brittle of houses is the house of the spider, if only they knew. (29 Al-'Ankabūt 41)

Many powerful similes and images appear in the Qur'ān's descriptions of the last things and final judgment. Qur'ānic eschatology typically depicts events at the end-time through metaphors, such as, in just one example, people being said to be like "moths blown" and the mountains like "carded wool" (101 Al-Qāri'ah 4–5).

When writing about a Qur'ānic simile, Al-Ghazālī approaches the subject systematically. He follows his preferred pious hermeneutical method, which is to probe the twofold external and internal realities of religious thought and practice. Ghazālī's treatment of the extended simile of the "verse of light" in *Al-Mishkāt Al-Anwār* ("Niche of Lights") shows the sophistication of his approach. The verse of light, 24 Al-Nūr 35, is, like *āyat al-kursī*, one of the best-known passages in the Qur'ān. It reads in English as follows:[43]

> Allāh is the Light (*nūr*) of the heavens and the earth. His Light is like a niche in which there is a lamp, the lamp is in a glass, the glass is like a glittering star. It is kindled from a blessed olive tree, neither of the east nor the west. Its oil will almost shine, even if no fire has touched it. Light upon light, Allāh guides to His Light whomever He

> pleases and gives the examples to humankind. Allāh has knowledge of everything. (24 Al-Nūr 35)

Ghazālī explains the similitude in terms of layers of experience and understanding. According to Martin Whittingham, Al-Ghazālī is here indebted especially to the philosopher Abū 'Alī Al-Ḥusayn bin 'Abd Allāh Ibn Sīnā (d. 1037) and his style of symbolic interpretation. Ibn Sīnā had previously used the verse to elucidate his theory of the intellect, and the "light" of knowledge possessed by those of differing capabilities such as prophets, those with understanding, and, ranked at the bottom, those us with merely ordinary sensibilities.[44] Al-Ghazālī writes:

> This similitude [of the "verse of light"] becomes clear only to the hearts of those who have faith or to the hearts of the prophets and the friends of God, not to the hearts of the unbelievers. After all, by "guidance" is meant light. That which is kept away from the path of guidance is falsehood and darkness – or rather, it is more intense than darkness, because darkness does not guide to falsehood any more than it guides to truth.[45]

Kristin Zahra Sands offers additional examples of many other esoteric interpretations of the same verse, including that of Ja'far Al-Ṣādiq, in her important book on Qur'ān interpretation.[46]

Esoteric interpretation, both Shi'ite and Sufi, that considers symbols in terms of many valences of meaning is often called *tafsīr bi'l-ishārah*, or "*tafsīr* of allusion." This designation is sometimes sought as an alternative to the otherwise negative connotations of the term "*ta'wīl*." In classical Shi'ite exegesis, the "hidden" meaning revealed by such interpretation often relates to ideas of the imamate. For example, there is the interpretation of the famous scholar Muḥammad Murtaḍā Al-Kāshī (d. ca. 1505) on the same "verse of light":

> It is said from (the Imām) [Ja'far] Al-Ṣādiq: What is involved here is a simile that God has coined for us (regarding God's words), *God is the light of the heavens and the earth*, Al-Ṣādiq said, God is thus. *His light*: Al-Ṣādiq says (what is meant by Muḥammad's breast). *Wherein is a lamp*, al-Ṣādiq says: wherein is the light of knowledge, that is, of prophecy. *The lamp in a glass*, al-Ṣādiq says: The knowledge of the Messenger of God issued from the latter into the heart of 'Alī ...[47]

And so forth, with "*light upon light*" referring to the transmission from *imām* to *imām* following 'Alī.

In another example of a Shi'ite interpretation of the same verse, *āyat al-nūr* (from an Ismā'īlī intellectual active in the tenth century whose ideas became widespread, Abū Ya'qub Al-Sijistanī), the images of the "verse of light" are interpreted in terms of figures in Shi'ite piety in a one-to-one correspondence:

> Light: Light of knowledge, radiating from the Command of God, and from the Intellect and the Soul
> Glass: The Imām, Al-Ḥasan [son of 'Alī, grandson of Muḥammad through his daughter, Fāṭimah]
> A glittering star: Imam Al-Ḥusain [brother of Ḥasan, martyred at Karbalā' in 680]
> Blessed Olive Tree: Imam 'Alī Zayn Al-'Abidin [son of Ḥusayn]
> Oil would almost glow forth: Imām Muḥammad Al-Bāqir [the next *imām*]
> Even if no fire touched it: Fire stands for Imam Ja'far Al-Ṣādiq [*imām* and a central figure in Shi'ite thought]
> Light upon light: Al-Qā'im [leader yet to come][48]

The scholar Ismail Poonwalla, who presents the excerpt above in an article, also quotes from an interpretation by a figure named Ja'far bin Manṣūr Al-Yaman, demonstrating that each of the same images may have different "*ishārah*," even within the same Shi'ite tradition of interpretation. (For example, "a glittering star" may, alternatively, be said to be Fāṭimah, daughter of the Prophet Muḥammad, wife of 'Alī, and mother of the two *imāms*, Ḥasan and Ḥusain.)

The classical science of exegesis known as "*tafsīr*" is considered to be legitimate when undertaken by a qualified authority and according to established methods. Who is said to be such an authority and what are the proper methods, however, have been differently understood across classical traditions. These notions have shifted dramatically in the modern era, and not only in terms of the fundamental "questions of authority" to undertake exegesis. Although not new to Muslim experience, translation of Qur'ānic meaning across language systems is a powerful mode of interpretation that is increasingly widespread, albeit masked by modern technologies and reading practices. All of the verses in this book that are not in the form of transliterated Arabic words have, after all, already undergone this interpretive process in having their meanings translated and rendered into English.

READING AND "TRANSLATION"

In pious understandings, any "translation" of the Arabic Qur'ān can be only a mere approximation of meaning of the words of God.[49] Tradition records that the question of "translation" was recognized early by the Prophet Muḥammad and his companions. The formulation of jurisprudential opinion on the status of "translations" came after that time. According to an article by the scholar A. L. Tibawi, one early controversy on the topic of "translation" that is recounted in the classical literature (which or may not be said to be supported by the historical record) was about the following incident. The figure who is known as the first Iranian convert to Islam, Salmān Al-Farīsī, was allegedly asked to write the Fātiḥah in the language of his homeland, Farsī. This report gave the opportunity to Muslims to ask the question, can one translate the Qur'ān? And, since the Fātiḥah is required to be read for the required act of worship, *ṣalāt*, could a Muslim use a non-Arabic translation for this prayer? It was known that the Prophet Muḥammad had said that the Qur'ān was "revealed in seven modes [*aḥrūf*]." Was this sanction to include non-Arabic reading, Muslims asked? Could *tilāwah* (recitation, as in the spoken words) be distinguished from a corresponding *ma'nā* (meaning), and if so what would be the implications of this for everyday religious life?

In his article on the history of Qur'ānic "translation," the contemporary academic scholar A. L. Tibawi writes that there were precedents for translating scripture in early Islamic tradition, even during the lifetime of the Prophet Muḥammad. First, he writes, there is an account that the Prophet had written to the Byzantine emperor a letter that included a passage, 3 Āl 'Imrān 63, apparently already knowing that it would be translated. Also, it was reported that the Prophet would "read Torah" in debate with Jews (for example, regarding the punishment for adultery in a widely known instance); it is presumed in these cases that the Hebrew scriptures were translated into Arabic, and, quite possibly, the Arabic Qur'ān to Hebrew. As Tibawi also observes in his article, however, the Prophet mainly dealt with other Arabic speakers, so there is little material in the *sunnah* that would offer a basis for a legal position on the matter. The meaning of a Qur'ānic verse like 14 Ibrāhīm 4 (i.e. that God sends no messenger but that he uses the "tongue of own people") may be interpreted as either expanding or restricting the parameters for linguistic diversity for rendering the Qur'ān's message, he notes.

Tibawi explains that Abū Ḥanīfa (d. 765), for whom the "Hanafi" school of law is named (see Chapter 4), began a controversy with his ruling that it was permissible to recite the Qur'ān in the Persian language in canonical prayer (*ṣalāt*). Abū Ḥanīfa himself was Persian; and the Hanafi school became well known for finding flexible solutions to real problems on the Iranian geographical periphery of the Muslim lands of the earliest period of Islam. Others extended this ruling to include Turkish, Hindi, Syriac, Hebrew, and other languages, according to Tibawi. By this time, there had already been a translation of Qur'ānic meanings into many other languages, across the geographic expanse of the growing Muslim world. Abū Ḥanīfa, however, meant to refer only to short passages expressly for prayer (like the Fātiḥah) in his ruling, not a complete translation of the entire Qur'ān, Tibawi states. His followers, notably Abū Yūsuf, clarified this position and further specified that recitation in Arabic was permissible only for those who were not yet capable of recitation of the Arabic words, which, Tibawi writes, would imply that this was intended just to be a temporary measure in order to ease the way for new Muslim converts. Nevertheless, he adds, there was still an important implication to this ruling, which was that "the Qur'ān" would be understood to be the meaning of the text, not its actual Arabic words. Tibawi observes that this perspective has some support in statements made by the Qur'ān itself, for example, that the Qur'ān is equivalent to previous revelations in other languages.

Tibawi writes that this single Hanafi opinion seems to have clarified what became the mainstream view, which is also the standard view today: the Qur'ān may not be "translated," whether ritually or semantically. Its "meanings" may only be said to be interpreted. Passages in the Qur'ān that affirmed that God revealed the Qur'ān in the Arabic language are taken to be textual verification of this position. According to Tibawi, the early jurists applied strong arguments, sometimes even prohibitions, to prevent Muslims from using translations in canonical prayer (*ṣalāt*), and further reaffirming that the language of religious learning was Arabic. The emerging Qur'ānic sciences of *i'jāz* ("inimitable" Qur'ānic expression) strengthened this view (see Chapter 5), and works such as that of Ibn Qutaibah on rhetoric elaborated the superior eloquence of Arabic over any other human language. By the fifth Islamic century, Tibawi writes, the issue was already settled.[50] The universality of Qur'ānic Arabic across the Muslim world has supported a plethora of "untranslated" pious expressions, found in countless languages. Many of these carry Qur'ānic forms like "*in shā' Allāḥ*" (if God wills), which is said about events that are hoped or expected to happen in the future (discussed further in Chapter 6).

Rendering Qur'ānic meanings into languages other than Arabic is called *tarjamah*. "*Tarjamah*" is best understood as a kind of *tafsīr*, an interpretation of Qur'ānic meaning.[51] In modern contexts, electronic media instantly translate Qur'ānic meaning and expression into many languages. New media that are visual, auditory, and time based amplify and enhance the meanings of the Arabic Qur'ān through emergent modes of reading. Recording technologies, for example, allow readings of the Qur'ān to cross boundaries quickly and to be accessed constantly for practices such as memorization. Digital study of basic Arabic has opened up new possibilities for learning the language of the Qur'ān with the innovation of not even having a living teacher present, at least for those who would be privileged to have access to such media.

NEW ACCESS AND ANALYSIS

The wide range of semantic meanings of a text that is *dhū wujūh* continues to be disputed in discussions today, such as with disputes about whether the Qur'ān's heavenly "houris" would be said to refer to the "wide-eyed virgins" in paradise or to the "white raisins" of Mecca. Under modern conditions, many simultaneous conversations about the nature of the Qur'ān and its reading can be heard as overlapping messages across mixed media. A few of these discourses could be said to be continued and direct responses to the challenges of colonialism, while many more are not. For example, the question of "*sūrah* coherence" represents a relatively modern view of the *sūrah* as a "unity" of expression.[52]

New media have forged unprecedented possibilities for rendering and apprehending the text of the Qur'ān. This produces effects that are at once both expansive and superficially limiting. The Qur'ān's accessibility in downloadable and searchable form leads to new, fast, and standardized possibilities of "reading," just as listening to recitations through recoding technologies has tended to homogenize vocalized style globally. Information and views also travel with increasing rapidity across geographical and other boundaries, creating a widening scope which can accompany what is otherwise a flattening of the depth of available knowledge through the redundancy of mirrored duplication. New media like the Internet open new communities of Muslim reading that would not otherwise have been in contact or been able to interact, especially through English-language media; correspondingly, another dimension of this trend is that the majority without access to new technologies will remain peripheral to the conversation.[53]

Distortions of access can themselves result in new dimensions of reading being introduced into the public sphere. Perspectives that previously were not representative of any mainstream can readily proliferate if they are propagated with persuasion or persistence by a priviledged few. An example of such a phenomenon is a contemporary approach to the mathematical "miracle" of the Qur'ān. This theory proposes a sort of Qur'ān code, premised on the axiom that the number nineteen (19) is a computational and interpretive common denominator. This perspective hearkens back to old traditions of esoteric analysis of the text, although probably not in a self-conscious way, in its assignment of numeric values to Arabic letters. Proponents of the view of the specialness of the integer nineteen make observations such as: the first verse of the Qur'ān, the Basmalah, contains nineteen letters; and, there are a total of 114 *sūrahs*, a value which can be expressed as the product of nineteen and six. Not surprisingly, calculations based on the "mysterious letters" are common to these algorithms. Information like this can move fast across the bounds even of faith communities. Exploiting the very same electronic formats, non-Muslims may also present themselves as authoritative interpreters of the Qur'ānic text as well, promoting their own ideological agendas about Islam.

In the contemporary period, Qur'ānic science maintains its symbolic prestige, while avenues of access and approach to the text extend and adapt across landscapes of knowledge and communication that are changing rapidly.[54] This has accelerated the formation of new and emerging Qur'ānic authorities, that is, contemporary interpreters of scriptural tradition. Continuing a shift that began in the colonial era, those who claim the mantle of such knowledge may or may not possess the training that once would have been recognized as necessary in the past (such as the study and memorization of *ḥadīth*, or traditional legal training as discussed in the chapter to follow). Some who would claim interpretive authority in fact possess primary training and credentials in non-religious fields such as natural science and computing. Supporting this innovative trend has been the multiplication and even commodification of possibilities for education, including the knowledge industries of secular and state-run universities and publishing.

A modern development that can be tracked as a long-term change in the practice of "reading" of Islamic scripture has been the proliferation of *tafsīr*. Major Muslim intellectual leaders of the twentieth century Muḥammad 'Abduh, Abū'l 'Alā Mawdūdi, Sayyid Quṭb, and many others who came before them in the colonial era (see Chapter 4) all produced long works of exegesis of the Qur'ān. Typically, these works reflected contemporary concerns such as "science" and "the West," nationalism and pan-Islamism, and models for ethics and behavior in the face of modern pluralism, both inside and outside Islam. These works were also part of projects of community-building, whether in support of or in opposition to the state. A widespread effort to render the Arabic Qur'ān into other languages (such as Malay/Indonesian, Farsi, Urdu, and English) should also be seen as a part of this larger phenomenon of new productions of "reading." This has accompanied the repositioning of global Islamic authority within areas like law and jurisprudence especially with respect to state or national systems, a topic discussed in the chapter to follow. Circulation and recirculation of Qur'ānic knowledge in these modes further decenters religious authorities overall, even as this fragmentation may have the tendency to focus reflection ever more narrowly on a few defined topics and issues.

For the Muslim mainstream, new media have allowed possibilities for the production of new certainties, including interpretations of the Qur'ān. For example, *faṭwā*s, which are non-binding legal opinions, proliferate today in the public sphere; increasingly these are sought as responses to questions relating to the private domain of personal conduct.[55] The supply of these answers meets an increasing demand for information that interprets the Qur'ān, as Muslims seek new perceptions of clarity. One religious trend in modern times seems to be an evidently diminishing comfort with ambiguity for some, and a correspondingly greater value placed on the quality of certainty itself. Related modes of religiosity connected to Islamic revival should not be viewed as necessarily restrictive, however. They represent a natural continuation under modern conditions of the pious need for confirmation that one is a good Muslim. As the horizons by which to assess or attain this certainty continually recede under increasing loads of symbolic and social complexity, however, traffic in the public authority of Qur'ānic readings can only increase accordingly.

NOTES

1. Qadhi, *An Introduction to the Sciences of the Qur'aan*, and Von Denffer, *'Ulūm Al-Qur'ān*.
2. Denny, "Exegesis and Recitation," p. 123.
3. Sells, *Approaching the Qur'an*.
4. For more general perspectives of "orality" in religious systems and Islam in particular, see Graham, *Beyond the Written Word*. See also his articles "Qur'ān as Spoken Word" and "Scripture as Spoken Word" as well as Denny, "Qur'ān Recitation: A Tradition of Oral Performance and Transmission."
5. See, for example, the foundational articles by Juynboll, "The Position of Qur'ān Recitation in Early Islam" and "The *Qurra'* in Early Islamic History."
6. Wild, "Spatial and Temporal Implications of the Qur'ānic Concepts of *Nuzūl*, *Tanzīl*, and *Inzāl*."
7. This is one of the *sūrahs* whose sound and meanings are treated in depth in the book by Sells, *Approaching the Qur'ān*.
8. Said, *Orientalism*.
9. Bell, *Bell's Introduction to the Qur'ān*.
10. Gwynne, *Logic, Rhetoric and Legal Reasoning in the Qur'ān*.
11. Saeed, ed., *Approaches to the Qur'an in Contemporary Indonesia*. See also representative global perspectives that are presented in Taji-Farouki, ed., *Modern Muslim Intellectuals and the Qur'ān*.
12. Source material is translated in Jeffery, *Materials for the Study of the History of the Text of the Qur'ān*.
13. For example, see Marcinkowski, "Some Reflections on Alleged Twelver Shi'ite Attitudes Toward the Integrity of the Qur'an." See also Mudarressi, "Early Debates on the Integrity of the Qur'an: A Brief Survey," and Motzki, "The Collection of the Qur'an."
14. Material presented here is after a typology originally given by Déroche, on which Solange Ory draws in an article which provides the basis for the presentation that is given here. I follow the article by Ory on "Calligraphy" from the *Encyclopaedia of the Qur'ān* throughout this paragraph and also in the one that follows. For more in-depth surveys of the historical development of calligraphy, see Blair, *Islamic Calligraphy*, and Lings, *Splendours of Qur'an Calligraphy and Illumination*.
15. Ory, "Calligraphy."
16. Ibid.
17. Denny, "Exegesis and Recitation."
18. These ideas are listed in von Denffer, *'Ulūm Al-Qur'ān*, p. 112.

19. These *ḥadīth*s are given in ibid.
20. Ibid., p. 116.
21. Rummānī, *Al-Nukat fī I'jāz al- Qur'ān*, excerpted and quoted in Rippin and Knappert, *Textual Sources for the Study of Islam*, pp. 49–59.
22. Ghazālī, *Jewels of the Qur'ān*, excerpted and quoted in Wittingham, *Al-Ghazālī and the Qur'ān*, p. 72.
23. Author's translation.
24. For example, Bell, *Bell's Introduction to the Qur'ān*, pp. 90–91. They take the passage 23 Al-Mu'minūn 12–16 to show "evidence of alteration."
25. For more discussion of classical categories in the light of the work of Al-Zarkāshī (d. 1392), see Gwynne, "Patterns of Address," in *Blackwell Companion to the Qur'ān*, pp. 73–87.
26. Both of these *sūrah*s are treated in detail in Sells, *Approaching the Qur'ān*, indicating variant possible translations as well.
27. Unlike other Qur'ānic citations in this book, this interpretation is not based on the translation by Fakhry, *An Interpretation of the Qur'an.*
28. McAuliffe, "Text and Textuality: Q. 3:7 As a Point of Intersection." See also Kinberg, "Muḥkamāt and Mutashābihāt (Koran 3/7)."
29. Cited in Peters, *A Reader on Classical Islam*, pp. 192–193.
30. An example of a later, abridged source that drew on Ṭabarī's work is a handbook, *Tafsīr "Al-Jalālayn" (The Tafsīr of the "Two Jalals").* This has been an introductory textbook for Muslims all over the world for hundreds of years. One of the "Jalāl"'s is Jalāl Al-Dīn [Jalāluddin] Al-Sūyūṭī, the author of the foundational text in Qur'ānic Sciences. For discussion on the development of classical *tafsīr* tradition, see also Saleh, *The Formation of the Classical tafsīr Tradition*. For a scholarly typology that has not been standard in the Islamic tradition, see Wansbrough, *Qur'ānic Studies*.
31. Adapted from the original translation of *Jami' al-bayān fī tafsīr al-Qur'ān* by Cooper as *The Commentary on the Qur'ān*, pp. 55–58.
32. Kamali, *Principles of Islamic Jurisprudence*, p. 27.
33. Ayoub, *The Qur'ān and Its Interpreters*, Vol. 1, pp. 246–252.
34. Excerpted and translated in McNeill and Waldman, *The Islamic World*, pp. 165–166 (the fuller excerpt is given on pp. 164–167). "Womb of Mary" seems to be a reference to the contested Christian doctrine of theotokos, central to the veneration of Mary in the Greek East by the time of the rise of Islam.
35. Ayoub, *The Qur'ān and Its Interpreters*, Vol. 1, pp. 246–252.
36. Whittingham, *Al-Ghazali and the Qur'ān*, pp. 78–79.
37. See Moosa, *Ghazālī and the Poetics of Imagination.*
38. For a scholarly treatment of facets of Al-Ghazālī's religious thought, see ibid.
39. Excellent introductions to Sufism are: Ernst, *What is Sufism?*; Knysh, *Islamic Mysticism*; and Schimmel, *Mystical Dimensions of Islam.*
40. Introductions are Halm, *Shi'a Islam*, and Momen, *An Introduction to Shi'a Islam* (which focuses on Twelver traditions).
41. Schimmel discusses the significance of the figure of Ja'far Al-Ṣādiq in the context of the special authority to interpret scripture, *Mystical Dimensions of Islam*, p. 41.
42. Sells, *Early Islamic Mysticism*, pp. 88–89.
43. This simile of the "niche of lights" is followed immediately in the Qur'ān by another one in 24 Al-Nūr 39, in which an unbeliever misperceives a false mirage for substantive reality.

44. Whittingham, *Al-Ghazali and the Qur'ān*, pp. 104–105.
45. This passage is excerpted from Buchman's transation of Al-Ghazālī, *The Niche of Lights* [*Mishkāt al-anwār*], p. 41. For a more general academic discussion, see Heer, "Abu Hamid Al-Ghazali's Esoteric Exegesis of the Koran."
46. Sands, *Sufi Commentaries on the Qur'ān in Classical Islam*, pp. 110–135.
47. This is excerpted and translated in Gätje, *The Qur'ān and Its Exegesis*, pp. 243–244.
48. Adapted from Poonwalla, "Isma'ili *Ta'wil*." See also Diana Steigerwald, "Ismā'īlī Ta'wīl," in *Blackwell Companion to the Qur'ān*, pp. 386–400. For a similar presentation of themes in "Twelver" tradition see Steigerwald, "Twelver Shī'ī Ta'wīl," in *Blackwell Companion to the Qur'ān*, pp. 373–385.
49. The summary to follow is based closely on the content of the article by Tibawi, "Is the Qur'an Translatable." See also Abdel Haleem, *English Translations of the Qur'an*.
50. This and previous discussion here relies on Tibawi, "Is the Qur'an Translatable."
51. Israeli, "Translation as Exegesis," discussing a case of the translation of the first *sūrah* into Chinese.
52. See Mir's book, *Coherence in the Qur'ān*, and his article, "The *Sura* as a Unity."
53. See two books by Bunt, *Virtually Islamic* and *iMuslims*, and also Anderson, "New Media, New Publics: Reconfiguring the Public Sphere of Islam" as well as contributions to Eickelman and Anderson, eds., *New Media in the Muslim World*.
54. Appadurai, "Disjuncture and Difference in the Global Economy."
55. Messick's article, "Media Muftis," considers a modern case of radio broadcast displacing textualities in Yemen. For discussion of the phenomenon of *fatwa*s and social change in an Indonesian context see Hooker, *Indonesian Islam*.

4

THE QUR'ĀN'S GUIDANCE

Among the many definitional terms for the Qur'ān are "*hudā*" or "*hidāyah*," words that both mean "guidance." Muslims understand these expressions in terms of the Qur'ān's statements to the effect that it engages all experience in this life and the life to come. Support for this comes in phrases such as "We have neglected nothing in the book [the Qur'ān]" (6 Al-An'ām 38) and "And We reveal the scripture unto you as an exposition of all things" (16 Al-Naḥl 89). It may therefore strike some beginning students initially as a paradox that there is actually relatively little information found in the Qur'ān that takes the form of statements of positive law. Muslim communities derive legal norms and rulings from the Qur'ān through various branches of jurisprudential religious sciences. Although these fields of law and ethics overlap with the "Qur'ānic sciences," in classical sources they are also treated separately. Jurisprudential sciences rely heavily on extra-Qur'ānic material, especially reports of the Prophet's experience and comportment (*ḥadīths*) that are the basis for knowing his exemplary model (*sunnah*). In addition, Muslim legal systems apply rigorous guidelines for reasoning and decision, and Shi'ite systems have enhanced this with the guidance of living authorities and interpreters.

Any action prescribed by God in the Qur'ān, including the exercise of faith and pious reflection, is ethical and legal.[1] Of course, Muslims also answer, and ask, wider ethical and legal questions with readings of the Qur'ān. As Muslims read the Qur'ān, its guidelines, fixed and flexible, are signposts for addressing questions such as: How do we do the right thing? How would we be able to know what is the right thing? The Qur'ān's solutions to problems like these come in many types of revealed language, not just the material that legal tradition recognizes formally to be "*aḥkām*," or clear jurisprudential rulings. Parables, narratives, and other Qur'ānic content issue multifaceted guidelines and models for thought and action, including the soteriological "promise and warning" about actions' ultimate consequences. Much of the Qur'ān's guidance comes in the form of general principles, such as the Qur'ānic call to "command the good and forbid the wrong." Legal and social thought establish their legitimate basis in such Qur'ānic norms, although the precise wording of a given ruling may often not actually be found in the Qur'ānic text itself, but instead has been derived through another mediating source.

Within the field of *fiqh* (jurisprudence), it is not the case that Muslims derive all law from the worded text of the Qur'ān. In addition, even positive law that is considered to be established definitively by the Qur'ān is subject to rules for derivation and application. For example, Muslims understand the changing circumstances of its being "sent down" in time to be reflected in "occasions of revelation" (*asbāb al-nuzūl*) of particular verses, and this is one of many criteria for "generalizing" or "specifying" legal and ethical content in application. A multiplicity of norms may thus be derived from the same text by a plurality of global Muslim communities, all of whom exercise sound and flexible Islamic principles such as those of Arabic grammar, legal theory and method, and moral aesthetics.

In teaching and learning about the Qur'ān and Islam in religious studies, the first questions many students pose about the Qur'ān are often legal in nature. Similar to the modes of questioning Muslims apply in religious settings, classroom learners tend to approach the text seeking certainty on matters such as, "Does Islam *really* require *x*," or, "What does Islam say about *y*," and so on. Without understanding long-established Muslim legal and interpretive frameworks for deriving legal rulings, however, students may attempt to find answers to their own questions directly from the text, by considering the Qur'ānic verses that are evidently relevant straight away. In effect, this is to act like a legal scholar, or *mujtahid*, who would derive a ruling based on a scriptural source, *Qur'ān*, and some exercise of independent reasoning. However, in bypassing established traditions of reading of the text, students naturally would not come into contact with the authoritative and historical models for understanding actual Muslim conversations on precisely the issues that are their own concerns about Islam. In addition, while the conclusions reached through this sort of ad hoc legal reasoning may actually be considered sound, the methods used to reach them are consistent with little that can be located within the mainstream of Islamic tradition historically. Confusion can arise for learners over time whenever they do not recognize contemporary discontinuities with a long tradition of Islamic religious thought that has had a rich history of development over a span of many centuries.

Paul R. Powers has explained "Islamic law" to students as a pious human task, an attempt to order human action and society (and to some extent, thought) in accord with revelation.[2] There are two key terms for Islamic law: *sharī'ah* and *fiqh*. For the purposes of the present Introduction, *sharī'ah* denotes transcendental ideals, the "will of God." Islamic law seeks the best approximation of these ideals within human lives and understanding. The word *fiqh* literally means "understanding." It is the pious effort to arrive at theory and method for rendering revelation (that is, *sharī'ah*) a part of human life, as in the definition of "Islamic law" above. Manuals of *fiqh* come in the form of lists of topics' rulings, often including some discussion of how the rules have been derived and what is the range of disagreement among scholars on any given point.

Islamic law is not a straightforward list of duties and prohibitions (*amr* and *nahy*), however. Most of the Qur'ān's guidance comes in the form of ideal and even transcendental perspectives. Even when they appear in the form of recognized rulings, it is not always clear whether the Qur'ān's laws should be seen as "general" or "specific," and following from that, what should be the steps for applying these rulings in everyday life. Among specific legal injunctions in the Qur'ān, there are the "five pillars," belonging to the class of legal action which pertains to worship (*'ibādāt*). In addition, there is another major class of social behavior and interaction covered in the Qur'ān known as *mu'āmalāt* (which treats matters such as marriage, criminal acts, etc.). To make determinations in both areas, jurisprudential tradition (*fiqh*) relies on more than the Qur'ān as a textual source. In fact, much of the textual basis for legal rulings, including the enactment of the "five pillars," comes from *ḥadīth* reports which recount the sayings, actions, and approvals and disapprovals of the Prophet Muḥammad.

"*Sharī'ah*" is a difficult term to understand and apply in modern contexts because it is also an expression commonly used in political rhetorics. In the global public sphere, students today will also commonly hear the term "*sharī'ah*" applied to law codes that are in fact the historical product of *fiqh* (jurisprudence). Many calls for "*sharī'ah* as the basis of the state" have an ideological appeal, but provide few immediate concrete answers to the questions of how to carry out the task of correlating the ideals of "Islamic law" with the political reality and social structures of the modern nation-state. It is not incorrect to say that the task of imagination, codification, and enforcement of "Islamic law" by the state to such an extent was unprecedented before the colonial era. Since that time, Muslim scholars have looked to the Qur'ān for positive law as well as for general guidance on political governance and principles, such as the idea of democratic or parliamentary process, consultative "*shūrā*" (42 Al-Shūrā 38 and 3 Āl 'Imrān 159 are the proof-texts that are usually given). However, it was also precisely the issue of the legitimate bases for political leadership that caused community devisiveness (in the form of "*fitnah*") in the first generations of Islam.

There is a social creativity to contemporary structures of Islamic law, including that whose basis is rationalized Qur'ānically. Some explicitly legal material in the Qur'ān that is non-ritual pertains to family law and punishment for criminal transgression, and so in modern contexts these areas have naturally been privileged whenever contemporary systems seek to innovate new statutory systems of religious "law codes," and especially so with respect to areas of gender and personal status law. In addition, Islamists who take on the symbolic system of "Islam" in order to critique extant structures have also tended to cast their calls for change in terms of highly charged categories of gender, personal status, and moral conduct. A growing modern trend for Muslims to wish to have all aspects of life matched against "Muslim" ideals, however understood, supports this phenomenon. Principled, progressive challenges to social injustice and environmental degradation are also heard by Muslims in new religious languages. At the same time, Muslims in Muslim-minority contexts, whatever their orientation, must work creatively in order to establish new mechanisms and channels just to solve the very same sorts of religious problems that were met by the first Muslims, such as in terms of fulfilling basic Islamic duties like paying, collecting, and distributing annual *zakāt* (legal alms).

THE "FIVE PILLARS OF ISLAM" AND THE QUR'ĀN

There are more than 6,000 verses in total in the Qur'ān. Of these, scholars estimate there to be more than 300 that convey legal rulings. The textual context of many of these verses also provides an accompanying explicit rationale (*ta'līl*) for the given ruling in many cases. The overall number of "legal" verses in the Qur'ān is thus relatively few, less than the total number of verses about the prophet Moses (Mūsā), for example. Some of these verses prohibit specific practices such as infanticide, usury, gambling, and unlimited polygamy. Others treat certain criminal transgressions and their penalties, known as *ḥudūd* ("limits"): illicit killing, highway robbery, fornication and adultery, and slanderous accusation. About seventy verses pertain to commercial and other transactions, and seventy to marriage and bequests. There are an additional 140 verses that relate to matters of worship, such as the "five pillars" of Islam.

The Qur'ān is unequivocal that every action will be assessed on the final day. After the period of the development of the intellectual foundations of law, called "*uṣūl al-fiqh*," in about the ninth century, there was an acceptance of the framework of "five attitudes" or five types of assessment for actions. This was not a formal scheme, but rather it is loose typology that emerged from the commentary within manuals of law. The framework reflects the fundamental idea that there could be an "attitude" assigned for everything a human does or would do, corresponding to the reward or punishment, if any, that the action deserves on the final day. The assessments range along a spectrum between two clear poles, from "obligatory" (*farḍ*, *wājib*) to "forbidden" (*ḥarām*). In between the two extreme ends would be actions that would be considered to be recommended, indifferent, or disapproved. The actions known as the "five pillars" are at one end of this continuum, and all required of all Muslim men and women. (In general, rulings of ritual law are not open to speculative or analogical reasoning.)

The "five pillars" are: *shahādah* (witnessing of faith); *ṣalāt* (canonical prayer, required five times daily); *zakāt* (legal almsgiving); *ṣawm* (fasting sunrise to sunset during the month of Ramaḍān for those who meet the conditions for this); and Ḥajj (pilgrimage to Mecca once in a lifetime, fulfilling the specified requirements). A verse found in the Qur'ān that sets forward most of these "five pillars" is the following:

> Righteousness is not to turn your faces towards the east and the west; the righteous is he or she who believes in Allāh, the last day, the angels, the book and the prophets; who gives of his or her money, in spite of loving it, to the near of kin, the orphans, the needy, the wayfarers and the beggars, and for the freeing of slaves; who performs the prayers and pays the alms-tax. Such are also those who keep their pledges once they have made them, and endure patiently privation, affliction and times of fighting. Those are the truthful and the God-fearing. (2 Al-Baqarah 177)

Of the "five pillars," this verse mentions three: "believing in Allāh" (*shahādah*), prayers (*ṣalāt*) and legal alms (*zakāt*). Within Muslim religious life, each of these provides an example of the intersection of the text of the Qur'ān and the living traditions of Islamic jurisprudence.

Law about worship is the Islamic legal area that is probably the most generally familiar among Muslims worldwide, since some knowledge of ritual law is required for anyone who tries to practice the religion of Islam. This knowledge would at least be expected to cover the required actions that comprise the "five pillars" of Islam. Any Muslim attempting to follow these requirements must ask how to "do the right thing," or put another way, know what is required to remove "speculation" and produce "certainty" that pious action will be approved of or accepted by God. However, just as much of "Islamic law" is not found written in the Qur'ān as such, complete information is not given in the Qur'ān regarding the precise application of these injunctions. Besides the Qur'ān, many types of persons and material answer Muslims' questions about how to carry out worship, and this also determines what will be the sorts of questions for which Muslims will go on to seek further clarification. Much of how Muslims practice their religion comes from the *sunnah*, not from a direct or reasoned textual ruling from the Qur'ān. And, in many cases, even the reports of the Prophet's comportment (*ḥadīth*), on which the legal and pious model of the Prophet's action, the *sunnah*, is based, are silent or ambiguous. Below is an introduction to derivation that would be necessary in order to stipulate clearly how to perform the "five pillars," considering some of the relevant Qur'ānic passages and also basic questions and approaches in *fiqh*.

The first act of worship is *shahādah*. This action takes the form of a statement, the declaration of faith, "There is no god but God," adding, "and Muḥammad is His messenger." As a "performative utterance," the idea already takes the form of an activity. As a spoken formula it is uttered during canonical worship, *ṣalāt*, and also comprises part of the act of accepting Islam as a convert. Both the *shahādah* and the intention (*niyyah*) that is required to be performed prior to some religious actions are ritual enactments that take the form of internal states. The entire Qur'ān and its message of the oneness of Allāh could be seen to be the basis of this act of worship, including its content pertaining to the prophets who relay the message of the *shahādah*, and also Muḥammad's own experience as a model of faith and practice.

In the Qur'ān, direct statements that affirm the "*shahādah*" ("there is no god but God") are found in 37 Al-Ṣāffāt 35 and 47 Muḥammad 19. The statement also appears in variant forms, such as in the well-known "verse of the throne" (2 Al-Baqarah 255, discussed in Chapter 3). The affirmation that Muḥammad is the "messenger of Allāh" is also found throughout the Qur'ān, and the statement appears in the same semantic form as the *shahādah* in 48 Al-Fatḥ 29. The entire verse reads:

> Muḥammad is the messenger of Allāh [*Muḥammadun rasūl Allāhi*] and those who are with him are hard on the unbelievers, merciful toward each other. You will see them kneeling and prostrating themselves, seeking bounty and good pleasure from Allāh; their mark is upon their faces, as a trace of their prostration. That is their likeness in the Torah and their likeness in the teachings of Jesus [*al-injīl*]; just as a seed which puts forth its shoot, strengthens it and grows stout, then rises straight upon its stalks, delighting in the sower, to vex thereby the unbelievers. Allāh has promised those who believe and do the righteous deeds forgiveness and a great wage. (48 Al-Fatḥ 29)

This verse, which also concludes the *sūrah*, also provides an example of a simile in the Qur'ān (in this case, that of the "good seed").

As for the word itself, "*shahādah*," there are many variants of the root *sh-h-d* found in the Qur'ān, often connoting "witnessing" (and sometimes meaning "martyr"). For example, there are two verses found in the *sūrah* 3 Āl 'Imrān that refer to the act of "witnessing": 3 Āl 'Imrān 18 and 3 Āl 'Imrān 86. This *sūrah* offers much material on the theme of religious identity and faith more generally, particularly with respect to Christianity and Islam. Nowhere in the revealed Qur'ān, however, is the statement ascribed the ritual status that it later came to have in Islamic tradition.

Second, there is prayer. There are countless types of prayers that Muslims perform, including many varieties of supplication called *du'ā'*. *Ṣalāt*, however, is an obligatory form of worship. The Qur'ān mentions the practice frequently (for example, it is commanded in 2 Al-Baqarah), and sometimes indicates the relevant times of day, such as the legal command to perform *ṣalāt* at the decline of the sun (that is, at the time just after the sunset), found in 17 Al-Isrā' 18 and in related commands elsewhere in the text. In addition, there is textual comment made on the change of the orientational direction to which prayer is to be performed to the "Sacred Mosque" (or Ka'bah) in Mecca in 2 Al-Baqarah 144 and again in 2 Al-Baqarah 149–150. These verses are considered to have been revealed about two years after the Hijrah. Prior to this, it is said that the direction of prayer (*qiblah*) had been toward Jerusalem.

The Qur'ān does not specify how to perform *ṣalāt*, however, nor what, precisely, would make any act of *ṣalāt* valid legally. What is explicitly given in the Qur'ān and *sunnah* about how to perform the ritual (such as, for example, facing the proper direction) is also less than what Muslims actually and usually do for the full ritual activity. The norms that are widely accepted for *ṣalāt* are outlined in Chapter 5, there considered in terms of the guidelines for the required practice of reciting from the Qur'ān during the act of worship.

Another legal requirement for *ṣalāt* is that it be performed when in a state of ritual purity (*ṭahārah*). In his article, "Impurity/No Danger," Kevin Reinhart explains that in Islamic religious thought, matters of purity and impurity are a mix of physical and "symbolic" concerns. However, within the tradition of Muslim jurisprudence, ritual "purity" and "impurity" also cannot be said to function as moral categories. They are factual statements about a condition. Reinhart points out that there is a necessarily limited duration of ritual purity; and, in fact, what are considered to be impurifying "events" that break this status are inevitable. While some causes of impurity in Islamic ritual law are, in principle, avoidable (such as contact with polluting substances and sex), many others are not (such as elimination, menstruation, and sleep). Removal of the condition of major impurity requires a full washing, *ghusl*, whereas minor impurity requires lesser ablution, *wuḍū'*. This lasts until it is broken once more. (*Ṭayammum*, the act of purification that may be performed if there is no water, lasts for one prayer.) Ritual acts that bring about a state of purification (*ṭahārah*), Reinhart explains, do not appear to have a direct physical connection to the causes of impurity.[3] Furthermore, these actions are not specified clearly in the Qur'ān.

One Qur'ānic verse about *wuḍū'* has been the center of vigorous debate about the practice of purification, as well as an even wider discussion over the method of interpretation of the Qur'ānic text overall. The key verse in the Qur'ān on *wuḍū'* is the following. It may be read in different ways, which has led to differing answers to the question of how one is to wash or wipe one's feet in everyday preparation for prayer:

> O believers [*yā ayyuhā alladhīna āmanū*], if you rise to pray, wash your faces and your hands up to the elbows and wipe your heads and your feet up to the ankles. If you are unclean, then cleanse yourselves; and if you are sick or on a journey, and if one of you has come from the rest-room, or if you have touched women and cannot find any water, then take some clean earth and wipe your faces and hands with it. Allāh does not wish to burden you, but to purify you and complete His grace upon you, that you may be thankful. (5 Al-Mā'idah 6)

As Mohammad Hashim Kamali explains in his book *Principles of Islamic Jurisprudence*, 5 Al-Mā'idah 6 is an example of a verse that is both "definitive" (*qaṭ'ī*) and "speculative" (*ẓannī*) in its meaning; that is, has aspects that are considered to be well defined for the law as well as aspects that are considered to be ambiguous. First, Kamali explains, the statement "… and wipe your heads" is "definitive" in that it is required to wipe the head during the act of *wuḍū'*. The rest of the verse does not, however, specify what part of the head is to be wiped, nor how this is actually supposed to be done.[4] Similarly, regarding feet, Muslims have asked questions such as are socks (if worn) to be removed, and if not, what kind of socks can stay on? These questions are not trivial since they pertain to an action performed many times a day, which is incumbent on all Muslims, and for which a mistake could invalidate prayer. It is known that the Prophet wore leather boots (*khuffayn*) that he did not remove, and some Muslims ask, how can this precedent be understood for today's practice? The answer to a question like this, however, can raise even further speculation in the practical and highly productive legal imagination.

The Qur'ān is clear that the act of *ṣalāt*, if it can be performed by meeting the prerequisite condition of *ṭahārah*, is obligatory.

Allegorization of these pious actions and concepts, while irrelevant from a purely legal standpoint, is not outside the sphere of Islamic religious thought and spirtuality. An example is a work by the famous mystic Ibn 'Arabī (Abū 'Abd Allāh Muḥammad bin 'Alī bin Muḥammad bin Al-'Arabī, 1165–1240) on *The Mysteries of Purity*.[5] In this work, "Ibn 'Arabī" reflects on many layers of the concept of "purity," including ritual actions, from a perspective that is "outward" as well as "inward." Despite the important Islamic maxim, which is based on a *ḥadīth*, that "actions are known by their intentions," the "inner" meaning of religious enactments like prayer and pilgrimage are nevertheless not ever considered to be a valid substitute for outward performance of required acts.

The verses treating the observance of fasting during the month of Ramaḍān, the third "pillar" of Islam, include instances of Qur'ānic "abrogation," when a ruling has changed in time (as it also did in the case of the direction of canonical prayer, for example). In one case, the Qur'ān permits sexual relations in the evening during Ramaḍ ān (2 Al-Baqarah 187), thereby cancelling out the validity of the ruling that had apparently prevailed prior to that (i.e. no sex was allowed all month long, just as sex invalidates Ḥajj). In legal tradition, David Powers explains, there has also been a well-known debate over the interpretation of the verses 2 Al-Baqarah 183–184, which state that a believer has the option either of fasting, or, if he or she happens to breaks the fast (perhaps because it is just too hard), then he or she may feed a poor person as a substitute for the ritual act of a day's fasting. However, Powers writes, in the very next verse, 2 Al-Baqarah 185 (quoted previously in Chapter 3), the same circumstance is mentioned again (breaking the fast), but without mentioning the option of feeding the poor person. Powers adds that scholars have differed as to whether this should be considered a case of abrogation, that is, whether the later verse "cancels out" the ruling in the previous verse, the one that would have allowed the option for an act of charity to take the place of fasting.[6] The verses read:

183. O you who believe [*yāayyuhā alldhīna āmanū*], fasting is prescribed for you as it was prescribed for those before you, so that you may be God-fearing;
184. For a fixed number of days. If any of you is sick or on a journey, then [an equal] number of other days. And those who find it extremely difficult [to fast?] should, as a penance, feed a poor person. He or she who spontaneously does even more good

deeds than this, it is even better for him or her. To fast is better for you, if you only knew.

185. The month of Ramaḍān is the month in which the Qur'ān was revealed, providing guidance for humanity, with clear verses to guide and to distinguish right from wrong. He or she who witnesses that month should fast it. But if anyone is sick or on a journey, [he or she should fast] a number of other days. Allāh desires ease and does not desire hardship for you, that you may complete the total number; glorify Allāh for His Guidance [*mā hadākum*], that you may be thankful. (2 Al-Baqarah 183–185)[7]

In addition, David Powers adds, there is also considered to be one more clear case understood to be an instance of abrogation here, relating to the duration of the days of the fast. In the verses above, the valid ruling appears to change from "a fixed number of days" (unspecified number, in verse 184) to the "whole month" (verse 185).[8]

Fourth, the Qur'ān puts forward many injunctions to give *zakāt* (legal alms). This annual tithe (usually paid at the end of the fasting month of Ramaḍān) differs from ordinary charity (called *ṣadaqah*) because it is required, and also because there are guidelines about who should pay, and how much, and to whom. Copious Qur'ānic material on helping the less fortunate and an expression of a vision of social justice forms an ethos that is a scriptural basis for the required practice. *Zakāt*, however, is an obligation that is difficult to translate in terms of past historical circumstances recast into new or present conditions. How does one compute the amount accurately and exactly, and in terms of what kinds of wealth? The rulings of the classical manuals of *fiqh*, themselves an attempt to render the general statements of the duty in the Qur'ān into clear rules, are in the language of the fiscal system of their day. They state requirements in measures for wealth that prevailed over a millennium ago, which are livestock, precious metals, etc., now antiquated for most Muslims in the urban cash economy. In addition, *zakāt* requires a social mechanism for collection and distribution, making tithing a highly variable contemporary practice in terms of accounting, systems of banking, and the state. Some modern Muslim thinkers, observing that the principle of *zakāt* represents an automatic system of wealth redistribution in Islam, see the fundamental practice to represent a challenge to Muslims, and humanity more widely, to implement a universalized vision of economic justice and equitable resource distribution.

Finally, the performance of the pilgrimage to Mecca, the Ḥajj, takes place over the course of several days. There are two sorts of pilgrimage to Mecca; Ḥajj is the "greater pilgrimage," and it is the one that is required at least once, if possible. Each action stipulated for Ḥajj must be carried out correctly in order for the journey to be considered a valid fulfillment of the legal requirement for the lifetime. Muslims understand most of the Qur'ān to have been revealed before the Prophet Muḥammad was able to undertake his Islamic pilgrimage in Mecca, which is said to have occurred near the end of his own life. Although there are quite a few Qur'ānic stipulations pertaining to the conditions of Ḥajj (such as 2 Al-Baqarah 196–203), as in the case of other ritual actions, few detailed instructions for the activity are actually given in the Qur'ān. Most of the basis for the required actions of Ḥajj comes from the *ḥadīth* reports that make up the *sunnah* (the exemplary model of the Prophet Muḥammad).

However, unlike other ritual actions discussed here, Qur'ānic narrative informs deeply the performance of Ḥajj. This material in the Qur'ān provides different kinds of expectations for Ḥajj than those that are strictly stipulative and legal. The paradigms of the sacred past establish an experiential relation of believers to their own enactments of sacred story. This occurs especially with the Qur'ānic accounts of the prophet Abraham (Ibrāhīm), such as the mention of a well-known site of *maqām* Ibrāhīm ("the station of Abraham") in 3 Āl 'Imrān 97. The Qur'ān establishes that Ibrāhīm built the Ka'bah ("The House of God" [Figure 2, p. 192]) at its place with his son, Ismā'īl, in 2 Al-Baqarah 127. Ibrāhīm's pilgrimage at this site is mentioned in 22 Al-Ḥajj 26–29; these verses include instruction from God to "purify My house" ("*waṭahhir baitī*," the Ka'bah), found in verse 26. Verse 29 contains the command to circumambulate the "ancient house" ("*al-bait al-'atīq*," the Ka'bah), corresponding to the practice of circling the Ka'bah seven times in greater or lesser pilgrimage, which is called *ṭawāf.* 37 Al-Ṣāffāt 101–109 recounts the near-sacrifice by Ibrāhīm of his son, who is not named in the Qur'ān but is usually understood to be the prophet Ishmael (Ismā'īl).

The figure of Ibrāhīm and his family permeates the active itinerary of Ḥajj, although not always directly in terms of technical stipulation of the actions required for Ḥajj to be valid. The pious relation to Abraham and his family that is established in Ḥajj also works through extra-Qur'ānic narratives that are commemorated and enacted during the pilgrimage. An example is Ḥajar running for water between two hills for her child, Ismā'īl, after she had been left by her partner Ibrāhīm in the desert at God's command; at this point the well of Zamzam is said to have been revealed to her. During Ḥajj, pilgrims are required to "run" between the hills of Aḷ-Safā and Al-Marwah, like a mother seeking to care for her child's needs with no other help but God's. They also drink from the well of Zamzam, and water from this source is a popular souvenir to take back to friends and relatives at home.

The prophetic model of Abraham energizes the model of Ḥajj functionally, genealogically, and geographically. For example, pilgrims undertaking Ḥajj stand for a day on the Plain of "'Arafat," where Ibrāhīm "knew" that the order to sacrifice his son was from God; they stone the pillars (*jamrāt*) representing the devil who tempted Ibrāhīm not to complete the sacrifice; and, on the "day of sacrifice" that ends the annual period of Ḥajj, they are responsible for the sacrifice of a real animal just like the one that God provided as a substitute for the human sacrifice of Ibrāhīm's son. This final action will be performed every year not only by pilgrims who are in the sacred precinct of Mecca, but in fact it is observed by Muslims worldwide as the second biggest holiday of the Muslim year, 'Id Al-Aḍḥā. Ḥajj enactments recall events in the sacred history of the Abrahamic narrative as well as the detailed stipulations of the Prophet Muḥammad's own purported model enactment in overlapping dimensions of myth and ritual. This renders Ḥajj a pious experience that is outwardly carried out according to precise formal detail and which at the same time also has potentially unbounded inner and transformative depth.

Every one of the "five pillars" of Islam, as considered above, points to a key question about the textual relation of required action to Qur'ānic guidance. These range from the semantic meaning of Arabic terms ("washing" or "wiping" feet), to the principle of abrogated rulings (as in fasting), to patterns of historical change (such as the terms of *zakāt*), and also how the lived ritual present occupies universal space and sacred time. In each of these cases, such as *ṣalāt*, all information Muslims seek about how to perform acts of worship correctly is not given in the Qur'ān. Not all the answers believers would need are provided even when the example of the Prophet (*sunnah*) is taken into account. There developed "schools" of jurisprudence (sing. *madhhab*, pl. *madhāhib*) in the first centuries of Islam that answered the questions that Muslims asked not only about worship but about the entire range of human activity. This came along with the formation of recognized branches of Islamic religious sciences more generally, including the developing divergences between Sunni and Shi'ite traditions.

In the formative period of jurisprudential tradition (the eighth to twelfth centuries), Islamic jurisprudence took shape in terms of many named "schools," some of which survived, and some of which did not. The "schools" were orientations in the law, a mixture of rulings and methods that were associated with authoritative named lineages. Knowledge and mastery in a legal school was not exclusive in the Muslim world of the past; that is, people would study in multiple schools of law, often traveling great distances in order to do so. However, there has been since early times an expectation not to conflate schools of law in a single context, that is, not to mix or match jurisprudential approaches in application.[9] In general, Shi'ite legal theory was systematized somewhat later than the first schools now considered to be Sunni. The Shī'a developed a tradition of Ja'fari law, along with schools in the "Twelver" tradition (that which is followed by most Shi'ite Muslims today, as in Iran), notably Uṣūlī (the mainstream) and also Akhbārī law. Traditions of the Shī'a tend to include the ongoing guidance that *imāms* and, in their absence, jurisprudential scholars, provide to religious community.

By the twelfth century the options for named jurisprudential schools had begun to narrow in the Sunni tradition. There are four accepted "schools" in the Sunni tradition, and some have said that no more independent approaches were accepted after this time (that is, that the "gate of *ijtihād*," or independent reasoned opinion, had been "closed"). However, even in the sense that this statement could actually be said to be valid, there was creativity required in order to adjust new situations and questions with the set parameters of the law, as the academic scholar Wael Hallaq has shown in his writings on legal history.[10] Within the Sunni world, which accounts for about ninety percent of the Muslim-majority and Muslim-minority populations today, four major legal schools are named for their eponymous founders: Hanafi (Abū Hanīfa d. 767, who developed early legal reasoning); Maliki (Mālik b. Anas d. 795, who was committed to the model of the Muslim community in Medina as *sunnah*); Shāfi'ī (Muḥammad bin Idrīs Al-Shāfi'ī, d. 820, whose legal theory is discussed in more detail below); and Hanbali (Aḥmad b. Ḥanbal, d. 855, a scholar of *ḥadīth* whose name appears in connection with the *miḥnah* over the nature of the Qur'ān). All of these "schools" can be found in practice, to a greater or lesser degree, in the present. There were also other legal options that continued past the formative centuries, such as the Ẓāhiri or "literalist" school that extended from students of Ḥanbal, along with many other smaller local groups.

GUIDELINES FOR DERIVING LAW IN SUNNI TRADITION

Islamic law is divided into "roots" and "branches." The "roots" are the theory and methods by which law is derived; "branches" are the areas of application of the law. The "roots" of Islamic law are known as *uṣūl al-fiqh* and were formalized in the Sunni schools in approximately the ninth and tenth centuries. Classical Islamic legal thought treats statements of the Qur'ān and *ḥadīth* as free-floating units or rules (*aḥkām*), in much the same way that verses are taken as discrete units in "traditional" Qur'ān exegesis. In jurisprudential practice, these "rulings" can be decontextualized (although the authority of the ruling as based in Qur'ān or *sunnah* is retained), and then recentered to provide legal norms. This process occurs, for example, through the reasonings of analogy.

The mainstream Sunni approach to *uṣūl al-fiqh* has come to be associated with the name of the legal scholar Al-Shāfi'ī (d. 820). In his treatise, the *Risālah*, Shāfi'ī standardized methods and assumptions of legal scholars at the time. This occurred in the same era as knowledge in Arabic grammar, *ḥadīth* study, and other fields of Qur'ānic and religious sciences were also being consolidated. There was a general trend toward piety in this period, seen in the rise of the movement of Sufism, which superseded previous intellectual traditions of philosophy in important respects. In addition, Shi'ite systems were developing key theories of the "imamate" in this period, as well as understandings of the designated authority of the trained legal scholar who interprets the law.

In the Sunni schools of law at the time of Al-Shāfi'ī, and after, there was a general trend increasingly to attempt to link all actions systematically to revelation (Qur'ān and *sunnah*).[11] The scope of "independent reasoning" is fairly circumscribed in Shāfi'ī's formulation, cast in terms of the treatment of the topic of legal analogy. Previously, the prevailing attitude had been that silence in these materials on any matter probably indicated God's approval of it. There was an increasing inclination to seek certainty and to theorize "revelation," especially with a growing tendency to view the *sunnah* as definitive guidance. Paul R. Powers has suggested this could possibly be explained by the growing temporal distance from the Prophet and his community in successive generations, and the related pious desire for confident affirmation that present Islamic practice, even far from the central lands, was still correct.

In the formulation offered by Al-Shāfi'ī, there are four basic ways of connecting revelation to human life.[12] The first is the Qur'ān; its statements provide prescription and proscription, guidelines and principles, and general norms. Scholars derive concrete legal rulings from the explicit rules of the Qur'ān, both from the "letter of the law" (*manṭūq*), as well as from the implied meaning, the "spirit of the law" (*mafhūm*). Statements in the Qur'ān that offer "duties and prohibition" provide legal norms to be understood through direct command, and also through promise and warning of the consequences of those actions. In general, Qur'ānic commands may represent actions that are required, recommended, or neutrally "permissible." Determining the level of assessment, Kamali writes, requires knowledge of the "objectives of the law" on the part of the legal scholar, which rests in turn on other sources as well as Arabic grammar and knowledge of the entire book. If an action is required or prohibited, the "means" or steps that would inevitably lead to those ends are also included as points of law that carry the same assessment, he adds.[13]

The second source of law in jurisprudential sciences of *uṣūl al-fiqh* is *sunnah*, the prophetic model. The *sunnah* is known through *ḥadīth* reports. This is a class of accounts of the actions of the Prophet in the context of his community. The term "*ḥadīth*" came to mean authoritative accounts of the sayings, actions, or tacit approvals or disapprovals of the Prophet Muḥammad (this is the standard definition). A *ḥadīth* report has two parts. First, there is the *isnād*, or the "support" for the account. This takes the form of a list of transmitters who successively passed along the information, extending back to the eyewitness to the authoritative source, the Prophet Muḥammad himself. The second part of the *ḥadīth* is the *maṭn*, or the content of the report. The audition and memorization of these accounts, along with their supports, would have been a first step in any scholar's religious education, after the study and memorization of the Qur'ān.

Historically, practices of aural *ḥadīth* transmission, audition, and memorization represent the origins of the development of institutions of Islamic education such as endowed legal colleges.

The project of *ḥadīth* criticism (the evaluation of their "soundness" based on transmission) and their compilation into collections was essential to the development and application of the law, since the *sunnah* is known through *ḥadīth* reports. Within the first centuries, there appeared "*muṣannaf*" collections, which are topically organized (rather than following a previous system, in which reports were identified by the names of their transmitters). The main collections in the Sunni tradition are six, including the *Saḥīḥ* of "Al-Bukhārī" by Muḥammad bin Ismā'īl Al-Bukhārī (d. 870), and a *Saḥīḥ* by "Muslim," or Muslim bin Al-Ḥajjāj (d. 875). Bukhārī's collection contains over 7,000 *ḥadīth* in hundreds of chapters, although Bukhārī worked through many thousands of reports and ended up retaining far fewer of them. However, there are still many repetitions in his collection due to independent chains of transmission, such as the *ḥadīth* report about the Qur'ān having been revealed in "seven modes" that was discussed in the previous chapter. Many Muslims first learn and memorize *ḥadīth* in short collections of "*arba'ūn*," or forty, *ḥadīth*.

The development of the sciences of *ḥadīth* reports, as well as the significance of the idea of *sunnah* to legal thought, meant that by the time of Al-Shāfi'ī, the two sources, Qur'ān and the *sunnah*, could be cited in the form of *naṣṣ* (authorititave "text," although the term is also somewhat misleading since transmission was primarily oral and aural). Qur'ān verses and *ḥadīth* reports were still open to the issue of discerning the meaning, applicability, and scope of a ruling, however. For this purpose, Muslim legal scholars developed sciences of interpreting *naṣṣ*, whether as literal or allegorical, for example, or how the ruling could be said to relate to other parts of the Qur'ān or to other statements in *ḥadīth*. Even what were apparently self-evident textual rulings were nevertheless subject to rules such as "abrogation."

Neither the Qur'ān itself nor the *ḥadīth* material that makes up *sunnah* represents a corpus of positive law, however. As suggested by study of the "five pillars" given above, most questions that Muslims have are not addressed explicitly by *naṣṣ*, whether in the Qur'ān or even by the *sunnah*. According to classical theory of *uṣūl al-fiqh* such as Al-Shāfi'īs, the interpreter of the law would turn to two other modes of reasoning whenever there was no clear textual ruling on a given question in Qur'ān or *sunnah*. The third approach of *uṣūl al-fiqh* as presented in Shāfi'ī's *Risālah* requires "independent reasoning" (*ijtihād*). It is analogical deduction (*qiyāṣ*), and it is actually the one area in which Al-Shāfi'ī admitted the permissibility of such an effort with respect to the Qur'ān. *Qiyās* is "ratiocination" from revealed statements, following methodical rules. With *qiyās*, one may derive law for an unprecedented case by way of an analogy from an established case. Performed correctly, it entails the application of a rigorous procedure.

Consider the example of deriving a ruling on the permissibility of drinking the beverage beer.[14] "Beer" is not mentioned in either the Qur'ān or the *sunnah*. Deriving a ruling on beer according to *qiyās* would begin with the comparison of two contexts: a question (such as, is it all right to drink beer?) and a *naṣṣ* (for example, the ruling derived from the Qur'ān in 5 Al-Mā'idah 90, which prohibits drinking wine). The next step would be to derive and affirm the applicability of an '*illāh*, or a "rational cause" for the ruling in the text. This exercise is one of the reasons why deriving law from the Qur'ān is considered to be a risky ethical responsibility in classical tradition: in order to state *why* wine would be forbidden by God, the scholar must now actually claim to determine the intent of the Lawgiver, i.e. God. In this case, he or she will first probably attempt to apply a guideline of Qur'ānic hermeneutics found across sub-fields: interpreting the Qur'ān by the Qur'ān itself. For this, there are two relevant Qur'ānic verses: 4 Al-Nisā' 43, which admonishes Muslims not come to prayer "when your mind is not clear" (i.e. drunk?); and 5 Al-Mā'idah 90, mentioned above, in which God prohibits "wine" entirely as an "abomination." Combining the meanings of these two verses, an '*illāh* could be derived: namely, that the rationale for prohibiting wine in 5 Al-Mā'idah 90 could be said to be the idea that it has the effect of intoxication (4 Al-Nisā' 43). The final step in analogical deduction would then be to consider whether the '*illāh* could apply to the new situation under consideration, such as the question of the permissibility of drinking beer. Beer's effect may be intoxication. Thus, the '*illāh* may be applied to the new question, and the final result would be a ruling prohibiting drinking beer, arrived at through the disciplined, "independent reasoning" of *qiyās*.

There are two further key points to mention here on *qiyās*. First, it is usually not applied to questions of ritual law, such as the "five pillars" of Islam. One does not attempt to understand the rationale of the Lawgiver on matters relating to worship. Scholars cannot automatically claim that *wuḍū'* when wearing nail polish, for example, is valid based on the precedent that the Prophet was known to have wiped over his leather boots without removing them when he traveled. In addition, questions such as why there are five required daily prayers in the first place have been addressed in mythic, ritual, and even esoteric modes (there is a story about this in the popular account of the Prophet's Isrā' and Mi'rāj). However, such matters are not rationalized in jurisprudential thought.

Second, there is scholarly dispute over the acceptable application of *qiyās*, even in its most rigorous and restricted forms. For example, there has been a Hanbali legal opinion that drinking beer is permissible.[15] This would actually represent a literalist or "fundamentalist" view, in that it conservatively avoids exercising human reasoning about any "rational cause" or *'illāh* whatsoever. Instead, the ruling relies on a literal reading of the word "*khamr*" (wine) that appears in the text of the Qur'ān. Since the beverage, beer, is not the same drink as the beverage specified by name in the Qur'ān ("wine"), this opinion holds that there is no clear Qur'ānic ruling against beer. This would represent a marginalized legal view today; any Muslim claiming that beer should be considered *ḥalāl* (permitted) rather than *ḥarām* (forbidden) could expect to hear this view corrected.

In the classical theory of *uṣūl al-fiqh*, finally, there is a fourth "root" of the law, called "*ijmā'*" or "consensus." This is a blurred area which denotes a generalized notion of "scholarly opinion." Shāfi'ī expected there to be differing legal opinions, and in fact included in his *Risālah* a section on "*ikhtilāf*," or the divergent views among jurists. *Ijmā'* is an idealized principle of a coherence of opinion. It represents a general notion that people with knowledge in the mainstream have, more or less, agreed on a given point. Legal scholars have not resolved whether this is meant to be a "consensus" for a particular place or whether it should be considered valid across the expanse of where Muslims live, or whether by "consensus" is meant the agreement of scholars in the past as well as those in the present. The principle of the authority of a perspective arrived upon through "consensus" appeared fairly early in the traditions of the interpretation of the Qur'ān, legal and otherwise. For example, Muḥammad bin Jarīr Al-Ṭabarī (d. 923), the great historian and exegete of the Qur'ān, commonly ordered points in reaction to a verse in terms of the "soundness" or overall acceptance of the perspective, as was demonstrated previously in Chapter 3.

One of the greatest changes in Islamic legal theory and practice in the modern period has been in the area of "questions of authority," a shift in the expectations of the authority of the interpreter of the Qur'ān and the law. In the past, Muslim legal scholars would be expected to have had an education that began with the memorization of the Qur'ān and knowledge of *ḥadīth*. In traditional Sunni systems, there were many types of recognized legal experts with specialized academic or practical training, such as: *qāḍī*'s (court judges, a position classically held ambivalently because of its proximity to state power); *mufti*s (who would issue legal opinions, *faṭwā*); and *mujtahid*s, who were sanctioned to exercise independent opinions. Depending on what fields of the "Islamic sciences" the scholar knew, he or she would be authorized in that area or in those areas. Within the realm of the exercise of "independent opinion" (*ijtihād*), some *mujtahid*s would specialize in certain types of law, such as the notoriously difficult area of inheritance law.

In the idealizations of the past, legal tradition spelled out criteria for what was thought to be required for a person to be considered a *mujtahid*, that is, in order to be authorized to exercise an "independent opinion." This would be a person who would be seen legitimately to be able to apply a disciplined reasoning, such as *qiyās*, to derive a ruling based on Qur'ān and *sunnah*. According to the scholar Mohammad Hashim Kamali, a classical text of the eleventh century by Abū'l-Ḥusain Al-Baṣrī became the standard for later works addressing this topic, such as those of Al-Ghazālī (d. 1111). The listing of such requirements below comprises knowledge of the sources and objectives of law as they would pertain to the special area which the particular *mujtahid* would claim authority. Here is a summary of points on the requirements for a *mujtahid* from this original source, following its presentation by Kamali in *Principles of Islamic Jurisprudence*. He or she must:

1. be Muslim, and of a mature age; ideally, he (or she?) should be trained in logic, but at least should be considered to be capable of making a sound judgment;
2. have a knowledge of Arabic, at least to the degree that he (or she) can understand the Qur'ān and *sunnah* with subtlety and accuracy;
3. be trained in the legal content of the Qur'ān and *sunnah*, including

sciences of relevant interpretation, *asbāb al-nuzūl* ("occasions of revelation"), Meccan and Medinan revelations, and abrogation;
4. have competence in *ḥadīth*, including knowledge of "sound" and "weak" *ḥadīth*, and which reports are accepted and which are not (from the texts cited in this treatise, Kamali reckons that this would mean mastery of over a thousand *ḥadīth* reports);
5. know the content of legal handbooks (*furū'*), the points on which there is agreement and disagreement; he (or she) should also know on what points there was consensus (*ijmā'*) in the early community;
6. possess a sound grasp of *qiyās*, which is analogical deduction;
7. understand the "objectives" (*maqāṣid*) of law, as well as principles that "counteract rigidity," such as the "removal of hardship" and the "primacy of certainty over doubt." The *mujtahid* must also further master the "spirit" of the law for matters such as public interest. This means preserving especially those objectives that are explicit in revelation itself, such as the "five principles" that are, namely, protection of life, religion, intellect, lineage, and property;
8. finally, he or she would be a trusted, upstanding person (*'ādil/ 'ādilah*) whose conduct is righteous; who is sincere; who does not seek any personal gain through the law; and, finally, who is free from any conflict of interest.[16]

Some popular interpreters of law in the modern period have not had the full opportunity to undertake the sort of training described above, especially in the areas of Qur'ānic sciences and *ḥadīth* study and criticism.

OCCASIONS AND APPLICATIONS OF REVELATION

Cross-referencing verses of the Qur'ān in terms of legal rulings on specific issues may lead Muslims to consider the stacked and recursive relations among the legal and ethical principles that are revealed in the text. In the case of the ruling on the prohibition on intoxicants above, the rationale adduced for one verse (prohibiting wine) was established in another textual context (not to pray when intoxicated). To determine specific rulings out of this, scholars observe that commandments occur both in a textual context (*maqām*) and also in the form of a worded statement (*maqāl*), or as a ruling that may be applied and qualified across contexts.

To consider the treatment of Qur'ānic verses within a single context (*maqām*), consider a section of *āyāt*, 215–256 of the second *sūrah*, Al-Baqarah. This passage of text offers some rulings and their applications. The occasion of the revelation of the verses is said in tradition to be questions that were posed to the Prophet about legal matters. The section includes one of the "wine verses" (to be discussed further below), as well as a mixture of references both to specific historical events as well as to universal principles. Material such as this has led Muslims to ask, how might one interpret these injunctions in their textual and historical context, especially in terms of "general and specific" scope and application? The first six of these verses are:

215. They ask you what they should spend. Say: "Whatever bounty you give is for the parents, the near of kin, the orphans, the needy and the wayfarer." And whatever good you do, Allāh is fully cognizant of it.
216. You are enjoined to fight, though it is something you dislike. For it may well be that you dislike a thing, although it is good for you; or like something although it is bad for you. Allāh knows and you do not.
217. They ask you about the sacred month: "Is there fighting in it?" Say: "Fighting in it is a great sin; but to debar people from Allāh's way [*sabīli Allāh*] and to deny Him and the sacred mosque [*al-masjidi al-ḥarām*], and to drive its people out of it is a greater sin in Allāh's sight. Sedition is worse than murder." Nor will they cease to fight you until they make you, if they can, renounce your religion. Those of you who renounce their religion and die, while they are unbelievers, are those whose works come to grief, [both] in this world and in the hereafter. And they are the people of the fire, abiding in it forever.
218. Those who believed and those who emigrated [*alladhīna hājarū*] and strove for the cause of Allāh [*sabīli Allāh*] are those who may surely hope for Allāh's mercy. Allāh is Forgiving, Merciful [*ghufūrun raḥīm*].
219. They ask you about wine [*al-khamr*] and gambling, say: "In both there is great sin and some benefit for people. But the sin is greater than the benefit." And they ask you about what they should spend, say: "What can you spare." Thus Allāh makes clear to you His revelations so that you may reflect
220. Upon this world and the hereafter. And they ask you about orphans, say: "To improve their condition is better for them.

> And if you associate with them, they are your brethren." Allāh knows the dishonest and the honest. And if Allāh had willed, he would have overburdened you with restrictions. Allāh is Mighty, Wise [*'azīzun ḥakīm*]. (2 Al-Baqarah 215–220)

The reading continues addressing matters of marriage to "believing women"; menstruation, sexual relations, oaths to avoid a spouse, and divorce; and more material on supporting the cause of Islam and fighting in a war, including some stories of past prophets. The section ends with the famous "verse of the throne" (2 Al-Baqarah 255, see Chapter 3) and also the verse that comes after it, also often cited, that affirms that there is "no compulsion in religion" (2 Al-Baqarah 256).

What stipulations given here are general, and what if any are relevant only to more specific circumstances and applications? The "verse of the throne" is cosmic and universal in scope, as is the Qur'ānic phrase appearing in the verse that follows after it, "There is no compulsion in religion," a general adage often quoted about and within Islam. However, the verses cited above that precede this material seem to be addressing changing historical circumstances. Verse 214, the verse which precedes the excerpt quoted here, for example, mentions "suffering and adversity," understood in tradition as a reference to the Battle of the Trench, and concludes with words that mean, "even the messenger [i.e. the Prophet Muḥammad] and those of faith who were with him cried, 'When will come the help of Allāh!' Truly, the help of Allāh is near." Verse 215 also has a specific occasion of revelation in tradition, which was a question that was put to the Prophet about how to spend wealth. Verses 217 and 218 are said to have been revealed after a raid on Nakhlah, an oasis between Mecca and Medina, just before the Battle of Badr. The raid was said to have occurred on the last day of Rajab, a sacred month. The Prophet was said to have been asked whether fighting was permitted, and this verse was sent down in response to the query. There was later a dispute among scholars about whether the legal ruling of the verse was abrogated by another, as well as a dispute about whether the scope of its application should be qualified to mean only those who observe the "sacred months" in the first place. Verse 219 is one of the "wine verses," discussed further below. One may observe here that its attitude toward wine does not seem to reflect the legal ruling that is in effect on the impermissibility of intoxicants. As for verse 200, even though it seems to be "general" in its application, it is in fact related in tradition that the verse was revealed specifically in response to a situation in which orphans (of which there were many at the time of the Prophet) had their food separated from that of the rest of the household's and were made to eat separately.[17]

"Occasions of revelation," called *asbāb al-nuzūl*, narrate a specific context in which certain verses of the Qur'ān were revealed, according to Muslim tradition. It is a classical mode through which narrative about the Qur'ān interacts with the text itself within interpretive tradition. The accounts actually take the form of a *ḥadīth* report, although historically many such accounts came widely into circulation only later in tradition in connection with the explanation of certain verses.[18] Their study is one of the "sciences of Qur'ān," along with the related field, "abrogation" (discussed below), and both are fundamental to the practice of legal interpretation. This information about the context of the revelation of certain verses sometimes appears within bound copies of the Qur'ān, running parallel to the text like a kind of commentary. As a genre, *asbāb al-nuzūl* did not come under suspicion or challenge, as did some other classes of information used by Muslims for understanding the Qur'ān, such as "*Isrā'īliyāt*" material (stories from other faith communities that supplemented interpretation of Qur'ānic stories of the sacred past). "Occasions of revelation" assist Muslims especially in discerning the generality or specificity of the application of norms in the Qur'ān, such as verse 217 above, whose meanings are quoted on "fighting on the sacred month."

The theory and application of "abrogation" (*nāsikh Al-Qur'ān wa mansūkhuhu*), or "*naskh*" for short, relies on knowledge of the accepted chronology of revelation in order to identify which are said to be the "abrogating" (*nāsikh*) and "abrogated" (*mansūkh*) verses. *Asbāb al-nuzūl* is the basis for determining whether a ruling on the Qur'ān is considered to be "abrogating," "abrogated," both, or neither. Abrogation is based on the religious premise that, naturally, the revealed message addressed the changing circumstances of the first Muslim community. The science of *naskh* developed historically along with traditions of jurisprudence and the study of *ḥadīth* and *asbāb al-nuzūl*.

The Arabic word "*naskh*" means to "cancel out" or "erase." In the Qur'ānic sciences, *naskh* means that the legal ruling of a certain verse of the Qur'ān is "abrogated," that is, superseded or suppressed by a later chronological ruling. The verses all remain in the Qur'ān, however; all that is relevant to this point is the present validity of the "ruling" associated with a given verse. This means that it is not possible just to read casually any verse in the Qur'ān that is in the form of a legal injunction, such as the verse on wine in 2 Al-Baqarah 219, above, and to be able to infer directly whether it is actually in effect for Muslims. One must first have knowledge of religious sciences such as "abrogation."

According to David Powers, whose article on *naskh* is the basis for the brief survey of the topic that follows here, there is evidence in Muslim sources that the issue of abrogation was discussed as early as the time of the community of the Prophet Muḥammad. The body of classical material on *naskh* began to develop with the following generation, and with disagreement. The genre emerged as a field of formal inquiry in the second century of Islamic experience. The first treatises that appeared at this time were probably handbooks for students to memorize, David Powers writes, and he describes them as having had a bipartite structure. The first part was an overview of the significance of abrogation and a survey of the disagreements among scholars about its meaning and scope. This was supported by relevant *ḥadīth*. The body of the text that followed this introduction conformed to the standard ordering of *sūrah*s, presenting each one in terms of where it was revealed (Mecca or Medina, or both), and the number of abrogating and abrogated verses it was said to contain. The text would provide either the entire verse or just the abrogated words in question, depending on the case. There would also be discussion of any relevant controversy, Powers writes.[19]

From the perspective of the religious science of *naskh*, a Qur'ānic verse would be said to have two properties: first, the actual words of the text; and, second, any "ruling" (*ḥukm*) that it may effect. Even if the *ḥukm* has been said to have been abrogated, that portion of the worded text is almost always read as a part of the Qur'ān. Following from this, there are recognized in tradition to be three different modes of abrogation. First there is the case of the abrogation of a ruling but not the wording, or "*naskh al-ḥukm*." This is the most common instance of abrogation. An established case of such an abrogated verse may be further considered to be "explicit or implicit," "complete or partial," and scholars have debated these terms.

The other two types of abrogation differ from this, and they are both considered to be rare. They are called "*naskh al-tilāwah*" (abrogation of the words but not the ruling) and "*naskh al-ḥukm wa'l-tilāwah*" (abrogation of both the wording and the ruling), respectively. The first type has an example in the "stoning verse," a punishment for adultery that is considered to be in effect (although rarely ever applied or enforced), but which nevertheless does not appear in the text of the Qur'ān. The punishment for fornication in the Qur'ān which appears at the beginning of 24 Al-Nūr is whipping. The second rare type of abrogation, of both wording and ruling, corresponds to the classical example of a companion of the Prophet Muḥammad claiming that he had received a verse, written it down, but that later it was lost or disappeared. For example, this is said to have occurred in the case of a report about a verse to the effect that breastfeeding from a woman ten times establishes a de facto kinship relation with her (known as the "verse of suckling"). The verse is now gone, and there is no such ruling usually considered to be in effect. Another instance that is possibly in the same class is the alleged case of the "satanic verses," based on the record of an event that is well known in classical Qur'ānic and legal theory. In this report, God annulled "what satan cast" into the Prophet's recitation of revealed verses (discussed below).

The application of the science of abrogation follows the following guidelines, as explained by Mohammad Hashim Kamali. In order for abrogation to be considered to be in effect at all for a given verse or verses, Kamali writes, the text itself must not prohibit the possibility of validity of abrogation for that ruling. For example, if a ruling is said explicitly within the Qur'ānic text to be one that is in effect "until the day of resurrection," it is not subject to any *naskh*. Second, the subject of the ruling must be a topic that is open to alteration. Some material, such as that which pertains to God's nature and moral imperatives, may not ever be said to be changed. Third, the abrogating text must be shown by accepted sources to have been revealed at a later time than the abrogated text; "occasions of revelation" establish this chronology. Fourth and last, the textual ruling of the Qur'ān may only be abrogated by another verse of the Qur'ān (or, according to a few legal scholars who have held that it is possible for the *sunnah* to abrogate the Qur'ān, by more than one strongly reliable *ḥadīth*).[20]

Classical sources state that the Qur'ānic basis or "proof" for the idea of abrogation is found in four verses of the Qur'ān itself.[21] One of them is the important verse 3 Āl 'Imrān 7: "It is He who sent down on you the book, wherein are *muḥkamāt* verses that are the essence of the book and others that are *mutashābihāt* ..." As was shown in the preceding chapter, this formulation has been incredibly productive for scholars within the Qur'ānic sciences. In this case, the categories of "clarity" and "ambiguity" (*muḥkamāt* and *mutashābihāt*) have been taken to refer to "abrogating" and "abrogated" verses. Another textual "proof" of abrogation is a verse in the Qur'ān which actually mentions the Arabic term *naskh*, 2 Al-Baqarah 106: "Whatever verse We abrogate [*nansakh*] or cause to be forgotten, We bring instead a better or similar one. Do you not know that Allāh has power over all things?" (The verse is said to have come in the Medinan period.)

Kamali writes that the "occasion of revelation" of both 2 Al-Baqarah 106 (above), as well as 16 Al-Naḥl 101 (below), is said to be a question put to the Prophet by non-believers about apparent inconsistency in practical religious norms. This could have been imagined to be, for example, a matter such as the change in the direction of prayer from Jerusalem to Mecca. When Muslim commentators considered the verse 2 Al-Baqarah 106 they asked, what is meant by the Qur'ānic term "abrogation," and to what does "abrogation" apply? As for the definitional issue (i.e. "What is meant by 'abrogation?'"), perspectives of classical commentators of the Qur'ān indicate both the accepted view as well as the wide range of thinking that there has been on the issue.[22] On this point many of the commentators have cited a *ḥadīth* on the authority of Ibn 'Abbās, who was a companion of the Prophet Muḥammad and a transmitter of a great deal of *ḥadīth* material, especially within traditions on Qur'ān interpretation. According to this report, the Prophet Muḥammad stated, "It [*naskh*] means that We [God] abolish, whether it be a verse or a precept of a verse; or it may mean that we substitute another for it."[23] This is consistent with what came to be the accepted definitions and practices in the Qur'ānic sciences.

The idea that abrogation only applies to the legal content of the Qur'ān, and not other kinds of Qur'ānic material, is generally accepted. In his explanation of "*naskh*" (abrogation), the commentator Al-Ṭabarī, for example, demonstrates the mainstream opinion that this is purely a legal term and concept, as here quoted and translated by Mahmud Ayoub:

> What We [God] abrogate regarding the precept of a verse which we change, or for which we substitute another, so that what is lawful

> may become unlawful and what is unlawful may become lawful; what is permitted may become prohibited and what is prohibited may become permitted. This, however, can only be done with regard to commands and prohibitions … but as for reports or narratives, they can neither be abrogated nor can they abrogate.[24]

Compare this with a more wide-ranging view of *naskh*, as expressed by the esoteric thinker Ibn 'Arabī (d. 1240), writing many centuries later. In *The Qur'ān and its Interpreters*, Mahmoud Ayoub quotes the commentary of Ibn 'Arabī as follows:

> Know then that the principles which are established in the "preserved tablet" [a reference to 85 Al-Burūj 21–22, quote marks added] are either particular or general. Particular principles appertain to particular persons or epochs. When these verses descend on the heart of the Apostle [Muḥammad], those which appertain to specific individuals remain operative so long as they live. Those belonging to specific epochs shall likewise be abolished with the passing of these epochs, be they short, such as those verses belonging to the Qur'ān, or long, such as the ancient sacred codes of law. This does not contradict their being inscribed in the preserved tablet because they are there inscribed for only the time during which they are operative here on earth. General principles, however, continue for all time. Some of these are, for example, the principles behind the faculty of speech in human beings, and the erectness of their stature.[25]

Ibn 'Arabī's concerns here seem to pertain more to cosmology than to *aḥkām*, relating categories of generality and specificity to principles of temporality. This is not to say that Ibn 'Arabī was not concerned with the law.[26] Characteristically, however, and as shown by his work on purity, his interests are esoteric rather than exoteric even in interpreting legal material. The most committed "fundamentalists" of tradition could even be said to be the mystics, like Ibn 'Arabī, who have sought to internalize Qur'ānic rulings and structures to their ultimate psychological limits in experiential modes.

Returning to Muslims' academic discussion of the science of Qur'ānic *naskh*, the third "proof" of abrogation in the classical sources is 16 Al-Naḥl 101. Here the Qur'ān mentions another term, "*tabdīl*" ("replacement"), however, and not *naskh*. Its meaning begins with, "And when We exchange [*baddalnā*] a verse in place of another …" This verse gave scholars an opportunity to theorize the idea of "replacement" in relation to "abrogation." David Powers writes that "*badā'*," the issue of the "mutability of divine will," was the key theological question problem related to *naskh*. The term is known in Judaic tradition, where it is considered impermissible. David Powers writes that Muslim scholars understood *badā'* to be like the rescinding of a proclamation, "changing one's mind."[27] In contrast, *naskh* was said to be an instance of something that was once forbidden now being made licit, or vice versa, in order to improve the condition of believers. For this, the original proclamation was only meant to be in effect for a specific period of time, with God having known all the while that the ruling (*ḥukm*) would be in effect only until circumstances changed, at which time the new one would be needed. An example would be the change in the direction of canonical worship (*qiblah*) from Jerusalem to Mecca, or the Qur'ān's sanction for sexual relations during the month of Ramaḍān after fasting hours, Powers explains.

Finally, according to David Powers, classical sources cite 22 Al-Ḥajj 52 in connection to the science of *naskh*:

> We never sent any messenger or prophet before you, but when he recited satan would intrude on his recitation. Yet Allāh annuls what the devil has cast. Then Allāh establishes his revelations [*āyātihi*]. Allāh is All-Knowing, Wise [*'alīmun ḥakīm*]. (22 Al-Ḥajj 52)

The verse above is taken by some in tradition to be a reference to the "satanic verses," an incident in which allegedly the Prophet Muḥammad began reciting after the verse of 53 Al-Najm 19 words which mentioned the polytheistic goddesses and a phrase with the following meaning, "These are the high-flying cranes; their intercession is to be hoped for." These words were not part of the Qur'ān. Their utterance has been explained by religious scholars in terms of the Prophet's sympathy for others and his heartfelt wish to have the unbelievers (who presumably would have worshiped goddesses) to enter into Islam. The incident is said by some also to be suggested by the Qur'ān's verse 17 Al-Isrā' 74 (which follows a verse about the unbelievers who were "about to lure you away from what We revealed to you"): "Had We not enabled you [singular] to stand firm, you might have inclined toward them a little." Later the matter was deemed controversial.

When considering the extent and application of "abrogation," scholars have disagreed historically over the actual verses that were said to be abrogating and abrogated, and also the type of material that would be affected. Some have said that nothing in the Qur'ān could ever be abrogated. Others have taken a view at the opposite extreme, holding that anything, even narrative, could be said to have been abrogated. (In fact, narrative was an area of much controversy on this point.) Another dispute was about the relation of *sunnah* to Qur'ān with respect to abrogation. Some held it was not possible for *sunnah* to abrogate Qur'ān, but there were also other opinions on the matter and it actually does occur in jurisprudential practice. (Even *ijmā'* overrules Qur'ān and *sunnah* in a few instances.) These points are all made by Kamali and Powers.[28]

In addition, David Powers also discusses one final sort of controversy among scholars: how much material in the Qur'ān may be considered either to be either "abrogated" or "abrogating" (or both), and which verses should they be said to be? He writes that between the eighth and eleventh centuries there was a great increase in the number of verses that were considered abrogating and abrogated, from less than 100 at the minimum to a maximum of about 250 verses. David Powers explains that this was likely due to the fact that the term *naskh* was understood to refer to a greater range of phenomena. For example, it came to comprise cases that were formerly seen as merely the specification of the content of one verse by another. Powers writes that the emergence of the sciences of jurisprudence (*fiqh*) in this period could also have influenced this trend.[29]

An example of this, analyzed at some length by David Powers in his article, is 9 Al-Tawbah 5, the "sword verse" (*āyat al-ṣaif*, quoted in Chapter 2), for which he claims Muslims have said there have been a hundred instances of other Qur'ānic verses whose rulings are abrogated by this one. Later, according to Powers, there seems to have been a reaction among scholars against the expansion of the number of instances considered to be abrogation. Later tradition sees a restriction on the number of such verses, coming along with a tendency to harmonize apparent contradiction rather than to claim full-blown "abrogation." For example, according to David Powers, around the year 1500 the scholar of Qur'ānic sciences Al-Sūyūṭī (d.1505) cited only twenty instances of abrogation in his work on the Qur'ānic sciences, and modern religious experts have tried to reduce the number much more.[30]

The classic case of abrogation that appears in standard Muslim religious textbooks is the prohibition on drinking wine (a question related to one considered previously in this chapter with respect to *qiyās*).[31] It is offered here as an example of both "occasions of revelation" and "abrogation." There are four verses in the Qur'ān that are directly relevant to this discussion, some of which have already seen some consideration. First, in 16 Al-Naḥl 67, wine is a sign of grace to humankind; then, in 2 Al-Baqarah 219 (cited previously), wine is presented more ambivalently; 4 Al-Nisā' 43 (also cited previously) states, do not come to prayer "when your mind is not clear"; finally, in 5 Al-Mā'idah 90 (cited previously as well), God prohibits wine entirely as an "abomination." Restated meanings of the first two of these verses are:

- 16 Al-Naḥl 67: "And from the fruits of palms and vines, you get wine and fair provision. Surely, there is a sign to a people who understand."
- 2 Al-Baqarah 219: "They ask you about wine and gambling, say: 'In both there is great sin and some benefit for people. But the sin is greater than the benefit.' And they ask you about what they should spend, say: 'What you can spare.' Thus Allāh makes clear to you His revelation so that you may reflect."

An occasion of revelation for the latter verse, given in the exegesis by Al-Zamakhsharī (d. 1144), the influential interpreter of the Qur'ān, is as follows. After 2 Al-Baqarah 219 was revealed, it is said that people prayed together as their intoxicated *imām* (prayer leader) recited in error, "Say, O rejecters of the faith, I worship what you worship," rather than correct Arabic words of the verse of the Qur'ān, which have the meaning, "I shall not worship what you worship" (109 Al-Kāfirūn 1–2).

It was then that the following verse that prohibits wine when praying was said to be sent down (4 Al-Nisa' 43, below), abrogating the ruling of the previous verse:[32]

- 4 Al-Nisā' 43: "O believers [*yā ayyuhā alladhīna amanū*], do not approach prayer while you are drunk, until you know what you say; nor when you are unclean – unless you are on a journey – until you have washed yourselves. And if you are sick or on a journey, or if any one of you has relieved himself, or you have touched women and could not find water, you might rub yourselves with clean earth, wiping your faces and hands with it. Allāh indeed is Pardoning, All-Forgiving [*'afūan ghafūr*]!"

The fourth and final verse to be revealed in accepted chronological order, however, forbids wine (*khamr*) categorically:

- 5 Al-Mā'idah 90: "O believers, wine, gambling, idols and divining arrows are an abomination of the devil's doing [*'amali al-shaiṭān*]; so avoid them that perchance you may prosper!"

The occasion of revelation for the final verse, above, is given by Zamakhsharī to be the following. Some companions began to boast about their ancestries. Intoxicated, the companion of the Prophet Muḥammad, Sa'd bin Abī Waqqās, recited a poem that insulted the *anṣār* (the "helpers" at Medina). One of the *anṣār* became angry and hit him with a camel whip, hurting the drunken Sa'd. Then, sources say, God revealed 5 Al-Mā'idah 90, forbidding wine entirely.[33]

Occasions and applications of revelation are one of many sciences of the Qur'ān that it is said a scholar must master in order to interpret any of its content in the form of a definitive legal ruling. A reader of the Qur'ān would need to know the chronology of the revelation of the verses above in order to determine that it is 5 Al-Mā'idah 90 and not 16 Al-Naḥl 67, for example, that determines the law on wine. According to information found in Al-Ṣūyūtī's seminal work on the Qur'ānic sciences, *Al-Itqān fī 'Ulūm Al-Qur'ān*, as well as other technical works on *naskh*, there is a report that the Prophet's son-in-law and cousin, the first Shi'ite imām and the fourth Sunni caliph 'Alī bin Abī Tālib, once ordered a man who was preaching in the mosque to stop doing so. This was because 'Alī had determined that this individual was not able to tell the difference between the "abrogating" and "abrogated" verses. According to the report, 'Alī approached the man and said to him, "You have destroyed yourself and others."[34]

OPEN QUESTIONS: SOCIAL CHANGE

Contemporary Qur'ānic social thought shows that believers recognize that there are problems still to overcome and questions still to answer about how to derive and apply legal and ethical norms from the text of the Qur'ān. Within the Qur'ānic sciences relating to Arabic language and grammar, for example, scholars of Qur'ānic language attempt to discern levels of certainty with respect to the interpretation of the words of the Qur'ānic text. This requires a highly advanced knowledge of Arabic, both its morphology and its syntax. Fields of learning especially relevant to contemporary conversations, as also suggested by the classical requirements for a *mujtahid* (above), include categories and principles of interpreting the Qur'ān's guidance such as "definitive and speculative" and "general and specific." The first distinction, that made between "definitive" (*qaṭ'ī*) and "speculative" (*ẓannī*) material, is one of the most important classifications with respect to rulings from the Qur'ān that are currently under global debate, including questions of gender and social change. For example, polygyny is a publicly contested issue along such lines in the world's most populous Muslim-majority country, Indonesia.[35]

By way of a definition, a "definitive" ruling is considered to be clear and precise, whereas one that is "speculative" may carry differing interpretations. These terms may thus describe how "open" any given religious question may be from a legal standpoint. The second set of terms above, "general" (*'āmm*) and "specific" (*khaṣṣ*), resolves issues such as for whom is a given ruling intended and under what conditions (i.e. universal or restricted) would it be said to apply? According to Kamali in *Principles of Islamic Jurisprudence*, in general, the "general" rulings are considered to be in effect for all members of a class (such as "all believing women") until or unless there is a specification (such as believing women who were the "wives of the prophet"). Specification (*takhṣīṣ*) of a general ruling found in the Qur'ān, Kamali goes on to explain, can be said to occur in the same phrase or clause in the text, or it may appear independently at some other point in the text of the Qur'ān. Such specification of general rulings across the text naturally brings up questions of the chronology of revelation, as was discussed in connection to abrogation, above.[36] Along with disciplines of *ḥadīth* criticism,[37] concepts like "definitive and speculative" and "general and specific" are applied widely in contemporary Muslim religious, political, and social conversation in formal and informal modes.

In contemporary law and ethics, on key points on which the Qur'ān is silent or on which it offers what would be called by scholars a "speculative" ruling or rationale, there can be many possible alternatives. Some of these perspectives may make claims to validity that are more exclusive (i.e. they claim to be "right" to the exclusion of other Muslim views), while others recognize and accept difference and pluralistic debate on principle (such as with the traditional idea of *ikhlitāf*). Also, as times change, more questions appear under new circumstances, which now require new (or old) answers. When working with norms that were contextualized in the past, many modern scholars turn to principles of historicization to derive "Qur'ānic" guidance for the present day. Some Indonesian scholars who were inspired by the teaching of Fazlur Rahman, for example, have developed a sophisticated methodology for such "contextualization." Others working within wider global progressive traditions also combine historical sensitivity with grounding in traditional Qur'ānic sciences in order to interpret Qur'ānic guidelines.[38]

For example, Amina Wadud, a womanist interpreter of the Qur'ān who has worked in Southeast Asia as well as North America, explains her progressive hermeneutical approach to the Qur'ān in her influential book *Qur'ān and Woman* as follows:

> My objective in undertaking this research was to make a "reading" of the Qur'ān that would be meaningful to women living in the modern era. By "reading" I mean the process of reviewing the words and their context in order to derive an understanding of the text. Every "reading" reflects, in part, the intentions of the text, as well as the "prior text" of the one who makes the "reading." Although each "reading" is unique, the understanding of various readers of a single text will converge on many points.[39]

Wadud continues in the same work, now detailing her methodology more fully:

> A hermeneutical model is concerned with three aspects of the text, in order to support its conclusions: 1. The context in which the text was written (in the case of the Qur'ān, in which it was revealed); 2. The grammatical composition of the text (how it says what it says); and 3. The whole text, its *Weltanschauung* or world-view. Often, differences of opinion can be traced to variations in emphasis between these three aspects.[40]

Farid Esack, another contemporary progressive Muslim thinker and activist (whose work is discussed below), also writes about "*Weltanschauung*" (world-view) as an interpretive principle in his book on the Qur'ān and liberatory praxis in the *jihād* (struggle) against racial oppression in South Africa in the time of racial apartheid. Esack has also applied Qur'ānic principles to engaged activism and advocacy related to HIV/AIDS.

One of the most productive, and contested, areas of legal interpretation in the twentieth century has been various stances on gendered issues. It has commonly been heard in Muslim settings since the colonial era that the gender norms that were first introduced by the Qur'ān, such as a woman's retention of personal property in and after a marriage, were more beneficial to women's social status than what had preceded them in pre-Islamic times. Whether women's roles were changing in the first years of Islam, and if so how much, times have certainly changed for all world social systems since the seventh century; and times have changed dramatically for Muslim men and women even since the nineteenth century, the age of worldwide European colonialism.

It was in this era, and under global regimes of colonialism, that gendered discourses of "liberation" of women became prominent within several types of ideological systems that all had a stake in evaluating Islamic "civilization" and its "progress" by the index "women in Islam." In the postcolonial era, gender still remains for many a measure of the status of religion vis-à-vis the state in Muslim-majority countries. As such, gendered politics of Islam in the public sphere often pertains to matters of modesty, personal status, and family law. The legacy of charged symbolic terms ("woman," "Muslim," "civilization") is also one factor that probably contributes to the dedicated interest students of the Qur'ān in the academic classroom tend to show with respect to the matter of what a Muslim woman ought to wear.[41] In addition, since dress is probably the most immediately apparent visible marker of Islamic identity in public life, naturally, students wish to know what is its Qur'ānic basis. Modest dress is therefore discussed here as an example of Qur'ānic norms and the open questions they support, in an exercise similar to the consideration of the acts of worship, the "five pillars" of Islam, that opened this chapter.

"The veil" or headscarf occupies a significant space in the global social imaginary of gender of the Muslim past and the present.[42] Modest dress, here called *ḥijāb* (which for present purposes will be said to comprise wearing a headscarf), is often said, for example, to be a Qur'ānic requirement. For some, further reasoning on the Qur'ān's position on the matter would be irrelevant; state systems, local norms, and other mechanisms have already determined how to dress. Sociological study of the growing phenomenon of modest dress and the headscarf worldwide has tended not to view the trend as a scriptural phenomenon, however; instead it is put forward as an indication of what are new roles and spaces for women's participation in modern public life. These global trends, such as women entering the workplace to support the family with a second (or first) wage, do not only affect Muslims. However, there are some typical Muslim religious responses to the perceived pressures to establish identity markers and codes that signal "respectability" within new sorts of socially hybridized and ambiguously gendered contexts. For most women in Muslim settings like those of Indonesia, Great Britain, Canada, and America, many influences shape personal choices contextually. Some of these forces may be seen to reflect global factors, such as the high cost of following fashion marketed as "Western"; anti-colonial, anti-consumerist, and nativist commitments; and practical considerations such as the convenience of not having to carry around a bag of extra clothing all day long just in order to be able to pray on time.

For those who have a choice, and make the choice, to look and feel like someone who wears *ḥijāb*, the state is an experienced bodily *habitus* can feel natural and may quickly become naturalized. In global discourse about the "choice" to wear *ḥijāb*, and when it is in fact presented as being a "choice" among modern alternatives, the practice is often rationalized only secondarily on the basis of the reactions of others. Specifically, global Muslims who support the headscarf as a chosen requirement stress that by doing so they are promoting positive ideals of dignified beauty as self-conscious alternatives to purportedly degrading "nakedness." Womanist rhetoric of this type has also been supported by "Third Wave" feminists such as, recently, the North American scholar Naomi Wolf. Muslim women who explain the "choice" to wear *ḥijāb* will also often claim that this determination is "individual" or "spiritual," tending to explain this in terms of a sense of personal liberation from messages of consumerism, commodification, and gendered humiliation through a male "gaze" of desire, as well as other forms of exploitation and oppression. Men who support the practice, such as those who comment within global Internet communities, can also be heard to speak in similarly personalized terms about their own sense of liberation in sharing a social environment that values dignity.

In addition to legal, symbolic, and sociological factors, these responses point to how modest dress may be a phenomenologically embodied sphere. Muslim mystics have long used metaphors of "veiling" in an interiorized sense, and some modern discussions of modesty as a "spiritual" choice seem to echo parts of this pious experiential rhetoric of the Muslim past. For those women who theorize publicly the practice as their own "choice," many assert that it creates a "safe space," as if the cloth's partition protects from misperception from without as much as forming a consciousness experienced from within. From this perspective, and when looking out from the inside, some women like to say *hijāb* is as much a "state of dress" as it is a "state of mind." As such, it could be described as an internalization of the Qur'ānic ideas of protecting dignity (by, for example, explicit Qur'ānic prohibitions that range from idle gossip to slanderous libel), and as a public performance of self-respect.

However, rationalizing *ḥijāb* along such "personal" or "spiritual" lines complements the apparent textual rationale given in the Qur'ān for the practice. With respect to "*ḥijāb*," the Qur'ān seems primarily to anticipate and regulate outward and contextualized social perceptions, not autonomous inner religious experience. Chapter 33 Al-Aḥzāb (discussed in Chapter 2) contains well-known verses that provide some Qur'ānic guidance on modest dress and conduct and indicate something of what these might be said to be, at least for the Muslim women of the past who carried a special status by virtue of being married to the Prophet Muḥammad:

> 32. O wives of the Prophet, you are not like any other women. If you are God-fearing, do not be abject in speech, so that he in whose heart is a sickness may covet you, but speak in an honorable way.
> 33. Stay in your homes and do not display your finery as the pagans of old did; perform the prayer, give the alms and obey Allāh and His messenger. Allāh only wishes to turn away abomination from you and purify you fully [*wayuṭahhirakum taṭhīra*], O people of the house [*ahl al-bait*]. (33 Al-Aḥzāb 32–33)

In discussions of the Qur'ānic basis of modesty norms, the passage above is usually paired with another verse that seems to have a more generalized application, and which appears elsewhere in the same *sūrah*:

> O Prophet, tell your wives and daughters and the wives of the believers to draw their outer garments [*jalābībihinna*] closer. That is more conducive to their being known, and not being injured. Allāh is All-Forgiving, Merciful [*ghafūran raḥīm*]. (33 Al-Aḥzāb 59)

Based on the wording of the two verses above from 33 Al-Aḥzāb, it would appear that the primary religious and revelatory rationale for wearing the garment(s) are contextual identification of faith affiliation ("being known") and an attempt to prevent insult and harm (i.e. not being "coveted" or "injured").

Those seeking Qur'ānic guidance in the present on ideals and realities of modest dress may also ask, should the injunctions in the verses above be read to apply only to "family of the Prophet" (i.e. "people of the house" of the Prophet) or "women in the Prophet's community" (who are also implied by these verses), or should this be extended further to include all Muslim women for all time most generally? To answer these questions definitively, the following verses are usually cited as the Qur'ānic imperative to modest dress and comportment for all Muslim men and women. For women, the verses provide some specification of an actual garment to wear as well as the bodily area to be covered with it, also citing what are the circumstances under which it may be removed, with a special concern shown for hidden jewelry that may jingle distractingly.

These verses appear in 24 Al-Nūr, the same *sūrah* that opens by addressing circumstances of an event of slanderous accusation, a crime of perception (in tradition, the victim was 'Ā'ishah, wife of the Prophet). The chapter also contains a ruling on the punishment for adultery, a transgression of sexual ethics (and a topic of traditional jurisprudential dispute in itself, regarding the relationship of the Qur'ān to the *sunnah*); and it is the *sūrah* that includes the "verse of light" (see Chapter 3) from which the chapter takes its name. The famous verses that state modesty norms read as follows in an English-language interpretation:

> 30. Tell the believers to cast down their eyes and guard their private parts [*furūjahum*]. That is purer [*azkā*] for them. Allāh is aware of what they do.
>
> 31. And tell believing women to cast down their eyes and guard their private parts and not show their finery, except the outward part of it. And let them drape their bosoms with their veils [*bikhumurihinna*] and not show their finery except to their husbands, their fathers, their husbands' fathers, their sons, the sons

> of their husbands, their brothers, the sons of their brothers, the sons of their sisters, their women, their maid-servants, the men-followers who have no sexual desire, or infants who have no knowledge of women's sexual parts yet. Let them, also, not stamp their feet, so that what they have concealed of their finery might be known. Repent to Allāh, all of you, O believers, that perchance you may prosper. (24 Al-Nūr 30–31)

The listing of males whose presence is an exception to the rule implies that a Qur'ānic rationale for women's *ḥijāb* could be said to be a variable perception of her sexuality. Justification for this idea also seems to appear later in the same *sūrah*, 24 Al-Nūr 60, in which the Qur'ān states that elderly women may cast aside some of these "outer garments" if they have "passed the prospect of marriage." This would imply a possible rationale for the ruling still to be perception of the woman in context (in particular, how available she is seen to be on the part of others).

Without any doubt, sincere religious Muslims would seek to imitate the Prophet in the form of the model of his community's practice to the best extent. For many, including Muslim religious scholars whose rulings on the subject based on *ḥadīth* became influential, the scarf is obligatory and this ruling is "definitive" and "general," not a "speculative" issue or one to be further "specified." This then leads directly to far less certain issues and many more open questions about actual application, such as how to interpret semantically the ambiguous Arabic words in the text that mean "veil," "outer garments," "bosom," etc., in terms of real bodies and apparel. Just as in the case of the "five pillars" of Islam, the Qur'ān's directives about how to adopt modest dress, for those who wear *ḥījāb* as a choice or requirement (or both), are open to interpretation by all. Many people who pay attention to Muslims' contemporary modest dress today make finely tuned assessments based on fairly fixed ideas about what is "good *ḥijāb*" and "bad *ḥijāb*," with examples of each now blogged in the worldwide public sphere daily.

Clothing choices that Muslims make represent everyday practical matters for real people, half of whom are female. Selection of color, texture and embellishment, fabric cut and pattern, drape and shape (neck, ears, bust or hairline, and the possibility of double-layering), and how to wrap, tie, or pin these bits of cloth nicely and securely indicate Muslim identities as much or even more today as they ever did in the past. At the time of this writing, the flowing *abaya* and wound rectangular *shaila* from the Gulf are becoming increasingly fashionable as Muslim international style Pacific to Atlantic, indicating sleek, chic, pious cosmopolitanism. On the other hand, in Muslim Southeast Asia, where head covering has become a part of mainstream Islamic norms only in the past thirty or forty years, *ḥijāb* can be observed on the street in a more strictly Qur'ānic manner; here, it is primarily the scarf itself (not necessarily coverage of other body parts like forearms or ankles) that until now has seemed to carry the main symbolic load as the signal of identity, faith commitment, and modesty. In just the last ten years in Indonesia, the signature scarf of piety has gone from "*jilbab putih*" (square white cloth folded diagonally and pinned close under the chin) to ready-to-wear fashion such as what was sometimes called the "*jilbab tsunami*" (one may put it on – and just go) or newer one-piece styles like the popular self-wrap "Kuwaiti" model.

If the scriptural rationale for the practice is really best said to be social assessment (which does appear to be the case in the relevant verses of the Qur'ān), then such norms and social trends are not trivial matters. Feminist theorists such as Judith Butler would be correct to say in this case that signifying expression is a process of gendered social self-making, especially under conditions of modernity in which identities are produced and reproduced contextually.[43] Viewed in this way, social perception can be seen to translate directly into piety, choice, and experience. At the same time, Qur'ānic principles that guide the practice, such as protection from misunderstanding, insult, and injury, may also take on new senses of meaning for women in contexts in which Islamaphobia can be a lived social fact.

Open and gendered questions based in the Qur'ān do not all relate to projects of the translation and adaptation of norms from long ago, like the *ḥijāb*, into the twenty-first century, however. Nor are the norms of the past always the best solutions Muslims find to twenty-first-century problems. In some cases, the practices of the past simply have changed, or they must change. This recognition is consistent with the ethos of the classical Qur'ānic science of abrogation, which accepts that norms were changing (about excessive alcohol consumption, for example) even during the time of the coming of Islam itself. To take a case that is self-evident, but also one that is still often heard mentioned in this regard, the Qur'ān was revealed in a time of slavery (there are fourteen verses that mention the practice). However, no one would condone the practice in order to carry out "Islamic law" according to the same social terms as the past. (And the Qur'ān encourages the manumission of slaves in any case.) The Prophet's wife 'Ā'ishah was just a child, according to reports, when she married him; such a practice is likewise not acceptable today. The same can said for the apparent Qur'ānic presentation of "*nushūz*" (spousal "rebelliousness") in a *jihād* (campaign) for justice.[44]

Contemporary Muslims who advocate on urgent social issues such as these develop principled norms from the Qur'ān. For example, Amina Wadud revisits the "*nushūz* verse" (4 Al-Nisā' 34) along with the *ḥudūd* punishments in the Qur'ān (such as cutting off the hand of the thief, etc.) in her recent book *Inside the Gender Jihad.* Wadud's hermeneutical move here is to interpret the Qur'ān by the Qur'ān in order to recognize revealed, consistent, and applicable norms that may translate into social policies and practices of nonviolence. She takes the Qur'ān's injunction to "stand up for justice" (which is found stated in the same *sūrah* as the "*nushūz* verse"), including gender justice, to be primary over other considerations. For this, Wadud cites the following verse:

> O believers [*yā ayyuhālladhīna āmanū*], stand up for justice [*qawwāmīna bi'l-qisṭi*] as witnesses for Allāh, even if it is against yourselves, your parents or kinsperson. Whether rich or poor, Allāh takes better care of both. Do not follow your desire to refrain from justice. If you twist [your testimony] or turn away, Allāh is fully aware of what you do. (4 Al-Nisā' 135)

This strongly stated imperative to "stand up for justice" appears more than once in the text of the Qur'ān (for example, see Chapter 5). Giving this emphatic statement categorical primacy follows the same approach that is typically found in other modern modes of Muslim social and political thought, such as giving the "public good" (*maṣlaḥah, istiṣlāḥ*) primacy in the religious imagination of the political state. Recently, Wadud has noted that the Qur'ānic framework of the "*ẓālim*" ("oppressor") is a concept that applies to any and all forms of coercion and abuse, and as such would additionally and categorically prohibit gendered injustice and harm.[45]

Some assumptions in Islamic law and ethics have simply ceased to be relevant in light of how social circumstances have changed since the seventh century. The theory, practice, and tactics of warfare, for example, at once changed immediately and irreversibly through the devastating acts of real and symbolic mass violence at Hiroshima and Nagasaki; in the atomic age, old global practices of unlimited war will, and must, stop. At the same time, new technologies and circumstances continually open up new moral questions and religious problems to solve, such as in the areas of medical ethics and the related status of human bodies,[46] or climate change and global human habitat. And, of course, for Muslims there still remain original Qur'ānic directives that, while clearly universal in scope, have also not yet been realized, such as care for the socially weak and vulnerable, or even peace (*salām*) itself. For Muslims, these represent human challenges to continued, committed, and creative striving in the way of Allāh in order to achieve their tangibility in the real world of the present. Within the mass politics of the nation and the state over just the past century of global change, "standing for justice" against oppression in many modes has been one of the key concerns of Muslim social thinkers worldwide.

QUR'ĀNIC RESPONSES TO GLOBAL CONDITIONS

Baghdad's central political structure collapsed in 1258, as the central Muslim lands rapidly came under new political systems. The coming of the Mongols, as led by members of the family of Genghis Khan, brought about dislocation in the middle of the thirteenth century that was felt from present-day Turkey to China and Vietnam. Some of those who saw their worlds changing fast asked at that time, had something caused Muslim civilization to become vulnerable to non-Muslim rule? (Put this way, the question is actually somewhat ironic, since new rulers rapidly accepted Islam in Muslim areas, and in fact in these regions became known as great patrons of Islamic learning and civilization.) In this period, a perspective like that of Ibn Taimiyya (1263–1328), which called for revitalization by reforming tradition, became influential among Muslims. Centuries later, when another non-Muslim power, the Europeans, had conquered and subjugated practically all Muslim lands from the Pacific to the Atlantic by the nineteenth century with relative rapidity, calls for reform in order to restore autonomy and greatness to Islamic societies again appeared at the forefront of global religious conversations. Once more, Muslims turned to the renewalist paradigm of the past in a number of modes in order to revitalize tradition, and all sought answers in the original source of the Qur'ān.[47]

Under regimes of European colonialism in the nineteenth century, there also came new opportunities for movement of Muslim people and Islamic ideas. Circumstances such as the rise of print capitalism and the opening of the Suez Canal facilitated connections in the colonial era, stimulating a rethinking of "pan-Islamic" bonds and Muslims' struggle worldwide against colonial subugation by the Dutch, the English, the French, the Portuguese, and others. Many Muslim "modernists" with liberationist ideas in this era had privileged educations that connected them to the very colonial systems that they wished to reform. Their social and religious appeals often came in the political language of educational reform, in order that Muslim societies could compete with the colonial systems in terms of shared ideals of "progress," but on a sound and nativistic Islamic basis. Many such reformers sought to translate the meanings of the Qur'ānic message into languages that were widely and popularly accessible, such as Bangla, Malay, Persian, Turkish, and Urdu. New questions and new answers relied on legal paradigms, especially as Muslims began to imagine possibilities for establishing independent new states in a postcolonial order. Anti-colonial movements underwent a corresponding transformation of ideals of pan-Islamism to territorial nationalism in the twentieth century.

Attention to modern social issues and political ideals and realities became typical of a new wave of Qur'ānic study in the colonial era. Works of exegesis of the Qur'ān, such as Muhammad 'Abduh's *Tafsīr Al-Manār*, proliferated, particularly among those who were activists for political and social change. Many of these figures came from families with Sufi pedigree, while they also called for "progress" in the form of a rejection of religious lifeways that could not be said to conform to the practice of the "pious ancestors" (*salāf*) who were among the Prophet's original community. In general, in newer practices of modern *tafsīr*, sacred narrative was considered relevant insofar as it was seen to provide moral or ethical guidance that was pertinent to projects of nation or community building (such as through, for example, the emancipatory exodus of the Prophet Moses). Along with what became standard themes of modernist Qur'ānic exegesis, such as social ethics and science, there came also a growing methodological tendency to interpret Qur'ān by Qur'ān, and to rely less on *ḥadīth* and other sources.

At the beginning of the era of nation-states, one global trend in the Muslim interpretation of the Qur'ān is represented by the career of Abū'l-A'lā Mawdūdī (1903–1979), a political voice of Pakistan and Bangladesh who was instrumental in the early years of a movement called Jamaati Islami. Mawdūdī's vision of just society echoes the rhetoric of nationalist freedom-fighting of the recent past, and his social theory rests on the public coherence of citizens' Islam comprising an "Islamic state." His work of Qur'ān interpretation was titled *Tafhīm Al-Qur'ān*.[48] There was an unprecedented intersection of the state and the law that took place in less than a few decades in this century of Islamic history, as nations like Pakistan and, later, Iran attempted variously to render Islamic law into statutory systems under the jurisdiction and enforcement of the state.

On the other hand, since the middle of the twentieth century, Muslim activists who did not participate directly in the project of state-building in places such as Egypt and Pakistan formed a self-conscious "alternative" to the Muslim mainstream. The appeal of these perspectives can often be seen to lie precisely in their oppositional stance. For example, in his influential writings in the mid-twentieth century, the Egyptian Sayyid Quṭb placed Islam in contrast to "*jahiliyya*" (pre/non-Islam), which could have meant Christians, capitalists, Communists, and even other Muslims. Such views are said to be radically modern, even as they appear to oppose innovation and claim to restore "Salafi" tradition. This is because it requires a great deal of social creativity in order to render conditions of the twentieth century in the same terms as those from over a millennium ago. Further, a claim that any one social vision is exclusively and unmediatedly "Qur'ānic" must necessarily also break with premodern jurisprudential traditions of difference and dispute while at the same time obscuring operative interpretive scriptural strategies.

If the term "fundamentalism" is to be applied to any of these Islamist or neo-"Salafi" orientations, it should be considered with respect to matters of law, which are usually the first concern of these ideologies whether in relation to private or public spheres. What such exclusionary viewpoints share with a plurality of global "fundamentalisms" (whether Christian, Hindu, or any other), as scholars like Mark Jurgensmeyer and Bruce Lawrence have suggested elsewhere, is their totalizing ideological scope that places them at odds with the inclusive values of pluralism.[49] Further, as Faisal Devji has shown in recent work, new "landscapes" of oppositional Islamism may now transcend the boundaries of nation, state, and even ideology itself.[50]

The career of Sayyid Quṭb can also be seen to represent wider trends in Muslim social thought of the later twentieth century that in fact span across many types of competing ideologies. Sayyid Quṭb had begun his early studies in rhetoric in Europe, and was captivated by the moralized aesthetics of the Qur'ān throughout his life.[51] Like many influential Muslim social thinkers of his era, he also completed a major exegesis of the Qur'ān, *Fī Ẓilāl Al-Qur'ān* (*In the Shade of the Qur'ān*). He shared a generally liberationist perspective with religious thinkers from diverse ideological stances, including revolutionary Marxists in Iran. His concern for emancipation from the oppression of existing systems can be seen through the example of his treatment of the figure of Moses, as presented by an article by Anthony H. Johns.[52] Sayyid Quṭb, however, became increasingly radicalized over the course of his career, which ended with imprisonment and execution by the Egyptian state in 1966. His dogmatic work, *Milestones*, was revised to reflect this increasingly combative attitude during his incarceration, putting forward a theory of the struggle of Islam stated in charged terms such as *jihād*, *dakwah*, and *jahiliyya* ("ignorance" or non-Islam). His work varied greatly in worldwide reception from Egypt to Indonesia, however; for example, the multidimensional concept of a "Qur'ānic generation" that is found in his writing has been variously understood. The challenge of "social justice in Islam," the title of one his works, still remains open today as Muslim communities are increasingly affected by conditions of global inequity.

In the modern era, there is another kind of phenomenon within Muslim social and religious thought that represents a turn to the Qur'ān with a liberationist agenda, a growing "progressive" movement. A key element of this trend, in stark contrast to the "othering" stance of the "Islamic alternative" of the twentieth century, is an inclusivist vision applied to diverse Muslims and Muslim groups, and which promotes the value of human diversity overall. This Islamic perspective on "standing for justice" embraces pluralism on a faith basis. A Qur'ānic proof for such a perspective is found in the expression of "*lita'ārifu*" (49 Al-Ḥujurāt 13) as well as numerous Qur'ānic statements that God's purpose in creating diversity is for the sake of "competition in goodness" (see Chapter 2). For example, Farid Esack, like Amina Wadud, is explicit in his writing about his progressive and inclusive Qur'ānic "hermeneutics" in his book on the Qur'ān, *Qur'ān, Liberation and Pluralism*. In this work, Esack interprets the Qur'ān's fundamental themes of diversity to present a platform of interreligious solidarity for liberatory praxis.

Esack's examples in *Qur'ān, Liberation and Pluralism* draw on experience of lived *jihād* in the struggle against racial injustice and apartheid in South Africa in the 1980s. Here, Esack discusses at length what he calls the "Exodus paradigm of solidarity" with the "marginalized and the suffering," based on the stories of the Prophet Moses in the Qur'ān. From this textual consideration of the Qur'ānic Moses, Esack derives a theology of struggle against the "oppressor Other" as well as a universal message of God's care that can be shared by many faiths.[53] Esack applies this Qur'ānic *Weltanschauung* to a concern with "liberative praxis," matters of "freedom and faith" that were key in the South African struggle. The turn to Islam in the fight for justice against racial oppression in the United States of America in the twentieth century, symbolized by the activist career of the Muslim Malcolm X, is another dimension of this worldwide liberationist trend. Malcolm X came to see this struggle for human rights as a global issue, as evidenced in the international appeal he made to African countries later in his career in the name of supporting Black Americans' cause in the civil rights struggle in the U.S.A.[54]

A tenet that guides the contemporary progressive Muslim perspectives on a number of issues is that human rights realized from one religious perspective will contribute to liberation for all. "Progressive Islam" continues a Muslim liberationist conversation that has lasted throughout the twentieth century, focusing on issues of moral conduct, human rights, and social obligation to "command the good and forbid the evil." It shares a commitment to struggle and social justice with many Muslim movements that attempted to "stand for justice" in the colonial and postcolonial era. Some of these goals, such as gender justice, probably would have been supported in principle by early modernists like the Egyptian Muḥammad 'Abduh, while others still remain controversial today even in the mainstream, such as the acceptance of same-sex love.[55] "Progressive Islam" affirms established methodology found in traditions of Islamic religious discourse and difference, and tends to appeal to a Qur'ānic and disciplined reasoning based on established tradition. As a mode of modern religious thought, it develops systematic theologies to address structural oppression, such as the hegemonies of colonialism, racism, patriarchy, and non-sustainable ecological practices. The movement is now strong in the Muslim-minority context of North America, as represented by the book edited by Omid Safi, *Progressive Muslims*, as well in Muslim-majority Southeast Asia.

Many Qur'ānic statements that call clearly for the redress of resource inequality, such as the text's appeals to support poor persons, orphans, and widows, are open to revitalized interpretations today from a "progressive" viewpoint. Qur'ānic perspectives inform religious practices of Islamic philanthropy, charitable giving, and relief just as they have since the earliest period, now reenergized as responses to new global conditions.[56] New and emergent trends in the theory and practice of "development" in Muslim settings are rapidly refocusing an Islamic religious response on issues of sustainability. This is evidenced by the contribution made by the winner of the Nobel Peace Prize in 2006, Muhammad Yunus, who developed the "Grameen Bank" microcredit system in Bangladesh. This paradigm is now embraced by NGOs across Muslim and non-Muslim communities worldwide. Since the turn of the twenty-first century, religious issues emerging at the start of a new era are responses to environmental degradation and climate change.[57]

Qur'ānic teachings to care for God's creation have a great urgency under present ecological conditions, presenting a personal, communal, and global problem. Some, such as Richard Foltz and Frederick Denny, have theorized the Qur'ānic idea of the "trust" that is mentioned in 33 Al-Aḥzāb 72 in this regard: "We offered the Trust (*al-amānah*) to the heavens, the earth, and the mountains, but they refused to carry it and were afraid of it, but humans carried it. They have indeed been unjust and ignorant." The "covenantal" relationship between humanity and its Creator (as depicted in 7 Al-A'rāf 172, see Chapter 6) also presents itself for interpretation along ecological lines. A "Qur'ānic perspective" on the environment usually also cites verses on the "stewardship" and responsibility that has been placed on humanity. For example, the Qur'ān affirms that creation is for human's use and benefit (see Chapter 6) in its theology of signification (God's "signs") and moral response. There is also the text's concept of God's designated "vicegerent": 38 Ṣād 26 begins, "O David, We have appointed you a vicegerent (*khalīfah*) on earth," and 2 Al-Baqarah 30–31 applies the same expression to a newly created humanity when the people are first presented to the angels. In each of these Qur'ānic instances of "vicegerency," however, there is also an ambivalence expressed in the text. In the first case, David is warned about the "desires of his heart" that would sway him from judging wisely; and, in the second instance, all the angels (who are almost always known for their obedience) protest to God that humanity can only bring trouble to the new earth.

The Qur'ān offers numerous deep ethical statements that theologians may use in the future to develop a religious platform for environmental responsibility. For example, many of the passages in the Qur'ān that relate the divine characteristics of God to the human experience in creation mention "*al-mulk,*" the divine worldly "dominion" (such as in, for example, the *sūrah* 67 Al-Mulk). Within the text, this concept often connects directly to the command for humans not to "corrupt the earth" (*lā fasidu fi'l-arḍ*). Similarly, a pervasive Qur'ānic command not to "transgress the balance" (see Chapter 6) links naturally to the Qur'ān's abundant description of the natural world, from tiny details like named plants and bugs to apocalyptic images of seas rising and lush gardens turning to desert.

The "oppressor" (*ẓālim*), a gender-neutral concept, is one that the Qur'ān invokes continually both in personal and political senses. The Qur'ān even psychologizes the idea, through its wisdom that he or she who acts as the "oppressor" has really harmed the self in willing harm to others. The Qur'ān's legal and ethical messages guide Muslims to address the questions of their time through the call to learn not to abuse or "oppress" God's creation and not to "corrupt the earth." In the present day, this could mean ceasing to do harm to oneself as well as the wellbeing of one's future descendants in the face of threatening environmental disaster. The final chapter of this book returns to the Qur'ān's depiction of individual and collective accountability as at this moment humanity, Muslims included, faces change in order to confront an unprecedented transformation of the natural order.

NOTES

1. See Denny, "Ethical Dimensions of Islamic Ritual Law"; Rahman, "Some Key Ethical Concepts of the Qur'an"; and, Reinhart, "Islamic Law as Islamic Ethics."

2. Many thanks to Paul R. Powers for discussion on introducing Islamic law in the religious studies classroom; his scholarly perspective has shaped the presentation of this chapter significantly.
3. Reinhart, "Impurity/No Danger."
4. Kamali, *Principles of Islamic Jurisprudence*, p. 23. Usually, in the act of *wuḍū'*, after stating the intention for the action, Muslims wash hands to the wrists three times, starting with the right; rinse the mouth and nostrils three times (in varying ways); wash the face three times; wash each arm to the elbow three times; wipe the head and ears just once, following conventions such as wiping behind the ears; then wash each foot three times up to the ankle.
5. See Winkel, *Mysteries of Purity*, a translation of Ibn Al-'Arabī's *Asrār al-ṭahārah*. For a more general discussion, see also Chodkiewicz, *Ocean Without Shore*.
6. The example is taken from David Powers, "The Exegetical Genre *Nāsikh Al-Qur'ān*," p. 128.
7. I changed the wording of the translation of verse 183 here significantly from what Fakhry gives in *An Interpretation of the Qur'an* for the sake of the clarity of the English meaning pertaining to the act and reward for spontaneous meritorious deeds.
8. David Powers, "The Exegetical Genre *Nāsikh Al-Qur'ān*," p. 128. I follow the content of this article in order to introduce abrogation later in this chapter.
9. An excellent source for further study is Bakhtiar, *Encyclopedia of Islamic Law*, which gives specific rulings on standard topics in *fiqh* manuals, giving resources to compare the four major schools of Sunni law and the Ja'fari school of Shi'ite tradition.
10. Hallaq, "Was the Gate of Ijtihad Closed?," reprinted in *Law and Legal Theory in Classical and Medieval Islam*.
11. See discussion in Hallaq, "Was Shafi'i the Master Architect of Islamic Jurisprudence?," reprinted in *Law and Legal Theory in Classical and Medieval Islam*. See also his book, *A History of Islamic Legal Theories: An Introduction to Sunni Usul al-Fiqh*.
12. Al-Shāfi'ī, *Risālah* is available translated by Khadduri in *Al-Shāfi'ī's Risāla*. A translated manual of *fiqh* also in the Shafi'ite tradition is under the title *Reliance of the Traveler* (*'Umdāt al-sālik*), in which the translator Keller shows in his annotations and notes generations of commentary and further rulings by scholars.
13. Kamali, *Principles of Islamic Jurisprudence*, p. 147.
14. For thorough consideration of wine in Islamic traditions, see Kueny, *The Rhetoric of Sobriety*.
15. Gätje, *The Qur'ān and Its Exegesis*, pp. 200–209, citing the commentator Rāzī's interpretation of 2 Al-Baqarah 219, which considers a Hanbali opinion.
16. Adapted from Kamali, *Principles of Islamic Jurisprudence*, pp. 374–377. Enumeration of the points as given is my own.
17. Mahmoud Ayoub, *The Qur'ān and Its Interpreters*, pp. 220–224.
18. See Rippin, "The Function of *Asbab Al-Nuzul* in Qur'anic Exegesis."
19. Powers, "The Exegetical Genre *Nāsikh Al-Qur'ān*," pp. 120–122. The discussion of *naskh* here relies heavily on this article, along with Kamali's *Principles of Islamic Jurisprudence*, throughout. Further sources are: Burton, *The Collection of the Qur'an*; and discussion given by Qadhi in *An Introduction to the Sciences of the Qur'aan*.

20. Kamali, *Principles of Islamic Jurisprudence*, p. 153.
21. The outline of the discussion to follow is based on David Powers, "The Exegetical Genre *Nāsikh Al-Qur'ān*," p. 118.
22. See, for example, the discussion of various interpreters, translated and presented by Ayoub, *The Qur'ān and its Interpreters*, Vol. 1, pp. 138–140.
23. This report may be found in the collection of exegetical perspectives presented by Ayoub, *The Qur'ān and its Interpreters*, Vol. 1, p. 139, citing Tabarsi.
24. Ayoub, *The Qur'ān and Its interpreters*, Vol. 1, p. 139, citing Ṭabarī.
25. Ibid., p. 140, citing Ibn 'Arabī.
26. A study of Ibn 'Arabi with respect to legal thought is Chodkiewicz, *Ocean Without Shore*.
27. David Powers, "The Exegetical Genre *Nāsikh Al-Qur'ān*," p. 127.
28. Kamali, *Principles of Islamic Jurisprudence*, p. 150 and David Powers, "The Exegetical Genre *Nāsikh Al-Qur'ān*," p. 126.
29. David Powers, "The Exegetical Genre *Nāsikh Al-Qur'ān*," pp. 122–123.
30. Ibid., p. 123.
31. There is one account that treats the occasions of the revelation of all of the wine verses together, which is attributed to 'Umar bin Al-Khattāb, but it is not followed here; instead, the accounts are treated in terms of disparate occasions of revelation. All of these accounts are given in Ayoub, *The Qur'ān and Interpreters*, Vol. 1. See also Kueny, *The Rhetoric of Sobriety*.
32. Ibid., p. 223.
33. Ibid.
34. See Qadhi, *An Introduction to the Sciences of the Qur'aan*, p. 248. David Powers also mentions the episode in "The Exegetical Genre *Nāsikh Al-Qur'ān*," p. 124.
35. For example, according to Nelly van Doorn-Harder's recent study, in contemporary Indonesia, many reformers (who come from settings of traditional education) apply the categories *qaṭ'ī* and *ẓannī* to rethink *fiqh* on social issues today. This is discussed in various places in van Doorn-Harder, *Women Shaping Islam*. A more global survey appears in Esposito and DeLong-Bas, *Women and Muslim Family Law*.
36. Kamali, *Principles of Islamic Jurisprudence*, p. 24.
37. See, for example, the analysis of a contemporary legal debate among Muslims in North America in Abou El Fadl, *And God Knows the Soldiers*.
38. Rahman, *Islam and Modernity*, and contributions to Saeed, ed., *Interpreting the Qur'an*.
39. Wadud, *Qur'ān and Woman*, p. 1.
40. Ibid., p. 3.
41. For discussion see Ahmad, *Women and Gender in Islam*.
42. For example, see recent perspectives represented in Heath, ed., *The Veil*.
43. Butler, *Gender Trouble*.
44. See Wadud's discussion of 4 Al-Nisā' 34 in *Qur'ān and Women*, pp. 74–78, in terms of the scriptural question of men having "a degree over women." For readings of the problematic verb that appears later in the verse, "*ḍaraba*," some modern exegetes have focused on the semantics of the term, while others have tried to reconsider the expression in light of a process of conflict resolution. Others contextualize the verse socially and historically in various ways. Considering the "*nushūz* verse," for example, Laury Silvers writes in her article "In the Book We Have Left Out Nothing" that there are sound reports that the

Prophet Muḥammad himself was personally uncomfortable with the content of the verse. Wadud still must remind readers of the obvious point, the "problem of domestic violence among Muslims today is not rooted in the Qur'ānic passage" (Wadud, *Qur'ān and Woman*, p. 76). See also Ali, *Sexual Ethics in Islam*, for a full survey of such perspectives as well as consideration of Muslim jurisprudential and interpretive tradition on the status of women in marriage, including also the issue of marital rape.

45. Amina Wadud has informally suggested this line of thinking, especially in connection to the idea of "patriarchy." Other works on contemporary Islamic religious thought and gender and Qur'ān are Abou El Fadl, *Speaking in God's Name*; Barlas, *"Believing Women" in Islam*; Stowasser, *Gender Issues and Qur'ān Interpretation.*
46. See material in two books edited by Brockopp, *Muslim Medical Ethics* and *Islamic Ethics of Life.*
47. Voll, "Revival and Reform in Islamic History."
48. See Adams, "Abū'l-A'lā Mawdūdī's *Tafhīm Al- Qur'ān.*"
49. See Jurgensmeyer, *Terror in the Mind of God*, and Lawrence, *Defenders of God.* Comparative theorization of "fundamentalism" in the study of religion has been influenced by the "Fundamentalism Project" at the University of Chicago; see Marty and Appleby, eds., *Fundamentalisms Observed.*
50. Devji, *Landscapes of the Jihad.*
51. Anthony H. Johns, "Let My People Go! Sayyid Qutb and the Vocation of Moses."
52. Boullata, "Sayyid Qutb and Literary Appreciation of the Qur'ān."
53. Esack, *Qur'ān, Liberation and Pluralism*, pp. 194–199.
54. For two works by a scholar of Islam working in the field of the academic study of religion, for example, see Curtis, *Islam in Black America*, and the more recent *Black Muslim Religion in the Nation of Islam, 1960–1975.*
55. Kugle, "Sexuality, Diversity and Ethics in the Agenda of Progressive Muslims" in Safi, ed., *Progressive Muslims.*
56. For a recent study of Muslim "NGOs," see Benthall, Jonathan and Jérôme Bellion-Jourdan, *The Charitable Crescent: Politics of Aid in the Muslim World.*
57. For religious responses to environmental issues from Muslim and Qur'ānic perspectives, see the important book edited by Foltz, Denny, and Baharuddin, *Islam and Ecology*. For views on religious eco-feminism, see Tahera, "Text and Practice: Women and Nature in Islam," and an influential work by Christian systematic theologian Sallie McFague, *The Body of God.*

5

THE PRESENT QUR'ĀN

The Muslim ontology of the Qur'ān as revelation links it directly to many religious modes of human experience. Through remembering and repetition, Muslims attest that the Qur'ān exerts a unique presence, and Muslims amplify the potential of the revealed Qur'ān in countless practices of reading and performance. These habitual practices may generate expectations and anticipations that are simultaneously embodied, affective, and intellectual. The agency of the Qur'ān may even be said to be palpable in some repeated acts of piety, such as memorization. Muslims affirm this experienced power of the Qur'ān in healing and worship; and a related impact is cultivated through the moral aesthetics of expert practices of expression. The presence of the Qur'ān pervades Muslim religious life-worlds as well as non-religious spheres, such as through cultural concepts and comportment and styles of speech and sound. Recognition of the social patterns of Qur'ānic presence and their potential to transform social attitude and ethical experience is the basis of many systems of *da'wah*, which are self-conscious programs among Muslim groups to deepen Islamic faith and identity in society. Qur'ānic expression pervades Arabic and non-Arabic systems with depth that is often intentional and which also "goes without saying." These form aesthetic patterns reflected in art like poetry, such as that of Jalāl Al-Dīn Rūmī (d. 1273), for example, a poet who relocated from Afghanistan to Turkey in the social disruption that swept across the continent of Asia in the mid 1300s. Rūmī composed in the cosmopolitan language of Muslim arts and learning, Farsi (Persian).[1]

Another example of the depth of Qur'ānic expression across non-Arabic language systems in the premodern era is the career of another poet from Asia, Hamzah Fansuri. Hamzah Fansuri lived in Aceh, Sumatra, Indonesia around the start of the seventeenth century, the beginning of the age of the European colonial presence in the Malay-speaking world and across Asia more widely. His writings reflect the leading edge of intellectual currents and religious conversations of his day, and its controversial status (his works were destroyed soon after his death) mirrors debates that were happening all over the Muslim world at the time, such as in Mughal India.[2] Hamzah Fansuri's poetic expression is consistent with an esoteric tradition of monistic mysticism that resembles the difficult system of Ibn 'Arabī (d. 1240).

Hamzah Fansuri's Malay-language work is based on impressive knowledge of the Qur'ān, Arabic language and grammar, and even Persian expression (which some say he could have studied with Muslim communities in Thailand within the globalized, cosmopolitan networks of the Indian Ocean and premodern Southeast Asia). Hamzah Fansuri's use of Qur'ānic Arabic throughout his poems demonstrates not only his advanced level of knowledge of the text and its grammar, but also the degree to which this information could be recognized as a common reference across the maritime world of the Indian Ocean. For example, here are two of his rhyming couplets, with the original translation they were given by Dutch scholars G. W. J. Drewes and L. F. Brakel:

> "*Wa 'llahu khalaqa-kum*" *dengarkan kata*
> "*Wa-ma ta'maluna*" *inilah nyata*
> "*Bi-kulli shay'in muhitun*" *di mata-mata*
> "*Kalam al-ashiqin*" *sedikitpun pada*
>
> "God has created you," listen to this word
> "And that which ye make" [37 Al-Ṣāffāt 96], a clear statement
> "He all things doth comprehend" [41 Fuṣṣilat 54], even with minute attention
> These mystical statements [or, "the speech of lovers"], however few, must suffice[3]

Each stanza of this lyric begins with an Arabic-language expression (appearing in quotations above), followed by a Malay gloss. The language and meaning of the Qur'ān is already internalized here to the extent that its embedded expression need only be referential. Only "a few [mystical] statements" suffice to convey Hamzah Fansuri's rich and textured Qur'ānic meanings in the Malay/Indonesian language (which, today, is the spoken language of about as many Muslims as those who are native speakers of Arabic). Hamzah Fansuri's mastery of irregular broken plurals and other aspects of Arabic syntax, evident elsewhere in the corpus of his works, show the depth of his knowledge of the Qur'ān on the one hand, as well as the expected proficiency and familiarity with this material within the reception and recognition of his audience on the other hand. These conditions came about within just a few centuries of Muslim history in Southeast Asia through the same practices of Qur'ānic reading and repetition that have had profound religious and historical impact across the Arabic- and non-Arabic-speaking worlds.

A pious tradition of "reading" that energizes Qur'ānic activity of the past and present emerged in the formative period of Islamic thought and practice alongside the development of more formal and rigorous academic approaches, such as the "Qur'ānic sciences" (discussed in Chapter 3). This has been especially evident in methods and materials produced by and for Sufis, but the authority for these classical modes of reading rests directly on the Qur'ān, not particular lineages of Sufi mysticism.[4] The scholar Al-Ghazālī (d. 1111), expert on the Qur'ānic sciences of recitation and interpretation, compiled selections of the Qur'ān, for example, in a work, *Jewels of the Qur'ān*. (There was some debate among scholars during this time about whether this genre was valid, that is, whether some verses could ever be singled out as being "more excellent" or "better jewels" than others in the Qur'ān.) It represents a mainstream in terms of its genre within traditions of Qur'ānically focused piety. In the introduction to this work, Al-Ghazālī gives an invitation to readers to heighten merely superficial academic knowledge in the religious sciences to an experiential appreciation of revelation:

> I then wish to rouse you from your sleep, O you who recite the Qur'ān to a great length, who take its study as an occupation, and who imbibe some of its outward meanings and sentences. How long will you ramble on the shore of the ocean, closing your eyes to the wonders of the meanings of the Qur'ān? Was it not your duty to sail to the midst of the fathomless ocean of these meanings in order to see their wonders, to travel to their islands in order to gather their best produce, and to dive into their depths so that you might become rich by obtaining their jewels? Do you not feel ashamed of being deprived of their pearls

> and jewels by your persistence in looking at their shores and outward appearances?[5]

In her survey of Sufi commentaries on the Qur'ān, Kristin Zahra Sands offers many similar and contemporaneous Muslim perspectives on the Qur'ān's experiential knowledge as an "ocean without shore."[6] These expectations of depth and sincerity formed ideals to which Qur'ānic artists and practitioners aspire in everyday practice.

The presence of the Qur'ān exerts incalculable religious power in the experience of people's projects of aesthetics, piety, and performance. The Qur'ān is believed to be transcendent as the "speech of God," while at the same time it was conveyed through the body and speech of Muḥammad and others who "follow" the reading. Muslims perceive the Qur'ān to exert an autonomous or independent power that relates to the experience of human hearts, minds, or bodies. For this there are many types of understandings of how heart and mind engage the active Qur'ān, as the Qur'ān forms a presence in the bodies of believers through practices like healing and prayer, listening and viewing, reading and writing. Practices like memorization indicate how embodied Qur'ānic presence (preserved in rehearsal and memory) has transformational moral effects for religious self and society. Dimensions of Qur'ānic ethical power include the aesthetic, ritual, and medical modes, often said to be realized through dyamics of disciplined and imaginative repetition. In modern contexts, diverse projects of piety self-consciously invite Muslims to enhance this experience of power in their own daily lives.

UNDERSTANDING THE NATURE OF THE QUR'ĀN

Pious, intellectual affirmation about the nature of the Qur'ān, such as the claim of the revealed text's *i'jāz* ("inimitability"), connects the text to the social and political lifeworlds of Muslim history. It was in fact a controversy over the nature of the Qur'ān that marked the end of the political and religious primacy of the rationalists known as the Mu'tazilites (introduced in Chapter 3), for example. Mu'tazilites had asserted that the Qur'ān was created separate from God, and in time. This was consistent with their fundamental proposition that nothing may be equivalent to God, who is transcendent. The position developed in part out of theorization of the Qur'ān's "speech" and the act of recitation, that is, the status of interlocution in the production of sound and recitation. "God's speech" of the Qur'ān was uttered in time, a rationalist position held, since *kalām Allah* was a contingent attribute of God.[7] Piety and understanding of the Qur'ān shaped Muslim history, and vice versa, in this case which took the form of the *miḥnah* ("trial" or "inquisition") over the nature of the Qur'ān.

In the first decades of the ninth century, Mu'tazilites vigorously defended the position that the Qur'ān was created in time. Otherwise, they claimed, it would be as if to say there were two divine realities (as some Christians had also successfully argued about divinity in the Greek-speaking East in prior centuries): first God, and then also His speech in the form of the "uncreated" Qur'ān. Mu'tazilis confirmed that the Qur'ān was the word of God, but that it was the created word, and not in any definitive sense a part of the godhead; the latter must be without attributes, they said, in accordance with their view of *tawḥīd* (divine unity). In contrast, there was an emerging movement of Sunni thought (characterized by Aḥmad bin Ḥanbal, the *ḥadīth* scholar and legal thinker, for example) that insisted that the Qur'ān was eternal and perfect as God's speech. This followed from the reasoning that, if the Qur'ān was created in time, then God's knowledge would be separate from His eternal nature, thus limiting God. This latter perspective won the debate but only after – and partially because of – the tactics of a bitter political struggle. It was one of the few instances in the history of Islam in the premodern world in which regulating and enforcing doctrine became a matter of state concern. Historically, it roughly coincided with a struggle over religion and state power in the "iconoclast" controversy over the divine presence in images in the neighboring Byzantine Empire, to which Christians in Muslim lands, such as John of Damascus (d. 749), had responded.

It was in part because of the conflict over the question of the Qur'ān's nature that the Mu'tazilites lost their influence with imperial power in Baghdad. The *miḥnah*, or "trial" or "inquisition," over the nature of the Qur'ān lasted under the reigns of 'Abbāsid caliphs Ma'mūn (r. 813–833), Mu'taṣim (r. 833–842), and Al-Wāthiq (r. 842–847). It ended with the ascendance of Mutawakkil in 847.

The official state position upheld Mu'tazilite doctrine, especially the "created Qur'ān." The 'Abbāsid caliph Ma'mūn had a genuine interest in *kalām* and learning. He was among the great patrons of a translation effort to render texts from Greek and Syriac into Arabic. He was also seeing political difficulties with pro-'Alids and others who were becoming disaffected politically. Many on the eastern boundary of the empire especially had come to see little benefit from the 'Abbasid revolution in 750, which had been supported by many on the claim of a return to genealogical closeness to the Prophet as a claim for legitimacy and rule (in contrast to the Umayyads who preceded them). Ma'mūn effectively tried to extend imperial power to the periphery by the enforcement of a doctrinal authority.

While the Mu'tazilites championed reason as the way to piety, and while their positions may now sound reasonable, their political methods were oppressive. In challenging prominent teachers, intellectuals, and religious leaders to accept their position, the state also imprisoned them. Many court *qadī*'s (judges) and scholarly authorities with pious allegiances, such as Aḥmad bin Ḥanbal (d. 855) himself, were required to testify about their claims. Reports document that Ibn Ḥanbal, who had been jailed during the *miḥnah*, had an outpouring of public support on the streets of Baghdad at his funeral by many who were not "Hanbali." This suggests the degree to which the *miḥnah* and its coercive methods had become popularly reviled in their time.

From the perspective of the *Ahl al-Sunnah wa'l-Jamā'a* ("The People of the Sunnah and the Community," the expression from which the term, "Sunni," is derived) the intellectual position on the "created" Qur'ān was impossible. Just because the Mu'tazilites were "rationalist" does not mean that the piety minded like Ibn Ḥanbal were irrational; they were looking rationally to "revelation," not "reason," for guidance. After the episode of the *miḥnah*, religious scholars, and others, became even more cynical regarding the piety of rulers, and a particular dislike of the Mu'tazilites and their positions was an outgrowth of this period. The "orthodox" doctrines that emerged from this formative era are represented by the work of Abū'l Ḥasan Al-Ash'arī (d. 935), who, in popular tradition it is said, defected from the intellectual tradition of Mu'tazilism. Pious and authoritative intellectual approaches become closely linked to the development of law, not philosophy, at about this time. For example, in this period the legal theorist Muḥammad Idrīs bin Al-Shāfī'ī (d. 820) theorized *sunnah* (the exemplary model of the Prophet) as revelatory guidance in jurisprudential thought and practice (Chapter 4). As pious people increasingly turned to revelation, not reason, speculative thought sought ways to interiorize revelation in the form of esoteric experience with a Sufi movement already spreading widely by the fourth century. Such an experiential focus was consistent with emergent piety across intellectual fields, from law to theology, and had its basis in the Qur'ān's own presentation of its active presence.

During the formative period, Qur'ānic sciences developed an independent field for the study of the "miraculous" nature of the Qur'ān. *I'jāz* is the theological doctrine of the "inimitable" Qur'ān. It is said that the Qur'ān is the "*mu'jizah*" or miracle of Muḥammad, who is reported in tradition to have been illiterate. *I'jāz* is the idea that the Qur'ān is a unique expression, different ontologically from poetry and prose, and which could only have been authored by God. The doctrine is based in the *taḥaddi* ("challenge") verses that appear in the Qur'ān itself. Such verses in the Qur'ān "challenge" others to imitate the Qur'ān, and they include, for example, 28 Al-Qaṣaṣ 49, "Say: Bring, then, a Book from Allāh giving better guidance than both [the Qur'ān and Torah], and I will follow it, if you are truthful." Elsewhere, the Qur'ān affirms that no one could ever actually do this, not even humans and *jinn* combined. In other examples, the Qur'ān enjoins its listeners to bring just ten *sūrah*s (11 Hūd 13) or even one *sūrah* (10 Yūnus 38 and 2 Al-Baqarah 23) like that of the Qur'ān.

Theologians began to elaborate formally the doctrinal positions of *i'jāz* in the ninth century. This also coincided with the rise of polemics and conversations among religious communities of Jews, Christians, and Muslims and others in cosmopolitan urban centers. Muslim theologians, for example, theorized the nature of the Qur'ān through the following question: why was the Qur'ān's own challenge to "bring another Qur'ān" not met? Astute scholars surmised that there must have been an "abundance of motives" among those who would have wished originally to prove the Prophet, and the Qur'ān, to be wrong. One answer to the question, popular among Mu'tazilites, was *ṣarfah*, meaning "turning" or "aversion." With this argument, it is claimed, it would have been possible for some to imitate the Qur'ān, but God constructed an "aversion" which prevented them from doing so. The "miracle" was thus this very aversion or prevention.[8]

The religious doctrine of *i'jāz* supports claims for the overall "eloquence" of the entire Arabic language. It has long been said that there are three types of expression in Arabic: poetry, prose, and the unique discourse of Qur'ān (this phrase is sometimes heard attributed to the litterateur of the early modern era, Taha Hussein). Some Muslims could try to be "like the Prophet" in their aspiration to poetic and rhetorical eloquence, as suggested by the nickname of the great poet of the 'Abbasid era, "Al-Mutanabbī" (d. 965), but they could also be sure they would never reach the ultimate horizon, the unique Qur'ān. The science of *i'jāz* inspired classical rhetorical analysis such as that of Ibn Qutaibah; in the modern period, Islamist thinker Sayyid Quṭb was originally fascinated by the persuasive rhetorical power of the Qur'ān.[9]

On the point of *i'jāz*, tradition emphasizes the Qur'ān's nature as a miracle. For example, the Qur'ān's unique guidance (*hidāyah*) is said to be proof of its divine nature. There are classical lists of the miraculous properties of the Qur'ān, such as Al-Qurtubī's (d. 1258) ten aspects of the Qur'ān's inimitability: its language excels over all other language (*fasāḥah*); its style excels over all other study (*naẓm*); its comprehensiveness cannot be matched, not can its arrangement (*tartīb*); its legislation cannot be surpassed; its narrations about the unknown can only come by revelation; there is no contradiction with sound natural sciences; the validation of its promises and warnings; its knowledge (legal and about the created world); it fulfills human needs; and its effects on the hearts of people.[10] Other religious formulations, such as Baqillanī's (d. 1013), include mention of the Qur'ān's knowledge of the unseen world (e.g. apparent foretelling of a defeat of the Greek Byzantine army, "Rūm," in 30 Al-Rūm 2–3).

Through the rational efforts of scholars considering the nature of the Qur'ān, theological positions on its status and the proofs of that status had been developed by the end of the formative period of Islamic intellectual traditions. It was at this time that theories of experiential knowledge and piety, such as those of Al-Ghazālī, arose as reflections on pious practice. Or, stated another way, it was in this period that religious practice and experience formed new avenues for pious intellectual explanation within related traditions of religious thought.

QUR'ĀNIC EXPERIENCE

Many of the Qur'ān's self-referential statements indicate qualities of scripture and its related effect on sensory and moral experience. The Qur'ān also highlights the transformation or transparency of affective and moral states rendered by the encounter with the recited book. Three examples of this idea, each taken from the text of the Qur'ān, describe prostration and weeping accompanying the recognition of revealed truth:

> Those are the ones whom Allāh favored from among the prophets of the progeny of Adam, of those We carried with Noah, or the progeny of Abraham and Israel and of those We have guided and elected. When the revelations [*āyāt*, i.e. the Qur'ān] of the Compassionate [*al-raḥmān*] were recited to them, they fell down prostrate and weeping. (19 Maryam 58)

> 106. It is a Qur'ān which We have divided into parts that you may recite it with deliberation, and We revealed it piecemeal.
> 107. Say [*qul*]: "Believe or do not believe in it. Surely when it is recited those, who were given the knowledge before it, fall down prostrate on their faces."
> 108. And they say [*wayaqūlūna*]: "Glory be to our Lord [*subḥāna rabbinā*]. Certainly the promise of our Lord is fulfilled." (17 Al-Isrā' 106–109)

> And when they hear what was revealed to the Messenger [the Qur'ān], you see their eyes overflow with tears on account of the truth they recognize. They say: "Our Lord, we believe, so write us down among the witnesses." (5 Al-Mā'idah 83)

Each of the verses that appears above refers to members of past communities who have recognized the validity of the persuasive discourse of the Qur'ān. The terms of this encounter are the "*āyāt*" (scriptural "verses" or natural "signs") from God. Typically, as in the examples above, the Qur'ān portrays this recognition as being emotional and kinetic as much as it is intellectual.

In Muslim religious traditions, an autonomous moral, spiritual, and social power is ascribed to the Qur'ān. For example, the Qur'ān is witnessed to be an agent of persuasion that draws people to enter Islam. The companion of the Prophet 'Umar bin Al-Khaṭṭāb is said to have turned from opposing the Muslims and embraced Islam after hearing Qur'ānic recitation, a report that appears in the accounts of *sīrah* (religious biography of the Prophet) by Ibn Hishām and Ibn Kathīr.[11] Some classical Asian court chronicles from the premodern era sometimes describe the coming of Islam in terms of the sudden ability of a local king or ruler to recite the book.[12] In contemporary religious biographical writing, the Qur'ān is reported to effect conversion to Islam as well. For example, this is a common feature of reports from contemporary North American women embracing Islam as documented in the book by Carol Anway, the mother of one such convert. Anway reports that typical responses to her survey questions on conversion related to the power of the Qur'ān. One woman, for example, answered Anway's questions about the conversion experience in terms that might have been familiar to a Sufi living a millennium ago:

> My conversion began as the result of a challenge by a Muslim to read the Qur'ān in order for us to have a debate on the position of women in Islam. I held the stereotypical view of Muslim women as being oppressed and in a bad position relative to their Christian counterparts. I was nominally Christian, raised in a Catholic environment … The reading of the Qur'ān and *ḥadīth* of the Prophet is what captured me. I went through a very odd experience whereby for the whole week it took me to read the Qur'ān I couldn't sleep and seemed to toss and turn all night in a feverish sweat. I had strange and vivid dreams about religious topics, and when I would get up all I wanted to do was continue reading the Qur'ān. I didn't even study for my final exams which were happening at the same time![13]

Modern Muslims recognize the phenomenon of perceptions of potential power of the Qur'ān, and develop strategies of *da'wah* (religious outreach) for Muslims based on this presumed fact. The Qur'ān's descriptions of its very own effects on listeners, such as falling down and weeping (even as it is being recited), function prescriptively and through sentimental and embodied modes.

Classical Islamic sources analyze the power of the Qur'ān *sūrah* by *sūrah*, and even verse by verse. This information belongs to a genre known as "*Faḍā'il Al-Qur'ān*," or "Excellent Properties of the Qur'ān," which typically relates the merits of *sūrah*s, compounded through expected repeated recitation over time to rewards at the end-time, although the effect of the Qur'ān's verses may also be said to be more direct, as suggested above. The material is based on *ḥadīth* reports. Although it is not popularly elaborated in the modern era, such statements remain an influence on practices ranging from everyday selection of verses to recite in prayer to the practice of traditional medicine. A well-known example of such *ḥadīth*, included by Al-Ghazālī, is the following statement, transmitted in tradition on the authority of Abū Huraira, an original companion of the Prophet and a source cited for many such traditions:

> Surely the house in which the Qur'ān is recited provides easy circumstances for its people, its good increases, angels come to it [in order to listen to the Qur'ān] and satans leave it. The house in which the book of God is not recited provides difficult circumstances for its people, its good decreases, angels leave it, and satans come to it.[14]

Rewards are not just said to come by reciting the Qur'ān *sūrah* by *sūrah* or *āyah* by *āyah* in this system. Muslim tradition preserves statements to the effect that rewards may even be achieved letter by letter in another statement that Al-Ghazālī cites:

> Ibn Mas'ūd said: [The Prophet] said, "Read the Qur'ān for you will be rewarded at the rate of ten good deeds for reading every letter of the Qur'ān. Take notice, I do not say that *alif lām mīm* constitute one letter [this is a reference to the 'abbreviated letters']. Rather, I should say that *ālif* is one letter, *lām* is another, and *mīm* is [still] another."[15]

This information would be received within Muslim theologies of the miraculous nature of the Qur'ān, including doctrine within the field of the "inimitability" of the Qur'ān. In addition, "Sufis," among the heirs to this early Qur'ānic tradition of piety, developed especially the soteriological and interiorized dimensions of Qur'ānic traditions. Some well-known Sufis represent the Qur'ān as having a palpable presence in the consciousness of practitioners: waking, dreaming, and in the life to come.

Islamic traditions of piety have at times portrayed the Qur'ān as the present criterion by which moral states may be evaluated for any individual, in statements that personalize the meanings of labels for the Qur'ān such as "criterion" and "proof." For example, a companion of the Prophet and a transmitter of important information about the first Islamic community, Anas bin Mālik, allegedly stated: "It often happens that a man recites the Qur'ān, and the Qur'ān curses him." This would ascribe an autonomous power or agency to the Qur'ān, in revealing the sincerity of those who enagage it. There is another similar report included in Bukhārī's collection of *ḥadīth*, that the Prophet Muḥammad himself made a statement to the effect that the test of inner virtue is found in voicing the Qur'ān: "There will be such people among you that when you compare your prayers with theirs, your fasts with theirs, your good deeds with theirs, you will consider yours to be very inferior. [However] they will read the Qur'ān, yet it will not sink deeper than their throats." This can be read, and was read by Muslims like Al-Ghazālī, as a pious elaboration of the primacy of the direct Qur'ānic power, experience, and encounter.

"CARRYING" THE QUR'ĀN IN MEMORY[16]

The Qur'ān's power in Muslim systems shapes practices of piety that are physically embodied, sentimentally affective, and intellectually cognitive. One mode of these processes is repetiton. Through memorization, for example, the "preserver" of the Qur'ān continually rehearses in order to keep the text fixed in memory, an effort that reflects a more universal Qur'ānic theme of "remembrance," which also forms the basis of countless other Muslim religious practices as well. A Qur'ān "preserver" (*ḥāfiẓ*/*ḥāfiẓah*) takes upon himself or herself the religious community's responsibility to "carry" the Qur'ān in memory. Traditionally, such Muslims would memorize the Qur'ān at a young age before undertaking other kinds of formal religious study. The process of Qur'ān memorization thus provides both a specific and an idealized model of "traditional" education, established by structures of textual transmission, orality, aurality, and memory.

In the early centuries of Islam, the expert memories of Qur'ān "readers" were the benchmark for the standardization of the written text and the accepted science of its "readings" and vocalization. Although every practicing Muslim must memorize some of the Qur'ān in order to perform the daily required duty of canonical worship (*ṣalāt*), memorization of the entire Qur'ān is the achievement of a few. Even among educated Muslims who do not manage to memorize the entire Qur'ān, it is still a basic goal to have memorized the final *juz'*, and at the very least to have read the entire Arabic

Qur'ān through once with a teacher; the latter, known as "*khatm Al-Qur'ān*," is marked by life-cycle celebrations in some parts of the Muslim world. Memorizers and expert readers of the Qur'ān are said in classical sources to be held to higher moral standards than others in this world and the next by virtue of "holding" the entire Qur'ān in memory, and these individuals are viewed with special respect.

Memorization of the Qur'ān, known as its "preservation" (*taḥfīẓ*), was encouraged from the earliest time of Islam. The wives of the Prophet, for example, were among those known especially for memorization and preservation of the Qur'ān. The material on the early Muslim community and later pious figures echoes the important social role of the Qur'ān reader, especially in education and transmission of the text. Bukhārī's and other major collections of *ḥadīth* reports, for example, relate (on the authority of 'Uthmān bin 'Affān) that the Prophet stated, "The best of you is one who has learnt the Qur'ān and has taught it." There are many *ḥadīth* reports that encourage Muslims to read and know the Qur'ān by heart.

According to traditions of Islamic law, memorization is a recommended act of piety; it is classified as *farḍ kifāyah*, which designates it as an obligation always to be observed by a community by some of its members on its behalf. Muslims understand the act of reading the Qur'ān to cultivate the self as well as community. Sources in Islamic tradition emphasize that ordinary Muslims may affect others' religiosity, and thereby build religious community, simply by reading the Qur'ān aloud. 8 Al-Anfāl 2 is the verse usually cited in connection to such claims:

> The true believers are those whose hearts, on mention of Allāh, quiver with fear; and when His revelations [*āyātuhu*] are recited to them, they strengthen in faith. They put their trust in their Lord. (8 Al-Anfāl 2)

The Qur'ān's statement that reading for others causes them to "multiply in faith" indicates that engaging the Qur'ān is fundamentally not just a personal practice of piety, but also a communal one.

As "preservers," those who carry the Qur'ān have a responsibility to contribute to the ethical order of society. Classical literature illustrates their moral responsibility to the community through a portrayal of unending commitment, which continues night and day: Qur'ān reading by night and constructive moral action by day. Literature on the norms of memorizaton (*adab*), for example, considers the question of how to earn a livelihood by teaching or reading the recited Qur'ān. This includes the problem of whether to accept payment for this practice. *Ḥadīth* reports on this point that were cited by the pious in the formative period underscore that the Qur'ān is to be cherished for its own sake, and should not be deployed for worldly gain.

One of the greatest challenges a *ḥāfiẓ* ever faces, however, is just to remain one. Tradionally, children who memorize the Qur'ān do so around the age of seven, and under the direction of a certified *ḥāfiẓ*.[17] In Indonesia, memorization usually takes place in Islamic boarding schools known as *pesantren*, some of which are famous for their students' memorization. Memorization also tends to run in families, passing from father/mother to daughter and son. The reason for this is the need for careful supervision at all times by a teacher, who can catch any mistakes. Simply not to forget any part of the Qur'ān already memorized represents an ongoing task due to the uniquely nonlinear structure and style of the Qur'ān, which causes textual patterns to shift and refract in human thought and memory. Qur'ānic structure and style "improvises" structurally on semantic themes according to its own rhetorical style (even as melody is improvised in its vocalization), which may actually frustrate automaticity and demands vigilant attention. This occurs even as the recited text persuasively addresses its listeners to "ponder," "reflect," and to listen and to react to the recited message. Memorizers encounter and address these internal challenges of the recited Qur'ān through ritual repetition and rehearsal.

Qur'ānic statements allude to its own design to require continual attentive "reminding" (*dhikr*) in order to remain firmly grounded in human consciousness. Although internalizing the text is suggested by the Qur'ān to be an "easy" task for those whose hearts are open, features of the text also ensure that maintaining the ability to recite from memory will be a lifelong process of highly focused engagement. Evidence of the difficulty for memorizers in holding Qur'ānic structure in memory is the frequency with which variants of a certain *ḥadīth*, found in the canonical collections of Bukhārī and Muslim, is cited in the literature. The account reports that the Prophet Muḥammad stated that memorizing the Qur'ān is more difficult than tethering a camel that is trying to run away. This report is related in variants such as one quoted in one influential manual, "Guard this Qur'ān, for, by He who has the soul of Muḥammad in His hand, it is easier for it to escape from the mind than for a camel to escape."[18] There is an enormous amount of material in the Qur'ān to memorize, and then to be rehearsed continually. To read the complete text straight through at the rapid pace of a memorizer's rehearsal, and with only the necessary breaks, takes about eight or nine hours. Memorizers often follow the recommendation to repeat the entire Qur'ān every week, one-seventh each day.

Nonlinear syntax and structure of the Qur'ān fragment automatic recall and require continuous attention. Carried away by rhythm and pattern, reciting or chanting with a flow from memory may actually produce a *mistake* rather than a correct rendition, as when the patterns are broken, whether by semantic ruptures or by other irregular structures. When discussing these challenges, Indonesian memorizers often cited the particular difficulty of retaining material in narrative mode, such as with accounts of the prophet Mūsā (Moses), which comprise about 500 out of the approximately 6,000 verses of the Qur'ān. Structural characteristics and sheer amount of narrative material make it difficult to remember any one account of Mūsā through multiple repetitions of the entire text, especially stylistic phrases, or concepts that may trigger other passages.

There are famously tricky passages highlighted by memorizers based on sentences, phrases, and even individual words. Passages that closely resemble one another and are repeated with a slight variation are among the most difficult for the memorizer. For example, variants of the phrase gardens "underneath which rivers flow" (*tajrī min taḥtihā al-anhār*, a description of heaven) appear dozens of times across the text. The formula that repeats in Sūrat Hūd (verses 28, 63, and 88) is an example of formulaic expression ending each of the accounts of prophets presented sequentially in the *sūrah*, but each has a slightly different wording. Such variations may appear at the beginning, middle, or end of an *āyah*. For memorizational practice, such cases fall under the technical heading of "difficulties" (*mushkilāt*), enumerated in classical sources, and memorizers may commit such handbooks to memory along with the Qur'ān itself.

Here is an example taken from such a handbook, the verses 4 Al-Nisā' 135 and 5 Al-Mā'idah 8. The first is in *juz'* 5 whereas the second is in *juz'* 6 (there are thirty of these partitions overall), meaning that if a memorizer repeats one *juz'* a day (repeating the Qur'ān over the course of a month, for example), these passages would be rehearsed on separate days. In these verses, two prepositional phrases are transposed, thus permuting the order of the final three words of the *āyahs*. The statements should be familiar from the discussion of law and ethics given in the previous chapter:

> *Yā'ayyuhā alladhīna āmanū kūnū qawwāmīn bi-l-qisṭi shuhadā' lillāhi* O you who believe! Stand up for **justice** as witnesses to **God**. (4 Al-Nisā' 135)
>
> *Yā'ayyuhā alladhīna āmanū kūnū qawwāmīn lillāhi shuhadā' bi-l-qisṭi* O you who believe! Stand up for **God** as witnesses to **justice**. (5 Al-Mā'idah 8)

The potential reversal is straightforward, and these are the only two *āyahs* in this class in the Qur'ān. The memorizer could easily commit this single instance of inversion to memory as an exceptional case.

Another, more complex, example is 2 Al-Baqarah 136 (and the beginning of 137) and 3 Āl 'Imrān 84 (and the beginning of 85). Compare these subtle differences:

> 136. Say [*qālū*, plural imperative] (O Muslims): We believe in Allāh and that which is revealed unto us [*'ilainā*, preposition with suffix] and that which was revealed unto [*ilā*, preposition] Abraham, and Ishmael, and Isaac, and Jacob, and the tribes, and that which Moses and Jesus received, and that which the prophets received [*wamā ūtī an-nabiyina*] from their Lord. We make no distinction between any of them, and unto Him we have surrendered (in Islam). [137:] So if they believe in the like of which you believe, then they are rightly guided [*fa'in āmanū bimithli mā 'amantum bihi faqad ihtadā*] ... (2 Al-Baqarah 136–137)
>
> 84. Say [*qul*, singular imperative] (O Muḥammad): We believe in Allāh and that which was revealed unto us [*'alainā*, a slightly different preposition than above] and that which was revealed unto [*'alā*, a slightly different preposition than above] Abraham and, and Ishmail, and Isaac, and Jacob, and the tribes, and that which Moses and Jesus and the prophets [*wan-nabiyina*] received from their Lord. We make no distinction between any of them, and unto Him we have surrendered (in Islam). [85:] And whoever seeks as a religion other than Islam it will not be accepted from him [*waman yabtaghi ghair al-islāmi ilkh*] ... (3 Āl 'Imrān 84–85)

Here, an inattentive memorizer could mistakenly skip at similar points from one *āyah* to the other, which is located elsewhere, and in another *juz* in the Qur'ān. Or, the memorizer may simply substitute the preposition that belongs in one verse into the other verse at some point, especially if his or her knowledge of Arabic grammar is shaky.

Those who "carry" the Qur'ān manage the text through ongoing repetition so that it does not, like the camel in the *ḥadīth*, slip away from them. Complementing the challenges of Qur'ānic structure are those of poetics and style. The unique syntax of Qur'ānic style makes it difficult to apply internalized principles of grammatical consistency as a mnemonic technique, even in coherent registers such as narrative. Syntactically as well as structurally, the Qur'ān refracts in memory, breaking linear patterns even as they are established. In the Qur'ānic sciences, the technical term for this kind of rupture in syntactical pattern is "*iltifāt*" (a literal meaning of the term is to "turn" or "turn one's face toward").[19] The contemporary scholar Muhammad Abdel Haleem defines "*iltifāt*" as "a sudden shift in the pronoun of the speaker or the person spoken about." In addition to shifts in deictic category ("person"), the phenomenon includes the Qur'ān's changes in verb tense, change in number (between singular, dual, and plural), change in case marker, and other features.[20] According to Abdel Haleem, Al-Zarkāshī (d. 1391) defined *iltifāt* as "the change of speech from one mode to another, for the sake of freshness and variety for the listener, to renew his interest, and to keep his mind from boredom and frustration, through having one mode continuously in his ear."[21] The poetics of the Qur'ān demand attention of the reader through what Abdel Haleem calls its "dynamic style;" these are also the very poetics of attention that ensures that the memorizer will embody the Qur'ān in an ongoing way.

In addition to continued circulation of traditional handbooks that offer to students practical information for memorizing, such as by listing cases of the inversions above, popular handbooks published in recent decades address the practice of memorization in modern contexts. One of the first contemporary guides to appear in Indonesia in the 1980s, for example, outlines the ways in which the memorizer can make time for study and practice in the home (such as by avoiding the television and telephone), and suggests psychological tricks to manage and counteract inevitable discouragement.[22] Newer handbooks available in Indonesia since the 1990s, some translated from Arabic, suggest regimens and sample schedules for practice.[23] One feature of these contemporary guides is that they reflect the new global circumstances for memorization, which no longer can be expected to take place in an Islamic boarding school such as an Arabic-language *madrasah* or *pesantren.*

Sources that were widely available in Indonesia in 2009 in mainstream, non-religious settings (like chain stores in shopping malls) encouraged Muslims to memorize the Qur'ān by way of practical advice within the context of modern, urban life. For example, the book by Ahmad Salim Badwilan, *Panduan Cepat Menghafal Al-Qur'an dan Rahasia-rahasia Keajaibannya* (*Quick Guide to Memorizing the Qur'an and the Secrets of its Miracles*, a work translated from Arabic), describes in detail how one can "realize the dream" ("*wujudkan mimpi*") of memorizing all thirty *juz'* of the Qur'ān. Although this book mentions the setting of the traditional Islamic school, the adult reader seems mostly to be expected to undertake individual study from the text (which traditionally is not recommended), and to practice in pairs or in groups along with the aid of sound recordings and electronic media like computer software. In the course of my own research on the theory and practice of Indonesian Qur'ān memorization in the 1990s, I heard no objection to using such modern tools and technologies when it was discussed in interviews. Religious scholars did, however, always stress that memorizational study is not possible all on one's own because of the frequency of unnoticed errors that would inevitably be committed.

Nevertheless, the *Quick Guide* is still intended primarily for personal use in settings outside the support and frameworks of Islamic schooling. This is indicated in the book's chapter that lists points of "helpful advice" for memorization, which I present in translated summary form as follows:

1. Before even starting anything or doing anything, feel humility before Allāh may He be Praised and Exalted. Be hopeful of success in this undertaking, and pray for God's help and guidance in it.
2. Read at least *juz'* a day (of unmemorized material, straight from the text) during your daily supplications. Do not begin your daily regimen of (memorization) study before you have read from the text of the Qur'ān. Do not let the task of memorization occupy you more, in balance, than reading the text of the Qur'ān.
3. Make it your "routine" (*rutin*) to read in the morning (*dzikir pagi*), in the afternoon, and before bedtime. Also make it a habit

to read verses that protect you from satan. This is because (the text explains) "*dzikir*" is the enemy of satan, and here there is citation of a verse of the Qur'ān, 5 Al-Mā'idah 91.

4. Attend meetings of religious groups (*majelis majeliṣ ulama*). There is much discussion here on this point, addressing the subject's unwillingness to attend such gatherings (due to being "*uzur*", lit. "feeling feeble"). Just suppose, the text states, that you were going to get ten thousand "*riyal*" (this is a translated text in Indonesian) for attending a "*majelis*." In that case, you would just go, wouldn't you? And suppose that you were invited to a naming/circumcision ceremony or a wedding, well then you would be sure to accept the invitation right away. But if you were to be asked to attend a study group (*majelis ilmu*), well, then you resist it. A lot of people would object at that moment, the text explains, "But I can just listen to recitation on cassette recordings at home." Any poor, unfortunate person (who would say this) has prevented himself/herself from attaining a great reward. (And the text here cites a *ḥadīth*: that the Prophet said one should go to a house where people gather to recite the Qur'ān because one feels close to others and is surrounded by angels.)
5. Find friends who help you to remember Allāh. Some people will want to tell you that your constant Qur'ānic practice makes it inconvenient for them to plan their social activities whenever and however they please. In contrast to people like this, your other friends who help you read the Qur'ān are like a treasure beyond value.
6. When you are in congregational prayer, standing behind the *imām*, and if you have already memorized the verses he recites, be a listener and not a tutor. The text here quotes a *ḥadīth* that the Prophet said: "Anyone who studies a certain 'knowledge' just so that he or she can show off with scholars, or in order to debate with ignorant/stupid people, or just so that he or she can attract a personal following, Allāh will cast that person into hell."
7. Know that the first, and original, knowledge is to preserve the Qur'ān. Each verse that you memorize opens a door to Allāh, may He be Praised and Exalted. Every verse that you do not memorize or that you forget represents a closed door that obstructs you from God (*Tuhan*). Make it your wish better to know new, unknown verses rather than (just to) remember only the shortest *sūrah*s in the Qurān.

8. Make *wuḍū'* before your read the Qur'ān. This is the *sunnah* of the Prophet Muḥammad, God's peace and blessings be on him.
9. Always ask for forgiveness (*beristighfar*), and do this more frequently all the time. This is because one big reason that people forget verses that they have already memorized is on account of sin. At this point, the text includes quite a number of accounts that narrate the statements of great figures of religious learning. These discuss cases of persons who were inhibited from gaining or preserving knowledge, including several instances of forgetting the memorized Qur'ān (and more than one self-reference in this regard), because of bad morals, bad acts, or just by having a bad attitude.
10. Beware of deluding yourself about your Qur'ānic memorization, and always remain vigilant about this point. Your capacity with the Qur'ān is for the sake of seeking God's pleasure (being upon you) and for feeling the sentiments of earnest piety (*rasa khasyah*) and calm contentment (*ketenangan*), not arrogance. Also, watch out for those people who would try to put you down or who insult you (*dengan pandangan menghinakan dan merendahkan*). They do this only for the simple reason that you memorize the Qur'ān and they do not. Being around people like this is the worst of all misfortunes (*hal itu merupakan musibah yang paling besar*).
11. "Know, O Brother/Sister! Memorizing the Qur'ān is a great satisfaction for those who attain it! Because, God rewards it." With this, the book's the section on advice on memorizing the Qur'ān closes, citing a verse from the Qur'ān (in Arabic and Indonesian translation), 14 Ibrāhīm 7. In conclusion, there is a final supplication: "O Allāh, make the Qur'ān a light for our hearts, remove all our sadness, and help us on the last day!"[24]

Many of these points update into the modern setting the religious difficulty of finding like-minded, upstanding Muslim companions. For this, there is citation of much material from the Islamic traditional genre of the "*adab*" (customary comportment) of teaching and learning, as in Point 9 above.[25] This also represents a distinctively modern adaptation of memorizational "tradition," however, since this would never have been a problem that would have been addressed in classical handbooks for memorization, which would presume the aspiring *ḥāfiẓ* already to be in a setting of religious learning (and not around people who have busy social calendars or who would ever treat the project of reading the Qur'ān with any disrespect). The list of "advice" above ends with motivational words and, appropriately, a Qur'ānic quote and final invocation in the form of a prayer.

Large portions of the *Quick Guide* (which, while it contains some 300 pages, is still cheap in paperback), a book which encourages people to try to memorize, are actually about how to get other people to memorize the Qur'ān. The second section of the book is titled "Children and Qur'ān Memorization." These chapters carry headings such as, "Why Children Don't Like to Go to Qur'ān Classes" (Chapter 24), and "Summer Vacation: An Opportunity to Teach the Qur'ān to Your Kids" (Chapter 28). In traditional systems of Islamic education, a child would have memorized before beginning any other formal schooling.[26] Now, however, modern circumstances are different, and middle-class Muslim children have other "extracurricular" pastimes, like playing popular computer games, that would compete with memorization.

Two separate chapters found in two different locations in the *Quick Guide*, 16 and 29, each bear the same Indonesian title, "How We Can Plant Love for the Qur'ān in the Hearts of Our Children." Both give specific advice to modern-day parents who aspire to get their kids to memorize the Qur'ān. Chapter 29, for example, offers five points of instruction to Muslim parents, which include: read the Qur'ān to your child while you are still pregnant, and also read after your baby is born; pray that your child will want to memorize, and that he/she will be able to do it; and give your son or daughter lots of little presents (*hadiah*) for his/her memorizational effort. At another point, parents are told to take their children to Qur'ān class once or twice a week, and to treat this just the same as regular practice for any sports team (rather than to show up only infrequently). Finally, Chapter 29 (and in fact the whole second section of the book) concludes with the following tip for encouraging one's child to memorize. Get him or her his or her very own special little stereo, one with a real microphone. The reason for this, the text explains, is that kids just love it. Every boy or girl, the text reminds its readers, really loves to hear his or her own voice coming through a sound system. So, have him or her first listen to someone reading the Qur'ān and then, when it's the child's turn, ask him or her repeat it into the microphone, and so on. The trick with this practice, the text continues, is just to make sure that your child knows that this special equipment is only for the purpose of Qur'ān reading and memorizing … and that it is not to be used for anything else.[27]

Memorization, while still hoped for in children, is also now becoming increasingly encouraged as a pious activity, or as a kind of religious hobby, for Muslims of all ages. Another popular source by the same author, Ahmad Salim Badliwan, widely available in Indonesia, was titled *Seni Menghafal Al-Qur'an: Resep Manjur Menghafal Al- Qur'an yang Telah Terbukti Keampuhannya* (*The Art of Memorizing the Qur'an: A Powerful Recipe with Proven Effectiveness*, also a work translated from Arabic). Its jacket cover boasts that it contains "66 *KISAH NYATA*" ("66 TRUE STORIES"). Chapters are comprised mostly of first-hand accounts by people who memorized, with many passages quoted as if they had been excerpted from actual interview transcripts. These include some stories of children memorizing, but most of the book is about adults. Just a few of the chapter headings of the book's "true stories" of success are: "A Woman Who was Able to Memorize at the Age of Eighty Years" (pp. 58–61); "A Blind Woman Who Memorized in Five Years" (pp. 61–63);"A Woman of Sixty Years Who Memorized Just by Hearing the Qur'ān" (i.e. only by ear, pp. 84–85); "A Fifty-Year-Old Woman Who Was Able to Memorize in Just One Year Once Her Husband had Passed Away" (pp. 71–74); and "A Mother Who Memorized the Qur'ān Right Along with Her Children" (pp. 118–121), namely one "Ummu 'Abdirrohman," who managed to do this by staging competitions with her kids every afternoon in the family's living room.

As suggested by the list of subjects above, about half the book seems to be taken up with "true stories" of women who are about or above the age of fifty, such as one narration found under the striking heading, "Women of Seventy or Eighty Years are the Class of People Who are the Most Hard-Working in Memorizing the Qur'ān." This particular account quotes the words of "Ummu Ahmad," including a statement that is set in boldface type, "I Carried the *Mushaf* Around for My Husband to the Point that I Wanted to be Able to Read it [for myself]" (p. 90). Once she had memorized, Ummu Ahmad says, she then went on to teach in a religious school specializing in memorization, "in order to help produce as many Qur'ān memorizers as possible."

In another of the book's accounts, titled "Tears of Joy Fall from the Eyes of a Woman Who Memorized the Qur'ān," a woman named

"Ummu LH" relates her experience, presumably while weeping, with the following words, which have been translated from Arabic to Indonesian and then into English:

> Ever since they were small, about four years old, I would work with my children to memorize the Qur'ān. Every day I would carry the youngest into the kitchen with me. I would explain the meaning to them as they would repeat *surah*s. Each day, I would listen to two *juz'* from each one of my children … [and "Ummu LH" memorized in this way, right along with her kids. She continues:] I often tell people around me to stop acting like those who just waste their time with things that have no use, with "*shopping*," becoming immersed in their worldly lives. I hope for their sake they would try to draw closer to Allāh by memorizing the Qur'ān."

The comment on "shopping" as the alternative to Qur'ānic study is a theme common across many of these accounts, suggesting a politics that would view memorization as a contrast to consumerism. This also would be consistent with the classical Islamic *adab* literature, which sees religious and Qur'ānic learning as antithetical to corruption in many forms, whether political, public, or personal.[28]

QUR'ĀNIC POWER IN HEALING, PIETY AND WORSHIP

According to Islamic systems of law and ethics, a spectrum of "assessments" may be applied to any action a Muslim performs, from a forbidden or questionable act, to one that is recommended, to acts that are required. Qur'ānic practices are perceived to occupy the full range of assessed actions, and they are understood potentially to exert a palpable, effective, and instrumental power in all. "Prophetic healing" and canonical worship (*ṣalāt*) are two types of examples of efficacious Qur'ānic practice that can be seen to point to different poles across a spectrum of "assessments of actions."

The instrumental power of the Qur'ān works within the human body, representing an explicit area of knowledge in the field of the "prophetic medical sciences." This is a field of learning established on *ḥadīth* that relate to the Prophet's known activities as a healer. The practices that are based in this tradition, along with others that have similar roots in piety, are sometimes treated with religious skepticism, however. One cause of controversy is the perception that some acts are overly instrumental (that is, performed, for the sake of self-interest rather or to achieve a desired goal other than for the sake of Allāh), and the debate is supported on both sides by the legal adage from a *ḥadīth* that "actions are known by their intentions."

Healing through traditional Qur'ānic practices may be a doubly controversial area in contemporary times. First, many of the practices come under religious suspicion as "innovation" (*bid'ah*) that is said to deviate from original Islamic practices, even though these practices were introduced long ago in the past. Second, they are additionally criticized as superstitious old traditions that have no place in a revitalized Islam, or next to new technologies of modern medicine. A practice such as drinking water in which paper inked with Qur'ānic writings has been soaked, for example, could be challenged on both grounds simultaneously. Nevertheless, many of these practices do have a history that extends back to the earliest reports of Muslim communities, and some religious scholars have considered them to be acceptable in the past. In addition, these practices are known to a great many people and undeniably remain widely practiced by Muslims today.

A mainstream example of the sort of practice about which one would expect to hear some controversy comes from a popular book from Pakistan (printed in English) that carries the simple title *Ṭibb Al-Nabawī* (*Prophetic Medicine*). As examples of the many properties attributed to specific *sūrahs*, the book states that Sūrat Al-'Ankabūt (number 29) and Sūrat Luqmān (number 31) may cure malaria if written and the soaked ink is drunk, and that writing Sūrat Al-Burūj (number 85) on paper and tying this to an infant will cause the child to wean all on its own. This sort of information extends the logic of the "excellences" and advantages of the genre *Faḍā'il Al-Qur'ān* to specific desired outcomes. One reason why such practices have been controversial is that these instrumental ends could overshadow their Qur'ānic means. For example, the following practice for bringing back a missing person would probably not be condoned by most contemporary scholars. The text describes the target of the practice to be a "runaway," which would apply, for example, in the situation of a husband's desertion without providing for continuing family support, nor having previously arranged for a divorce:

> For bringing back a runaway person, one should recite *Sūra* Yaseen [*sūrah* 36] seven times and call the name of the person concerned while uttering "*mukremina*" [sic]. This should be blown over to a lock and then get it closed and thrown into the air afterwards so that it come down after revolving in the space [sic]. *Sūra* Yaseen should be recited in its complete form and the lock should be thrown in the direction of the wind.[29]

The text also provides an associated chart on which would be written the name of the missing person along with his or her own mother's name. Across the Muslim world from Africa to Asia, it is common to see charts of transcribed *sūrah* numbers and numeric equivalents represented as values in written matrices of power that are used as amulets, talismans, and decorations. In other everyday modes, *sūrahs* of the Qur'ān are used for many functions formalizing and Islamicizing activity and rendering it auspicious. For example, the recitation of Al-Fātiḥah is used to seal binding contracts such as marriage. *Sūrahs* 113 Al-Falaq and 114 Al-Nās, the final chapters of the Qur'ān, are commonly recited with their protective themes in mind.

Qur'ān reciting, context notwithstanding, is rarely ever considered to be a questionable act in itself. Some memorization and recitation of the Qur'ān is required simply in order to carry out minimal daily ritual observances always required for valid *ṣalāt*, which places this activity at the positive extreme of "assessed action." The Qur'ān itself also encourages reading the Qur'ān, indicating that the recitation of the Qur'ān carries the status of an action rewarded by God. Recitation is a dimension of religious "remembrance" of Allāh, and Muslims read the Qur'ān frequently as an act of supererogatory piety. Recitation especially at night is performed by committed Muslims, as recommended in the Qur'ān in 3 Āl 'Imrān 113–114, a verse which contrasts the actions of believers ("people of the book") with the unbelievers:

> 113. They are not all alike. For the people of the book [*ahl al-kitāb*], there is an upright nation who recite Allāh's revelations [*āyāt*] throughout the night, while prostrating themselves.
> 114. They believe in Allāh and the last day, bid the right and forbid the wrong and hasten to do good deeds [*wayanhūr 'an al-munkar wayusāri'ūna fī al-khairāt*]. These are among the righteous people! (3 Āl 'Imrān 113-114)

During the fasting month of Ramaḍān, the Qur'ān is read through over the course of the month in nighttime prayers called *tarāwiḥ*. In addition, during Ramaḍān and also during the days of Ḥajj, the whole Qur'ān may be recited through in one night by pious Muslims anywhere. "Readings" of the Qur'ān customarily heard on public occasions include 36 Yā Sīn (discussed in Chapter 6), recited for the deceased or dying in a (sometimes controversial) practice known as *taḥlīl*, and 12 Yūsuf, which can mark rites of passage in some parts of the Muslim world. Sūrat 18 Al-Kahf, analyzed in Chapter 6, is sometimes read communally as a weekly observance.

Although terms for the act of Qur'ān recitation differ across the Muslim world, there are a few expressions that are common to denote the practice of recitation. First, the term *tajwīd* designates the technical guidelines for recitation, representing one of the "Qur'ānic sciences" connected to the field of vocalization or "readings" (*qirā'āt*). *Tajwīd* makes the recited Qur'ān sound different from ordinary Arabic speech and song. It includes rules for the assimilation and partial assimilation of consonants, elongation of some vowels, and permissible and recommended starts and stops in reciting. Its Arabic root means to "make beautiful" or correct. A semantic form derived from the same linguistic root, "*mujawwad*," is the term most commonly heard for a slow, ornamented style of recitation. In this style, reciters modulate according to the pitch classes and melody types of musicalized "modes," or *maqām*, which are required to be improvised.

Other common terms for recitation are "*tartīl*" and especially "*tilāwah*." The verbal form of *tartīl* appears in the Qur'ān in 25 Al-Furqān 32, where it describes the reading of the Qur'ān as an act of chanting distinctly:

> 32. The unbelievers say: "If only the Qur'ān had been sent down on him [the Prophet] all at once." That is how we wanted to strengthen your heart with it and we recite it deliberately [*warattalnāhu tartīlan*]. (25 Al-Furqān 32)

A verb that is related to "*tartīl*" also appears in 73 Al-Muzzammil 1–4, verses which are said to be among the very first revelations that the Prophet Muḥammad received:

> *Bismillāh Al-Raḥmān Al-Raḥīm*
> 1. O enwrapped one [Muḥammad]
> 2. Keep vigil throughout the night, except for a little while;

3. Half of it, or a little less;
4. Or add a little thereto and chant the Qur'ān loudly [*warattili Al-Qur'āna tartīlan*]
5. Indeed, We shall deliver unto you a weighty discourse [*qawlan thaqīf*] (73 Al-Muzzammil 1–5)

In addition, the term *tilāwah* appears in the Qur'ān many times, as both a noun and a verb. In the Qur'ān, the term often refers to the signs of God that are "rehearsed," the stories of previous messengers and communities, as well as the actual reading of the verses of the Qur'ān aloud. In the Qur'ān, when "*tilāwah*" refers to reading the Qur'ān, this conveys the idea of "following" the meaning of the text as it is shaped in sound. Finally, another word for faster, less melodically ornamented recitation is "*tadarus*," a term connoting study. In all of these forms, pitch variation may be regular, while nevertheless the cantillation is still considered to be improvisatory.

Qur'ān recitation has its effect through aesthetic modes, and the classical literature indicates that readings were to be valued for beautiful and compelling qualities. In fact, the force of religious injunctions concerning the beauty of recitation renders it a legal norm for many reciters who wish to "beautify the Qur'ān in voice." Tradition has preserved many separate accounts relating that the Prophet Muḥammad appreciated beautiful voices among readers of the Qur'ān, such as the following report of a statement attributed to the Prophet (collected by Bukhārī and others): "Allāh has not heard anything more pleasing than listening to a prophet reciting the Qur'ān in a sweet loud voice." Compilers of traditions also relate accounts about the Prophet's reaction to hearing the recited Qur'ān, such as his shedding tears.

Norms of practice known as *adab* structure performance and response in the recitation of the Qur'ān, as work by Frederick Denny has shown, and this includes the comportment of Qur'ān memorizers as well. During the act of reading the Qur'ān aloud, expectations include respectful silence while listening, facing the direction of prayer (if possible) when reading, and observing *sajdah al-tilāwah*, which is prostration that is to be performed at fourteen or fifteen *āyāt* in the Qur'ān. As the example of just one of these verses, 41 Fuṣṣilat 37 (the example quoted in Chapter 1), shows, these are *āyāt* that refer to created beings who bow before their Creator. The practice is based on a *ḥadīth* report. A prostration is performed, facing the *qibla* (the direction of Mecca); after standing, the reading continues.

The standard opening and closing formulae are also part of the *adab* of recitation. These are, first, the opening statement, the *ta'awwudh* ("I take refuge in God from the accused satan," "*a'wudhu bilLāhi min ash-shaiṭān ir-rajīm*"), which is always followed by the Basmalah, "*Bismillāhir-Rahmānir-Rahīm,*" no matter where in the Qur'ān the reader begins. The Basmalah also opens every *sūrah* except one, although not as a numbered *āyah* (except in the case of the Fātiḥah). The reciter closes a reading with the formula *ṣadaq Allāhu'l-'aẓīm*, meaning,"Thus Almighty God has spoken truly." In some places, the readings of women reciters are quite popular (such as Indonesia); in some other parts of the Muslim world, there are reservations expressed about whether men should be allowed to listen to the voices of women reciting out of concern that they might find themselves too easily distracted from Allāh's speech in the Qur'ān. Ritual law about the Qur'ān treats the question disputed in tradition about whether one must be in a state of ritual purity in order to touch a *muṣḥaf* (written text) of the Qur'ān.

Most of the requirements found in the law regarding recitation (*fiqh*) relate to recitation for canonical prayer (*ṣalāt*), one of the "five pillars" of Islam and thus a practice clearly assessed as being "required" (*farḍ*, *wājib*) by all practicing Muslims. These are the five daily prayers, required for male and female Muslims who are not otherwise excused from prayer for reasons such as menstruation (these missed prayers are not required to be made up), travel (for which the missed prayer should later be made up), or incapacity. Prayers are also performed in connection to funerals and eclipses, and it is also obligatory to observe the communal prayers that fall on the mornings of the two annual festivals known as "'Īd." Muslims should observe the noon prayer on Friday in a communal setting, *jamā'ah*. Each and every one of these acts of *salāt* requires more than one recitation of the first *sūrah*, the Fātiḥah (see Figure 1, p. 69 and Figure 5, p. 194).

Each prayer also requires that some other excerpt of the Qur'ān besides the Fātiḥah be recited, although it is left to the discretion of the worshiper what that reading is to be, if one is not following the audible recitation of a prayer leader (*imām*). For prayers that are said aloud (*fajr* in the morning and the first part of *maghrib* and *ishā'* prayers in the evening), the worshiper will follow the reading of the *imām* or prayer leader, if there is one. For silent prayers (*ẓuhr* and '*asr* in the afternoon and also the latter parts of evening prayers) and for prayer that is conducted alone, the worshiper will determine what material to recite. Often worshipers select short *sūrah*s from *Juz' 'Ammā*, such as one of the three *sūrah*s that conclude the book of the Qur'ān, which includes 112 Al-Ikhlāṣ (see Figure 6, p. 196), or well-known verses such as *āyat al-kursī* (2 Al-Baqarah 255 [Figure 4, p. 194]) or *āyat al-nūr* (24 Al-Nūr 35). *Ḥadīth* material contains detailed information on what *sūrah*s the Prophet Muḥammad himself was said to have recited during certain prayers; this material functions as prescription since the action is assessed with the status of being the recommended "*sunnah*" of the Prophet's model.

Each of the five canonical prayers is made up of units of action called *rak'ah* (pl. *rak'āt*). A required prayer might have two *rak'āt* (*fajr*), or three (*maghrib*), or four *rak'ah*s (*ẓuhr*, *'asr*, *ishā'*). Prayer begins with the statement of intention, naming the prayer; the supplicant must face the *qiblah* (direction of the shortest route over land or water to the Ka'bah in Mecca [Figure 2, p. 192]), be in a state of purity (usually requiring *wuḍū'*), and be dressed in clothes that cover the body appropriately (men may expose heads, chest, arms and calves, although they tend also to cover up parts of the body, such as by donning a cap to pray after *wuḍū'* is complete; women may expose face, hands and feet). Each *rak'ah* begins with standing, reciting "*Allāhu ākbar*," and then reciting the Fātiḥah, the opening *sūrah* of the Qur'ān. This would be followed by some recitation of the Qur'ān. The *rak'ah* includes bowing once (*rukū'*) and two prostrations (*sajdah*). Two *rak'ah*s are coupled together in practice with a transitional formula, whose wording in practice varies, but does include the *shahādah* and greetings and praise on the Prophet Muḥammad. As with many of the "five pillars" of Islam, the Qur'ān does not supply complete instructions for prayer; it states only that it is necessary. Some perform extra *rak'āt* of that it is known that the Prophet conducted. Some also perform a prayer at bedtime called *witr*, with an unspecified number of *rak'āt* (usually said to be three), and there are other occasions for performing additional recommended *ṣalāt*, many of which are said to be "*sunnah*" to perform, including extra *rak'āt* that may be added at times of canonical worship.

In every act of *ṣalāt*, the Fātiḥah is recited with each *rak'ah*; the prayer is not considered complete without this. The *sūrah* is thus actually rehearsed in worship, by practicing Muslims, at least seventeen times every day, the figure which is the sum of the minimum number of required *rak'āt* daily. The Fātiḥah reads as follows (note that the Basmalah is actually the first *āyah* of this *sūrah*):

Sūrat Al-Fātiḥah

1.	In the Name of Allāh, the Compassionate, the Merciful	*Bismillāhi Al-Raḥmān Al-Raḥīm*
2.	Praise be to Allāh, the Lord of the Worlds,	*Al-ḥamdu lillāhi rabbi al-'ālamīn*
3.	The Compassionate, the Merciful,	*Al-raḥmān al-raḥīm*
4.	Master of the day of Judgment,	*Māliki yawmi al-dīn*
5.	Only You do we worship, and only You do we implore for help.	*Iyyāka na'budu wa iyyāka nasta'īn*
6.	Lead us to the right path,	*Ihdinā al-ṣirāta al-mustaqīm*
7.	The path of those You have favored	*Ṣirāṭa alladhīna an'amta 'alaihim,*
	Not those who have incurred Your wrath or have gone astray	*ghairi al-maghḍūbi 'alaihim wa lā al-ḍāllīn*

There is here a shift in deictic category to direct address in verse 5, heightening Al-Fātiḥah's supplicatory tone. A study of the Fātiḥah by Mahmoud Ayyoub emphasizes its nature as an essential Islamic prayer.[30] There are many types of prayers that Muslims perform, including supplicatory prayers called *du'ā'*. Muslims may also perform *rak'āt* at any time they wish, such as to thank and praise God or to ask for guidance in a personal matter.

Across a spectrum of ritualized observances, ranging from what are potentially questionable pious practices from a legal standpoint to the required acts of worship, the Qur'ān occupies the bodies of believers. This comes from an engagement that is not primarily in terms of the meanings of the Qur'ān, but rather through its direct effect on human experience in ritual. Repetition of these Qur'ānic actions, such as recitation and prayer, deepens the presence of the Qur'ān in believers' hearts, minds, and physical bodies.

QUR'ĀNIC AESTHETICS: CULTIVATING AND DISCIPLINING EXPRESSION

In Qur'ānic aesthetic practices that are cultivated to the expert level, such as calligraphy and recitation, religious Muslims develop disciplined expression to achieve compatible ideals of art and ethics, both linked experientially to revelation. Traditions of Qur'ānic arts like these cast the practitioner's own understanding and practical ability with respect to the unparalleled power and beauty of the Qur'ān. In the theorization of aesthetic "ideals" (such as what Kristina Nelson has called the performance of the Qur'ān's "ideal recitation"),[31] the human agent or his or her artistry will usually be said to be erased under the Qur'ān's own expressive force. The word of God, ideally, is to be conveyed aesthetically through a transparent mode such as speech or writing. The practitioner, such as the reciter or calligrapher, mediates this expression through maximal expressive or emotional receptivity in terms of moralized and affective states. For this task, Qur'ānic arts like calligraphy and recitation develop regimes of discipline that follow and meticulously render the Qur'ān "letter by letter." In practical expression, the artist does not aspire merely to technical virtuosity, but rather to render the actual presence of the Qur'ān through a balance of experiences of formalism and inspiration.

In Qur'ānic calligraphy, the religious practitioner cultivates the capacity to render the word of God as an artifact of visual culture. In addition to what can be highly elaborate artistic expression such as that found in illuminated manuscripts (Figure 5, p. 194), Qur'ānic inscriptions have been rendered exquisitely in materials ranging from stone, wood, animal skin, and metal to tile and ceramics since the earliest period of Islam. Calligraphy was in fact central to Muslim religious material culture and monumental architecture since the Umayyad period in the first centuries of Islam. A well-known example from the early era is the Dome of the Rock in Jerusalem (completed in 691), said in tradition to have been the destination of the "night journey" of the Prophet Muḥammad and the site from which he made his heavenly "ascent." Another famous example of exquisite Qur'ānic inscription on a building is the tomb from the Mughal era in Agra, India, the Taj Mahal.

In esoteric Qur'ānic visual piety, the forms of the letters of the Arabic alphabet themselves become infused with meaning, and this often occurs through homology with the forms of the human body. For example, the initial "standing *ālif*" (the first letter of the alphabet), the vowel that produces the open "ā" sound that begins the Name of God, Allāh, as well as the name of the first human and prophet, Ādam, was imagined in esoteric traditions to correspond to the standing human figure. Other Arabic letters were also rendered as bodies, especially in terms of positions of prayer, such as the restive letter *dāl* performing the kneeling *jalsah* posture between prostrations. Further extending the esoteric systems of "*ḥurūfī*" (letter) piety were numerical letter equivalents that were reckoned for Arabic words and even entire chapters of the Qur'ān. These equivalences were used in producing efficacious and talismanic diagrams.

Naturally, the Qur'ān is expressed visually in arts that are both "high" and "low." Many factors come to bear on pious aesthetics besides the refinement of "high art," however.[32] From a religious perspective, an example of some of the most prestigious Qur'ānic calligraphy in the Muslim world could be said to be the *kiswāt*, black cloths that drape over the Ka'bah in Mecca (Figure 2, p. 192). The Ka'bah is the orientation of canonical worship (*ṣalāt*), and it is the focus of the practices of Ḥajj and '*umrah* (lesser) pilgrimages in Mecca. These coverings are restitched each year in threads of brilliant gold by embroiderers in Saudi Arabia. Some pilgrims are lucky to get a glimpse of this practice, or even a bit of thread to take home as a souvenier (Figure 3, p. 192).

The piety displayed on and at the House of God ("*Bait Allāh*" is a name for the Ka'bah) is replicated as a presence in the homes of ordinary believers worldwide, particularly as images representing the Ka'bah itself or as renderings of verses of the Qur'ān on cloth and other materials. Qur'ānic wall-hangings often depict the Names of God, or popular verses like those of the Fātiḥah and the "verse of the throne," *āyat al-kursī* (2 Al-Baqarah 255, quoted and discussed in Chapter 3). One reason for the visual popularity of the throne verse is said to be its expression of the ever-wakeful and protective presence of God. Some calligraphic renderings place verses, *sūrah*s, or the entire Qur'ān in the shapes of objects like boats, crescent moons, mosques, or even animals like birds and horses.

Two examples of *āyat al-kursī* rendered in cloth from Indonesia suggest a range of styles within formal parameters, also indicating how local materials shape the hand-rendered yet still mass-produced arts of Qur'ān decorations. One example on a bright pink

Figure 2 The Ka'bah in Mecca. Photo by S. M. Amin/Saudi Aramco World/SAWDIA. Used with permission.

Figure 3 Embroidering the *Kiswah* for the Ka'bah in Mecca. Photo by S. M. Amin/Saudi Aramco World/SAWDIA. Used with permission.

cloth measures about one meter by one and a half meters. The letters are stitched in a gold lamé thread with borders that are reminiscent of Indonesian double-weaving (*ikat*) patterns. Another example is a smaller, mass-produced object: a rolled scroll of velveteen with shiny plastic ends colored gold. The calligrapher worked in the primary medium of a squeeze bottle of desk glue, dusting the letters with gold glitter as it dried (Figure 4, p. 194). In Indonesia, the indigenous rendition of illumination has been the focus of major projects in the past decade, such as with the enormous *muṣḥaf* from Wonosobo, central Java, and the "Mushaf Istiqlal" project in the 1990s that was designed as a "national Qur'ān," decorated with floral motives from across Indonesia.[33]

In high arts of calligraphy, ideally the calligrapher approaches the Qur'ānic word while maintaining a balance of inner states that may achieve the appropriate combination of spontaneity and discipline in outward form. Illustrating these ideas is a manuscript by an Iranian calligrapher of the seventeenth century, Bābā Shāh Iṣfahānī, presented and discussed by the scholar Carl Ernst. The work, *Ādāb al-mashq*, treats the progressive stages, internal and external, for mastery of a calligrapher's art. Ernst writes the work is "an unusually complete presentation of the aesthetic and religious basis of Islamic calligraphy," representing "a visionary method of concentration strongly influenced by Sufism."[34] The author was an expert in the *nasta'līq* style of calligraphy, which is highly developed in Persianate contexts (Figure 1, p. 69, is a rendering in a style like this). He himself was also likely a practitioner of Sufism, and, Ernst surmises, possibly associated with a school known for mystical letter-symbolism and related theories and practices of piety.

According to the text by Bābā Shāh Isfahānī, which Ernst describes as being "practical," moral and spiritual cultivation allow the practitioner to carry out his work with perfection. Ernst translates and quotes the original source, "Because blamable qualities in the soul are the sign of imbalance, God forbid that work proceed from an imbalanced soul, for there will be no balance in it."[35]Attributes like "purity" lead to mastery of the calligraphic arts. However, just as in Qur'ānic recitation at the most advanced level, "imagination" (here called *mashq-i-khayālī*) and improvisation are integral to the art of expression (as opposed to what Bābā Shāh Isfahānī calls formal "pen-practice"). Ernst translates the following passage from Bābā Shāh Isfahānī's treatise that explains the contrast:

Figure 4 "Ayat Al-Kursi" (37.5 × 24.5 cm, 1996, glitter and glue on velveteen), Java, Indonesia. Photographic image design by Michael Kodysz. Photo by author.

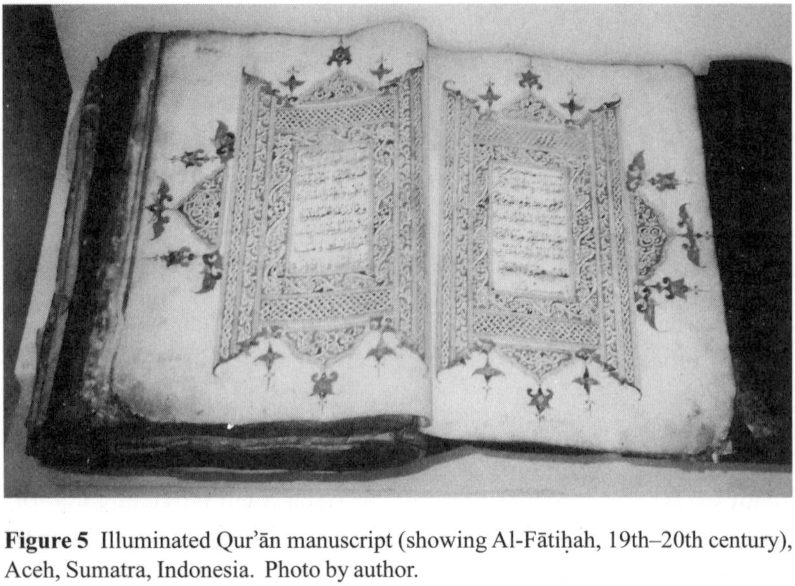

Figure 5 Illuminated Qur'ān manuscript (showing Al-Fātiḥah, 19th–20th century), Aceh, Sumatra, Indonesia. Photo by author.

> "Imaginative practice" is when the scribe writes not according to a model but with reference to the power of his own nature, and he writes every composition that appears [to him]. The benefit of this practice is that it makes the scribe a master of spontaneity (*taṣarruf*), and when this practice mostly takes the place of pen practice, one's writing becomes non-reflective (*bi-maghz*). If someone makes a habit of pen practice and avoids imaginative practice, he lacks spontaneity, and is like the reader who grasps the writing of others but himself cannot write. Spontaneity is not permitted in pen practice.[36]

The calligrapher's ideal technical development here progresses from a formal, disciplined base to the freer exercise of imaginative and improvised choice. The process moves from mastery of formal features of the art to an improvisational "imagination." As similarly described in classical treatises on the art of vocal recitation, such a non-reflective state may achieve a sort of erasure of the "reflective" self in the Qur'ānic art.

The artistic career of influential modern Muslim painter A.D. Pirous, from Aceh in Sumatra, Indonesia (the home of Hamzah Fansuri centuries ago), has followed a calligraphic development that was shaped by themes of moral aesthetics, and which also complements the progression described above by Bābā Shāh.[37] In his "Conversations with Pirous," Kenneth George invited Pirous to reflect on his development as an artist; George has translated and presented their Indonesian-language discussion in the book *Picturing Islam*. In an early period (the 1970s), the painter experimented with calligraphic forms in the context of modernist abstraction. Pirous says that during that time he avoided intelligibility in order better to express the figurative shapes of Arabic letters. He comments that he felt with this he had more "freedom," and also felt a sense of "satisfaction in the dynamic of the lines themselves." He explains to George that he was trying to build an "atmosphere" for the "unexpressed word," imagining this to be something like the same "atmosphere" in which the process of revelation itself occurred.[38]

Once his works began to be viewed publicly, however, Pirous explains that he underwent a religious and artistic transformation. Comments he said he heard from his audience led him to consider the "message" of his work. In order to maintain expressive potential in his painting, he says that at first he still resisted forms that could be recognizably read, here mentioning the example of writing *sūrah* 112 Al-Ikhlāṣ specifically. Then, he adds, "Suddenly I woke up."

Pirous explains to George his aesthetic and moral determination to combine what he calls, in English words, "aesthetic" and "ethical" sensibilities:

> And so I decided to be useful. This is the concept of "*khairuqum anfa'aqum linnas*" [the original phrase is in Arabic] – a person useful to others ... I planted in the paintings concepts and philosophical values that would make them more enjoyable.[39]

Pirous's painting of 112 Al-Ikhlāṣ from the year 1989 (Figure 6, below) highlights the "meaning" of the *sūrah* in its clear intelligibility,[40] and its formal creativity plays with the very sociality of this expression.

Pirous's rendition of 112 Al-Ikhlāṣ makes a visual allusion to the social life of the *sūrah*, the theme he himself brings up in his discussion with George, above. The Arabic calligraphy appears against

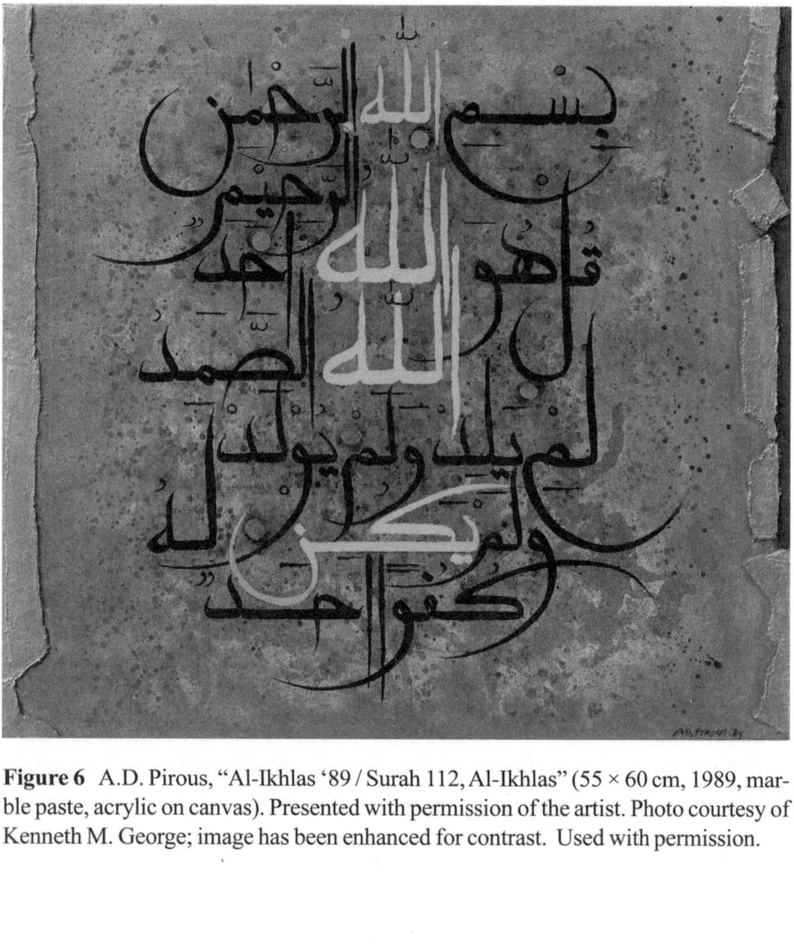

Figure 6 A.D. Pirous, "Al-Ikhlas '89 / Surah 112, Al-Ikhlas" (55 × 60 cm, 1989, marble paste, acrylic on canvas). Presented with permission of the artist. Photo courtesy of Kenneth M. George; image has been enhanced for contrast. Used with permission.

a rich golden background and on a surface with uneven edges, reminding the viewer of the "*kitab kuning*" ("yellowed books") read in dictation for traditional study in the Malay-speaking world (see Figure 5, p. 194, for an example of a *muṣḥaf* that originated from Aceh). The colors of the painting render a sharp contrast between this background, the appearance of the black ink, and then the brilliant red color of the Name, "Allāh," that is repeated in the *sūrah* and arranged vertically down the canvas. Handwritten religious texts that are traditionally recited publicly in Muslim Southeast Asia, such as those in the "Mawlid" cycle, will offset the Name in red (not the usual black) ink in just this way. Pirous has referenced this participation in the social reading and transmission of the *sūrah*. In addition, Pirous applies his spatial insights about letters and words to create a visual emphasis on semantic meaning in the painting. In the formal composition, he has arranged the repeated Name, Allāh, vertically. The word "*yakun*" is aligned under this, also in the same dark red color as the Names that appear stacked above it. Besides emphasizing God's unique existence (the word is a form of the verb "to be"), this rendering also invites reflection on the same word as it appears elsewhere in the Qur'ānic text. For those who know the Arabic Qur'ān, one would expect the word highlighted in the context of divinity (with the visual emphasis on the word "Allāh") to trigger association with the expression of God's omnipotence as Creator in the phrase "'*kun*' *fa yakun*" ("[He only needs to state] 'Be,' and it is.").

In his conversation with George, Pirous has described a long-term process that balances a progression outlined by Bābā Shah (and, below, also Al-Ghazālī almost a millennium ago). Form and meaning, beauty and response, and the tension of moral transformation and spontaneous expression are long-standing themes in the theory of expert performance across Qur'ānic arts. These moral aesthetics expand on the Qur'ān's own internal theory of its own effect, such as making its listeners ponder and reflect, weep and recognize the "truth," and as a result affirm with sincerity a place in creation and the desire to help others and to do good works.

The aesthetics of artistry in the practice of Qur'ānic recitational arts (*tilāwah*) is theorized in similar terms by scholars such as Al-Ghazālī. Recitation according to the rules of *tajwīd* is part of early religious schooling, although, as expert readers (*qārī*'s) can often be heard to say, real mastery of proper vocalization is a lifetime achievement. Experts who perform for others develop heightened technical artistry which, within the bounds of proper *tajwīd*, includes spontaneously improvised melodic forms. These melodic and aesthetic qualities are not covered by the formal guidelines of either *tajwīd* or *qirā'āt* (Chapter 3). In fact, according to Qur'ānic norms, the "melodic" aspects of Qur'ān recitation may not be fixed in any one performance or in an overall system. This is in order that God's speech in the form of the revealed Qur'ān will not be associated with human technical artistry. Scholars, however, wrote a great deal about what Kristina Nelson calls the "ideal performance" of the Qur'ān reciter (*qārī'*) who recites in a slow, ornamented style known in the Arabic-speaking world as *mujawwad*.

It is actually not known what melodic structures were used in the recitation of the Qur'ān in the earliest period. Sources show that expert styles of melodic recitation developed systematically in the 'Abbasid period. The question of "recitation with melody" (*qirā'ah bi'l-alḥān*) appears in the literature at this time, indicating that reciters were using the developing system of musical modes (*maqām*, *maqāmāt*) of Arab art music. Today, recitation in the *mujawwad* style relies on melodic structures that are heard in Arab art music. Recorded performances of the recited Qur'ān reading in the style called *mujawwwad* have been increasingly accessible in recent decades due to broadcast and recording technologies and other trends. The development of the "first recorded version" of the recited Qur'ān in Egypt in the 1970s is documented by Labīb Al-Sa'īd. In her book *The Art of Reciting the Qur'ān* Kristina Nelson examines the practices of Egyptian reciters, the same figures who have become influential the world over because of the dissemination of their recordings through broadcast and cassettes, and now electronic media. The singing of the great women vocalists from the Arab world, such as Fairouz, Warda, and above all Umm Kulthūm (as well as men such as 'Abd Al-Wahhāb), has influenced the improvisational styles of these performers. Across the Muslim-majority and Muslim-minority worlds of Islam in the latter twentieth century, the recitation recordings of a few such reciters (many of whom trained in classical Arabic music) have been the most influential models for aspiring reciters.

With recitational arts, questions that lie at the intersection of theology and technique arise naturally. The doctrine of the "created Qur'ān" about which the *miḥnah* focused, for example, came about at least in part due to the theorization of the status of a speech act that repeats God's words. In classical Islamic tradition, normative questions relating to musical practice, its application, and acceptability, have been tied to the issue of *samā'* or "spiritual audition." Such debates usually have centered on the intents and contexts of practice, and cover not just Qur'ānic arts, but, more widely, the appreciation of poetry (like that of Rūmī) accompanied by high art music. For Qur'ān recitation, the most authoritative sources on what Kristina Nelson has termed the "*samā'* polemic" highlight a tension between the cultivation of experiential perceptions related to "listening" (*samā'*) on the one hand and the ideal of the absolute separation of transcendent revelation from human components on the other.[41] Al-Ghazālī discusses the controversial question of *samā'* at length in his treatise on the practice of reciting the Qur'ān (the eighth book of the *Iḥyā' 'Ulūm Al-Dīn*). In the case of Qur'ān recitation, a key issue in classical religious literature has been the problem of the reciter's technical artistry potentially being confused with the divine power of the Qur'ān.

Al-Ghazālī theorized the intersection of the reciter's real and idealized experience using notions about religious piety, aesthetics, and performance that were common among learned Muslims by the latter twelfth century. As Martin Wittingham shows, with Al-Ghazālī's work across many fields of the religious sciences, an exterior analysis typically runs alongside an interpretive internal discourse. This is especially the case in his discussions of many forms of practical piety, including recitation. Al-Ghazālī's "rules" for recitation in the eighth book of his *Ihyā' 'Ulum Al-Dīn* describe both an "external" and an "internal" dimension to the act of voicing God's speech. His scheme is a stepwise path, like the process outlined by Bābā Shāh for calligraphic arts, and here the intents, consciousness, and sensibilities of the reciter are subordinated to the divine presence of the word of God through purposive effort. In other words, while maintaining "external" disciplined form, the advanced reciter is supposed to follow an "internal" process that will diminish the aspects of performance that are not pure amplifications of the manifestation of an idealized presence.

Al-Ghazālī's treatise on recitation, the two sets of "tasks" incumbent upon the reciter (the "External Rules of Recitation" and the "Mental Tasks of Recitation"), prescribe parallel dimensions of affective and technical activity. Al-Ghazālī juxtaposes the categories of formal, technical rules on the one hand and cultivated experience expression on the other. Treatises on Qur'ān recitation often delineate similar lists of "tasks," many also with apparent Sufi influence. Al-Ghazālī's ten "external rules" discuss: being in the state of ritual purity; the amount of reading to be completed; the proper vocalization of the Arabic text; to weep (especially when reciting the Qur'ān's threats and warnings); to perform prostrations as required; to read aloud but without bothering other people; and trying to read beautifully and with control.[42] At the end of Al-Ghazālī's "external" system, objective and quantitative instructions have begun to elide into subjective and qualitative instructions with the requirement of "beauty."

After the "external tasks" of recitation, Ghazālī's *Iḥyā' 'Ulūm Al-Dīn* turns to the ten "mental tasks" incumbent upon the reciter.[43] They are as follows:

1. The reciter should "magnify the divine speech" (in order to do this, the reciter considers the attributes of God).
2. Once the reciter has magnified the divine speech, he or she amplifies the speech within himself or herself (called the "magnification of the speaker"); this prepares him or her to impart the speech of God to listeners.
3. The reciter releases the "inner utterances of the soul"; for this, the reciter pays attention to the text and follows the Qur'ān closely, recognizing that each individual letter is an affective landscape to be explored.
4. The reciter should ponder the recited verse, listen to it (*samā'*), and read it aloud.
5. The fifth mental task is understanding.
6. The sixth mental task is to remove all obstacles to achieving this understanding; here, Ghazālī warns the reciter of the four "veils" of obstruction that satan uses to lead the reciter astray: mispronunciation, dogmatic convictions, pride, and unreflective reliance on *tafsīr* (exegesis).
7. The reciter needs to render the teachings specific by recognizing that the entire Qur'ān is intended for him or her individually.
8. The reciter must be affected emotionally by the meanings of the verses, rather than simply narrate them.
9. The reciter ascends into a state in which the speech of recitation is not from the reciter but from God. Ghazālī explains at this point that there are three grades of recitation: reading at God,

reading such that God hears, and reading such that God's speech is actually present in the words.

10. Last, the tenth mental task is for the reciter to abandon not only his or her outward pride but sincerely to lose more completely all sense of personal agency and power.[44]

These ideas are not abstract, but just like the instruction of Bābā Shāh or description of a religious turning point in the career of A.D. Pirous, they come out of practical contexts. The strategies of affect and performance that Al-Ghazālī describes may be applied as real practical techniques in order to achieve performative and religious ideals. For example, Al-Ghazālī discusses at length the reciters' practical technique of "weeping." He states that while sentimental affectation may at first be false, its "ends are true" as it becomes emotion experienced in the reality of the heart.[45] Consistent with this attitude, reciters can be heard to "choke up" purposively as a common vocal technique when performing in the *mujawwad* style.

Actual Qur'ānic performers strive to balance spontaneous, expert performance with formal discipline, including always to follow the rules of vocalization known as *tajwīd*. For example, melismatic ornamentation, while always improvised, nevertheless must correspond to proper sectioning and syllabic length and measure. In contemporary global systems of recitation in the *mujawwad* style, melodic structure corresponds to the modal system of Arab art music of the past century (with named *maqāmāt* such as *bayati*, *rast*, *sika*, *soba*, *jiharka*, *hijaz*, and *nahawand*). New technologies, like cassettes and CD sound recordings, have allowed the performances of master readers like 'Abd Al-Bāsiṭ 'Abd Al-Ṣamad to become the benchmark for aspiring reciters all over the world. Former regional styles are coming rapidly to conform to international style as a result. In contemporary systems for teaching and learning recitational arts, emotional and ethical cultivation remain closely linked to expressive style, just as they have been in calligraphic art.

Southeast Asians, including Indonesians, are known as some of the most proficient reciters of the Arabic Qur'ān in the world. Coaches at the top level try to develop reciters' technical artistry through a combination of rigor and personal "*variasi*," meaning individual improvisational style. The latter is usually identified through named correspondence with the style of a famous global performer from the Arab world. In learning settings, such as preparation for competition at the national and international levels, teachers instruct students' moral and aesthetic sentiments in order to heighten skill and performance. A key emotion term used by Muslims in this setting, "*rasa*," predates the coming of Islam to southern Asia. The concept, however, reflects global ideals of expressive Qur'ānic arts: one must cultivate an affective, disciplined capacity in order to achieve the improvisatory and expressive possibilities of performance. As evidenced by the classical writings, such ideas have deep roots in pious aesthetic traditions of the embodied Qur'ān.

In an interview conducted with an international champion *qari'* (reciter), H. Hasan Basri of Makassar, Indonesia, the master explained how he trained aspiring top performers by cultivating their *rasa*. The important thing here, he explained, is to balance creativity with discipline. I asked him if it was ever hard to teach the kids who showed natural talent (*bakat*). He said:

> There are some who want to be given more [improvisatory modes to study] right away. They don't even have fix on the first one [musicalised mode, melody type] yet, but then they keep wanting to add on the next and the next. The first one isn't even set yet, but they already want to change to another one. It's all still hazy with them and still they want more ... Yes, it's very hard. It takes a student like this a very long time because it's the *rasa* that must improve. It's his or her own *rasa* that has to be improved.[46]

H. Hasan Basri here emphasized cultivation of capacity (a moral sentiment, *rasa*) over curricular content of any type. Just like the pupils one could imagine were tutored by Bābā Shāh Isfahāni centuries ago, these students also cannot try to move too fast with Qur'ānic expression, but instead they must learn to exert discipline to match capacity with moral aesthetics and formal technique. In each of these cases of Qur'ānic expressive arts, the ultimate goal may be expressive spontaneity that transcends human consciousness as Al-Ghazālī describes. However, as suggested by Pirous's painting, "Al-Ikhlas '89," the power and agency of the Qur'ān works through morally disciplined and socially recognized modes of transmission and repetition. The goal of Qur'ānic expressive arts is a cultivated moral aesthetics that delivers the message of the Qur'ān with affect and effect, and with tangible religious benefit for others as well as the self.

QUR'ĀN AND *DHIKR*

Remembering and repetition are essential to a range of Qur'ānic pious practice, including memorization. Repeated "remembrance" defines many sorts of Muslim religious practices that are all known as *dhikr*. These usually take the form of a modulated and repetitive contemplation of Qur'ānic, prophetic, and divine realities, ideally under the mediation of a guide, for whom the best model ultimately would be the Prophet Muḥammad himself. One common goal of *dhikr* is thus to deepen a Qur'ānic presence and awareness of the prophetic experience of the Prophet Muḥammad who bore the Qur'ān's message. Many such practices are also contested in tradition, along the lines of the "*samā*' polemic," and also on the grounds that they seem to have confused the basic principle of the worship of Allāh alone. Related practices of contemplation and performance range from the accepted act of piety rehearsing the enumerated Names of God, to entertaining public and participatory performances that are highly aestheticized or experiential.

Most often, when Sufis are criticized it is for such practices and not, in fact, their speculative theologies or radical anthropologies of homologized micro- and macrocosms.[47] A "way" (*ṭarīqah*) is the lineage of a particular *shaikh*, and this may be understood in terms of his or her *dhikr*. *Dhikr* may be communal or individual within the context of a Sufi order. In many places, including Egypt and Indonesia, Thursday night is an expected time for a communal *dhikr* observance. The text of the Qur'ān is the basis for utterances during such shared acts of piety, and a *dhikr* above all is an expression intended to internalize the reality revealed in the Qur'ān. One of the names the Qur'ān gives for itself is "*dhikr*," or "reminder," just as its discourse continually reminds listeners to ponder, reflect, and respond to the message. Qur'ānic expressions, such as *ṣubhān Allāh* ("glory to God"), *Allāhu ākbar* ("God is great"), and others, are used as everyday personal *dhikr* and also in group observances.

One kind of practice of *dhikr* closely associated with the text of the Qur'ān is the recitation of the Most Beautiful Names of God (*Al-Asmā' Al-Ḥusnā*). These are listed in Table 2, overleaf. God has many divine characteristics and attributes in the Qur'ān, with more than fifty of these mentioned by name in the text, such as Creator, Benefactor, Helper, Judge, Most High, Clear-Sighted, Generous, Forgiver, Light, and so on. Many of these are mentioned multiple times in the text.

Besides Al-Raḥmān and Al-Raḥīm,[48] the Names meaning "The Exalted," "The Omniscient," "The All-Seeing," and "The Wise" each appear more than fifty times, for example. Such Names that appear in the Qur'ān are the basis for lists of the "Most Beautiful Names" (*al-asmā' al-ḥusnā*) in Muslim traditions. The Qur'ānic proof-text for the practice of reciting these Names is 17 Al-Isrā' 110: "Say: 'Call on Allāh or the Compassionate [*al-raḥmān*]. By whatever name you call [Him], His are the Most Beautiful Names [*al-asmā' al-ḥusnā*].' And pray neither with a loud nor low voice, but follow a middle course." The idea of the "Most Beautiful Names" also appears in the Qur'ān in 7 Al-A'rāf 180: "And to Allāh belong the Most Beautiful Names [*al-asmā' al-ḥusnā*]; so call Him by them and leave those who distort His Names. They shall be punished for what they used to do." And, even more succinctly, the expression also appears in 20 Ṭa Ha 8: "Allāh, there is no God but He. His are the Most Beautiful Names."

Table 2 Ninety-nine "Most Beautiful Names" of God (*Al-Asmā' Al-Ḥusnā*)

1. Al-Raḥmān, "The Beneficent"
2. Al-Raḥīm, "The Merciful"
3. Al-Malik, "The King"
4. Al-Quddūs, "The Holy"
5. Al-Salām, "Peace-Giver"
6. Al-Mu'min, "Faith-Giver"
7. Al-Muhaymin, "The Guardian"
8. Al-'Aziz, "The All-Mighty"
9. Al-Jabbār, "The Compeller"
10. Al-Mutakabbir, "The Tremendous"
11. Al-Khāliq, "The Creator"
12. Al-Bāri', "The Maker of Order"
13. Al-Muṣawwir, "The Fashioner of Forms"
14. Al-Ghaffār, "The Forgiving"
15. Al-Qahhār, "The Subduer"
16. Al-Wahhāb, "The Bestower"
17. Ar-Razzāq, "The Providing"
18. Al-Fattāḥ, "The Opener," "The Giver of Victory"
19. Al-'Alīm, "The All-Knowing," "The Omniscient"
20. Al-Qābiḍ, "The Restrainer"
21. Al-Bāsiṭ, "The Expander"
22. Al-Khāfiḍ, "The Abaser"
23. Ar-Rāfi', "The Exalter"
24. Al-Mu'izz, "The Giver of Honor"
25. Al-Mudhill, "The Humiliator"
26. Al-Samī', "The Hearing"
27. Al-Baṣīr, "The Seeing"
28. Al-Ḥakam, "The Judge"
29. Al-'Adl, "The Just"
30. Al-Laṭīf, "The Kind"
31. Al-Khabīr, "The Aware"
32. Al-Ḥalīm, "The Forbearing"
33. Al-'Aẓīm, "The Magnificent"
34. Al-Ghafūr, "The Forgiving"
35. Al-Shakūr, "The Grateful"
36. Al-'Alī, "The Highest"
37. Al-Kabīr, "The Great"
38. Al-Ḥafīẓ, "The Preserver"
39. Al-Muqīt, "The Nourisher"
40. Al-Ḥasīb, "The Reckoner"
41. Al-Jalīl, "The Majestic"

42. Al-Karīm, "The Generous"
43. Al-Raqīb, "The Watchful"
44. Al-Mujīb, "The Answerer"
45. Al-Wāsi', "The Vast"
46. Al-Ḥakīm, "The Wise"
47. Al-Wadūd, "The Loving"
48. Al-Majīd, "The Glorious"
49. Al-Bā'ith, "The Resurrector"
50. Al-Shahīd, "The Witness"
51. Al-Ḥaqq, "The Truth," "The Real"
52. Al-Wakīl, "The Trustee"
53. Al-Qawi, "The Strong"
54. Al-Matin, "The Steadfast"
55. Al-Walī, "The Protector"
56. Al-Ḥamīd, "The Praiseworthy"
57. Al-Muḥṣi, "The Accounter"
58. Al-Mubdī, "The Initiator"
59. Al-Mu'īd, "The Reinstater"
60. Al-Muḥyī, "The Giver of Life"
61. Al-Mumīt, "The Bringer of Death"
62. Al-Ḥayy, "The Living"
63. Al-Qayyūm, "The Self Subsisting"
64. Al-Wājid, "The Perceiver"
65. Al-Mājid, "The Illustrious"
66. Al-Wāḥid, "The One," "The Manifestation of Unity"
67. Al-Aḥad, "The One," "The Indivisible"
68. Al-Ṣamad, "The Everlasting"
69. Al-Qādir, "The Powerful"
70. Al-Muqtadir, "The Dominant"
71. Al-Muqaddim, "The Expediter"
72. Al-Mu'akhkhir, "The Delayer"
73. Al-Awwal, "The First"
74. Al-Akhir, "The Last"
75. Al-Ẓāhir, "The Manifest"
76. Al-Bāṭin, "The Hidden"
77. Al-Wāli, "The Patron"
78. Al-Muta'ālī, "The Exalted"
79. Al-Barr, "The Most Kind and Righteous"
80. At-Tawwāb, "The Ever-Returning"
81. Al-Muntaqim, "The Avenger"
82. Al-'Afuw, "The Pardoner"
83. Al-Ra'ūf, "The Compassionate"
84. Mālik-Al-Mulk, "The Owner of All Sovereignty"
85. Dhū Al-Jalāli wa'l-Ikrām, "The Lord of Majesty and Generosity"
86. Al-Muqsiṭ, "The Equitable"
87. Al-Jāmi', "The Unifier"
88. Al-Ghanī, "The Rich," "The Independent"
89. Al-Mughnī, "The Enricher"
90. Al-Māni', "The Defender"
91. Al-Ḍarr, "The Distressor"
92. Al-Nāfi', "The Propitious"
93. Al-Nūr, "The Light"
94. Al-Hādī, "The Guide"
95. Al-Badī', "The Incomparable"
96. Al-Bāqī, "The Abiding"
97. Al-Wārith, "The Inheritor of All"
98. Al-Rashīd, "The Guider"
99. Al-Ṣabūr, "The Patient"

The actual terms that comprise the Names may typically be found at the end sections of Qur'ān, often appearing as contrasting pairs. There is a partial list of the Names in the final verses of 59 Al-Ḥashr, 22–24, which in context follows directly after the statement in *āyah* 21 (cited previously) that "Had we sent down this Qur'ān upon a mountain," it would have been broken by the power of the revelation and the "fear of Allāh." Note that here, each *āyah* (22–24) begins with the repeated formula, He is Allāh:

22. He is Allāh; there is no god but He, the Knower [*al-'alīm*] of the unseen and the seen. He is the Benificent [*al-raḥmān*], the Merciful [*al-raḥīm*].
23. He is Allāh. There is no god but He, the King [*al-mālik*], the Holy [*al-quddūs*], the Peace-Giver [*al-salām*], the Faith-Giver [*al-mu'min*], the Guardian [*al-muhaymin*], the All-Mighty [*al-'azīz*], the Compeller [*al-jabbār*], the Tremendous [*al-mutakabbir*]. May Allāh be exalted above what they associate.
24. He is Allāh, the Creator [*al-khāliq*], the Maker of Order [*al-bāri'*], the Fashioner of Forms [*al-muṣawwir*]. His are the Beautiful Names [*al-asmā' al-ḥusnā*]; whatever is in the heavens and on the earth glorifies him. He is the All-Mighty [*al- 'azīz*], the Wise [*al-ḥakīm*]. (59 Al-Ḥashr 22–24)

In tradition, there are said to be ninety-nine names, some of which appear in the Qur'ān. The other Names that complete the list of ninety-nine are derived from Qur'ānic themes.

The number ninety-nine is based on a *ḥadīth*, narrated on the authority of Abū Huraira and which is found in the major collections like Bukhārī's: "To God belong ninety-nine names – one hundred less one, for he, the odd number [i.e. the Unique] likes [to be designated by these enumerated names] one by one – whosoever knows the ninety-nine names will enter Paradise." The "Ninety-Nine Names" or "*asmā' al-ḥusnā*" ("Most Beautiful Names") are elaborated in tradition in practices such as chanting and the enumeration of Names with prayer beads. The Names are commonly recited on beads in a string of thirty-three, as are other formulae praising God (such as "*al-ḥamdu lillāh*," which opens the Fātiḥah, and "*ṣubḥān Allāh*," which opens 17 Al-Isrā'). They are also the basis for common Muslim given names, with prefixes in the form, "'Abd," meaning "servant of," as in "Abdurrahman" ("Servant of Al-Raḥmān"), for example.

The Names have also provided a rich area for theological reflection. In intellectual traditions, the nature of the relationship of divine "essence" to the "attributes" of divinity was a theological question taken up by thinkers such as Al-Ghazālī. Philosophers had asked, are the divine "attributes" of the essence, but not actually the essence themselves? Alternatively, how are the "names" that signify related to that which they signify (i.e. their divine essence)? Are they naturally in a hierarchy, and, if so, of what kind? For those whose goal is the practical internalization of divine perfection, who actively seek to replace their own "attributes" with transcendent ones, such questions entered deeply into structured understandings of esoteric piety, such as with the Sufi tradition.

In his canonical treatise on the ninety-nine Names of God, Al-Ghazālī offers what would have been a mainstream presentation of the Names by the twelfth century, categorized by imagined levels of the depth of their potential interiorization. In his introduction to this work, Al-Ghazālī skillfully shifts theorization away from questions about the nature of God Himself and on to the capacities of the subject who strives to apprehend Him. At the crudest level of understanding, Ghazālī explains, the Names are simply Arabic words, just as they are memorized by rote and discussed by "most scholars" as such. Even theologians, Al-Ghazālī adds, are arguing merely superficial semantics in their conversations about the essence and the attributes that the Names connote.[49] Another type of person, however, would long to understand their subtle meanings and effects, he continues. And, for a third group that is even more spiritually advanced, Al-Ghazālī states that the Names are an access to understanding divinity itself through experiential modes. He writes the following in his treatise on the "Ninety-nine Names," as translated by David B. Burrell and Nazih Daher:

> The third share [of persons] follows upon the effort to acquire whatever is possible of those attributes, to imitate them and be adorned with their good qualities, for in this way a person becomes "lordly" – that is, close to the Lord Most High, and so becomes a companion to the heavenly host of angels, for they are on the carpet of proximity to God. Indeed, whoever aims at a likeness to their qualities will attain something of their closeness to the extent that he or she acquires some of the attributes which bring them [the angels] closer to the Truth most high.[50]

Ghazālī's introductory discussion then moves rapidly from listing and defining initial terms to the pious possibility of recognizing the Qur'ān's own active agency in human experience by acquiring something like the divine attributes represented by the Names. Most of his book is comprised of reflection on each of the Names, considered sequentially.

Lists of the "Ninety-nine Names" are not absolutely fixed in Muslim tradition, and Names do differ across lists. For example, there has been a question of whether the Name "Allāh" is to be included or not. The list of the "Most Beautiful Names" in Table 2, p. 204, is a well-known version. Following a usual ordering, the first thirteen Names (Names 2–14, if the first is understood to be "Allāh") correspond to a list derived from 59 Al-Ḥashr 22–24 (which was cited above). The ordering that follows this is ruled by pairs of correspondences or contrasts. A few examples of such dialectical meanings are: "Al-Qabīd" and "Al-Bāsiṭ" ("Restrainer" and "Expander") as in Names 20 and 21; "Awwal" and "Akhīr" ("First" and "Last") as in Names 73 and 74; and "Ẓāhir" and "Bāṭin" ("Manifest" and "Hidden") as in Names 75 and 76. Related verbal forms and assonances may also form such consecutive pairings.

Another type of practice of *dhikr* venerates the Prophet Muḥammad, such as in the cycle of "Mawlid" performances (mentioned previously in regard to the rendering of Pirous's painting). These are enactments of the Qur'ānic injunction to invoke peace and blessings on the Prophet Muḥammad. The genre, known since the first generations of Islam, has been particularly influential in southern Asia since the nineteenth century, when a number of texts in the cycle also appeared. These recited texts combine biographical material of the Prophet Muḥammad with sections of formulaic praise, along with repeated expressions such as "*Allāhumma ṣallī 'alā Muḥammad*," and "*Yā nabī salāmun 'alaika*," which are also both commonly repeated daily as part of standard supplications during canonical prayer (*ṣalāt*).

An example of a complete performance of a communal *dhikr* associated with a branch of a global Sufi order known especially for its outreach in Muslim and non-Muslim contexts is a Naqshbandi observance. It is selected because it is transcribed in English and available as a musical score under the title *Remembrance of God Liturgy of the Sufi Naqshbandi Masters*. It is presented here (rather than others) because this text with standard musical notation is available to students for study, along with an accompanying sound recording. This single recorded performance demonstrates a typical interaction between leader and group during the *dhikr*, with dynamics modulated by the *shaikh*.[51] The *dhikr* also shows characteristic repetition of Qur'ānic formulae. In the case of this performance, and also typical of communal *dhikr*s more widely, there is an intensifying tempo, such as when the statement "*Allāhu Akbar*" becomes shortened to "*Allāhu*" and then finally pronounced in rapid repetition only as the case ending on the Name of God, "*hu*" (which is also the pronoun "He"). In general, Naqshbandis have been known worldwide for observing more restrained public *dhikr*s, in comparison to their counterparts in other named orders.

The performance as recorded and transcribed begins with the *shahādah*, repeated twenty-five times. There is then a supplication by the leader, followed by the Fātiḥah, which is recited seven times. Next, for ten minutes the participants invoke peace and blessings on the Prophet Muḥammad and his family. Then, the leader calls for the "Chapter of the Expansion" (94 Al-Sharḥ, quoted in Chapter 2), which is repeated seven times. After this, *sūrah* 112 Al-Ikhlāṣ is recited (ten times), followed by the Fātiḥah again (seven times). Then, there are ten more repetitions of the invocation for peace and blessings on Muḥammad and his family.

Next, the dynamics of the enactment accelerate. The Fātiḥah is recited again, but now it functions as a transition; it is not chanted on a variation of a few pitches, but rather it is spoken rapidly. Then, for a hundred times or more, the group repeats, "*Lā illāha illā Allāh*" ("There is no god but God," the first part of the *shahādah*), with slightly increasing tempo (this lasts for about five minutes). A call and response pattern follows after this, in which the leader praises the Prophet as one of the line of prophets, as the intimate friend of God, as the chosen friend of God, as the beloved friend of God, as the intercessor with God, with this praise punctuated by congregational responses that are repetitions three times in Arabic of the phrase "There is no god but God." Another transition follows, marked by chanting the Fātiḥah.

At this point, repetition becomes more abbreviated. About half an hour has passed since the beginning of the *dhikr*. The group now repeats the Name of God one hundred times ("*Allāhu, Allāhu*"), followed by "*Hu, Hu*" (thirty-three times, the number of beads on a standard string), then some more Names of Allāh such as "*Ḥaqq, Ḥaqq*" (The Truth, The Truth), and "*Ḥayy, Ḥayy*" (The Living, The Living), each repeated thirty-three times. Then the group moves into a recitation of the complete, standard list of the Names of God. Finally, as the tempo reaches a crescendo, the leader adds a supplication, accompanied by the congregation calling peace and blessings on the Prophet. At this time, the performance slows and finally ends with the Fātiḥah, supplications, and the word *Amīn*.

DA'WAH

The Naqshbandis are a global Sufi order especially well known for missionization, as well as other activities, including political engagement. Naqshbandis are spread today from Central Asia to Southeast Asia, and have a growing presence in North America and Europe under one lineage. Speaking historically, since about the thirteenth century and until the nineteenth century, Sufi thought and practice was one of the most effective modes of *da'wah*, or the propagation of Islam, worldwide.

Qur'ānic *da'wah* represents a recognition of the intrinsic power of the Qur'ān and its message to persuade and engage. "*Da'wah*" is a Qur'ānic term interpreted and applied in different ways in different global contexts. The Qur'ānic basis for the idea of *da'wah* is usually taken to be 16 Al-Naḥl 125, understood to be a verse that addresses prophets along with ordinary Muslims: "Call [same root as "*da'wah*"] thou to the way of thy Lord with wisdom and good admonition, and dispute with them in the better way." The term means a "call" to deepen one's own, or encourage others', Islamic piety. It has been a crucial concept in the historical propagation of the Islamic religious tradition, and especially within certain historical traditions of the past and the present. There are different views about whether *da'wah* should be considered to be "outreach" to other Muslims, to non-Muslims, or to both. There are also many different forms of *da'wah* in the mainstream. However, just as Qur'ānic *dhikr* deepens pious awareness in the self, it could be said that the goal of Qur'ānic *da'wah* is to enhance piety in everyday religious life across communities.

Global *da'wah*, when undertaken with respect to non-Muslim faith communities, often highlights the text and meanings of the Qur'ān as scripture. For example, Ahmed Deedat, a preacher from South Africa, was known for his polemical engagement in the English language with other faith communities along these lines, such as in one well-known debate held in Louisiana, U.S.A. in the 1990s with American preacher Jimmy Swaggart.[52] In this instance, available on videocassette, Deedat highlighted the "inimitable" nature of the Qur'ān, using the assumptions of Islamic scripture to put forward his argument. Deedat challenged Swaggart's Christian approach to the English-language Bible as the unmediated "word of God," focusing, for example, on discrepancies of translation among popular North American biblical texts, from the King James version to the

Good News Bibles. (Deedat had previously written tracts that took the same approach.) In contrast to initiating formal public debates in the Anglophone tradition, most Muslims see the best *da'wah* to invite others to Islam simply by acting in the model of the Prophet Muḥammad as much as possible in the way of justice, truthfulness, and kindness, in the spirit of disputing "in a better way."

Most global "*da'wah*" is aimed at other Muslims. In some locations, such as the world's most populous Muslim-majority nation, Indonesia, "*dakwah*" (now an Indonesian word) represents a formal academic field as represented in departments of major universities as well as a popular culture industry. Typical Indonesian definitions, for example, deploy categories of "general" and "specific" application. Typically, they divide the concept "*dakwah*" into its "restricted" form (for within Islam) and its "open" form (for all of humanity). *Da'wah*, according to this framework, carries the basic meaning of persuading people to commit to Islamic values and, by extension, to the improvement of all of human existence. In Indonesia, the Qur'ān is recognized to be powerful as both a means and an end of mainstream *da'wah*.

Contemporary Indonesians in the mainstream have emphasized the appreciation of Qur'ānic beauty and enjoyable Qur'ānic activities like memorization, recitation, and calligraphy as a highly effective means to "motivate" ("*memotivasikan*") Muslims to deepen religious piety. In curricula such as that for teaching and learning recitation at all levels, from Qur'ānic kindergartens to major recitation competitions at the national level, aesthetics and performance have been primary modes by which Indonesian Muslims have approached the project of contemporary Qur'ānic *da'wah*. At the forefront of these reinvigorated Indonesian projects of Qur'ānic *da'wah* have thus been what is sometimes called "Arts with an Islamic Flavor" (*Kesenian yang Bernafaskan Islam*). This includes arts like recitation, calligraphy, and manuscript illumination, and other types of performance (Figure 7, p. 212). Across Muslim-majority nations of Southeast Asia (which includes the nations of Brunei, Indonesia, and Malaysia), competitions in the recited Qur'ān and other Qur'ānic arts and activities like memorization have been immensely popular.

Globally, some of the most effective movements of Islamic *da'wah* in the twentieth century have been based on the presumed transformational power of the Qur'ān, especially through embodiment and repetition, and the related possibility for Qur'ānic projects to inspire attention and commitment. Models of religious teaching and

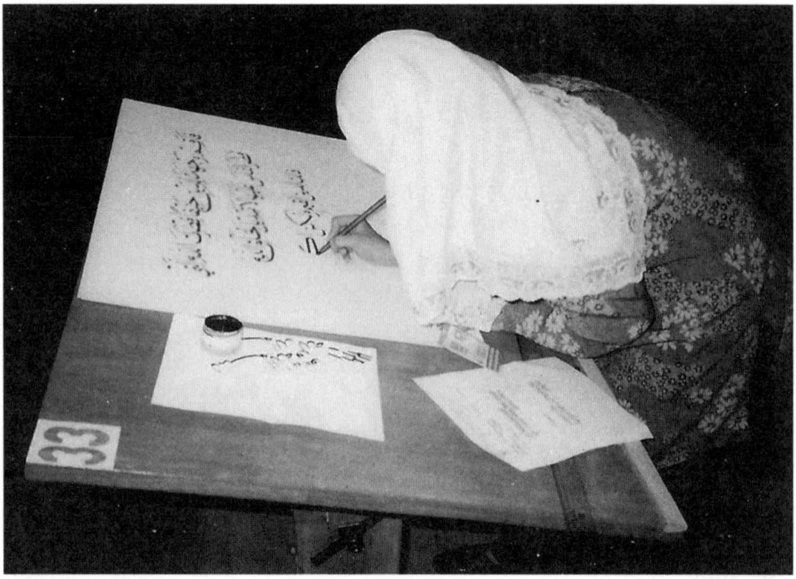

Figure 7 Competition in Calligraphy ("Khatt Al- Qur'ān"), National Competition for the Recitation of the Qur'ān, Sumatra, Indonesia, 1996. Photo by author.

learning that focused on the Qur'ān were the basis, for example, of the voluntary associations first imagined by the schoolteacher Ḥasan Al-Bannā (who established the Muslim Brotherhood in Egypt), and the Deobandi and Jamaati Tablighi communities in South Asia (Pakistan, Bangladesh, India), the latter having spread far more widely. The shared goal of many types of programs of Qur'ānic *da'wah* is not just to be religiously active, or even to acquire a visible symbol of Islamic identity, but instead to attain a positive transformation of the self and society through a lived Qur'ānic presence.

CONCLUSION

Qur'ānic experience, whether through intellectual, moral, embodied, or affective and aesthetic modes, is understood by Muslims to enhance capacity in non-Qur'ānic fields of knowledge, action, and expression. For example, it is said that the great Egyptian singer of the twentieth century, Umm Kulthūm, sang Arabic so beautifully because she had studied Qur'ān recitation (*tajwīd*) as a child.[53] Such influences, real and idealized, affect everyday worlds of sound, sense, thought, and practice in Qur'ānic systems, in a process that mirrors the self-referential structure of the text itself. When experiences of Qur'ānic power feed back into the very systems of Qur'ānic expression that support them, the effect can be a deepening, or what Al-Ghazālī might call an increasingly focused or "subtle," intensity.

Within some Qur'ānic arts, such as the phenomenon of recitational *da'wah* in Indonesia, Muslims have come to expect the Qur'ān to exert this power to captivate attention and to inspire a person, and for him or her then in turn to inspire others to a more engaged and sincere religious practice. For some, such a process may even emerge unexpectedly such as when, pursuing a goal like expression in art, a moral reorientation suddenly takes place by sharing with others a Qur'ānic reality. Such increasingly inspired engagement comes quite naturally to religious, or at least to a Qur'ānic, presence. I myself witnessed it happening first hand, one night during Ramaḍān.

Understanding the text to say that the Qur'ān, preserved on a "tablet," was also revealed in a night, a night in the month of Ramaḍān (see Chapter 1), leads Muslims to seek "*lailat al-qadr*" (as in 97 Al-Qadr) in the last ten days of that holy month (see discussion in Chapter 2 and also in Chapter 3). In some contexts, that night is said to be known, and formal celebrations and performances for "*Nuzūl Al-Qur'ān*" are scheduled long in advance (such as in Muslim Southeast Asia). In other contexts, *lailat al-qadr* is "sought" on odd-numbered nights in the hearts of believing Muslims who observe prayers. This year on the last night of *tarwiḥ* prayers that were held here in Wellington, New Zealand, a preschool child told me excitedly that she could hear the sound of angels. It happened at one moment when she was standing alongside the others in the mosque, listening to the *imām* recite *Juz' 'Ammā*, she said. I asked what the music that angels make sounds like. She said it was soft and tinkly, like a music box.

When she woke up the following morning, the child kept telling her story: a little pink glittery star had somehow appeared on her pillow. She told me that she supposed that the angels had probably just left it behind when they went back up to heaven at the break of dawn. I quoted for her the *ḥadīth*, that angels come to visit a house in which the Qur'ān is recited. She quickly replied yes, she already knew that. And then, she added, she would be sure to recite lots of the Qur'ān during Ramaḍān next year so that the angel would come back down from the stars to meet her again in the mosque *in sha' Allah*.

NOTES

1. On composition and style in the poetry of Rūmī, see Keshavarz, *Reading Mystical Lyric*; Mojaddide gives a survey of poetry in relation to the Qur'ān in his article in the *Blackwell Companion to the Qur'ān*, "Rūmī," pp. 362–372.
2. For discussion, see Riddell, *Islam in Malay-Speaking World*, pp. 101–138.
3. These verses and original English translation are from "Malay Poem No. 13," found on pp. 82–83 of the collection translated and annotated by Drewes and Brakel, *The Poems of Hamzah Fansuri*. "The speech of lovers," which is a gloss that has been added here, is a key expression in Islamic religious mysticism, relating to the lover's desire for unity with the divine beloved.
4. Sells, *Early Islamic Mysticism*.
5. Al-Ghazālī, *Jewels of the Qur'ān*, trans. Abul Quasem, p. 19.
6. The examination made by Kristin Zahra Sands in *Sufi Commentaries on the Qur'ān in Classical Islam* includes discussion of the popular metaphor of the Qur'ān as the "Ocean of all Knowledge" (pp. 7–13) and the importance of reading the Qur'ān with and by the "heart" (pp. 29–34).
7. See J. R. T. M. Peters, *God's Created Speech*, on the thought of the Mu'tazilite scholar 'Abd Al-Jabbār, and also the survey by Madelung, "The Origins of the Controversy Concerning the Creation of the Koran."
8. Al-Jāhiẓ, excerpted in Peters, *A Reader on Classical Islam*, p. 174.
9. See articles by Boullata, "Sayyid Qutb amd Literary Appreciation of the Qur'ān" and "Rhetorical Interpretation of the Qur'ān."
10. Von Denffer, *'Ulūm Al-Qur'ān*, p. 149.
11. For this and other conversion stories related to the Qur'ān, see Navid Kermani, "The Aesthetic Reception of the Qur'ān as Reflected in Early Muslim History."
12. Levtzion, ed., *Conversion to Islam*.
13. Anway, *Daughters of Another Path*, p. 34.
14. Al-Ghazālī, *The Recitation and Interpretation of the Qur'ān*, trans. Abul Quasem, p. 23.
15. Ibid., p. 24.
16. Parts of this section are adapted from Gade, *Perfection Makes Practice*, pp. 60–113.
17. For general discussion from an anthropological perspective, see Eickelman, "The Art of Memory."
18. Al-Nawawī, "The Explanation of the Proper Comportment for Carrying the Qur'ān" [*Al-tibyān fī adab ḥamalat Al-Qur'ān*], excerpted and translated by Rippin and Knappert in *Textual Sources for the Study of Islam*, p. 105. I have changed the translators' "possessor" to "possessing."
19. Abdel Haleem, "Dynamic Style," in *Understanding the Qur'ān* and "Grammatical Shift for Rhetorical Purposes." Treatments of *iltifāt* are to be found especially in the writings of the linguist and exegete Al-Zamakhsharī (b. 1075) and others.
20. Abdel Haleem, "Dynamic Style," p. 184 and pp. 186–188.
21. Ibid., pp. 186–187, translating Al-Zarkashī's *Al-burhān fī wujūh al-bayān*.
22. Zen, *Tata Cara / Problematika Menghafal Al Qur'an*, discussed more fully in Gade, *Perfection Makes Practice*, pp. 103–111.
23. For example, a recent work popularly available is Sa'dulloh, *9 Cara Praktis Menghafal Al- Qur'an* (*Nine Practical Ways to Memorizing the Qur'an*).

24. This is my translation and summary of the material in Chapter 15 of Badwilan, *Panduan Cepat Menghafal Al- Qur'an dan Rahasia-rahasia Keajaibannya* (*Quick Guide to Memorizing the Qur'an and Secrets of its Miracles*), pp. 161–169.
25. For perspectives from the field of religious studies, see Denny, "The *Adab* of Qur'ān Recitation: Text and Context" and Graham, "Those Who Study and Teach the Qur'ān."
26. For example, see the story depicted in Eickelman, *Knowledge and Power in Morocco*.
27. Badwilan, *Panduan Cepat Menghafal Al- Qur'an*. The advice about stereo equipment is given on p. 256.
28. Badwilan, *Seni Menghafal Al-Qur'an: Resep Manjur Menghafal Al- Qur'an yang Telah terbukti Keampuhannya* (*The Art of Memorizing the Qur'an: A Powerful Recipe with Proven Effectiveness*). The account "*Wanita Berusia 70 dan 80 Tahun Tergolong Pelajar Tahfiz yang Paling Rajin*" is on pp. 89–90, and the woman who taught and learned Qur'ān with her children while she was cooking the family's meals appears on pp. 102–103.
29. Dehivi, *Prophetic Medical Sciences*, p. 39. According to Marcia Hermansen, traditions of pious practice in South Asia at time use words and phrases from 36 Yā Sīn, which might explain the reference to the expression "*mukremina*" in this text. However, since the word "*mukramīna*" also appears as the last word of verse 27 in 36 Yā Sīn, it seems more likely in this case that the instruction is to stop reading at that point, pause to ask for the return of the runaway, then continue with the reading of the *sūrah*. Thanks to Arthur Buehler for assistance. The other citations from this source mentioned above are from p. 63 (treating malaria) and p. 29 (weaning a baby/toddler).
30. Ayoub, "The Prayer of Islam"; see also Abdel Haleem, "*Al-Fātiḥah*: The Opening of the Qur'ān," in *Understanding the Qur'ān*, pp. 15–28.
31. Nelson, *Art of Reciting the Qur'ān*.
32. See perspectives on theorizing religious material culture in Christian context in the book by Freedberg, *The Power of Images*.
33. George, "Designs on Indonesia's Muslim Communities."
34. Ernst, "The Spirit of Islamic Calligraphy."
35. Ibid., p. 283.
36. Ibid., p. 284.
37. Pirous has incorporated text from the Malay-language poems of Hamzah Fansuri as well as reference to other classical Sumatran (Indonesian) Muslim writing into a few of his works.
38. George, *Picturing Islam*, forthcoming.
39. Ibid.
40. The meanings of *sūrah* 112 are considered in Chapter 2 in relation to the theme of God's unity, *tawḥīd*; the Arabic is transliterated in Chapter 3. 112 Al-Ikhlās is one usually first taught to children in order to start to pray regularly.
41. Nelson, *Art of Reciting the Qur'ān*, pp. 32–51.
42. These "External Rules" are given in Al-Ghazālī, *The Recitation and Interpretation of the Qur'ān*, trans. Abul Quasem, pp. 34–47.
43. Al-Ghazālī's "Mental Tasks" are given in *The Recitation and Interpretation of the Qur'ān*, trans. Abul Quasem, pp. 56–82.
44. Adapted from Gade, *Perfection Makes Practice*, pp. 138–140, drawing on Al-Ghazālī's work.

45. Nelson, *Art of Reciting*, pp. 89–100.
46. Cited in Gade, *Perfection Makes Practice*, p. 209. In the 1980s, H. Hasan Basri took first place in the world competition that was held in Saudi Arabia.
47. For case studies, see analysis by Sirriyeh, *Sufis and Anti-Sufis*, and articles presented in de Jong and Radtke, eds., *Islamic Mysticism Contested.*
48. "Al-Raḥmān" is a special case of an attribute of God in the Qur'ān, since the Qur'ān states "Call on Allāh or Al-Raḥmān" (see text, above). In the Qur'ān, the name "Al-Rahman" is used more than ten times in the place of the Name of God, "Allāh."
49. Al-Ghazālī, *The Ninety-Nine Beautiful Names of God*, trans. Burrell and Daher, pp. 30–31.
50. Ibid., p. 32. I have changed the wording of the translation by Burrell and Daher slightly in order to be gender inclusive.
51. For discussion, see Buehler, *Sufi Heirs of the Prophet.* Videography of *dhikr* performances that are considered both "high" and "low" in Egypt can be seen on the videorecording by Valerie Hoffman, *Celebrating the Prophet in the Remembrance of God*, or in the written descriptions of *dhikr* by Earl Waugh in *The Munshidin of Egypt*. See also Waugh's more recent study, *Memory, Music and Religion*, for North African perspectives.
52. *Is the Bible God's Word?* (videorecording).
53. Danielson, *A Voice Like Egypt.*

6

SPACE, TIME, AND THE BOUNDARIES OF KNOWLEDGE

The Qur'ān's moralized aesthetics link the presentation of the past (prophecy) and the future (judgment) with the present. Through narratives, for example, the Qur'ān's internal time frames of the past and the future merge to convey a message of accountability, that is, the "promise and the warning" of the inevitable consequences for actions. "Signs" in the present underscore humans' relation to God as Creator, Judge, and Sustainer in dimensions that transcend time itself. The Qur'ān connects themes of time and experience through modes such as stories of the prophets; through its eschatology, descriptions of the final hour and the last things; and through depictions of the natural world. Such themes and content mutually reflect and refract in the Qur'ān's unique presentation, as beginnings and endings continually shift, blend, and overlap.

The Qur'ān's verse 7 Al-A'rāf 172 connects a primordial moment experienced by all generations to the inevitable experience of judgment at the end of this creation. The event that the verse relates to, which escapes any definable time frame, is known in tradition as the "Day of Alast." Is it called the day of "Alast" because the first word of the question that the Creator poses to His creation in the verse "Am I not?" is, in Arabic, "*Alastu.*" It reads:

> And [remember] when your Lord brought forth from the loins of the children of Adam their posterity and made them testify against themselves. [He said:] "Am I not your Lord?" [*Alastu bi rabbikum?*] They said: "Yes, we testify." [This] lest you should say on the day of resurrection: "We were in fact unaware of this." (7 Al-A'rāf 172)

The passage relates knowledge and responsibility on individual as well as collective levels; it also establishes the religious reality of the primordial past with reference to the future, both of which are to be recalled in the ongoing present.

The condition of the "children of Adam" to their Creator is "Islam" ("surrender, peace"); this is a timeless state. The Qur'ān also describes the entirety of creation as having a "*fiṭrah*" (original or inborn nature) which is naturally good, and inherently Muslim. One Qur'ānic verse expressing such a meaning is the following:

> So, set your face toward religion [*li'l-dīni*] uprightly. It is the original nature [*fiṭrata*] according to which Allah fashioned humankind. There is no altering Allah's creation. That is the true religion [*al-dīnu al-qayyimu*]; but most people do not know. (30 Al-Rūm 30)

The last *āyah* of Sūrat Al-Ḥajj also connects the state of being "Muslim" with the religion of the prophet Abraham in the past, as well as the future hour of judgment:

> And strive for Allāh [*wajāhidū fī Allāhi*] as you ought to strive [*ḥaqqa jihādihi*]. He elected you, and did not impose on you any hardship in religion – the faith of your father Abraham. He called you Muslims before and in this [the Qur'ān], that the messenger may bear witness against you and you may be witness against humankind … (22 Al-Ḥajj 78)

This *āyah*, which also ends this *sūrah*, concludes with a prescription for action, stated in terms of obligatory duties: "So, perform the prayer, give the alms and hold fast to Allāh. He is your Master; and what a Blessed Master and a Blessed Supporter [*mawlākum fini'ma al-mawlā wani'ma al-naṣīr*]" (22 Al-Ḥajj 78). This verse is a typical Qur'ānic expression of religious identity and commitment, cast in terms that are temporal yet timeless, and from which a command to a specific righteous action in the present follows directly.

In the Qur'ān's narratives about the past, the present, and especially the time to come, some depictions are challenging for modern students to grasp, regardless of religious background. This is especially the case for representations of hell (*al-nār*). In the context of the degradation of the created world coming with today's growing environmental crisis, however, the soteriological and even eschatological imperative to change attitude and behavior in the present in order to conform to Qur'ānic principles of accountability may reveal another contemporary "face" of the multifaceted Qur'ān for readers in the present.

GOD THE CREATOR IN THE PRESENT

The Qur'ān emphasizes the role of God as Creator and the signs (*āyāt*) of His created world. Fazlur Rahman develops the idea that God's signs are apparent "proofs" of the Maker in his book *Major Themes of the Qur'ān*. "Signs," like other clear proofs (*bayyināt*, *burhān*), are persuasive and convincing, he writes, and the Qur'ān also shows them to be palpable and real. The signs in the created world point to how God's command, "Be," is the basis of ethical order. The Qur'ān refers often to this utterance and cosmogonic event, as well as the external power that Allāh has over His dominion. In contrast to God's "signs," Fazlur Rahman points out, magic and sorcery are never real in their Qur'ānic presentation, even though they may be shown to have some effect in people's minds. The present, past, and future are all dimensions of the "signs" of God the Qur'ān.[1]

The Qur'ān suggests that the structures and signs of the created world also inspire the maintenance of the human moral order. In an article "Some Key Ethical Concepts of the Qur'ān" Fazlur Rahman links closely "faith" (*imān*) and "action" (*islām*), and in Rahman's presentation these are both connected to "*āyāt*," the "signs of God" in His creation.[2] The Qur'ān often references the influence on attitudes and behavior that comes from God's "signs." For example, the Qur'ān links belief and signs in many repeated statements about past communities, to the effect, "This is a sign but people still do not believe."

An example of a listing of "signs" in the Qur'ān, following in the text after a call to "glorify Allāh" in the evening, morning, end of the day, and at "noontide," is 30 Al-Rūm 20–25 (a passage which is also quoted by Rahman in this regard). Every verse in this section begins with the mention of "signs," coming with the repeated formula, "And of His signs":

20. And of His signs [*āyāt*] is that He created you from dust; and behold, you are mortals scattered all round.
21. And of His signs is that He created for you, from yourselves, spouses to settle down with and He established friendship and

mercy between you. There are in all that signs for people who reflect.

22. And of His signs is the creation of the heavens and the earth and the diversity of your tongues and colors. Indeed there are in that signs for people who know.
23. And of His signs is your sleeping by night and day and your seeking some of His bounty. There are in that signs for people who hear.
24. And of His signs is showing you the lightning, to fear and to hope; and He brings down from the sky water with which He revives the earth after it was dead. There are in that signs for people who understand.
25. And of His signs is that the heavens and the earth shall arise at His command. Then, if He summons you once, behold, you shall be brought out of the earth. (30 Al-Rūm 20–25)

Signs of creation, reproduction, and resurrection are typical of Qur'ānic expression, whether considered in this passage or throughout the Qur'ān. This section of text from 30 Al-Rūm stands out in the Qur'ān for mentioning social "signs," such as spouses' partnership and the very fact of human diversity, along with those of the natural world.

Many listings of signs in the natural world explicitly compel "reflection" for "faith" and "understanding," as in the verses whose meaning is quoted above. Characteristic of many of the Qur'ān's verses on the natural world, and also an emphasis apparent in this passage from 30 Al-Rūm above, is the affirmation of the reality of future resurrection of the dead. Such verses remind believers that God creates and re-creates life in the present and the future. Many passages in the Qur'ān link an everyday event ("rain," which "brings life to the dead earth") to creation of a human form, and then this to the inevitable future event of bringing the dead to life at judgment.

The perfection of the natural world, apparent in "signs," points directly to the perfection of its Author, an idea also emphasized by Fazlur Rahman in his discussion of "nature" and signs in *Major Themes of the Qur'ān*. In the Qur'ān, part of the visible expression of this perfection is symmetry. The Qur'ān repeats themes like the balanced divisions and proportions of the created world (such as the heavens and the earth, celestial motion and the divided day, gendered creation). The following verses, 2 Al-Baqarah 163–164, show a typical Qur'ānic collection of celestial and everyday "signs":

> 163. Your God is One God. There is no god but He [*lā illāha illā huwa*], the Compassionate [*al-raḥmān*], the Merciful [*al-raḥīm*]
> 164. In the creation of the heavens and the earth; in the ships which sail in the sea with what profits humans; in the water which Allāh sends down from the sky in order to bring the earth back to life after its death and disperses over it every type of beast; in the continuous changing of winds; and in clouds which are driven between heaven and earth – surely in these are signs for people who understand. (2 Al-Baqarah 163–164)

Many signs, like the sailing ships mentioned in the verses above, have utility. Their qualities of usefulness are shown in the Qur'ān to be another reminder of the nature of God and the necessity to be thankful to Him.

The *sūrah* 16 Al-Naḥl offers an especially strong presentation of these themes, to be surveyed here. This is a late Meccan *sūrah*, said to have been revealed after 18 Al-Kahf and before 71 Nūḥ. The *sūrah* contains many verses on the themes of lying and hypocrisy, demonstrating that the actions of "liars" have no lasting value (and with implicit reference to the historical situation of the Muslim emigrants to Medina). For example, verses 57–59 expose the hypocrisy of the unbelievers in gendered terms. The Qur'ān does this by calling out the nonbelievers for polytheistic worship of female goddesses ("and they ascribe to Allāh daughters"), and then with irony takes note of their desire only to have male sons with words of pointed critique, "… and if the birth of a daughter is announced to any of them, his face turns black, and he is enraged" (verse 58). In the same *sūrah*, the Qur'ān expresses related themes in parables, such those which begin in *āyah* 74 (on God's power and human knowledge) and in 112 (one of the Qur'ān's stories of a "disbelieving town" that was punished). The *sūrah* is one of many in the Qur'ān that expresses the idea that God only needs to say "Be" for a thing to come to existence (verse 40). Finally, 16 Al-Naḥl has several self-referential features that include recitational direction, coming as instruction to take refuge from satan before reading the Qur'ān (verse 98); a verse of "*sajdah*" that requires prostration (verse 49); and there is a key verse on abrogation (verse 101, discussed previously in Chapter 4). Finally, the *sūrah* contains the verse that is commonly cited as the proof-text for the prohibition against Muslims eating pork (verse 110).

The first verses of 16 Al-Naḥl express the themes being considered here, the idea of the created world, its utility, and the proper human response to God's creation. Following an opening verse of praise, there is a first person singular "voice" ascribed to Allāh in verse two. God speaking in the singular is a relatively rare occurrence in the Qur'ān, but here it is consistent with the theme of the verses that follow, of a personalized benefit in Allāh's creation:

> *Bismillāh Al-Raḥmān Al-Raḥīm*
> 1. Allāh's decree will be fulfilled; so do not hasten it. Glory be to Him and may He be exalted above what they associate [with Him]!
> 2. He sends down the angels with the Spirit by His command upon whom He pleases of His servants [saying]: "Warn that there is no god but I; so fear Me."
> 3. He created the heavens and the earth in truth; may He be exalted above what they associate [with Him]!
> 4. He created humanity from a fertilized egg and, behold, he [a human] is a professed disputant. (16 Al-Naḥl 1–4)[3]

The verses that follow these in the *sūrah* list benefits God gives to humankind, with particular emphasis on livestock and domesticated animals. Here the Qur'ān offers to its readers a poetics of abundance in both its content and its structure, as example builds on example:

> 5. And the cattle He created for you. Therein are warmth and other advantages, and from them you eat.
> 6. And in them you witness beauty, when you bring them back [home], and when you drive them out for pasture.
> 7. And they carry your burdens to a distant land which you could only reach with great hardship. Surely your Lord is Clement [*ra'ūf*] and Merciful [*raḥīm*].
> 8. And horses, and mules, and asses [He created] for you to mount, and as an adornment; and He creates what you don't know.
> 9. It belongs to Allāh to show the straight path; some, however, deviate from it. Had Allāh pleased he would have guided you all. (16 Al-Naḥl 5–9)

Livestock here provide "warmth and other advantages" (verse 5). With this, however, the Qur'ān also establishes dimensions to the gift of "cattle" that go well beyond their obvious utility. In verse 6, they are said to be beautiful, and moreover they may be appreciated for their beauty at different times of day. In verse 7, domesticated animals further provide to humans the potential to do what they otherwise could not (reach a "land you could [otherwise] only reach with great hardship"). In other words, they increase human capacity. With this, the Qur'ān also mentions two of God's Names (Al-Ra'ūf and Al-Raḥīm). Following this, in verse 8, there is a suggestion coming in yet another emotional register: looking and feeling good when riding (instead of, presumably, walking on foot), enhancing further the sense of benefit. And, in verse 8, the Qur'ān's exhaustive persuasion about "cattle" surpasses even the limits of human knowledge with "what you do not know." The section concludes in verse 9, an acknowledgement of the power of Allāh in a statement that also affirms God's determination of faith.

The verses that follow in this section of 16 Al-Naḥl provide additional proof of the bounties of God, here pivoting on the idea of "feeding cattle" (verse 10), but now coming to express the familiar Qur'ānic theme of water and its utility. The discourse rapidly moves on to cosmic gifts, offering unexpected details such as an unusual reference coming in verse 13, which conveys the notion that the fullness of the visual spectrum of light and color is a "sign" of God:

> 10. It is He who sends down water from the sky; from it you drink, and through it grow the plants on which you feed your cattle.
> 11. From it He brings forth for you vegetation, olives, palms, vines, and all kinds of fruit. In that, surely, there is a sign for a people who reflect.
> 12. And He has subjected to you the night and the day, the sun and the moon, and the stars are subjected by His command. In that there are signs for a people who understand.
> 13. And what He created for you in the earth is of multifarious colors; in that there is, surely, a sign for people who are mindful.
> 14. And it is He Who subjected the sea, so that you may eat from it tender meat and bring out from it jewelry for you to wear; and you see the ships cruising therein. [He subjected it for you] so that you may also seek His bounty and give thanks. (16 Al-Naḥl 10–14)

This description of God's bounties is characteristic of the Qur'ān's treatment of God's "signs." Rather than concluding the section at this point, however, which the reader might expect from his or her familiarity with Qur'ānic pacing and poetics, instead the Qur'ān continues in this instance to deepen and develop further:

15. And He laid up in the earth firm mountains [*rawāsī*], lest it shake under you; as well as rivers and pathways that, perchance, you may be guided.
16. And He [laid] landmarks; and by the stars they are guided.
17. Now is He who creates like him who does not create? Do you not take heed?
18. Were you to count Allāh's blessings [*ni'mat Allāhi*], you will not exhaust them. Allāh is truly All-Forgiving [*ghafūr*], Merciful [*raḥīm*]. (16 Al-Naḥl 15–18)

The established stability of the world itself (as in the "tent pegs," *rawāsī*, that God placed to anchor the moving tectonic crust of the earth), that is, the very fact that mountains stay fixed at all and do not drift about, is a "sign" and also a mercy of God. The interruption of two sudden, challenging rhetorical questions in verse 17 draw the listener into the exposition and actively mark the end of the section of this material. At the conclusion of the section, the Qur'ān cites two Names of God. The discourse ends with a Qur'ānic reference to its own persuasive strategy and style as demonstrated in the previous verses of the section, namely, that, "Were you to count Allāh's blessings, you will not exhaust them." God's signs and their beneficence are simply beyond any human reckoning.

The Qur'ān recapitulates similar themes later in the same *sūrah*, Sūrat Al-Naḥl, in at least two passages: verses 64 to 70, which includes the unique reference to "the bees" from which the *sūrah* derives its name, "Al-Naḥl" ("The Bees"); and verses 78–81. With its mention of tiny insects like spiders, ants, and "the bees" (each of these is the traditional title of a *sūrah*), the Qur'ān is said by religious Muslims not to leave out any example, whether on the scale of little bugs or on the scope of entire worlds. In 16 Al-Naḥl, bees illustrate a sign of God. After mentioning the book of guidance (i.e. the Qur'ān), water from the skies being a "sign," and also cattle and fruit in verses 68–69, the Qur'ān then states that Allāh commanded the bees to build hives and eat fruit. Verse 69 states: "From their bellies comes out a syrup of different hues, wherein is a healing for humans [i.e. honey]. Surely, in that there is a sign for a people who reflect." Further reflection on the power of Allāh over life and over death follows directly from this:

> Allah created you, then He will cause you to die. For some of you will be brought back to the worst age, so that they will no longer know

> anything, even after having acquired knowledge. Surely Allāh is All-Knowing [*'alīm*], All-Powerful [*qadīr*]. (16 Al-Naḥl 70)

Here, consideration of the human process of aging, memory, and forgetting shows God's power over the very faculty of knowing. Immediately after this, there follow parables that illustrate this theme, now presented in terms of differing human capacities: in particular, the Qur'ān compares the status of a slave to a free person; and it compares the capabilities of an impaired and an unimpaired person (verses 75–76).

In later verses of Sūrat Al-Naḥl, "signs" of God are once again affirmed, but now expressed in a cosmic frame and in terms of the eschatological urgency of the entire Qur'ānic message. In verse 77, which follows immediately after the parables mentioned above, the Qur'ān emphasizes God's power over the imminent end of all creation:

> To Allāh belongs the unseen of the heavens and the earth. The coming of the hour is only like the twinkling of the eye, or nearer. Surely, Allāh has power over everything. (16 Al-Naḥl 77)

After the shocking effect of this statement, that the End could be sooner than one thinks, perhaps nearer than the blink of an eye, the next verse transitions back to the *sūrah*'s original themes: signs that have utility and beauty, highlighting biological reproduction. With this, however, the Qur'ān seems still to place a special emphasis on the faculty of knowledge, mirroring concepts that were expressed in verse 70 previously:

> And Allāh brought you out of your mothers' bellies knowing nothing; and gave you hearing, sight and hearts, that perchance you might give thanks. (16 Al-Naḥl 78)

The faculties by which all sensory knowledge is gained are God's gifts. The following verses invoke the mystery of birds held aloft in the sky by the power of Allāh (79); and God's gift of tent dwellings made from cattle hides and the other furnishings as well as the "means of enjoyment" these animals provide (80); and, finally, how the "perfection" of God's blessings is manifested in shade from the hot sun, mountains for retreat, clothing that protects from heat and cold, and coats of mail for bodily defense during warfare (81). This combined imagery echoes the exposition of "cattle" that was found in the *sūrah*'s opening verses.

The passages discussed above from 16 Al-Naḥl, on the utility of the created world, mirror Qur'ānic statements that affirm that all of creation is for a purpose. Creation, from the perspective of humanity, is described often by the Qur'ān as being a "test," sometimes even as a competition in human terms. Elsewhere the Qur'ān also adamantly claims that life is not a trivial game, as in the words of its direct challenge to readers, "So you think that We created you in sport and that you will not be returned to us?" (23 Al-Mu'minūn 115). Another passage indicating God's role as purposive Creator, a passage which guides the reader and listener through appropriate reactions to the "signs" it mentions, are the following verses (11–17) from the beginning of 35 Fāṭir. They read:

> 11. Allāh created you from dust, then from reproductive fluid, then made you into couples. No female bears or gives birth, save with His knowledge, and no one advances in years or his or her life-span is diminished, except as ordained in a book. That indeed is an easy matter for Allāh.
> 12. The two seas are not the same; one is sweet, clear and delectable to drink and the other is salty and bitter. Yet from both you eat tender flesh and extract ornaments which you wear, and you see the ships cruising therein, that you may seek His bounty, and that perchance you may be thankful.
> 13. He causes the night to phase into the day and the day to phase into the night and He has subjected the sun and the moon, each running for an appointed term. That is Allāh, your Lord to whom belongs the dominion [*al-mulk*], whereas those you call upon, apart from Him, do not possess a date's crust.
> 14. If you call upon them, they do not hear you call; and were they to hear they would not even answer you. On the day of resurrection they will repudiate your idolatry. None will inform you like the Well-Informed One [*khabīr*].
> 15. O people [*yā ayyuhā al-nās*], it is you who have need of Allāh, whereas Allāh is the All-Sufficient [*al-ghanī*], Praiseworthy One [*al-ḥamīd*].
> 16. If He wishes, He will annihilate you and bring forth a new creation [*bikhalqin jadīd*].
> 17. That for Allāh is not a grave matter. (35 Fāṭir 11–17)

The passage blends general and specific reference in indication that God is the Creator of the extant world, and also speaks of a potential "new creation" of a world to come. The *sūrah*'s name, Fāṭir, means "Originator," and the word first appears in the opening verse, in a phrase describing divinity, "Originator of the heavens and the earth"; by the third *āyah*, the concept has already turned back on the listener in the form of direct address, "Is there any Creator [*khāliq*] other than Allāh, providing for you from heaven and earth?" The passage above from 35 Fāṭir expresses the twofold and balanced nature of creation, such as in male and female gender (verse 11), fresh and salty bodies of water (verse 12), and the symmetrical regularity and cyclical periodicity of celestial phenomena (verse 13). God also destroys as well as He creates, as in the idea of a "new creation," found in verse 16 above.

The connection, and dislocation, between this world and the hereafter is essential to the imagination of Qur'ānic cosmology. 55 Al-Raḥmān, a *sūrah* that is well known and commonly recited, juxtaposes the events of creation and destruction in balanced terms, presenting these with stylistic and rhetorical continuity through the device of a repeated refrain. The *sūrah* is characterized by many grammatical and conceptual "duals" or pairings, and many Arabic nouns also appear in dual form in the *sūrah*, which assists the end-rhyme on each verse. For example, the sound shape of the opening verses, ones which are commonly memorized by Muslims, is:

Al-raḥmān
'Alama al-qur'ān
Khalaqa al-insān
'Allamahu al-bayyān
Al-shamsu wa al-qamaru bi husbān
Wa al-najmu wa al-shajaru yasjudān
Wa al-samā'a rafa'aha wa rada'a al-mizān
Alā taṭghaw fī al-mizān
Wa aqīmū al-wazna bi'l-qisṭi wa lā tukhsirū al-mizān

Early in the *sūrah* (in the last three lines shown above, which are verses 7 to 9), the *sūrah* introduces the idea of the "balance" (*al-mizān*) that is not to be transgressed. This is one of the Qur'ān's richly open theological concepts, inviting moral philosophy. In context, the term appears embedded into the description of created forms, pointing in the modern present to a responsibility to the "balance" of natural creation. This, in turn, is found in a *sūrah* that elsewhere depicts the destruction of the created world and the experience of the next world, as determined by the consequences of present action.[4]

In English, meanings of the verses transcribed from Arabic above are as follows, now continuing with verses up to the first instance of the *sūrah*'s repeated alternating refrain, which begins in *āyah* 13:

Bismillāh Al-Raḥmān Al-Raḥīm

1. The Compassionate [*al-raḥmān*]
2. He taught the Qur'ān
3. He created humanity;
4. And taught people elocution.
5. The sun and the moon move according to plan.
6. The shrubs and the trees prostrate themselves.
7. And the sky, He raised and He set up the balance [*al-mizān*]
8. That you may not transgress the balance.
9. Conduct your weighing with equity and do not stint the balance [at this point, the Arabic transliteration that was shown above ends]
10. And the earth, He set up for all humankind.
11. In it are fruit and palm trees in buds;
12. And grain blades and fragrant plants.
13. So which of your Lord's bounties would you, both, deny [*fa bi'ayyi alā'i rabbikumā tukadhibān*]? (55 Al-Raḥmān 1–13)

These opening lines establish both the sonic and semantic patterns of the *sūrah*, which continue to its close.

Doublets in this *sūrah*, 55 Al-Raḥmān, couple nouns (within lines, like "easts and wests"), and also pair verse lines themselves. There is even a doubling of a section of substantive content, when two "gardens" of paradise, not one, appear to be described twice in succession. In the course of the *sūrah*, exposition moves from the created world to the destroyed world, and then from down in the fire back up to the garden. All events are linked rhetorically through the continual refrain that underscores God's beneficence throughout while it also voices a moral imperative ("which of your [dual] Lord's favors would you deny?"). The refrain is consistent with the *sūrah*'s scheme of rhyme, ending on "*-ān*": "*Fa bi ayyi ala'i rabbikumā tukadhibān*?" The continuation of the refrain across positive and negative subject matter (i.e. heaven and hell) makes the expression seem at times practically ironic.

The refrain first appears in verse 13, and it will be read thirty-one more times until the end of the *sūrah*, with the exception of one *āyah* that alters the pattern of repeated refrain. This one instance, verse 60, breaks rhetorical pattern and ruptures established expectation with a challenge in words that mean: "Is the reward for goodness anything but goodness?" After this, the refrain resumes. An extended refrain structure is uncommon in the Qur'ān overall, and nowhere else is the pattern sustained for such a lengthy portion of the text. However, refrain does occur elsewhere, such as in 77 Al-Mursalāt, a *sūrah* which repeats an *āyah* meaning, "Woe betide on that day, those who denounce [*wailun yawm'ithin li'l-mukadhdhibīn*]" (verses 15, 19, 24, 28, 34, 40, 45, 47, 49). Just like the case of the unexpected *āyah* number 60 that interjects into 55 Al-Raḥman, after building this patterned structure the Qur'ān also breaks it in 77 Al-Mursalāt. The final verse of 77 Al-Mursalāt (*āyah* 50) challenges unbelievers with a confrontational rhetorical question, "What discourse will they believe in after this [*fa'ayyi ḥadīth ba'dhu yu'uminūn*]?"

The connection of a moral imperative (such as not to "deny" "your Lord's favors") to times that are past, present, and future does not only occur through the Qur'ān's material that describes divinity and creation. It is also a principle that structures narrative material in the Qur'ān. Stories of prophecy also introduce another kind of soteriological moment into the ethical and temporal relation of the beginning and end of creation. The Qur'ān's narratives show that the natural order may be suspended or altered in historical or sacred time, such as with the destruction of a community that did not bother to heed the warnings of a messenger, or people who did not care to read the "signs" of God and the natural world, even when these were shown to them clearly.

THE QUR'ĀN'S STORIES

Although the Qur'ān is not structured as a narrative text, stories of many types work through and about the Qur'ān in Islamic traditions. There are stories in the Qur'ān, such as the narratives of prophets; there are also the Qur'ān's parables; in addition, there are stories Muslims relate about the Qur'ān, such as the "occasions of revelation"; and there are stories used to interpret the Qur'ān (such as "*Isrā'īliyāt*" material, sources recognized as originating from non-Islamic traditions). Further, Qur'ānic material is rendered into other traditional forms of religious narrative, such as the genre of *Qiṣāṣ Al-Anbiyā'* ("Stories of the Prophets").

When studying the prophetic past that Qur'ānic materials represent, considering the relationship to biblical accounts can help students of Islam to understand how Muslims have used the Jewish and Christian sources in order to understand and interpret the Qur'ān. From this perspective, the primarily question would not be, How do Muslims retell the "original" stories of the Bible?[5] Instead, it is to grasp how material that was available to Muslims from other faith communities was preserved in early Islamic hermeneutical tradition as "*Isrā'īliyāt*". This genre was formative within more than one branch of Islamic religious sciences, including supporting the Islamic theological claim that the coming of Muḥammad had been foretold in the scriptures of other faith communities. This material was also a rich resource for esoteric speculation in Muslim religious thought. Later in tradition, especially once the nature and position of Islamic scripture had been clarified intellectually by Muslim academics, these sources were generally set aside, and with the formation of doctrine such as *i'jāz* (the "inimitable" Qur'ān), former scriptures were more likely to be approached with the attitude that these were prophetic revelations whose readings had been "corrupted" in historical time.

According to an article by the scholar Gordon Newby "*Isrā'īliyāt*" material was transmitted among Muslims on authority that was attributed to companions of the Prophet Muḥammad. An example is the figure Ibn 'Abbās, whom Newby writes was cited to the degree that even traditions that were previously held to be anonymous over time came to carry his name. Much material originated from converts to Islam from Judaism and Christianity; the majority of the *isnād*s ("supports" for transmission) include the names of non-Arab Muslims, according to Newby. There was a rapid early growth in the amount of this material due to the vocation of some converts (*mawālī*) who earned a living as *quṣṣāṣ* (storytellers), and thereby further propagated Islamic tradition. Historically, *Isrā'īliyāt* material was accepted only for a time among scholars, then it came to be approached with more skepticism. Newby writes that classical sources on heresiography evidence that almost all transmitters of this material came under scholarly doubt for their methodology or thought in later times. According to Newby, this shift occurred at the beginning of the 'Abbāsid period in the latter eighth century, the age of the beginning of the consolidation of religious sciences, including ideas like *i'jāz*. It was also in this period that the idea of *sunnah* came to be restricted to reports about the person of the Prophet Muḥammad, as in law, and the genre of studies about other prophets became more closely tied to the formal genre, *Qiṣāṣ Al-Anbiyā'*.[6]

Within Islamic traditions, each exemplary religious figure in the Qur'ān is appreciated uniquely, and every one is recognized with a special emphasis. Most of these religious figures appear multiple times in the Qur'ān, with some exceptions. Figures for whom extensive material appears in just one or two *sūrah*s, for example, are the Prophet Joseph (Yūsuf), and Mary (Maryam), mother of Jesus. The frames for the accounts of Yūsuf and Maryam stay relatively stable in Qur'ānic context; that is, they are not mixed contextually with other material that ranges across sacred history, and the Qur'ān narrates them chronologically as "stories."

The *sūrah* 12 Yūsuf is an instance of an entire *sūrah* of the Qur'ān that takes the form of a single sustained narrative.[7] It actually introduces itself in terms of being a "narrative" in its opening verses (verse 3), as being "the most beautiful of stories." The *sūrah* carries several important characteristics that are typical of a Qur'ānic narrative. For example, many of the figures are unnamed (such as the brothers of Yūsuf). Also, an elliptical style advances the plot, in which action starts and stops abruptly. For instance, the narrative begins suddenly with the words in verse 4, "When Joseph said to his father: 'O my father, I saw [in my dream] eleven planets and the sun and the moon, I saw them prostrating themselves before me.'" Also typical, the actions and moral states of people are commonly expressed through their elocution, or what it is that they say. Finally, there appear to be coherent and sustained themes throughout the narrative, to which the Qur'ān draws attention through a sort of internal commentary. In this case, there is a theme of "knowability": what knowledge is hidden, what becomes revealed, and the "*ta'wīl*" or interpretation of the unseen (such as dreams). There are also themes of the Qur'ānic *sūrah* on which broader Muslim religious traditions, like Sufism, have traditionally elaborated, like the "beautiful patience" enjoined on the prophet Jacob (Ya'qūb) during the time he had to wait for news of his son.

Comparison in emphasis with the biblical account in Genesis 37–50 shows the strongly thematic (rather than genealogical) focus of the Qur'ān's account of Yūsuf. For example, while the biblical account ends with the command for Joseph and the tribes to "Go into Canaan," the *sūrah* of Yūsuf ends on a distinctively Qur'ānic theme: this story is a "sign" indicating the unseen and the revealed. 12 Yūsuf concludes with an emphasis on the message of faith and *tawḥīd* as related by the Prophet Joseph himself in the Qur'ān. The Qur'ān states that stories and events like these are a guide and a mercy for others, and instruct those who would believe and understand.

Qur'ānic prophets are illustrative as *'uswāt* or "models" to follow, as are other religious figures in the Qur'ān. The characterization of Maryam (Mary), the mother of Jesus (who is not considered a prophet in tradition, although she is greatly revered) also tends toward certain distinct themes in the Qur'ān. However, the fact that there is more than one account given also suggests contextual variations. Material about Mary appears in at least three locations in the text of the Qur'ān, the *sūrah*s 3 Āl 'Imrān, 5 Al-Mā'idah, and 19 Maryam, the *sūrah* which has her name. Across these three instances the Qur'ān offers thematic continuity within the overall narrative and religious presentation of material about the figure of Maryam, such as with the theme of "purity," despite differences in what is the relative emphasis across all three of these *sūrah*s.

The *sūrah* 19 Maryam contains much material about mercy and mercy-giving, for example. When Mary gives birth, events that help her (see Chapter 2) are said in the Qur'ān to be a "mercy." Sūrat 5 Al-Mā'idah, in contrast, offers much about the theme of judging fairly, especially how God judges communities (including Christian ones), an idea expressed in the refrain that appears in verses 46–50. On the other hand, there are commonalities in these differing contexts in terms of the content and style of stories of Mary and her son, the prophet Jesus, and all together they read as thematically coherent. For example, verses found in two separate accounts of Jesus and Mary, 3 Āl 'Imrān 47 and 19 Maryam 35, are statements that underscore that whatever Allāh commands to "Be" will come to be. This act of creating of life applies to the conception of Jesus with no help to Mary but God's, and who, the Qur'ān emphasizes, is not the "son" of God, since the deity does not reproduce biologically (a charge against which some early Christians, especially those in the East, defended as well). In 3 Āl 'Imrān, when angels announce to Mary she will have a child, these tidings in the Qur'ān are a "word" (*kalīmah*, as in the Greek expression *logos*):

45. When the angels said: "O Mary, Allāh bids you rejoice in a word [*kalīmah*] from Him, whose name is the messiah [*al-masīḥ*], Jesus, son of Mary. He shall be prominent in this world and the next and shall be near to God.
46. "He shall speak [*yukallimu*] to people from the cradle and while an old man will be one of the righteous." (3 Āl 'Imrān 45–46)

Throughout the accounts of Mary, Zakariyā', and their families, the Qur'ān depicts many facets of "word," "speech," and silence.

Neither the narrative of Maryam nor Yūsuf has a "punishment story" attached. Likewise the stories in 18 Al-Kahf, which are to be discussed below, also do not depict the destruction of any prophet's community. However, all of these accounts are somewhat atypical of the Qur'ān's stories of the sacred past in this respect. In fact, the primary theme of many of the presentations of religious figures in the Qur'ān is the "warning" that they bring to communities. The Qur'ān presents these prophetic figures both in terms of a revelation that they bear and the ultimate ends of the communities who heard, but did not heed, the warning.

HISTORY, COMMUNITIES, AND MESSENGERS

In the presentation of Qur'ānic prophets and communities that are judged in past time, the sacred histories of the past tend to overlap textually with the Qur'ān's depiction of ultimate judgment in the future. A group of *sūrah*s called in tradition the "hair-whitening *sūrah*s" illustrate these ideas (the name comes from a report in which the Prophet Muḥammad allegedly claimed that their revelation caused his hair to begin to turn grey). In this type of material, the Qur'ān's narrative structures superimpose layers of destruction, judgment, "weighing," and account. Such depictions open the question for mystics and moral philosophers, how can humans apprehend the relationship among the religious remembrance of previous communities, an individual person's death, and the shared experience of the last day and final hour? The Qur'ān's narratives refract all of these dimensions of the past and the future as promise and warning in the present.

In the Qur'ān, the role of a prophet is expressed by several Arabic terms, reflecting the multilayered function of these figures.

For example, they are messengers (*nabī*, *rasūl*); warners (*nadhīr*); and bearers of tidings or news. In the Qur'ān's "punishment stories," the past communities of particular messengers are judged in time, such as the "peoples of" Nūḥ (Noah), Lūṭ (Lot), Shu'aib, Hūd, and Sāliḥ. Examples of named communities thus destroyed are: 'Ad (Hūd's people); Thamūd (Sāliḥ's people); the people of Ḥijr (possibly the same as Thamūd); Midian (Shu'aib's community); "the people of the wood" (who appear in four *sūrah*s and seem much like Midian); "the cities of the plain" (Lot's people); Pharaoh's people, who encounter the Prophet Moses; Korah and Haman (also associated in the Qur'ān with Pharaoh); Al-Rass (they are in two *sūrah*s); Sabā' (Sheba, who appears only in *sūrah* 34, the *sūrah* called Sabā'); Al-Mu'tafikāt (found in three *sūrah*s). Below is a comparison of a few Qur'ānic instances, considering narratives from the seven principal accounts: 7 Al-A'rāf, 11 Hūd, 15 Al-Ḥijr, 21 Al-Anbiyā', 26 Al-Shu'arā', 46 Al-Aḥqāf, and 54 Al-Qamar.[8]

The section 7 Al-A'rāf 59–102 treats the messengers Noah, Hud, Sāliḥ, Lot, and Shu'aib. The Qur'ān presents an account of each figure in turn. This version of the group of stories of past communities in the Qur'ān carries much dialog between the respective prophet and his community, and each case specifically mentions that the messenger came bearing a "sign." Every one of the accounts specifies what was the transgressive act or behavior of that particular community, and the presentation of these groups in 7 Al-A'rāf emphasizes the attitude of disbelief of the spokespeople. A destruction of the peoples follows their rejection of the prophet's message in every case, and after this the Qur'ān usually reflects in some way on the interpretation of the stories. In its relative emphasis, the account found in this *sūrah* highlights questions of leadership rather than punishment (7 Al-A'rāf 94–102), calling attention to the false sense of security that may come when Allāh gives good fortune to a people. This occurs through the string of rhetorical questions which appear in this account, interrogating the reader directly as to whether these people were in fact smugly complacent in their confidence that judgment would not come to them (and previous statements given by their political leaders show that indeed they were). The section concludes in verse 101, making clear reference to the narration of the stories of the past: "Those cities, We relate to you some of their tales; their messengers came to them with clear signs, but they would not believe in what they had denied earlier. Thus Allāh seals the hearts of unbelievers." The more general themes established in this section of 7 Al-A'rāf continue through the end of the entire *sūrah*, however, focusing on the theme of actions and their consequences and the differences between believers and unbelievers in the past, present, and future.

One example of the thematic extension following the "punishment stories" in 7 Al-A'rāf is its telling of the story of Moses, which appears right after the section in the *sūrah* discussed above. The link to the previous material comes with a transitional phrase: "Then after them, We sent Moses with his revelations to Pharaoh and his people" (verse 103). In this account of Moses in 7 Al-A'rāf, which is one of the many such accounts that the Qur'ān gives, there is much dialog quoted between Moses and Pharaoh, along with descriptions of the "signs" that Moses brings, and through which God exposes the superficial tricks of Pharaoh's magicians. Just as in the other accounts of previous communities that precede this story in the same *sūrah*, here the arrogant people deny the message of Moses and threaten to harm his followers. In *āyah* 130, Pharaoh's people suffer from drought, but they still will not change their ways. In verse 133, punishment comes to them in the form of a flood. There is respite when they promise that now they will believe Moses, but when they break their pledge they are finally drowned, which happens in verse 137. Then there follows an excursus, which continues to verse 171, discussing the Israelites and their difficulties as a people with respect to the message of the Prophet Moses. This section ends with the verse 7 Al-A'rāf 172, which is the verse of the "Day of Alast." The conclusion to the *sūrah* returns to the theme of the truth of revelation (the Qur'ān) and its denial by some members of communities, whose course no one, not even the Prophet Muḥammad himself, can alter. In this wider context of 7 Al-A'rāf, the punishment stories appear as instructive tales illustrating moral inertia among communities, past and present.

In another Qur'ānic telling of the "same" stories of past warners, 11 Hūd 25–95, the emphasis seems subtly different. These narrations also relate a great deal of dialog, but here there is more discourse coming in the way of formulaic speech. This creates a sense of rhetorical continuity within the section's narration. The tone of these accounts also appears to be more intimate. For example, in the story of the prophet Noah (which is the first to appear in this series), the Qur'ān renders the experience of Noah as a wrenching tale of human loss. In verse 38, for example, as Noah makes the ark, passers-by mock him to his face. When the flood starts, Noah gets on to the ark at God's command, but then in verse 42 he calls out to his own son across the rising waters. The verse reads, "And as it sailed along with them amid waves like mountains, Noah called out to his son, who stood apart: 'My son, embark with us, and do not remain with the unbelievers.'" In the next verse, the Qur'ān continues: "He [Noah's son] said: 'I will seek refuge in a mountain that will protect me from water.' He [Noah] said: 'Today there is no protector from Allāh's decree, except for him on whom He has mercy.' Then the waves came between them and so he was one of those who were drowned." This is a vivid picture both of a parent's loss of a child and also of a human catastrophe on a global scale.

Noah even appeals directly to Allāh in verse 45 in his anguish over losing his son (this material echoes the theme of the test put to Ibrāhīm elsewhere in the Qur'ān, to sacrifice his child by his own hands). The verse reads, "Noah then called out to his Lord saying: 'My Lord, my son is of my family; and Your promise is surely the truth and you are the Best of Judges.'" However, in terms that appear similar to those in which the Prophet Moses is instructed by Khiḍr in the narrative of 18 Al-Kahf, Noah here is told by Allāh not to ask about things "of which you have no knowledge." Noah asks for forgiveness. There is also a mirroring here of another Qur'ānic presentation of Noah, 71 Nūḥ, which is a more sustained telling of the story, and also one which highlights his personal experience. Personalized prophetic accounts like these in Qur'ānic context naturally reflect the experience of the Prophet Muḥammad himself.

11 Hūd's prophetic narratives continue after relating the story of Noah. There follows the account of Hūd and 'Ad; Sāliḥ and Thamūd; and Abraham's (unnamed) wife, who laughs at the amazing news that she will mother a child (Isaac, who will become the father of Jacob, who is the father of Joseph). There is a smooth transition to the story of Lot and his family (with gendered references, as when Lot offers his daughters to ransom the city, and his wife looking back in defiance of the clear command not to do so), followed by the story of Shu'aib and Midyan. In each of these accounts in 11 Hūd, messengers approach people with words of formal address, "O My People," and these accounts all seem to carry something like the personal and intimate tone found in the opening story of Noah. The stories, and also the entire *sūrah*, end with an account of Moses and

Pharaoh (in a version that is much shorter than those that are found in other *sūrah*s).

In the concluding material about Pharaoh in 11 Hūd, the Qur'ān once again effects a narrative transition to the theme of ultimate, final judgment, here turning on the question of when Pharaoh's own punishment will come. This occurs in the following verses:

> 98. He [Pharaoh] shall be at the head of his people on the day of resurrection; thus he shall lead them into the fire. How wretched is the place to which they will be led!
> 99. And they are followed in this life with a curse and on the day of resurrection too. What is the support they shall be given?
> 100. That is part of the tidings of the towns We recount to you; some of them are still standing and some have been reduced to rubble. (11 Hūd 98–100)

Finally, with these overlapping the frames of experience of the sacred past and inevitable future, the *sūrah*'s ending turns its personalizing and apocalyptic tone back on to the present listener. The penultimate verses of 11 Hūd establish a lasting and haunting moral suspense:

> 121. And say to the unbelievers: "Continue with what you are doing, and we shall continue with ours.
> 122. "And wait; We too are waiting."
> 123. To Allāh belongs the unseen in the heavens and on earth, and to Him the whole affair shall be referred. So worship Him and put your trust in Him; your Lord is not unaware of the things you do. (11 Hūd 121–123)

There are many other sections of the Qur'ān in which a moment of past judgment elides into a future judgment, imminent in the present.

As a comparison, 44 Al-Dukhān also tells the story of Pharaoh and his judgment in the last *āyah*s of the *sūrah*, transitioning here to a vivid description of future punishment in which the damned, who also doubted the reality of the consequences for their actions, are engulfed in boiling water. In contrast, the Qur'ān shows that those who rest in the garden are in a "secure place," and have only "tasted their death" one time (that is, on earth). The *sūrah* ends with the following verses:

> 57. We have made it [the Qur'ān] easy in your own tongue, so that you may remember [*la'allahum yadhakkarūn*]

58. So wait and watch; and they are waiting and watching. (44 Al-Dukhān 57–58)

The Qur'ān affirms its own clarity, explains that the reason for this clarity is in order to make it easy to "remember" (or repeat), and then issues another final, eerie challenge to its readers to out-"wait" and to out-"watch" unnamed others.

Contrasting the individualistic terms of 11 Hūd, the short *āyah*s that relate the "punishment" narratives of 15 Al-Ḥijr 45–99 emphasize much more a shared communal or group experience. Verse 87 of this *sūrah* mentions the perplexing idea of the "Seven *Mathānī*," an open Qur'ānic concept that has been the subject of much interpretive speculation. These are seven "folded" or "repeated" (*mathānī*) things. Some Muslims have wondered whether these could be said to be the "oft-repeated" verses of the Fātiḥah (the opening *sūrah*, used in canonical prayer); some have said that it refers to the whole Qur'ān; and some have said the referent is the punishment stories themselves.

Two further examples of punishment stories in the Qur'ān show more of a schematic development. In 26 Al-Shu'arā' 69–191, the first instance of a prophetic account is detailed (Lot), but the narratives are highly regular after that. The *sūrah* includes accounts of Abraham, Noah, Hūd, Sāliḥ, and Lot. The Qur'ān's speech is highly stylized in these accounts, with a repeated structure that opens with the formula "and the people called [the prophet] a liar," and transitioning at seven points with the expression "There is surely in that a sign, and most of them were not believers." In a similar way, the accounts of prophets and punishment in another *sūrah*, 54 Al-Qamar 9–55 (which includes stories of Noah, Thamūd, Lot, and Pharaoh), emphasize details of the calamities that befall those who rejected the message. This *sūrah* carries a rhetorical statement repeated three times, "And we have made the Qur'ān easy to remember [*qalaqad yassarnā al-qur'āna lil-dhikri*]. Is there, then, any one who will remember?"

In all five of the major accounts considered above, collective judgment led to the destruction of the past communities, and all are said in the Qur'ān to be signs on which to reflect in the present. At times, the Qur'ān makes the clear connection of these past events in sacred time to future judgment. At the end-time, the Qur'ān evidences, the same prophets of the past will appear to testify in regard to their communities, especially with respect to their individual responsibilities in bearing the message (for example, Jesus swears that he never taught his community that he had a divine nature in 5 Al-Mā'idah 116; and the text seems to imply that the Prophet Muḥammad himself testifies in 4 Al-Nisā' 41). The Qur'ān's thematic link between these temporal communities and ultimate judgment seems to be, first, the complacent, prevalent doubt of the truth of accountability among the unbelievers of the past and the present, and, second, the inevitability of the destruction of God's created environment that humanity inhabits in some future – or perhaps even natural destruction within the present moment as well.

QUR'ĀNIC ILLUSTRATIONS OF THE FINAL HOUR

Eschatological scenarios in the Qur'ān represent some of most difficult material for students to grasp in the academic classroom. (This was apparently also the case for some Muslim philosophers, a few of whom seemed to wish to deny the idea of the corporeality of judgment.) Contemporary Muslim apocalyptic literature shows an updated attempt to come to terms with this material.[9] It is possible, however, that Muslims living at an early period had in fact expected an imminent end (as evidenced by some statements made by the Prophet himself). It is also the case that Qur'ānic material that is said to have been revealed earlier in the career of the Prophet Muḥammad is more eschatological. About one-fifth of the Qur'ān's content is about judgment and the hereafter. Heaven and hell are presented in roughly the same proportions throughout this material: there are between 300 and 400 verses on each, with a few more treating the fire than describe the garden. The "punishment stories," discussed above, weave through many of the Qur'ān's primary depictions of final judgment, offering multiple dimensions to themes of accountability and inevitable judgment, past and future.

The Qur'ān relates that no one knows the final hour, but that it is certain to come, and it could possibly be here very soon. In 7 Al-A'rāf 187 and elsewhere, the Qur'ān confirms that the knowledge of the hour is with God alone. There is also the challenge issued repeatedly by the Qur'ān to "wait" for this time while God also "waits," and the Qur'ān issues a reminder that those who would ever try to second-guess against this plan would always be outdone by Allāh Himself, who is the "Best of Plotters." Typically, a thunderclap or blast heralds the final hour. Notably, satan (who has been given a respite by Allāh himself to tempt people until this very moment, judgment) does not have much of a role in the Qur'ān's depiction of this day, at which time all beings are ultimately consigned to heaven or to hell. 50 Qāf, as just one example, contains material that affirms the future event of bodily resurrection at this time, a reality that the Qur'ān vigorously claims is in God's power, sometimes by reminding readers that Allāh brings the dead earth to life in an everyday and ordinarily miraculous way whenever rain comes from the sky. There are several names for the "Day" in the Qur'ān, conveying many facets of its significance, such as the "Hour," "Great Day," "Great Calamity," the "Sorting Out," "Raising Up," "Inevitable Event," "Date of Meeting," "Mutual Loss and Gain," and others, including some terms that do not have any meaning that is immediately evident at all, such as "Al-Qāri'ah" (which is the title of *sūrah* 101).

In *Major Themes of the Qur'ān*, Fazlur Rahman offers a way to approach the concept of judgment as depicted in the Qur'ān. Since reality is ultimately moral and just, according to Rahman as well as traditions of Islamic religious thought, there must be an ultimate judgment, otherwise fairness in this life is not ensured. "Ends" must be clarified in terms of objectives and results, and without a doubt, so that people can see with certainty what they should strive for in the present purpose of life.[10] Fazlur Rahman emphasizes a key idea, that judgment creates an effect and awareness within the experienced present. On the final day, he adds, it will already be too late, since on that day "excuses will not profit the wrongdoers" (40 Ghāfir 52). Viewed in this way, Qur'ānic material on judgment, of which there appears quite a bit, represents one of many strategies within the Qur'ān to persuade people to acknowledge and to act in accordance with God's will.

Qur'ānic scenarios of judgment depict an instant of unprecedented self-awareness. There is nothing that remains between God and the self except the ontological separation of Creator and created as affirmed by the covenantal pledge of the "Day of Alast." This is an evident moral reality, with no more denials or distortions of this state. The Qur'ān states that there has been a palpable weighing and scaling of records at this time; these documents are read at judgment, sometimes depicted in the Qur'ān as an actual book being delivered to the judged, received in the right or the left hand. Past actions are now reckoned in terms of this final "account." Minds, words, and bodies testify physically as the long-range results of actions in the present world are known in terms of their future "*akhirāt*" or ends. In addition, through this process, all disputes, dissensions, and conflicts are resolved, whether between religious communities (22 Al-Ḥajj 17, for example) or in terms of interpersonal relations. Believers in the garden and unbelievers in the fire also interact in these moments in vivid Qur'ānic dialog, each group and each person within it confirming that God's promise and warning were true.

The Qur'ān quotes people talking a great deal at judgment, holding conversations either as individuals or as representatives of generations or communities. These presentations invite readers in the present to wonder how to imagine the apocalyptic speech and its space. The ambiguity of the Qur'ānic eschatological depiction and in fact its vivid portrayal of the disorientation of this experience opens up a productive area for such reflection. The opening verses of the Meccan *sūrah* 81 Al-Takwīr demonstrate the bizarre confusion of a world undergoing a moment of its final transformation (the verses ending the *sūrah* were given in Chapter 2):

Bismillāh Al-Raḥmān Al-Raḥīm

1. When the sun shall be coiled up;
2. And when the stars shall be scattered about;
3. And when the mountains shall be set in motion;
4. And when the pregnant camels shall be discarded;
5. And then the beasts shall be corralled;
6. And then the seas shall raise mightily;
7. And when souls shall be paired off;
8. And when the buried infant shall be asked:
9. "For what sin was she killed?"
10. And when the scrolls shall be unrolled;
11. And when heaven shall be scraped off;
12. And when hell shall be stoked;
13. And when paradise shall be brought near;
14. Then each soul shall know what it had brought forth.
15. No, I swear [*falā uqsimu*] by the alternating stars,
16. Which circle then hide;
17. And the night when it recedes;
18. And the morning when it breaks,
19. It is truly the discourse of a noble messenger (81 Al-Takwīr 1–19)

In this depiction, layering on to the rent skies, strewn stars, exploded geography, rising seas, and vacant tombs that are found in other Meccan *sūrahs* (e.g. 82 Al-Infiṭār, which follows this *sūrah*), is a theme of the natural order in the process of going wrong. No one who is sensible, for example, would leave a valuable pregnant camel unattended (verse 4). The murdered baby girl (verse 8), presumably a victim of gendered infanticide, is not yet raised up, but it is as if she is just coming alive again under the ground in order to begin the process of universal question and answer for the sake of final justice.

The Qur'ānic topography of the afterlife is unclear. In the Qur'ān, heaven is called "*al-jannah*" ("the garden"), *jannat 'adn* ("Eden"), *firdaws* ("Paradise), but spatially it is ambiguous. There are some stylized features of the description of heaven in the Qur'ān, on which the text's separate accounts improvise in terms of typical images such as couches of brocade on which to recline, idealized companionship, and cool flowing rivers. Hell also has several Qur'ānic names, such as *al-nār* ("the fire") and *jahannam*. Rhetorically, hell also has its own stylized features in the Qur'ān that complement heaven's formulaic imagery, such as the "tree of Zaqqum," and it is characterized by suffocating heat and boiling water (a counterpart to the cool rivers that flow under the garden, and even the water that falls as a mercy from God in the form of the earth's rain). In several instances, God's voice affirms that He will fill hell to its capacity. Hell even talks back to God, reporting on its own present status, as in 50 Qāf 30, "On that day We shall say to hell: 'Are you full?', and it shall respond: 'Is there more to come?,'" implying that some space could be made for more.

The Qur'ān gives the impression that there is no middle ground between heaven and hell, whether as moral geographic destinations. That said, the topography of judgment is not entirely clear; this matches the disorientation the Qur'ān depicts for the emotional and intellectual experience of the day. 7 Al-A'rāf treats the confusing landscape of judgment at length, and its title, meaning "The Heights," in fact comes from a reference to an apocalyptic space. Amid the shouting back and forth between residents of heaven and hell, verses 46 to 49 of 7 Al-A'rāf mention the people of "the heights" or "the ramparts" (*al-a'rāf*), which appears to be a wall, perhaps one that has been set up right on a spot located in between heaven and hell. These verses read:

46. Between them [the people of paradise and the people of the fire] there is a veil [*ḥijāb*], and on the heights [*al-a'rāf*] are beings who know everyone by his or her mark. And they will call out to the people of paradise: "Peace be upon you [*salāmun 'alai-kum*]." That is, before they enter it, though they hope to do so.
47. And when their eyes are turned towards the people of the fire, they will say: "Lord, do not place us among the wrongdoing people."
48. And the people of the ramparts [*aṣḥābu al-a'rāf*] will cry out to some people whom they will recognize by their marks stating: "Your amassing [of wealth] and your arrogance are of no avail to you."
49. "Are those the people on whom you swore Allāh will have no mercy?" [To these people it will be said]: "Enter paradise, you have nothing to fear, and you shall not grieve." (7 Al-A'rāf 46–49)

Who are these people? What are they saying, and to whom? Where is this "wall" between heaven and hell, and is it permanent or only set up for the time being on judgment day?

Even stable spaces are hard to map in the transformative cosmology of Qur'ānic judgment. For example, the *sūrah*s 55 Al-Raḥmān and 56 Al-Wāqi'ah both imply that there could be in fact two gardens, or perhaps a special sub-garden within the one big garden that is heaven. In addition, the final verses of 56 Al-Wāqi'ah appear to describe a transitional space of "waiting," from individual death to the experience at judgment, thereby possibly adding to all this the dimension of a prior human death on earth before judgment day:

83. Would that when the soul leaps into the throat [at death?]
84. And you are, then, waiting;
85. While We are closer to him [the dead person?] than you, but you do not see.
86. And would that, not being subject to judgment,
87. You are able to bring them [souls?] back, if you are truthful!
88. However, if he or she [the dead person?] is one of those who have drawn near [*al-muqarribīn*];
89. Then ease and delight, and gardens of bliss are his or hers.
90. But if he or she is one of the companions of the right;
91. Then "Peace be upon you" [a greeting] from the companions of the right.
92. However, if he or she is one of those who denounce and err;
93. Then he or she will be served boiling water.
94. And will be scorched by the fire. (56 Al-Wāqi'ah 83–94)

The distinction made between "people who attain" or who have "drawn near" in verse 88 and those who are "companions of the right" is a concept upon which some, particularly in esoteric and philosophical traditions, have long reflected. Verses 7 to 14 (cited in Chapter 2) already established such categories at the beginning of this *sūrah*, now recapitulated in the verses whose meanings are quoted above.

Testimony at judgment is shown in the Qur'ān to come primarily through speech, and also through the written record and "accounts" of past deeds. The latter weighs heavy if there is much merit, and light if there have been only a few good actions. However, these are not the only forms of truth that are told. Even the earth itself testifies about its own witness, being "inspired" on that day, as in 99 Al-Zalzalah, here quoted in entirety:

Bismillāh Al-Raḥmān Al-Raḥīm

1. When the earth shall quake violently,
2. And the earth shall bring forth its burdens;
3. And a person shall say: "What is happening to it?"
4. On that day, it [the earth] shall relate its tales;
5. That the Lord has inspired it [*awhā lahā*]
6. On that day, people shall emerge in clusters to see their works.
7. Then whoever has done an atom's weight of good shall find it;
8. And whoever has done an atom's weight of evil will find it.

The Qur'ān's dialogic style in presenting judgment, naturally, depicts most vividly the statements of the judged as they talk and shout. The earth's testimony, as in the example above, is a rare instance of an otherwise inanimate entity's speech at that time.

In the Qur'ān's judgment scenarios there is particular emphasis on the true testimony of visible and seen bodies, coming along with, and sometimes contradicting, corresponding voices and the statements that they utter. This bodily experience is first to be understood in terms of the corporeal experience of resurrection. The dynamic experience of judgment day in the Qur'ān is a reawakening in the form of a second creation, as expressed in the riddle of a famous verse in the text that mentions "two lives" and "two deaths," 40 Ghāfir 11, "They will say: 'Our Lord, you have caused us to be dead twice and brought us to life twice, and so we have confessed our sins. Is there now a way out?'" At this time, bodies themselves participate in the process of judgment and testimony, as the same *sūrah* attests:

16. The day on which they will emerge, nothing of their being concealed from Allāh. "Whose is the sovereignity today?" "It is Allāh's, the One, the Conqueror" [*al-wāḥid al-qahhār*]
17. Today, every soul will be rewarded for what it has earned. There is no injustice today. Allāh is surely Quick in reckoning.
18. Warn them of the day of imminence, when the hearts shall come up to the throats. The wrongdoers will have then no intimate friend and no intercessor who will be heeded.
19. He knows what the eyes betray and what the breasts conceal. (40 Ghāfir 16–19)

Bodies themselves may also testify against their persons at that time, as in the following verse from the *sūrah* known well to many Muslims (and discussed further below), 36 Yā Sīn:

> Today, We set a seal upon their mouths, and their hands will speak to Us and their feet will bear witness, regarding what they used to earn. (36 Yā Sīn 65)

In the Qur'ān, body parts like hands and feet may tell the truth even while speech fabricates lies. After all, it does stand to reason that liars in one creation are likely still to be lying in the next one. In one amazing scenario in 41 Fuṣṣilat, the Qur'ān depicts a contest between persons and their own bodies, as skins start to talk, and to testify against their very persons:

19. And when the enemies of Allāh are mustered into the fire, they shall be held in check
20. When they reach it, their hearing, sights and skins shall bear witness against them regarding what they used to do.
21. And they will say to their skins: "Why did you bear witness against us?" They will say: "Allāh Who gave everything speech gave us speech, and He is the One Who created you the first time and unto Him you shall be returned."
22. You did not try to hide from the witness that your hearing, sights and skins would bear against you; but you thought that Allāh does not know much of what you do. (41 Fuṣṣilat 19–22)

It is as if bodies, made of the substance of God's creation, and always present and aware witnesses, will now speak truth at judgment as their physicality is reclaimed by their Creator.

The Qur'ān renders awareness of judgment primarily in terms of individuals, as clarified, for example, in 6 Al-An'ām 94:

> You have come to Us one by one, just as We created you initially, and you have left behind what We granted you. We do not see with you your intercessors whom you claimed were [Allāh's] partners. Certainly what held you together is now cut off, and that which you claimed has failed you. (6 Al-An'ām 94)

The Qur'ānic depictions of the moment of human realization at judgment are likewise personal and immediate, as two examples excerpted from *sūrahs* 37 Al-Ṣaffāt and 39 Al-Zumar show below.

37 Al-Ṣāffāt is said in tradition to have been revealed after 6 Al-An'ām and before 31 Luqmān. It contains a lengthy excerpt on the near-sacrifice by Abraham of his son, with the section following this on various prophets punctuated by the refrain, "Thus We reward those who act kindly" (110, 121, 131). 37 Al-Ṣāffāt 50–57 also portrays judgment in personal and sometimes even quite tender terms. After describing the people in the heavenly location of the garden in the Qur'ān, it states:

> 50. Then, they will advance one towards the other asking each other.
> 51. One of them will say: "I had a comrade;
> 52. "Who used to say: 'Are you then one of the confirmed believers?
> 53. 'Will we, once we are dead and have become dust and bones, be really judged?'"
> 54. He said [speaker ambiguous]: "Are you looking down?"
> 55. He looked and saw him [his old friend] in the center of hell.
> 56. He said: "By Allāh, you almost caused my perdition.
> 57. "But for my Lord's grace, I would have been one of those brought forward." (37 Al-Ṣāffāt 50–57)

With this narration, the Qur'ān draws the listener into the interiorized experience of a soul who had only narrowly escaped the same fate as that of his friend. It is here as if he looks back physically over the edge of a precipice over which he himself had nearly fallen a moment before.

In 39 Al-Zumar, a *sūrah* that concludes with a vision of people being drawn into heaven and hell in throngs and masses, there is also a portrayal of personal sentiment and individual feelings, especially the soul's potential regret, on judgment day. Verses 55–59, which switch in their reference to God to the first person singular in the course of the passage, read:

55. And follow the fairest of what has been sent down to you from your Lord, before punishment visits you suddenly while you are unaware.
56. Lest any soul should say: "Woe betide me for what I have neglected of my duty to Allāh and for having been one of the scoffers."
57. Or it should say: "Had Allāh guided me, I would have been one of the God-fearing."
58. Or it should say, when it sees the punishment: "If only I had a second chance, then I would be one of the beneficent."
59. Yes indeed! My signs [*āyātī*] came to you, but you denounced them as lies and waxed proud and were one of the unbelievers. (39 Al-Zumar 55–59)

This is the same *sūrah* that includes the reference to the sensation of skins "shivering" at the "remembrance" of their Lord (verse 21). 39 Al-Zumar also includes another Qur'ānic instance of bodily testimony at that time:

> On the day of resurrection, you will see those who told lies against Allāh with their faces blackened. Is not there in hell a resting place for the arrogant? (39 Al-Zumar 60)

The Qur'ān commonly depicts faces of the righteous becoming shining and illuminated at judgment, while the faces of those who acted badly are automatically rendered darkly obscure in shadow.

The experience of Qur'ānic judgment is described in many social frames; when collective, the Qur'ān usually portrays a dialog among peoples being judged and consigned to their fates. On judgment day, the judged do not merely converse, however. They really do shout. They confirm that the promise (of the garden) and the threat (of the fire) have been true all along. For example, there is the following verse in *sūrah* 7 Al-A'rāf:

44. And the people of paradise will call out to the people of the fire: "We have found what our Lord promised us to be true; so have you found what your Lord promised to be true?" They will say: "Yes." Thereupon a caller [*mu'dhdhin*] from their midst shall call out: "May Allāh's curse be upon the wrongdoers." (7 Al-A'rāf 44)

Following this there are the verses that include the mention of "heights," quoted above. At this point, in verse 50 of 7 Al-A'rāf, the interaction between heaven and hell becomes even more tangible:

50. Then the people of the fire will call out to the people of paradise: "Pour out on us some water or part of what Allāh has provided you with." They will say: "Allāh forbids them both to the unbelievers, (7 Al-A'rāf 50)

And, next, the Qur'ān explains why:

51. "Who take their religion as an amusement and sport, and the present life deludes them. Today, We forget them as they forgot the encounter of this Day and used to deny Our revelations [*biāyātinā*]." (7 Al-A'rāf 51)

Although close enough to interact in voice, the kind people who are in heaven cannot reach out to help those in hell, not even with just a little sip of water, not even if they wanted to.

Sūrat 7 Al-A'rāf also depicts this form of conversation among the judged, that is, among those consigned to the same, given fate. The section, verses 34–39, begins with a general statement in an ambiguous time frame, "For every nation there is a [fixed] term, so that when its term comes, they will not be able to put it back or bring it forward a single hour." Then, individuals are shown to enter the fire as parts of collectives and groups, historical peoples following one after another, beginning with a rhetorical question:

37. For who is more unjust than he who fabricates lies about Allāh or denies His revelations [*biāyātihi*]? Those will get their share of the punishment ordained for them. When Our messengers [*rusulunā*] come to take their souls they will say, "Where are those upon whom you called besides Allāh?" They will say: "They have left us," and they will bear witness against themselves that they were unbelievers.
38. Allāh will say: "Enter together with nations who have gone before you, *jinn* and men, into the fire." Every time a nation enters it, it curses its sister-nation; so that when they shall have followed each other into it, the last of them will say of the first: "Our Lord, these led us astray; inflict on them a double punishment in the Fire." He will say: "A double [punishment] to each, but you do not know."
39. And the first of them shall say to the last: "In no way are you better than us; so taste the punishment for what you did." (7 Al-A'rāf 37–39)

Even with the sentence doubled all round, the wicked are still making excuses for themselves or trying to blame others. The Qur'ān offers many such examples of petty bickering in hell, or on the road leading there.

Having once arrived in hell, the damned still whine and they complain. An example is 38 Ṣād 55–64, verses which follow directly after a description of those in heaven:

55. That is that, but the addressors shall have the worst resort.
56. Hell, in which they roast. Wretched is their couch.
57. That, let them taste it, as boiling water and pus.
58. And another, of the same kind, manifold.
59. This is another throng marching with you; no welcome to them, they will roast in the fire.
60. They will say: "No welcome to you; you have offered it to us in advance, and what a wretched resting-place!"
61. They say: "Our Lord, whoever has offered this to us, multiply his punishment in the fire."
62. And they say: "What is it with us that we do not see the people here whom we used to reckon to be among the wicked?
63. "We took them for a laughing-stock, or have our eyes been diverted away from them?"
64. This is perfectly true, the feuding of the people of the fire." (38 Ṣād 55–64)

Those consigned to the fire, even when there and tasting the boiling water and the pus, still seek out others whom they can look down upon, those who they are sure must now be even worse off than them – but who are conspicuously absent. The Qur'ān gives another example of disputation in the fire in 40 Ghāfir 45–52. The passage comes at the end of a somewhat lengthy account of the story of Moses and Pharaoh, with a transition from this narrative of the sacred past to the determined apocalyptic future coming in verses 45–46:

45. Then, Allāh guarded him [Moses] against the evils of their scheming; and the evil punishment encompassed Pharaoh's folk;
46. The fire to which they shall be exposed morning and evening. And the day of the hour shall come to pass, it will be said: "Admit Pharaoh's folk to the worst punishment." (40 Ghāfir 45–46)

After this introduction to the depiction of the hereafter, a reflection on the past that comes from the preceding account is now placed in a generalized future moment of disputation and responsibility. At this point, some of those who have already found themselves in hell now try to negotiate a lighter sentence for themselves, turning first to those in their own cohort:

> 47. And while they dispute in the fire, the weak will say to those who waxed proud: "We were followers of yours. Will you, then, withhold from us a part of the fire?"
> 48. Those who waxed proud will say: "We are truly all in it. Allāh has judged between the servants."
> 49. Those in the fire will say to the keepers of hell: "Call on your Lord that he may remit a day of punishment for us."
> 50. They will reply: "Did not your messengers bring you clear proofs?" They will say: "Yes indeed." They will reply: "Call then, although the call of the unbelievers is in vain." (40 Ghāfir 47–50)

In verses 49–50 above, the damned even try to convince hell's wardens to deflect from them the consequences of their own actions, but to no avail. They did not listen to the message and the warning and now, as a result, their own voices will go unheard.

Eschatological expression in the Qur'ān addresses levels of individual, collective, and universal drama as well as disorientation. The Qur'ān also renders the future palpable in these same textual modes. To see these ideas in effect within the context of a single *sūrah*, consider the chapter Muslims often recite publicly, 36 Yā Sīn. This *sūrah* differs from 55 Al-Raḥmān, discussed above, in which the Qur'ān's depiction of creation flows linearly into destruction and then back into a new creation. In 36 Yā Sīn, in contrast, the ideas and principles of moral accountability are apparently presented on each imaginable homologized level concurrently. 36 Yā Sīn is often read ritually for the sake of the dead, perhaps even to instruct the dead, in many parts of the Muslim world. The unexplained letters that begin the *sūrah*, "*Yā Sīn*," are (like "*Ṭa Ha*," the name for the twentieth *sūrah*) also considered to be a name for the Prophet Muḥammad, and is thus also a relatively common boys' name.

36 Yā Sīn starts with an oath sworn by the Qur'ān on itself (verse 2). Immediately, the Qur'ān presents the *sūrah*'s theme of accountability, stating that the Qur'ān is a revelation sent to warn humanity. The Qur'ān then presents parables, beginning in verse 13. Here there is an anonymous town that was warned, and a righteous man who testified there and was told to enter into paradise, while the fate of

this anonymous people is recounted in verse 29, "It was only one cry; and behold they were silenced."[11]

After verse 33 of 36 Yā Sīn, the Qur'ān highlights the signs of God's natural creation with its familiar images, but also here placing a particular emphasis on God's power to destroy just as He creates, as suggested by the following verses:

> 37. And a sign unto them is the night, from which We strip off the day; and lo, they are in darkness (36 Yā Sīn 37)

And,

> 39. And the moon, We have determined its phases, until it became old like a twig (36 Yā Sīn 39)

This section also includes an elliptical reference to the time of the prophet Noah:

> 41. And a sign unto them is that We carried their progeny in the laden ark
> 42. And We created for them the like of it that which they could not board.
> 43. And if We wish, We would drown them; then there is none to deliver them, nor will they be rescued
> 44. Except for a mercy from Us and enjoyment for a while. (36 Yā Sīn 41–44)

Next, the Qur'ān mentions those who did not heed the warning when it is given. In verse 51, the scenario of Yā Sīn shifts to judgment, heralded by a trumpet blast:

> 51. And the trumpet is blown, then behold how from their graves, unto their Lord, they slink away (36 Yā Sīn 51)

The Qur'ān now recapitulates language that appeared previously in the chapter's parable of the ruined city. In verse 53, it states, "It was only a single cry, and behold they were all brought before Us." Then there is an address coming from the voice of God, speaking in the singular. A transition comes in verses 69–70, with mention of the Prophet Muḥammad and a reminder that the Qur'ān is a warning. The rhetorical frames here seem to be expanding to become more generalized and even universal.

In verse 71, Sūrat Yā Sīn presents themes of God's creation and His power to create, as in verse 82, which states that Allāh only needs to say "Be" for something to come to be. In its final verses, as often happens at the conclusion of its *sūrah*s, the Qur'ān's discourse reaches out from the text to its reader. "Signs" here are presented in the form of rhetorical questions, persuading listeners that a Creator who made humanity from a drop can "bring bones to life" (verses 77–78) and, in verse 79, the Prophet Muḥammad (and by extension, believers) is instructed to state:

> 79. Say: "He Who originated them the first time will bring them back to life and He has knowledge of every creation." (36 Yā Sīn 79)

The *sūrah* ends with the eighty-third *āyah*, calling to praise Allah, with mention of His own "hands" in which the whole world rests, and a reminder of the final state of all being: "Glory, then, to Him in Whose hands [*biyadihi*] is the dominion [*malakūt*] of everything and unto Whom you will be returned."

The *sūrah* 36 Yā Sīn relates the cosmic scenario of judgment to a human's life and death across shifting textual references, aligning *ẓāhir* (outward) and *bāṭin* (inward) dimensions of experience. An Islamic tradition that has theorized precisely such correspondences analytically is that of the Sufis. The mystic's goal is to internalize the ascetic goal of death even in life (as in the Prophet's instruction, "die before you die"), and to follow specific regimens in order to bring the self to annihilation or extinction in the awareness of the only one reality of divinity. To this end, Sufis attempt systematically to replace perception and experience that is oriented to this world with that which is oriented to the next.

Sufis have been particularly fond of the verse of the "Day of Alast," recognizing that the primordial moment of standing before the Creator also stands for the moment at the ultimate end of all things. Further, their spiritual techniques attempt to render that imagined moment real in their lived present. Whether within esoteric traditions or in rhetorical, normative, and jurisprudential modes, Qur'ānic accountability at judgment cannot be said only to be allegorical; it is a palpable moral reality for religious Muslims, and one that is anticipated self-consciously as an affective encounter. The Qur'ān stretches its listener's ability to grasp and accept the immediacy of messages of promise and warning through every available persuasive strategy. Such Qur'ānic material and its representation across the text push the boundaries of human religious knowledge out to their very limits.

THE BOUNDARIES OF KNOWLEDGE: SPACE AND TIME IN 18 AL-KAHF

To understand the meanings of the Qur'ān is, by pious accounts, an impossiblity. A religious approach to the Qur'ān is always asymptotic, an approximation. Even the Qur'ān itself, while it asserts its own clarity, also points to its inaccessibility as divine speech. Sūrat 18 Al-Kahf, a chapter that expresses themes of the limits of knowledge in space and time, is located in the middle of the Qur'ān; it is in fact said that if one opens the *muṣḥaf* to its very center, one will discover Sūrat Al-Kahf. Like the themes of 12 Yūsuf, this *sūrah* similarly leads its readers to consider the question: what can be known, and by whom? However, whereas Sūrat Yūsuf seems to emphasize the scope and limits of human knowledge as represented by prophets within a single story (Yūsuf's dreams, Isḥāq's awareness of his son), 18 Al-Kahf is more global in perspective. Sūrat Al-Kahf seems to stretch the theme of known and knowable events to embrace the whole universe.

The narratives in Sūrat Al-Kahf, of which there are three principal stories, lead in the *sūrah* itself to questions about what can be "known" about such events and by which persons, and as members of what communities.[12] The first story, and title of the *sūrah*, implies a story known to Christians at the coming of Islam called the "sleepers of the cave" ("sleepers of Ephesus"); the story of the Prophet Moses is similar to a Jewish story known in *midrash*; and a Greek or possibly even Zoroastrian story is connoted by the Qur'ānic account of the world-conqueror "Dhū'l Qarnain" (who in Islamic tradition is said to be Iskandar or Alexander the Great). The *sūrah* opens with a Qur'ānic refutation of the Christian doctrines of the divine nature of Jesus, and mentions several times disputes about the interpretations of the very stories it will relate throughout the chapter. Parts of the *sūrah* imply controversy in an inter-faith revelatory context, as when the prophet is told to "say" what about them can be known and what can not (such as in material that functions as transition between accounts in *āyah*s 45 to 49).

Sūrat Al-Kahf contains verses and concepts influential in Muslim traditions outside the scriptural context of the reading of the Qur'ān. Two that are among the best known both relate to the themes of knowledge and knowability. First, there is the common expression "*in sha' Allah*." Many Muslims state this formula habitually when mentioning something they plan or expect in the future. Its appearance in 18 Al-Kahf is both descriptive and directive. The expression is presented as a prescribed utterance, then its significance is immediately illustrated in verses that follow. At the end of the *sūrah*'s first narrative, that of the "sleepers of the cave," and after having considered the impossibility of answering questions about the narrative of the sleepers, the Qur'ān offers these verses:

23. And do not say of anything: "I will do that tomorrow" [unless you add]:
24. "If Allah wills" [*in shā' Allāh*]. Remember your Lord, if you forget, and say: "Perhaps, my Lord will guide me to something closer to this in rectitude?" (18 Al-Kahf 23–24)

With this, the Qur'ān gives the command to use the expression. The Qur'ān then returns to address further the question of speculation about the story of the sleepers.

In the verses that follow this, however, the Qur'ān also further embellishes the idea "*in shā' Allāh*." Following after more instructional content, such as an injunction to recite the Qur'ān, the Qur'ān now begins to blend in observations about the fixity of revealed knowledge in contrast to human speculation. Finally, *āyah*s 30–31 end this opening section with Qur'ānic promise and warning. Then, there begins another parable of "two gardens." This short story, which is not considered to be one of the *sūrah*'s three major narratives, illustrates the principle of unknowability, and provides a rationale for saying "*in shā' Allāh*." At the beginning of the story, God has given each of two men an irrigated garden; a field separates their lands. One man boasts that he has more harvest than the other when in 18 Al-Kahf 35 the Qur'ān states, "Then he entered his garden, wronging himself. He said: 'I do not think this will ever perish.'" His companion responds that he trusts and believes in Allāh, stating in verse 39: "If only you were to say, upon entering your garden: 'What Allāh pleases (*mā shā' Allāh*) [shall come to be]; there is no power save in Allāh …" After this parable, the Qur'ān next shifts to teaching that is more cosmological in tone, but which still corresponds to the same theme: the unknowability of the future that God wills. In *āyah* 45, the Qur'ān offers a reminder of the transience of life in the world, also related to the idea of the utterance "*in shā' Allāh*." Immediately after this, the Qur'ān recapitulates the story of Iblīs (satan) in one *āyah*. A final section (*āyah*s 54–59), appearing just before the first major story in the *sūrah*, affirms the truth of the Qur'ān's revelation and the destruction of communities that denied the message.

Second, there is another well-known expression introduced by 18 Al-Kahf relating to the question of what may be known, and by whom. The phrase is "*'ilmu ladunnā*," often translated as "knowledge from Ourselves [God]." This comes in the narrative introduction to the figure whom the Prophet Moses encounters, who is called "one of Our Servants" in this, the second major story in Sūrat Al-Kahf. He is said to be the quasi-prophetic figure Khiḍr (Al-Khāḍir) in Muslim readings. The key verse in which the expression appears, 18 Al-Kahf 65, explains that Moses and his own companion encountered this mysterious figure by the river's edge: "And so, they found one of Our servants whom We had accorded a mercy of Our own and had imparted to him knowledge from Ourselves [*'ilmu ladunnā*]." In Sufi systems, this concept, "*'ilmu ladunnā*," is defined in relation to various levels and types of knowledge.[13] Elsewhere in 18 Al-Kahf, textual commentators have found occasion to reflect more directly on the nature of divine knowledge, such as in the Qur'ān's mention in 18 Al-Kahf 12 of God's seeking knowledge about the sleepers' own ability to understand their circumstances (an issue mentioned previously in Chapter 2).

Sufi traditions have elaborated on the stories that are found in this *sūrah* to a great extent, as suggested by the book by Kristin Zahra Sands on Sufi commentaries on the Qur'ān in classical Islam. This phenomenon has influenced the popular experience of the *sūrah* in Muslim lifeworlds; like 36 Yā Sīn (often read in remembrance of the dead) and 12 Yūsuf (often read as part of life-cycle observances), 18 Al-Kahf is known for being read on a weekly basis in some parts of the Muslim world, such as in recitations traditionally held every Thursday night in some parts of Indonesia. One Indonesian source (translated from an Arabic original) which was available on the front table of a major chain bookstore in 2008, *The Mystery of Surat Al-Kahf*, introduces the *sūrah* in the first paragraph of Page One as follows:

> Surat Al-Kahf is a sura in the Qur'an that conceals many mysteries of meaning. Allah has compiled within this sura many types of meanings on which we must reflect and ponder [*kita renungkan dan fikirkan*] so that we may discover the many sorts of meaning and wisdom that are contained within it. If we are able to discern [*menyingkapnya*, lit. "unveil"] these meanings, surely then there must be many secrets [*rahasia*] coming from this sura that Allah wishes us to comprehend.[14]

Groups no longer meet for regular Thursday night *dhikr* in the same traditional settings that they once did in Muslim Indonesia, although renewed pious forms of Qur'ānic and recitational practice are very popular. This mainstream book on Sūrat Al-Kahf, however, found in the "Religion" section, along with books on "Prophetic Life Management" and other "Keys to Success," shows how a tradition of Islamic thought and practice centered on this *sūrah* continues in the twenty-first century.

The *sūrah*'s structure of three principal narratives is rather unusual in Qur'ānic perspective as an arrangement. With exceptions like 12 Yūsuf and 71 Nūḥ, *sūrah*s are rarely shaped in terms of narrative at all. Each of the main stories in 18 Al-Kahf relates in some way to the theme of space, time, and the boundaries of knowledge of the seen and unseen. The first main story in 18 Al-Kahf is the account of the "sleepers of the cave," in which the fact of time itself is distorted and questioned. In the second story, in which the Prophet Moses follows the mysterious "servant of God," reasoned principles of cause and effect are apparently suspended, then restored. Finally, the third narrative is the story of "Dhū'l Qarnain" ("he of the two horns/epochs"), interpreted to be Alexander the Great. The geography of this narrative traverses space to the ends of the earth. These stories are interspersed with parables, like that of the two gardens and a short account of Iblīs, as discussed above.

Expressions of the theme of knowability are multifaceted throughout this *sūrah*, suggested even by formal aspects of structure and style. The Qur'ān's words and grammar, structure and style, shatter their own coherence at times for the reader of 18 Al-Kahf. Examples are the sleepers' groggy speech and disorientation upon waking up, and Moses' confused and confounded reaction as he is baffled by the actions of his guide. The Qur'ān's internal commentary throughout the chapter reinforces a religious awareness of the inexhaustible knowledge in the Qur'ān that is beyond human comprehension, a limitless potential of revealed word that, like drops in an ocean, is beyond any human accounting.

Take, for example, the narrative of the sleepers of the cave. As often occurs in Qur'ānic narrative (for example, the extended story of the Prophet Joseph told in 12 Yūsuf), this story starts suddenly. It begins with a rhetorical question, then continues:

> 9. Or did you think that the people of the cave and *al-raqīm* [meaning unclear] were the wonders of Our signs [*āyātinā 'ajaba*]?
> 10. When the youths took refuge in the Cave saying: "Our Lord, accord us from Yourself mercy, and guide us well in our affair."
> 11. Then We sealed their hearing in the cave for many years.
> 12. Then We roused them to learn who of the two parties was able to calculate the time they had lingered. (18 Al-Kahf 9–12)

With these verses, the Qur'ān establishes the narrative to follow as being one about which one may wonder, and in *āyah* 12 it is not known who within the story will be able to reckon time. *Āyah*s 13–16 turn to the theme of the sleepers' identity and faith. Then action of the story begins with the account of the sleepers themselves asking questions:

> 13. We relate to you their story in truth. They were youths who believed in their Lord and We increased them in guidance.
> 14. And We strengthened their hearts when they arose saying, "Our Lord is the Lord of the heavens and the earth. We will not call on any god besides Him. For then we would be uttering an enormity.
> 15. "These our people have taken other gods besides Him. Why do they not bring a clear authority for them? Who is, then, more unjust than he who invents lies against Allāh?"
> 16. When you withdraw from them and what they worship, apart from Allāh, take refuge in the cave and your Lord will extend to you some of his Mercy and prepare you for a suitable course in your affair. (18 Al-Kahf 13–16)

Already in these verses, coherence begins to break. It is unclear exactly who is the addressee in verse 16, for example.

Together, *āyah*s 9–16, above, establish a context for the story of the "*ahl al-kahf*" ("companions of the cave"). This section, and the account overall, is characterized by two modes of narrative voice. First are active verbs in the first person plural. These verbs often appear at the beginnings of *āyah*s and they mark the progression of narrative events as God's actions (e.g. "We sealed" [11], "We awoke them" [12], "We strengthened" [14]). There is also a mode of narration in which the actions of the *ahl al-kahf* are rendered in the third person plural, recounting what "they" did (verse 10, for example).

There are two *āyah*s in this section that signify the relation of the narrative to the story's listeners as well as to the wider context of revelation itself. These are: first, in 9, "Or do you think," in which a second person singular (the Prophet?) is being addressed; and, second, in 13, "We relate," which is in the first person plural indicative, and which is an explicit reference to the act of narration with the Arabic root *q-ṣ-ṣ*. These utterances mark both the act of narration as well as the presence of narrative, emphasizing the significance of the story itself as one of God's signs (*āyāt*).

The utterances of the *ahl al-kahf* themselves, however, comprise most of the story in this section. Each *āyah* in which they speak (10, 14, 15, and 16) effects a different mode of speech. In verse 10, the sleepers address God in the vocative ("our Lord") and the imperative ("guide us") at the time when they withdraw into the cave. In 14, after God has fortified their resolve, they do not address Him directly again, however, but rather they describe Him and their relationship to Him, as in the phrases, "our Lord is the Lord of the heavens and the earth" and "we would not call on any god besides Him." In *āyah* 15, the sleepers articulate the relationship of those outside the cave to God; in this instance, both "our people," meaning the sleepers, and God are signified in the third person. The meaning of *āyah* 16 parallels 10 in that it relates the withdrawal of the sleepers into the cave and the mercy and guidance that God grants to them. Verse 16, however, is in the second person plural voice and is also conditional ("when/if you withdraw"). It is unclear who is the authoritative speaker in 16 who instructs the (other?) sleepers to enter the cave. In this section, *āyah*s 9–16, the verses in which the sleepers speak, if taken together, implicitly render the relationship of the sleepers to their faith and actions, God's agency, and the outside world. Together, however, they present an unstable narrative frame even as the Qur'ān emphasizes its own telling of a story.

With the next verses, there is a sudden switch to a more immediate narrative. *Āyah*s 17–18 describe the state of the *ahl al-kahf* while they are asleep:

17. And you might have seen the sun, when it rose, inclining from their cave towards the right, and when it set, inclining to the left, while they were in an open space inside it. That was one of Allāh's signs [*āyāt Allāh*]. He whom Allāh guides is well-guided; and he whom Allāh leads astray, you will not find a friend to direct him.
18. You would think them awake, whereas they were sleeping. We turned them over to the right, then to the left, while their dog was stretching its paws in the yard. If you looked at them, you would have turned away from them in flight, and would have been filled with fear. (18 Al-Kahf 17–18)

Time here has an eerie, suspended quality. The *sūrah* states that any witness to the events would be scared and would want to run away, his or her sense of reality so distorted by the scene. Both *āyah*s above begin with addresses to a second person singular addressee (the Prophet), which heightens the sense of narrativity. It also invites the listener to imagine actively the conditions of the sleepers and their cave, as in 17, "you would see," and, 18, "you would think/consider." *Āyah* 17 refers to God in the third person rather than in the first, perhaps emphasizing the sun's movement as an *āyat Allāh* (sign of God). In 18, there is a return to the first person plural voice within the narrative, with the phrase "We turned them over" marking the end of the hypothetical situating of the listener among the sleepers, and the return of the original narrative voice of the account.

In *āyah*s 19–20, the sleepers awake in confusion. The Qur'ān's elocution mirrors this state. In fact, the text says that they are disoriented precisely so that they might ask questions:

19. Thus We roused them, that they might question each other. One of them said: "How long have you lingered?" They said: "A day or part of a day." They said: "Your Lord knows best how long you have lingered. So send someone with this silver [coin] of yours to the city, and let him see what food is purest. Then let him bring you some provision thereof, and let him be gentle and let him apprise no one about you.
20. "Surely, if they learn about you, they will stone you or force you back into their religion and then you will never prosper." (18 Al-Kahf 19–20)

Āyah 19 begins with the verb in the first person plural, advancing the narrative, with "We roused them." The rationale for the action is given immediately with the verbal phrase that follows, "so they might question." The *āyah*s that follow relate the mutual questioning and address among the sleepers. They discuss two matters: first, the duration of their sleep from which God has awakened them (in which the voice is ambiguous); and, second, instruction to the one who is to go into the city (in which the identity of the interlocutor is ambiguous).

The first discussion among the sleepers, regarding the length of their sleep, contains three principal utterances. The first is made by an individual ("one of them"), who addresses the others (all or some of them) in the second person plural: "How long have you lingered?" The response to the question now comes from more than one speaker (*qālū*, "they said"). Third, another group of interlocutors (perhaps including all of the above) addresses a second person plural (as in "your Lord" knows). There is no clear correlation between grammar and context in these three utterances (although the second utterance does follow from the first), depicting the searching confusion among the sleepers upon their awakening. At this point, the understanding of the figures who are depicted within the story itself is confounded.

The second cluster of utterances in this section, *āyah*s 19–20, employs one voice consistently, even though the identity of the speaker(s) is not indicated explicitly. These statements address the group of sleepers (or part of it) in the second person plural (e.g. "with this money of yours"), while there is also instruction given to the one who is to travel into the city. In *āyah* 20, the verse which suggests the results of the potential discovery of the sleepers by those outside the cave, the consequences for the entire group are expressed in address to a second person plural ("they will stone you"; "you will not prosper") rather than the first person. This gives the sense that there may be a privileged voice among the sleepers that leads the others. This voice carries the same authoritative sense as the address to the sleepers previously in *āyah* 16.

Āyah 21 concerns those outside the cave. It reads:

> 21. That is how We made them known [to people] so as to know that Allāh's promise is true and that the hour is undoubted. As they were arguing among themselves concerning their affair, they said: "Build over them an edifice; their Lord knows best their condition." Then those who prevailed over them said: "Let us build over them a place of worship."

Now, more figures within the story debate what it is they know. The narration begins here, as it did in 19 and elsewhere, with an active verb in the first person plural ("We made it known"), and quotes the words of the people's dispute about what action they should undertake with respect to the sleepers. There seem to be two main factions here; one group speaks in the second person plural imperative ("build over them"), while the group that "prevails" speaks in the first person emphatic imperative ("let's all build").

*Āyah*s 22–26 then shift outside the narrative frame entirely. They still depict the human act of questioning, however. These verses address the problem of epistemology in general and questions with respect to the sleepers in specific.

> 22. Some say: "[The sleepers were] three; their dog was the fourth of them"; and [others] say: "Five, their dog was the sixth of them," casting at the unseen [*rajman bi 'l-ghaib*]. And they say: "Seven; their dog being the eighth of them." Say [O Muḥammad]: "My Lord knows best their number; none knows them, save a few." Do not, then, dispute concerning them, except with reference to that which is clear to you, and do not question, concerning them, any of them.

Then the verses of "*in shā' Allāh*" (discussed above) appear, in *āyah*s 23–24. Following this there is a final return to the narrative of the story known to Christians as the "sleepers of Ephesus":

> 25. And they lingered in their cave three hundred years, and [some] added nine.
> 26. Say: "Allāh knows best how long they lingered. His is the unseen of the heavens and the earth. How clear is His sight and His hearing! Apart from Him, they have no protector, and He has no associates in His sovereignity." (18 Al-Khaf 25–26)

Together, all of the verses in *āyah*s 22–26 compare multiple perspectives about what may, or may not, be known about the sleepers. *Āyah* 22 begins by contrasting the statements of two groups of speakers on the matter of the number of sleepers. A second person singular imperative (to the Prophet) resolves the controversy as to what to say (*qul*), as well as providing instruction to him about whether and how even to get involved in such disputes.

However, these statements are not directly related to the questions asked within the narrative of the *ahl al-kahf.* Rather, they are direct addresses to God, reflecting a more encompassing theme of what may not be presumed or even ever be known about the context of God's omniscience, omnipotence, mercy, and guidance. After this, when the Qur'ān returns to the *ahl al-kahf* and the matter of the duration of their stay in the cave, there are multiple perspectives given. Although it is stated that the sleepers stayed in the cave for three hundred years, this statement is followed by a verb in the third person plural, indicating that "they" added nine. This may be a reference to solar and lunar calendrical computations; in any case, it underscores once again the inadequacy of human understanding to comprehend matters that only God may know. *Āyah* 26 concludes the whole episode of the sleepers of the cave, and affirms that God knows how long the sleepers remained in the cave, and that, most important, all the mysteries in heaven and on the earth (*ghaibu as-samāwāti wa'l-arḍ*) are with Him alone. The next verses, which appear just before the parable of the two gardens begins, concern what cannot be known except by God, connecting God's knowledge to His power as well.

The other accounts in the *sūrah*, on Moses and Khiḍr and "Dhū'l Qarnain," present other dimensions of the boundaries of knowledge across space and time. The account of Moses and Khiḍr, a figure well known especially among those who would interpret the "mysteries" of the journey allegorically, relates to the understanding of actions' causes and their effects. The account begins in *āyah* 60 with Moses and his own servant seeking the "confluence of the two seas," where they "forget the fish" they were about to eat. The "fish" is interpreted in a variety of ways in tradition, and if it is said to be anything more than just a "fish," it is then a metaphor for knowledge.

The account then continues as Moses encounters with "one of Our servants" who possesses "knowledge from Ourselves" (*'ilmu ladunnā*). This figure is usually said to be Al-Khiḍr or Al-Khāḍir. Moses asks to follow him, and, after expressing his reservations, at last this mysterious figure agrees:

65. And so, they found one of Our servants whom We had accorded a mercy of our own and had imparted to him knowledge from Ourselves [*'ilmu ladunnā*].
66. Moses said to him [Khiḍr]: "Shall I follow you so that you may teach me of the good you have been taught?"
67. He [Khiḍr] said: "You will not be able to bear with me.

68. "And how will you bear with that of which you have no knowledge?"
69. He [Moses] said: "You will find me, *in shā' Allāh*, patient and I will not disobey any order of yours."
70. He said: "If you do follow me, do not ask me about anything, until I make mention of it." (18 Al-Khaf 65–70)

Once the agreement is struck between Moses and Khiḍr, their journey continues with three episodes that confound Mūsā. First, Khiḍr puts a hole in a boat, and Moses questions his actions, observing that this act could endanger others at a future time:

71. So, they set out; but no sooner had they boarded the ship than he made a hole in it. He [Moses] said: "Have you made a hole in it so as to drown its passengers? You have indeed done a grievous thing."
72. He [Khiḍr] said: "Did I not tell you that you will not be able to bear with me?"
73. He [Moses] said: "Do not reproach me for what I have forgotten, and do not overburden me with hardship." (18 Al-Khaf 71–73)

Moses has apologized for forgetting, and has asked Khiḍr please not to be too hard on him. Then, Khiḍr takes the life of a child, and Moses' reaction is outraged:

74. Then they departed; but when they met a boy he [Khiḍr] killed him. Moses said: "Have you killed an innocent person who has not killed another? You have surely committed a horrible deed."
75. He [Khiḍr] said: "Did I not tell you that you will not be able to bear with me?"
76. He [Moses] said: "If I ask you about anything after this, do not keep company with me. You have received an excuse from me." (18 Al-Khaf 74–76)

Moses here promises that if he does it again, he would expect his journey with Khiḍr to be over. Finally, Khiḍr rebuilds a wall along their way, and the Prophet Moses, who could possibly be hungry as a result of having been denied hospitality by the local townsfolk, wonders out loud why he did not ask to get paid for the work:

77. So, they went on, until they reached the inhabitants of a town. Whereupon they asked its inhabitants for food, but they refused to offer them hospitality. Then, they found in it a wall about to fall down, and so he [Khiḍr] straightened it. He [Moses] said: "Had you wished, you could have been paid for that."

In all three instances, Moses has questioned Khiḍr's actions, just as he promised he would not do.

Khiḍr now addresses Mūsā, reprimanding him but also explaining what were his actions with his own "*ta'wīl*":

> 78. He [Khiḍr] said: This is where we part company. [Now] I will tell you the interpretation [*bita'wīl*] of that which you could not bear patiently with.
> 79. As for the ship, it belonged to some poor fellows who worked upon the sea. I wanted to damage it, because on their trail there was a king who was seizing every ship by force.
> 80. As for the boy, his parents were believers; so we feared that he might overwhelm them with oppression and unbelief.
> 81. So we wanted that their Lord might replace him with someone better in purity and closer to mercy.
> 82. And as for the wall, it belonged to two orphan boys in the town; and beneath it there was a treasure for both of them. Their father was a righteous man; so your Lord wanted them to come of age and dig up the treasure, as a mercy from your Lord. What I did was not of my own will. This is the interpretation [*ta'wīl*] of that which you could not bear patiently. (18 Al-Khaf 78–82)

The story concerns cause and effect, limitations and boundaries, and the potential of a knowledge even greater that that which a prophet may be said to possess.

Immediately after the story of Moses and Khiḍr, the story of "Dhū'l Qarnain" appears in Sūrat Al-Kahf. It is not clear who this figure is, and in fact the section opens in *āyah* 83 with a reference to questions being asked about him: "And they ask you about Dhū'l Qarnain. Say: 'I will give you this account of him.'" This figure is said in the Qur'ān to follow his "course" to the "setting place of the sun" (verse 86) and then to the "rising place of the sun" (verse 90), encountering peoples along the way. Finally, when he reaches a "point separating the two barriers" in verse 93, he comes upon a people whose speech is so foreign it is practically unintelligible:

> 94. They said: "O Dhū'l Qarnain, surely Gog and Magog [*jūj wa ma'jūj*] are making mischief in the land. Shall we pay you a tribute so that you may build a barrier between us and them?"
> 95. He said: "What my Lord has empowered me to do is better. So help me forcefully and I will build a barrier between you and them.

96. "Bring me large pieces of iron." So that when he had leveled up [the gap between the two sides], he said: "Blow." And having turned it into fire, he said: "Bring me molten brass to pour on it."
97. Then, they could neither scale it nor make a hole through it.
98. He said: "This is a mercy from my Lord; but when my Lord's promise comes to pass, He will turn it into rubble, and the promise of my Lord is ever true." (18 Al-Kahf 94–98)

The figure offers a technology of protection along with a universal message of promise and warning, bringing together communities at the ends of the earth. The end of the story serves as a transition to the *sūrah*'s concluding soteriological themes.

Material about the last day, confirmation of God's promise and threat follows, and then the *sūrah* at last concludes. At this point, Sūrat Al-Kahf again takes up themes of the awareness of the limits of knowledge. The final verse of the *sūrah* reads:

110. Say: "I am only a mortal like you. It has been revealed to me that your God is One God. Let him who hopes to meet his Lord, do what is good and associate none in the worship of his Lord."

The human humility expressed in this verse ("I am only a mortal like you") contrasts the preceding, penultimate verse of the chapter, which represents one of the most well-known statements in the Qur'ān about the Qur'ān itself. It relates the inexhaustibility of the Qur'ān's wisdom, and conveys that even for all of the information contained in the *sūrah*, there are even more mysteries that humanity, those who are "merely mortal," will never understand. This verse, *āyah* 109, reads, "Say: 'Were the sea to become ink for my Lord's words [*likalimāt rabbī*], the sea would be exhausted before the words of my Lord are exhausted, even if We were to bring its like to replenish it.'" As was suggested previously in Chapter 5, the image of an endless ocean, one without a shore, is a foundational metaphor in Islamic religious thought.

CONCLUSION

Dimensions of narrative in the Qur'ān, such as 18 Al-Kahf, suggest a scriptural principle of time that is stacked and nested, referencing the past and future in the present, as occurs, for example, in readings of the single verse of the "Day of Alast." As in 36 Yā Sīn, this cosmology relates to the individual and his or her actions in the miscrocosmic experience of a person's life and death. The Qur'ānic message of accountability is universal and communal, but it is also expressed most vividly in the text in terms of the person, his or her speech, body, and feelings. A well-known verse from 41 Fuṣṣilat (also known as "*Hā Mīm Al-Sajdah*," see Chapter 1), for example, offers a religious correspondence of micro- and macrocosm in the moral order. Its famous, penultimate verse reads:

> We shall show them Our Signs [*āyātinā*] in the distant regions and in their own souls, until it becomes clear to them that it is the Truth [*al-ḥaqq*]. Does it not suffice your Lord that He is a Witness of everything [*bikulli shay'in shahīd*]? (41 Fuṣṣilat 53)

This is the same *sūrah* that includes the refrain "among his signs"; which contains a "*sajdah*" or prostration; and this is the chapter that includes a verse about skins testifying, mentioned previously. The idea, "signs on the horizons and in themselves," is a favorite of Sufis in its "multifaceted" expression, stretching knowledge and accountability across space and time, both inwardly and outwardly.

The Qur'ān often expresses the limits of human knowledge and imagination in language that is apocalyptic and eschatological. This can present some of the most difficult religious material in the Qur'ān for students to study in the academic classroom. However, for those students who prefer a palpable reading, it may not be necessary to imagine esoteric or internalized interpretations in order to grasp a Qur'ānic meaning of the end of creation as we know it, and the unknown and undetermined state of a world yet to come. Like any expression of the natural world or eschatology in the Qur'ān, such as in the example of 55 Al-Raḥmān, "signs" in the text focus meaning on to the reader's present. One facet of this message of attention, especially if considered in terms of the "signs" imminent upon the horizon, may be read as the oppressive changes brought to the natural world for which Muslims, along with all humans, are responsible. Readers of the Qur'ān coming from any global community may recognize this as an Islamic warning about the impossibility of unsustainable consumption, and a universal call to embrace an ethic that sustains the earth's "balance" for future generations.

NOTES

1. Rahman, *Major Themes of the Qur'ān*, pp. 70–74.
2. Rahman, "Some Key Ethical Concepts of the Qur'ān."
3. Here I have changed Fakhry's phrase "sperm-drop" to "fertilized egg," interpreting the Arabic term "*nutfah*," to be more like a zygote before its implantation.
4. Abdel Haleem, "The Qur'ān Explains Itself: The Sūrat Al-Raḥmān," in *Understanding the Qur'ān*, pp. 158–183.
5. Waldman, "New Approaches to 'Biblical' Materials in the Qur'ān" and Rippin, "Interpreting the Bible Through the Qur'ān."
6. Newby, "Tafsīr Isra'iliyyāt," and McAuliffe, *Qur'ānic Christians*.
7. Johns, "The Qur'ānic Presentation of the Joseph Story" and Mir, "Irony in the Qur'ān: A Study of the Story of Joseph."
8. Rahman, *Major Themes of the Qur'an*, pp. 52–60, discusses these narratives. See also Bell, *Bell's Introduction to the Qur'ān*, revised by Watt, pp. 127–135, and Welch, "Formulaic Features of the Punishment Stories."
9. For example, see Cook, *Contemporary Muslim Apocalyptic Literature*.
10. Rahman, *Major Themes of the Quran*, p. 116.
11. There is speculation in Muslim tradition about what could have been this place, such as Antioch in the Christian Bible's book of Acts, or in relation to the Qur'ān itself with respect to Ilyas (Elias) in 37 Al-Ṣāffāt 130.
12. My thanks go to Professor Wadad Kadi, with whom I had the opportunity to study this material.
13. Sands, *Sufi Commentaries on the Qur'ān in Classical Islam*, pp. 82–88.
14. Muhammad Mutawalli Asy-Syarawi, *Misteri Surat Al-Kahfi* ("The Mystery of Surat Al-Kahf"), p. 1. Translation from Indonesian is mine. There are fine literary and historical studies of this *sūrah* in the English language, including Brown, "The Apocalypse of Islam," and Roberts, "A Parable of Blessing."

CONCLUSION

This book has presented basic material for an introductory academic study of the Qur'ān at the beginning of the twenty-first century. It invites readers to appreciate the dynamic connections across the Qur'ānic text that have been at the core of Muslim approaches to the Qur'ān and Islamic religious sciences, whether in terms of language and rhetoric, history and narrative, law and guidance, or other themes in religious thought and practice. This book, written in a "Muslim world" of the Asia-Pacific region (New Zealand), is a product of its time and place, even as it tries to consider a timeless and "multifaceted" text and tradition in global perspective. Many of the book's examples of Qur'ānic social reception and expression have come from Southeast Asia, a region of the world where about as many Muslims reside as in the entire Arabic-speaking word. However, the classical sources that have been presented are also the shared heritage of Muslims across the vast expanse of the Muslim-majority and Muslim-minority worlds.

One of the themes of the presentation has been, self-consciously, time. Chapter 2, for example, included discussion of Muslims' narratives of the time in which the Qur'ān has appeared in human history. Chapter 3 showed how traditions of "Qur'ānic sciences" developed historically, and also how Muslims use a principle of temporality to interpret and understand the text, such as with "occasions of revelation." Chapter 4 demonstrated how law was derived in terms of universal principles and changing times, in both classical and contemporary traditions. Chapter 5 considered some ways in which Muslims internalize Qur'ānic principles in their own present time through persistent modes of embodiment, aesthetics, and piety. Finally, Chapter 6 explored the Qur'ān's internal presentation of cosmic, narrative, and present time – including experience of the end of time itself – as well as what are the limits of temporal knowledge in the Qur'ān and about the Qur'ān. In addition, and as the text of the Qur'ān constantly reminds its Muslim religious readers, our own time may also be running out. "Signs" that are visibly very apparent in the present connect to the Qur'ān's central themes of countering "oppression" and the sustainable "limits" that are set by God and to the theological and human problem of global times to come: environmental change.

For many years I taught this material as a course with students of religious studies at Oberlin College, which is located close to a city on America's "rust belt," Cleveland, Ohio. The area is known for a river, the Cuyahoga, that became so polluted with industrial waste decades ago that it caught fire and burned for days. Teaching the class on the Qur'ān, which inspired this book, in Oberlin's pioneering building, the Environmental Studies Center, reminded me and my students that apocalyptic imagery like fire and water, and the emphatic warning not to "be an oppressor" or to "corrupt the earth," might not be so distant to our present experience. The waters are starting now to rise again, as they did in the Qur'ānic narrative past, while rains elsewhere cease to fall. These real phenomena can only exacerbate global inequities, and are sure to impact communities of Muslims especially severely in regions of Africa, Asia, and Oceania.

Future religious responses to conditions of ecological crisis by Muslims will certainly draw on the text and guidance of the Qur'ān, which offers to religious readers new horizons for thought and action. Whether or not Muslims, or any of us, are ready to hear the message, the Qur'ān does appear already to have anticipated these urgent issues of our time with a final question that challenges denial, defeatism, and disbelief:

> Have you considered who, if your water drains away,
> will bring you pure running water? (67 Al-Mulk 30)[1]

NOTES

1. See also Abdel Haleem, "Water in the Qur'ān," in *Understanding Qur'an*, pp. 29–41, and Faruqui, Asit, and Murad, eds., *Water Management in Islam*. Thanks to Frederick Denny for the latter reference.

GLOSSARY

Abbreviated letters discrete Arabic letters that appear at the beginning of twenty-nine *sūrahs* of the Qur'ān

Adab cultivated comportment; many disciplines of learning and practice have an "*adab*," from music to teaching and learning the Qur'ān

Ahl Al-Bait "people of the house"; the immediate family of the Prophet Muḥammad

Ahl Al-Kahf "people of the cave," the "sleepers" whose story is told in 18 Al-Kahf

Ahl Al-Kitāb "people of the Book"; this is usually glossed as meaning believers across faith communities including Islam, Judaism and Christianity

Aḥrūf "modes": the Qur'ān is said to be revealed in seven "modes," and there have been a number of opinions about what this means

'Ā'ishah wife of the Prophet Muḥammad

'Alī Alī bin Abī Ṭālib, cousin and son-in-law of the Prophet Muḥammad

Asbāb al-nuzūl "occasions of relevation," traditional accounts of the circumstances of the reception of certain verses of the Qur'ān

Al-Ash'arī Abū'l Ḥasan Al-Ash'arī (d. 935), Sunni theologian

Al-Asmā' Al-Huṣnā the "most beautiful Names" of God; in tradition, there are ninety-nine of these

Āyah (pl. āyāt) a verse of the Qur'ān; a "sign" of God

Āyat Al-Kursī "verse of the throne"; 2 Al-Baqarah 255

Āyat Al-Nūr "verse of light"; 24 Al-Nūr 35

Bukhārī Muḥammad bin Ismā'īl Al-Bukhārī (d. 870); collector of *ḥadīth* reports

Caliph leader of the community in Sunni tradition; there were four "caliphs" who followed Muḥammad: Abū Bakr, 'Umar, 'Uthmān, and 'Alī

"Day of 'Alast" expression referring to the episode described in 7 Al-A'rāf 172

Dhū wujūh "multifaceted" (lit. "having faces")

Al-Fātiḥah "The Opening," first *sūrah* of the Qur'ān

Fātimah daughter of the Prophet Muḥammad, wife of 'Alī

Faṭwah non-binding legal opinion

Fiqh jurisprudence

Fitnah strife within the community

Al-Ghazālī Abū Ḥāmid Al-Ghazālī (d. 1111), prolific and influential Sunni scholar

Ḥadīth an authoritative report of the sayings, actions or tacit approvals or disapprovals of the Prophet Muḥammad, from which the *sunnah* is known

Hāfiẓ(ah) Qur'ān memorizer

Ḥajj pilgrimage to Mecca, performed under the correct conditions to fulfill the requirement to enact this at least once in a lifetime (one of the "five pillars" of Islam)

Ḥalāl permissible; a legal category for the "assessment of action"

Ḥarām forbidden; a legal category for the "assessment of action"

Ḥijāb a state of modest dress; cloth that may be worn on the head and body

Hijrah "emigration" of Muslims from Mecca to Medina in the year 622 C.E.

Ḥudūd Qur'ānic term for the "limits" set by God; punishment for certain criminal acts

Ibn 'Arabī Abū 'Abd Allāh Muḥammad bin 'Alī bin Muḥammad bin Al-'Arabī (d. 1240), mystical thinker

Ibn Ḥanbal Aḥmad bin Ḥanbal, (d. 855), collector of *ḥadīth*; founder of what came to be one of the four principal Sunni schools of law

I'jāz doctrine of the "inimitable" nature of the Qur'ān

Ijmā' consensus of legal opinion

Ijtihād independent reasoning in the law (one who is recognized for doing this is a "*mujtahid*")

"Al-Ikhlāṣ" *sūrah* 112

Ikhtilāf difference of scholarly opinion on a point

'Illah "rational cause" for a legal ruling; this is derived as part of the process of *qiyās*

Imām prayer leader; Shi'ite authority

Imān faith

Isrā' and Mi'rāj the "Night Journey and Ascent," an episode in which the Prophet Muḥammad was transported to Jerusalem and from there ascended to heaven

Isrā'īliyyāt material preserved from non-Muslim faith communities about figures named in the Qur'ān

Jibrīl Angel Gabriel, who conveyed the revealed Qur'ān to the Prophet Muḥammad

Juz' a section of one-thirteth of the Qur'ān; "*Juz' 'Ammā*" is the last thirtieth

Ka'bah structure in Mecca that is the focus of Ḥajj and *ṣalāt*

Kalām dialectical theology

Khadījah first wife of the Prophet Muḥammad

Khiḍr (Al-Khāḍir) said to be the mysterious "servant of God" whom the Prophet Moses encounters in 18 Al-Kahf

Kitāb book; a name for the Qur'ān; "Ahl Al-Kitāb" are "people of the Book"

Lailat Al-Qadr "Night of Power," understood to be a night in the month of Ramaḍān in which the Qur'ān was revealed

Mawlid celebration of the birthday of the Prophet Muḥammad; a text cycle venerating the Prophet that may be read at any time

Mecca (Makkah) site of the Ka'bah; town that was the original home of the Prophet Muḥammad

Medinah city in which the Prophet Muḥammad resided in the latter part of his life

Miḥnah "trial" or "inquisition" over the nature of the Qur'ān during the ninth century

Muṣḥaf a bound Qur'ānic text, in Arabic

Mu'tazilite designation for a rationalist philosophical orientation in the first centuries of Islam

Nabī prophet

Naskh "abrogation" of the words or the application of legal ruling of a verse of the Qur'ān

"*Nushūz* Verse" 4 Al-Nisā' 34

Orientalism the heritage of European knowledge of the non-Christian "other" in eastern and western Asia (including the "Middle East")

Qiblah directional orientation following the shortest route over the earth to Mecca; direction for performing *ṣalāt*

Qirā'āt variant "readings" of the standard text of the Qur'ān

Qiyās ratiocination; legal analogy

Rak'ah gestural unit of Islamic worship, *ṣalāt*; different prayers have different numbers of required rak'āt (two, three, or four depending on the time of day)

Ramaḍān Islamic lunar month; month of the fast, in which the Qur'ān is said to have been revealed

Rasūl messenger of revelation; Muslims will sometimes refer to the Prophet Muḥammad as "*Al-Rasūl*," such as in *ḥadīth* reports

Ṣalāt canonical worship, performed five times daily (*fajr*, *ẓuhr*, *'asr*, *maghrib*, *ishā'*)

Ṣawm fasting from dawn to dusk during the month of Ramadan (one of the "five pillars" of Islam)

Al-Shafi'ī Muḥammad bin Idrīs Al-Shāfi'ī (d. 820), developer of legal theory and founder of what came to be one of the four principal Sunni schools of law

Shahādah "Witnessing" of faith with the affirmation, "There is no god but God and Muḥammad is the messenger of God" (one of the "five pillars" of Islam)

Sharī'ah divine will; law

Shi'ite an orientation in Islamic thought and practice that upholds the authority of 'Alī and his successors as *imāms*; Isma'ili (sevener) Shi'ism developed doctrines of esotericism; Ithna' 'Ashari Shi'ism is the orientation of the majority of Muslims in Iran today

Shūrā participatory consultation

Sīrah religious biography of the life of the Prophet Muḥammad

Sufi following esoteric piety, including veneration of the Prophet Muḥammad and holy figures; following a guided path; and, known in terms of "lineages"

Sunnah model of the exemplary comportment of the Prophet Muḥammad; a legal category for the "assessment of action"

Sunni approach of the majority of Muslims, who are not Shi'ite

Sūrah chapter of the Qur'ān; there are 114 of these

Al-Ṣūyūtī Jalāluddīn Al-Sūyūṭī (ca. 1445–1505), scholar of Qur'ānic sciences

"Sword verse" *āyat al-ṣaif*, 9 Al-Tawbah 5

Al-Ṭabarī Muḥammad bin Jarīr Al-Ṭabarī (d. 923), historian and Qur'ān interpreter

Ṭahārah state of ritual purity

Tafsīr exegesis of the Qur'ān

Tajwīd system for vocalizing the Arabic sounds of the Qur'ān

Tarwīḥ community observances during the evening during Ramaḍān in which the entire text of the Qur'ān is read by a prayer leader over the course of the month

Tawḥīd the Unity of God

Ta'wīl interpretation (for example, of the Qur'ān)

Tilāwah recitation of the Qur'ān

'Usūl al-fiqh intellectual foundations of jurisprudence

Wudū' a form of ritual ablution

Zakāt legal almsgiving (one of the "five pillars" of Islam)

Al-Zamakhsharī Abū'l-Qāsim Maḥmūd bin 'Umar Al-Zamakhsharī (d. 1144), grammarian and interpreter of the Qur'ān

BIBLIOGRAPHY

SELECTED INTRODUCTIONS TO THE QUR'ĀN

Campanini, Massimo. *The Qur'an: The Basics*. London, Routledge, 2007

Cook, Michael. *The Koran: A Very Short Introduction*. Oxford, Oxford University Press, 2000

Draz, Mohammad Abd Allah. *Introduction to the Qur'an*. London, I. B. Tauris, 2000

Esack, Farid. *The Qur'an: A User's Guide* (2nd ed.). Oxford, Oneworld Publications, 2002

Lawrence, Bruce. *The Qur'an: A Biography*. London, Atlantic, 2006

Leaman, Oliver. *The Qur'an: An Encyclopedia*. London and New York, Routledge, 2008

Matteson, Ingrid. *The Story of the Qur'an: Its History and Place in Muslim Life*. Oxford, Blackwell, 2008

McAuliffe, Jane Dammen, ed. *The Cambridge Companion to the Qur'ān*. Cambridge, Cambridge University Press, 2006

Rippin, Andrew, ed. *The Blackwell Companion to the Qur'ān*. Oxford, Blackwell, 2006

Robinson, Neal. *Discovering the Qur'ān: A Contemporary Approach to a Veiled Text*. Washington, D.C., Georgetown University Press, 2003

Saeed, Abdullah. *The Qur'an: An Introduction*. London and New York, Routledge, 2008

Siddiqui, Mona. *How to Read the Qur'an*. New York, W. W. Norton & Co., 2008

GENERAL REFERENCE

Encyclopedia of Islam

Kassis, Hanna E. *A Concordance of the Qur'ān.* Berkeley, University of California Press, 1982

McAuliffe, Jane Dammen, ed. *Encyclopaedia of the Qur'an* (5 vols.). Leiden, Brill, 2001–2006

Mir, Mustansir. *Dictionary of Qur'ānic Terms and Concepts*. New York, Garland, 1987

SUGGESTED FURTHER READING

Chapters 1 and 2: The Written Qur'an and The Multifaceted Qur'ān

Abdel Haleem, Muhammad. *Understanding the Qur'ān: Themes and Style.* London, I. B. Tauris, 2001

Cook, David. *Understanding Jihad.* Berkeley, University of California Press, 2005

El-Awa, Salwa M. S. *Textual Relations in the Qur'an: Relevance, Coherence and Structure*. London, Routledge, 2006

Haykal, Muhammad. *The Life of Muhammad.* Translated from 8th edition of the Arabic work by Isma`il Ragi A. Al Faruqi. North American Trust, 1976

Ibn Isḥāq (d. ca. 768). *The Making of the Last Prophet: A Reconstruction of the Earliest Biography of Muhammad.* Gordon Darnell Newby. Columbia, S.C., University of South Carolina Press, 1989

Rahman, Fazlur. *Major Themes of the Qur'ān*. Minneapolis, Bibliotheca Islamica, 1980

Chapter 3: Readings of the Qur'ān

Bunt, Gary R. *Virtually Islamic: Computer-mediated Communication and Cyber Islamic Environments*. Cardiff, University of Wales Press, 2000

Devji, Faisal. *Landscapes of the Jihad: Militancy, Morality, Modernity*. Ithaca, N.Y., Cornell University Press, 2005

Qadhi, Abu Ammaar Yasir. *An Introduction to the Sciences of the Qur'aan*. Birmingham, U.K., Al-Hidaayah, 1999

Saleh, Walid A. *The Formation of the Classical Tafsir Tradition: The Qur'an Commentary of Al-Tha'labi* (d. 427/1035). Leiden, Brill, 2004

Sands, Kristin. *Sufi Commentaries on the Qur'ān in Classical Islam*. New York, Routledge 2005

Von Denffer, Ahmad. *'Ulūm Al-Qur'ān: An Introduction to the Sciences of the Qur'an*. Leicester, U.K., The Islamic Foundation, 1983

Chapter 4: The Qur'ān's Guidance

Bakhtiar, Laleh. *Encyclopedia of Islamic Law: A Compendium of the Major Schools*. Chicago, ABC International Group, 1996

Chodkiewicz, Michael. *An Ocean without Shore: Ibn 'Arabi, the Book, and the Law*. Translated from the French by David Streight. Albany, State University of New York Press, 1993

Esack, Farid. *Qur'ān, Liberation, and Pluralism: An Islamic Perspective of Interreligious Solidarity Against Oppression*. Oxford, Oneworld Publications, 1997

Gwynne, Rosalind. *Logic, Rhetoric and Legal Reasoning in the Qur'ān: God's Arguments*. London and New York, RoutledgeCurzon, 2004

Kamali, Mohammad Hashim. *Principles of Islamic Jurisprudence* (3rd ed.). Cambridge, Islamic Texts Society, 2003

Rosen, Lawrence. *The Anthropology of Justice: Law as Culture in Islamic Society*. Cambridge, Cambridge University Press, 1989

Wadud, Amina. *Qur'an and Woman: Rereading the Sacred Text from a Woman's Perspective*. Oxford, Oxford University Press, 1999 [1992]

Weiss, Bernard G. *The Spirit of Islamic Law*. Athens, G.A., University of Georgia Press, 1998

Chapter 5: The Present Qur'ān

Blair, Sheila S. *Islamic Calligraphy*. Edinburgh, Edinburgh University Press, 2006

Ernst, Carl W. *The Shambhala Guide to Sufism*. Boston, Mass, Shambhala, 1997

Lings, Martin, *Splendours of Qur'an Calligraphy and Illumination*. New York, Thames and Hudson (distrib.), 2005

Nelson, Kristina. *The Art of Reciting the Qur'an*. Austin, University of Texas Press, 1985

Sells, Michael. *Early Islamic Mysticism: Sufi, Qur'an, Mi'raj, Poetic and Theological Writings*. New York, Paulist Press, 1996

Sirriyeh, Elizabeth. *Sufis and Anti-Sufis: The Defence, Rethinking and Rejection of Sufism in the Modern World*. Richmond, Surrey, Curzon, 1997

Waugh, Earle H. *Memory, Music and Religion: Morocco's Mystical Chanters*. Columbia, S.C., University of South Carolina Press, 2005

Chapter 6: Space, Time, and the Boundaries of Knowledge

Foltz, Richard C., Frederick M. Denny and Azizan Baharuddin, eds. *Islam and Ecology: A Bestowed Trust*. Cambridge, M.A., Center for the Study of World Religions, Harvard Divinity School, Distributed by Harvard University Press, 2003

Izutsu, Toshihiko. *Ethico-religious Concepts in the Qur'an*. Montréal, McGill University Press, 1966

Sells, Michael. *Approaching the Qur'an: The Early Revelations* [book with accompanying CD sound recording]. Ashland, O.R., White Cloud Press, 1999

Wheeler, Brannon M., ed. and trans. *Prophets in the Qur'ān: An Introduction to the Qur'an as Muslim Exegesis*. New York, Continuum, 2002

OTHER WORKS

Abdel Haleem, Muhammad A. S. *English Translations of the Qur'an: The Making of an Image*. London, SOAS, 2006

—— "Grammatical Shift for Rhetorical Purposes: *Iltifāt* and Related Features of the Qur'ān." Bulletin of South Asian Studies 60:3 (1992): 409–410

Abou El Fadl, Khaled. *And God Knows the Soldiers: The Authoritative and Authoritarian in Islamic Discourses*. Lanham, M.D., University Press of America, 2001

—— *Speaking in God's Name: Islamic Law, Authority and Women*. Oxford, Oneworld Publications, 2001

Abu Rabi', Ibrahim M. *Intellectual Origins of Islamic Resurgence the Modern Arab World*. Albany, State University of New York Press, 1996

Adams, Charles J. "Abū'l-A'lā Mawdūdī's Tafhīm Al- Qur'ān." In A. Rippin, ed. *Approaches to the History of the Interpretation of the Qur'ān*. Oxford, Clarendon, 1988, pp. 307–324

Aftab, Tahera. "Text and Practice: Women and Nature in Islam." In Alaine Low and Soraya Tremayne, eds. *Women as Sacred Custodians of the Earth? Women, Spirituality and the Environment*. Oxford, Berghahn Books, 2001, pp. 141–158

Ahmed, Leila. *Women and Gender in Islam*. New Haven, Yale University Press, 1992

Akbar, Ali. *Kaidah Menulis dan Karya-Karya Master Kaligrafi Islam*. Jakarta, PT Pustaka Firdaus, 1995

Ali, Kecia. *Sexual Ethics in Islam: Feminist Reflections on Qur'an, Hadith and Jurisprudence*. Oxford, Oneworld Publications, 2006

Anderson, Jon W. "New Media, New Publics: Reconfiguring the Public Sphere of Islam." *Social Research* 70:3 (2003): 887–903

Anway, Carol, L. *Daughters of Another Path: Experiences of American Women Choosing Islam* (4th ed.). Lee's Summit, M.O., Yawna Publications, 2000

Appadurai, Arjun. "Disjuncture and Difference in the Global Economy." In Bruce Robbins, ed. *The Phantom Public Sphere.* Minneapolis, University of Minnesota Press, 1993, pp. 269–295

Arberry, Arthur J. *The Koran Interpreted.* New York, Macmillan, 1955.

Asy-Syarawi, Muhammad Mutawalli. *Misteri Surat Al-Kahfi* (*The Mystery of Surat Al-Kahf*; original Arabic title given as: *Al-Qasas al-qur'ani fi surah al-kahfi*). Translated into Indonesian by Khoirul Amru Harahap Sochimin. Kedung Wuluh Purwokerto, Java, Indonesia, Pustaka Teladan / Jendela Wawasan Keagamaan, 2007

Atiyeh, George, ed. *The Book in the Islamic World: The Written Word and Communication in the Middle East.* Albany, State University of New York Press, 1995

Awn, Peter J. *Satan's Tragedy and Redemption: Iblīs in Sufi Psychology.* Leiden, Brill, 1983

Ayoub, Mahmoud "The Prayer of Islam: A Presentation of *Sūrat Al-Fātihah* in Muslim Exegesis." *Journal of the American Academy of Religion* Thematic Issue 47:4 (1979): 35–48

—— *The Qur'ān and Its Interpreters*, Vol. 1. Albany, State University of New York Press, 1984

—— *The Qur'ān and Its Interpreters: The House of 'Imrān*, Vol. 2. Albany, State University of New York Press, 1992

—— "The Speaking Qur'ān and the Silent Qur'ān: A Study of the Principles and Development of Imāmī Shī'ī Tafsīr." In Andrew Rippin, ed. *Approaches to the History of the Interpretation of the Qur'ān*. Oxford, Clarendon, 1988, pp. 177–198

Badwilan, Ahmad Salim. *Panduan Cepat Menghafal Al-Qur'an dan Rahasia-rahasia Keajaibannya* (*Quick Guide to Memorizing the Qur'an and Secrets of its Miracles*). Translated from Arabic into Indonesian by Rusli. Jogyakarta, Indonesia, DIVA Press (Anggota IKAPI), 2009

—— *Seni Menghafal Al-Qur'an: Resep Manjur Menghafal Al- Qur'an yang Telah terbukti Keampuhannya* (*The Art of Memorizing the Qur'an: A Powerful Recipe with Proven Effectiveness*, original Arabic title given as: *Nisaun la ya'rifnalya's*). Translated into Indonesian by Abu Hudzaifah. Solo (Surakarta), Indonesia, Wacana Ilmiah Press (WIP), 2008

Barlas, Asma. *"Believing Women" in Islam: Unreading Patriarchal Interpretations of the Qur'an*. Austin, University of Texas Press, 2002

Bell, Richard. *Bell's Introduction to the Qur'ān*. Revised by W. Montgomery Watt. Edinburgh, Edinburgh University Press, 1970

Benthall, Jonathan and Jérôme Bellion-Jourdan. *The Charitable Crescent: Politics of Aid in the Muslim World.* London, I. B. Tauris, 2003

Bonner, Michael. *Jihad in Islamic History: Doctrines and Practice.* Princeton, N.J., Princeton University Press, 2006

Boullata, Issa J. "Rhetorical Interpretation of the Qur'ān: *I'jāz* and Related Topics." In Andrew Rippin, ed. *Approaches to the History of the Interpretation of the Qur'ān.* Oxford, Clarendon, 1988, pp. 139–157

—— "Sayyid Qutb and Literary Appreciation of the Qur'ān." In Issa J. Boullata, ed. *Literary Structures of Religious Meaning in the Qur'ān.* Richmond, Surrey, U.K., Curzon Press, 2000, pp. 354–371

Brockopp, Jonathan E., ed. *Islamic Ethics of Life: Abortion, War and Euthanasia.* Columbia, University of South Carolina Press, 2003

—— ed. *Muslim Medical Ethics: From Theory to Practice.* Columbia, University of South Carolina Press, 2008

Brown, Norman O. "The Apocalypse of Islam." *Social Text* 8 (1983): 155–171

Buehler, Arthur. *Sufi Heirs of the Prophet: The Indian Naqshbandiyya and the Rise of the Mediating Sufi Shaykh.* Columbia, University of South Carolina Press, 1998

Bunt, Gary R. *iMuslims: Rewiring the House of Islam.* Chapel Hill, N.C., University of North Carolina Press, 2009

—— *Virtually Islamic: Computer-mediated Communication and Cyber Islamic Environments.* Cardiff, University of Wales Press, 2000

Burton, John. *The Collection of the Qur'an.* Cambridge, Cambridge University Press, 1977

—— *The Sources of Islamic Law: Islamic Theories of Abrogation.* Edinburgh, Edinburgh University Press, 1990

Butler, Judith. *Gender Trouble: Feminism and the Subversion of Identity.* New York, Routledge, 2006

Cook, David. *Contemporary Muslim Apocalyptic Literature.* Syracuse, N.Y., Syracuse University Press, 2005

Cook, Michael. *Studies in the Origins of Early Islamic Culture and Tradition.* Burlington, V.T., Ashgate/Variorum, 2004

Crone, Patricia. *Meccan Trade and the Rise of Islam.* Princeton, Princeton University Press, 1987

—— "What do We Actually Know about Mohammed?" Published online on www.opendemocracy.net, 30 August, 2006

—— and Michael Cook. *Hagarism: The Making of the Islamic World.* Cambridge, Cambridge University Press, 1977

Curtis, Edward IV. *Black Muslim Religion in the Nation of Islam, 1960–1975.* Chapel Hill, University of North Carolina Press, 2006

—— *Islam in Black America: Identity, Liberation and Difference in*

African-American Islamic Thought. Albany, State University of New York Press, 2002

Daftary, Farhad. *The Ismā'īlīs: Their History and Doctrines* (4th ed.). Cambridge, Cambridge University Press, 1999

Danielson, Virginia. *The Voice of Egypt: Umm Kulthum, Arabic Song, and Egyptian Society in the Twentieth Century*. Chicago, University of Chicago Press, 1997

Dehivi, [Hazrat Maulana] Ahmad Saeed ("Sehban-ul-Hind"). *Prophetic Medical Sciences*. Translated from Urdu to English by Badr Azimabadi. Karachi, Darul Ishaat, 1989

Denny, Frederick M. "The *Adab* of Qur'ān Recitation: Text and Context." In A. H. Johns, ed. *International Congress for the Study of the Qur'ān*. Canberra, Australian National University, 1981, pp. 143–160.

—— "Ethical Dimensions of Islamic Ritual Law." In Edwin B. Firmage, Bernard Weiss, and John W. Welch, eds. *Religion and Law: Biblical-Judaic and Islamic Perspectives*, Winona Lake, Eisenbrauns, 1990, pp. 199–210.

—— "Exegesis and Recitation: Their Development as Classical Forms of Qur'ānic Piety." In Frank E. Reynolds and Theodore M. Ludwig, eds. *Transitions and Transformations in the History of Religions: Essays in Honor of Joseph M. Kitagawa*. Leiden, E. J. Brill, 1980, pp. 91–123

—— "Qur'ān Recitation: A Tradition of Oral Performance and Transmission." *Oral Tradition* 4:1–2 (1989): 5–26

Donner, Fred M. "From Believers to Muslims: Patterns of Communal Identity in Early Islam." *Al-Abhath* 50–51 (2002–2004): 9–53

—— "The Sources of Islamic Conceptions of War." In John Kelsay and James Turner Jonson, eds. *Just War and Jihad: Historical and Theoretical Perspectives on War and Peace in Western and Islamic Traditions*. New York, Greenwood Press, 1991, pp. 31–69

Draz, M. A. *The Moral World and the Qur'ān*. London, Palgrave, 2008

Drewes, G. W. J. and L. F. Brakel, eds. and trans. *The Poems of Hamzah Fansuri*. Dordrecht, Holland and Cinnaminson, N.J., Foris Publications, 1986

Eickelman, Dale F. "The Art of Memory: Islamic Education and Its Social Reproduction." *Comparative Studies in Society and History* 20:4 (1978): 485–516

—— *Knowledge and Power in Morocco: The Education of a Twentieth-Century Notable*. Princeton, Princeton University Press, 1985

—— and Jon W. Anderson, eds. *New Media in the Muslim World: The Emerging Public Sphere*. Bloomington, Indiana University Press, 2003

Ernst, Carl. *Following Muhammad: Rethinking Islam in the Modern World*. Chapel Hill, University of North Carolina Press, 2003

—— "The Spirit of Islamic Calligraphy: Bābā Shāh Iṣfahānī's *Ādāb al-mashq*." *Journal of the American Oriental Society* 112:2 (1992): 279–286

Esposito, John and Natana J. DeLong-Bas. *Women and Muslim Family Law* (2nd ed.). Syracuse, N.Y., Syracuse University Press, 2001

Fakhry, Majid. *An Interpretation of the Qur'an: English Translation of the Meanings, A Bilingual Edition*. New York, New York University Press, 2002

Al-Faruqi, Lois Ibsen. "The Cantillation of the Qur'ān." *Asian Music* 19:1 (1987): 2–25

—— "Music, Musicians, and Muslim Law." *Asian Music* 17:1 (1985): 13–36

Faruqui, Naser I., Asit K. Biswas, and Murad J. Bino, eds. *Water Management in Islam*. Water Resources Management and Policy Series. New York and Paris, International Development Research Centre and Tokyo, United Nations University Press, 2001

Firestone, Reuven. *Jihad: The Origin of Holy War in Islam*. New York, Oxford University Press, 1999

Flügel, Gustav. *Corani – Textus Arabicus*. Ridgewood, Gregg Press, 1965

Foltz, Richard, C., Frederick M. Denny, and Azizan Baharuddin, eds. *Islam and Ecology: A Bestowed Trust*. Cambridge, Harvard University Press, 2003

Freedberg, David. *The Power of Images: Studies in the History and Theory of Response*. Chicago, University of Chicago Press, 1989

Gade, Anna M. *Perfection Makes Practice: Learning, Emotion, and the Recited Qur'ān in Indonesia*. Honolulu, University of Hawai'i Press, 2004

Gätje, Helmut. *The Qur'ān and Its Exegesis: Selected Texts with Classcial and Modern Interpretations*. Alford T. Welch, ed. and trans. Oxford, Oneworld Publications, 1997

Geertz, Clifford. *Islam Observed: Religious Development in Morocco and Indonesia*. Chicago, University of Chicago Press, 1968

George, Kenneth M. "Designs on Indonesian's Muslim Communities." *Journal of Asian Studies* 57:3 (1988): 693–713

—— *Picturing Islam: Art and Ethics in a Muslim Lifeworld*. Malden, Wiley-Blackwell, 2010

Al-Ghazālī, Abū Ḥāmid Muḥammad bin Muḥammad Al-Tūsī. *The Faith and Practice of Al-Ghazzali* [*Al-munkidh min al-dalāl*; *Badāyat al-hidāyah*]. W. Montgomery Watt, trans. London, G. Allen and Unwin, 1953

—— *The Jewels of the Qur'ān: Al-Ghazali's Theory* [*Kitāb Jawāhir Al-Qur'ān*]. Muhammad Abul Quasem, trans. London, Kegan Paul International, 1977

—— *The Niche of Lights* [*Mishkāt al-anwār*]. Arabic–English parallel text, trans. and annotated by David Buchman. Provo, U.T., Brigham Young University Press, 1988

—— *The Ninety-Nine Beautiful Names of God* [*Al-Mawāsid al-asna fī sharḥ asmā' Allāh al-ḥusnā*]. David B. Burrell and Nazih Daher, trans. Cambridge, Islamic Texts Society 2004 [1992]

—— *The Recitation and Interpretation of the Qur'ān: Al-Ghazzali's Theory* [*Iḥyā' 'ulūm al-dīn*, Book 8]. Muhammad Abul Quasem, trans. Boston, Kegan Paul International, 1983

Graham, William A. *Beyond the Written Word: Oral Aspects of Scripture in the History of Religion*. New York, Cambridge University Press, 1987

—— *Divine Word and Prophetic Word in Early Islam*. The Hague, Mouton, 1977

—— "Qur'ān as Spoken Word: An Islamic Contribution to the Understanding of Scripture." In Richard Martin, ed. *Approaches to Islam in Religious Studies*. Tucson, University of Arizona Press, 1985, pp. 23–40.

—— "Scripture as Spoken Word." In Miriam Levering, ed. *Rethinking Scripture: Essays From a Comparative Perspective*. Albany, State University of New York Press, 1989, pp. 129–169

—— "Those Who Study and Teach the Qur'ān." In A. H. Johns, ed. *International Congress for the Study of the Qur'ān*. Canberra, Australian National University, 1981, pp. 9–28

Hallaq, Wael B. *A History of Islamic Legal Theories: An Introduction to Sunni Usul Al-Fiqh*. Cambridge, Cambridge University Press, 1997

—— *Law and Legal Theory in Classical and Medieval Islam*. New York, Variorum, 1995

—— "Was Shafi'i the Master Architect of Islamic Jurisprudence?" *International Journal of Middle East Studies* 25 (1993): 587–605

—— "Was the Gate of Ijtihad Closed?" *International Journal of Middle East Studies* 16 (1984): 3–41

Halm, Heinz. *Shi'a Islam: From Religion to Revolution* (2nd ed). Princeton, Markus Wiener, 1999

Hawting, G. R. *The Idea of Idolatry and the Emergence of Islam: From Polemic to History*. Cambridge, Cambridge University Press, 1999

—— and Abdul-Kader A. Shareef, eds. *Approaches to the Qur'ān*. New York, Routledge, 1993

Heath, Jennifer, ed. *The Veil: Women Writers on its History, Lore, and Politics*. Berkeley, University of California Press, 2008

Heer, Nicholas. "Abu Hamid Al-Ghazali's Esoteric Exegesis of the Koran." In L. Lewisohn, ed. *Classical Persian Sufism: From its Origins to Rumi*, Oxford, Oneworld Publications, 1999, pp. 235–258

Hirtenstein, Stephen. *Unlimited Mercifier: the Spiritual Life and Thought of Ibn 'Arabī*. Ashland, O.R. White Cloud Press, 1999.

Hodgson, Marshall G. S. *The Venture of Islam: Conscience and History in a World Civilization* (3 vols). Chicago, University of Chicago Press, 1974.

Hooker, M. B. *Indonesian Islam: Social Change through Contemporary Fatāwā*. Honolulu, University of Hawai'i Press, 2003

Husaini, Syed Kaleemullah. *Easy Tajwid: A Text Book on Phonetics and Rules of Pronunciation and Intonation of the Glorious Qur'ān*. Syed Noorullah Khadri and Quadir Husain Khan, trans. Chicago, Muslim Community Center, 1990

Israeli, Raphael. "Translation as Exegesis: The Opening *Sūra* of the Qur'ān in Chinese." In *Islam: Essays on Scripture, Thought, and Society*, Peter G. Riddell and Tony Street, eds. Leiden, Brill, 1997, pp. 81–103

Izutsu, Toshihiko. *God and Man in the Qur'ān: Semantics of the Koranic Weltanschauung*. Tokyo, Keio Institute of Cultural and Linguistic Studies, 1964

Jeffery, Arthur J. *Materials for the Study of the History of the Text of the Qur'ān*. Leiden, Brill, 1937

—— "The Textual History of the Qur'ān." *Journal of the Middle Eastern Society* 1947, pp. 35–49

Johns, Anthony H. "Let My People Go!: Sayyid Qutb and the Vocation of Moses." *Islam and Christian–Muslim Relations* 1:2 (1990): 143–170

—— ed. "The Qur'ān on the Qur'ān." *In International Congress for the Study of the Qur'ān*. Canberra, Australian National University, 1981, pp. 1–8

—— "The Qur'ānic Presentation of the Joseph Story: Naturalistic or Formulaic Language?" In G. R. Hawting and Abdul-Kader A. Shareef, eds. *Approaches to the Qur'ān*. New York, Routledge, 1993, pp. 37–70

de Jong, Frederick and Bernd Radtke, eds. *Islamic Mysticism Contested: Thirteen Centuries of Controversies and Polemics*. Leiden, Brill, 1999

Juergensmeyer, Mark. *Terror in the Mind of God: The Global Rise of Religious Violence*. Berkeley, University of California Press, 2000

Juynboll, G. H. A. "The Position of Qur'ān Recitation in Early Islam." *Journal of Semitic Studies* 19 (1974): 240–251

—— The *Qurrā'* in Early Islamic History." *Journal of the Economic and Social History of the Orient* 16 (1973): 113–129

Kahle, Paul. "The Arabic Readers of the Koran." *Journal of Near Eastern Studies* 8 (1949): 65–71

Katz, Marion. *Birth of the Prophet Muhammad: Devotional Piety in Sunni Islam*. New York, Routledge, 2007

—— *Body of Text: The Emergence of the Sunni Law of Ritual Purity*. Albany, State University of New York Press, 2002

Kermani, Navid. "The Aesthetic Reception of the Qur'ān as Reflected in

Early Muslim History." In Issa J. Boullata, ed. *Literary Structures of Religious Meaning in the Qur'ān*. Richmond, Surrey, U.K., Curzon Press, 2000 pp. 255–276

Keshavarz, Fatemeh. *Reading Mystical Lyric: The Case of Jalāl Al-Dīn Rūmī*. Columbia, University of South Carolina Press, 1998

Khaleel, Muhammad and Andrew Rippin, eds. *Coming to Terms with the Qur'ān: A Volume in Honour of Professor Issa Boullata*. Islamic Publications International, 2008

Kinberg, Leah. "*Muḥkamāt* and *Mutashābihāt* (Koran 3/7): Implication of a Koranic Pair of Terms in Medieval Exegesis." In Andrew Rippin, ed. *The Qur'an: Formative Interpretation*. Aldershot, Ashgate Variorum, 1999, pp. 283–312

Al-Kisā'i, Muḥammad ibn 'Abd Allāh. *Tales of the Prophets* (*Qiṣāṣ Al-anbiyā'*). Wheeler M. Thackston, Jr., trans. Chicago, Great Books of the Islamic World, Inc., 1977

Knysh, Alexander. *Islamic Mysticism: A Short History*. Leiden, Brill, 2000

Kueny, Kathryn. *The Rhetoric of Sobriety: Wine in Early Islam*. Albany, State University of New York Press, 2001

Kugle, Scott Siraj Al-Haqq. "Sexuality, Diversity and Ethics in the Agenda of Progressive Muslims." In Omid Safi, ed. *Progressive Muslims: On Justice, Gender and Pluralism*. Oxford, Oneworld Publications, 2003, pp. 190–234

Lawrence, Bruce. *Defenders of God: The Fundamentalist Revolt Against the Modern Age* (1st ed.). San Francisco, Harper & Row, 1989

Lawson, B. Todd. "Akhbārī Shī'ī Approaches to *Tafsīr*." In G. R. Hawting and Abdul-Kader Shareef, eds. *Approaches to the Qur'ān*. New York, Routledge, 1993, pp. 173–210

Levtzion, Nehemia, ed. *Conversion to Islam*. New York, Holmes & Meier, 1979

Lings, Martin. *The Quranic Art of Calligraphy and Illuminations*. London, World of Islam Festival Trust, 1976

Makdisi, George. *The Rise of Colleges: Institutions of Learning in Islam and the West*. Edinburgh, Edinburgh University Press, 1981

Marcinkowski, Muhammad Ismail. "Some Reflections on Alleged Twelver Shi'ite Attitudes Toward the Integrity of the Qur'an." *The Muslim World* 91:1/2 (Spring, 2001): 137–154

Madelung, Wilferd, "The Origins of the Controversy Concerning the Creation of the Koran." In Wilferd Madelung, *Religious Schools and Sects in Medieval Islam*, London, Variorum Reprints, 1985, pp. 504–525

Martin, Richard C., ed. *Approaches to Islam in Religious Studies*. Tucson, University of Arizona Press, 1985

—— "Understanding the Qur'ān in Text and Context." *History of Religions* 21:4 (1982): 361–384

Marty, Martin and Scott Appleby, eds. *Fundamentalisms Observed.* Chicago, University of Chicago Press, 1991

McAuliffe, Jane Dammen. *Qur'ānic Christians: An Analysis of Classical and Modern Exegesis*. Cambridge, Cambridge University Press, 1991

—— "Text and Textuality: Q. 3:7 as a Point of Intersection." In Issa J. Boullata, ed. *Literary Structures of Religious Meaning in the Qur'ān*, Richmond, Surrey, U.K., Curzon Press, 2000, pp. 56–76

McFague, Sallie. *The Body of God: An Ecological Theology*. London, SCM Press, 1993

McNeill, William H. and Marilyn Robinson Waldman, eds. *The Islamic World.* Chicago, University of Chicago Press, 1973

Mernissi, Fatima. *The Veil and The Male Elite: A Feminist Interpretation Of Women's Rights In Islam*. New York, Basic Books, 1992

Messick, Brinkley. "Media Fuftis." In Muhammad Masud, Khalid, Brinkley Messick, and David S. Powers, eds. *Islamic Legal Interpretation: Muftis and their Fatwas*. Cambridge, M.A., Harvard University Press, 1996, pp. 310–322

Mir, Musansir. *Coherence in the Qur'ān: A Study of Iṣlāḥī's Concept of Naẓm in Tadabbur-I Qur'ān*. Indianapolis, American Trust, 1986

—— "Irony in the Qur'ān: A Study of the Story of Joseph." In Issa J. Boullata, ed. *Literary Structures of Religious Meaning in the Qur'ān*. Richmond, Surrey, U.K., Curzon Press, 2000, pp. 173–187

—— "The *Sura* as a Unity: A Twentieth-Century Development in Qur'an Exegesis." In G. R. Hawting and Abdul-Kader A. Shareef, eds. *Approaches to the Qur'ān*. London, Routledge, 1993, pp. 211–224

Al-Miṣrī, Aḥmad ibn Naqīb. *Reliance of the Traveler: A Classical manual of Islamic Sacred Law* [*'Umdāt al-sālik*]. Nuh Ha Mim Keller, ed. and trans. Beltsville, Maryland, Amana Publications, 1994

Momen, Moojan. *An Introduction to Shi'i Islam*. New Haven, Yale University Press, 1985

Moosa, Ebrahim. *Ghazālī and the Poetics of Imagination*. Chapel Hill, University of North Carolina Press, 2005

Motzki, Harald. "The Collection of the Qur'an: A Reconsideration of Western Views in Light of Recent Methodological Developments." *Der Islam* 78 (2001): 1–34

Mudarressi, Hossein. "Early Debates on the Integrity of the Qur'an: A Brief Survey." *Studia Islamica* 77 (1993): 5–39

Nasr, Sayyed Hosein. "Islam and Music: The Legal and Spiritual Dimensions." In Lawrence E. Sullivan, ed. *Enchanting Powers: Music in the World's Religions*. Cambridge, M.A., Harvard University Press, 1997, pp. 219–236

Al-Nawawi, Ab, Zakariya' Yahya ibn Sharaf Al-Din. "*Al-Tibyan fi Adab Hamalat Al-Qur'ān* [excerpt]." Translated into English in Andrew Rippin and Jan Knappert, eds. *Textual Sources for the Study of Islam*. Chicago, University of Chicago Press, 1986, pp. 100–105

Nelson, Kristina. *The Art of Reciting the Qur'ān*. Austin, University of Texas Press, 1985

—— "Reciter and Listener: Some Factors Shaping the *Mujawwad* Style of Qur'ānic Reciting." *Ethnomusicology* 26:1 (1982): 41–48

Newby, Gordon. "Tafsīr Isra'iliyyāt." *Journal of the American Academy of Religion Thematic Issue* 47:4 (1979): 685–699

Nöldeke, Theodor. *Geschichte des Qorāns* (reprint). Boston, Elibron Classics, 2005

Norris. "*Qisas* Elements in the Qur'ān." In A. F. L. Beetson, ed. *Arabic Literature to the End of the Umayyad Period*. Cambridge, Cambridge University Press, 1983, pp. 246–259

Ory, Solange. "Calligraphy" (8 pp.). Brill Online: Encyclopaedia of the Qur'ān (2001–2006)

Peters, F. E. *Muhammad and the Origins of Islam*. Albany, State University of New York Press, 1994

—— *A Reader on Classical Islam*. Princeton, Princeton University Press, 1994

Peters, J. R. T. M. *God's Created Speech: A Study in the Speculative Theology of the Mu'tazili Wadi'l-Qudat Abū'l-Ḥasan 'Abd Al-Jabbār b. Aḥmad Al-Ḥamdani*. Leiden, Brill, 1976

Poonawalla, Ismail K. "*Ismā'īlī ta'wīl* of the Qur'ān." In Andrew Rippin, ed. *Approaches to the History of the Interpretation of the Qur'ān*. Oxford, Clarendon, 1988, pp. 199–222

Powers, David S. "The Exegetical Genre *Nāsikh Al-Qur'ān wa mansūkh-uhu*." In Andrew Rippin, ed. *Approaches to the History of the Interpretation of the Qur'ān*. Oxford, Clarendon Press, 1988, pp. 117–138

Powers, Paul R. *Intent in Islamic Law: Motive and Meaning in Sunni Fiqh*. Leiden, Brill, 2006

Qureshi, Regula Burckhardt. "Sounding the Word: Music in the Life of Islam." In Lawrence E. Sullivan, ed. *Enchanting Powers: Music in the World's Religions*. Cambridge, M.A., Harvard University Press, 1997, pp. 263–298

Qutb, Sayyid. *In the Shade of the Qur'ān* [*Fi zilāl Al-Qur'ān*] (18 vols.) Translated into English. Markfield, Islamic Foundation, 2004

—— *Milestones*. Cedar Rapids, Iowa, The Mother Mosque Foundation (n.d.).

Rahman, Fazlur. *Islam and Modernity: Transformation of an Intellectual Tradition*. Chicago, University of Chicago Press, 1982

—— "Some Key Ethical Concepts of the Qur'ān." *Journal of Religious Ethics* 11 (1983): 170–185

Reinhart, A. Kevin. *Before Revelation: The Boundaries of Muslim Moral Thought*. Albany, State University of New York Press, 1995

—— "Impurity / No Danger." *History of Religions* 30:1 (1990): 1–24

—— "Islamic Law as Islamic Ethics." *Journal of Religious Ethics* 2:2 (1983): 186–203

Riddell, Peter. *Islam in Malay-Speaking World: Transmission and Responses*. Honolulu, University of Hawai'i Press, 2001

Rippin, Andrew, ed. *Approaches to the History of the Interpretation of the Qur'ān*. (Oxford, 1988)

—— "The Function of *Asbab Al-Nuzul* in Qur'anic Exegesis." *BSOAS* 51 (1988): 1–20

—— "Interpreting the Bible Through the Qur'ān." G. R. Hawting and Abdul-Kader A. Shareef, eds. *Approaches to the Qur'ān*. New York, Routledge, 1993, pp. 249–259

—— ed. *The Qur'an: Formative Interpretation*. Aldershot, U.K., Ashgate/ Variorum, 1999

—— ed. *The Qur'an: Style and Contents*. Aldershot, U.K., Ashgate/ Variorum, 2000

—— ed. *Textual Relations in Qur'ān*. London, Routledge 2005

—— and Jan Knappert, eds. and trans. *Textual Sources for the Study of Islam*. Chicago, University of Chicago Press, 1990

Roberts, Nancy N. "A Parable of Blessing: The Significance and Message of the Qur'ānic Account of the Companions of the Cave." *The Muslim World* 83:3/4 (1993): 295–317

Sa'dulloh, H. *9 Cara Praktis Menghafal Al- Qur'an* [*Nine Practical Ways to Memorizing the Qur'an*]. Jakarta, Gema Insani, 2008

Saeed, Abdullah, ed. *Approaches to the Qur'an in Contemporary Indonesia*. Oxford, Oxford University Press; London, in association with the Institute of Ismaili Studies, 2005

Safi, Omid. *Memories of Muhammad: Why the Prophet Matters*. New York, HarperOne, 2009

—— ed. *Progressive Muslims: On Justice, Gender and Pluralism*. Oxford, Oneworld Publications, 2003

Said, Edward. *Orientalism*. New York, Vintage, 1979

Al-Sa'id, Labib. *The Recited Koran* [*Al-Jam'al Al-Ṣawti l-Awwal li'l-Qur'ān Al-Karīm*]. Bernard Weiss, M. A. Rauf, and Morrow Berger, trans. Princeton, Darwin Press, 1975

Schimmel, Annemarie. *And Muhammad is His Messenger: The Veneration of the Prophet in Islamic Piety*. Chapel Hill, University of North Carolina Press, 1985

—— *Calligraphy and Islamic Culture*. New York, New York University Press, 1984

—— *Mystical Dimensions of Islam*. Chapel Hill, University of North Carolina Press, 1975

Sells, Michael. *Desert Tracings: Six Classical Arabian Odes by 'Alqama, Shānfara, Labīd, 'Antara, Al-A'sha, and Dhu Al-Rūmma*. Middletown, Connecticut, Wesleyan University Press, 1989

Al-Shāfi'ī, Muḥammad bin Idrīs. *Al-Shāfi'ī's Risāla: Treatise on the Foundations of Islamic Jurisprudence* (2nd ed.). Translated with Introduction and Appendices by Majid Khadduri. Cambridge, Islamic Texts Society, 1997

Silvers, Laury. "'In the Book We Have Left Out Nothing': The Ethical Problem of the Existence of Verse 4:34 in the Qur'an." *Comparative Islamic Studies* 2:2 (2006): 171–180

Smith, Jane I. and Yvonne Haddad. "The Virgin Mary and Islamic Tradition and Commentary." *The Muslim World* 79 (1989): 161–187

Stowasser, Barbara. *Gender Issues and Qur'ān Interpretation*. New York, Oxford University Press, 1998

—— *Women in the Qur'ān, Traditions, and Interpretation*. New York, Oxford University Press, 1994

Al-Ṭabarī, Muḥammad bin Jarīr. *The Commentary of the Qur'an* [*Jamī' al-bayān fī tafsīr al-Qur'ān*]. Abridged and trans. by J. Cooper. Oxford University Press, 1987

Taji-Farouki, Suha, ed. *Modern Muslim Intellectuals and the Qur'ān*. Oxford and London, Oxford University Press in association with the Institute of Ismaili Studies, 2004

Tibawi, A. L. "Is the Qur'ān Translatable?: Early Muslim Opinion." *Muslim World* 52 (1962): 4–16

Van Doorn-Harder, Pieternella. *Women Shaping Islam: Indonesian Women Reading the Qur'an*. Urbana, University of Illinois Press, 2006

Voll, John. *Islam: Continuity and Change in the Modern World* (2nd ed.). Syracuse, Syracuse University Press, 1994

Voll, John. "Revival and Reform in Islamic History: *Tajdīd* and *Iṣlāḥ*." In John L. Esposito, ed. *Voices of Resurgent Islam*. New York, Oxford University Press, 1983, pp. 32–47

Wadud, Amina. *Inside the Gender Jihad: Women's Reform in Islam*. Oxford, Oneworld Publications, 2006

Waldman, Marilyn. "New Approaches to 'Biblical' Materials in the Qur'ān." *Muslim World* 75 (1985): 1–16

Wansbrough, John. *Qur'anic Studies: Sources and Methods of Scriptural Interpretation*. Oxford, Oxford University Press, 1977

Waugh, Earle. *The Munshidin of Egypt: Their World and their Song*. Columbia, S.C., University of South Carolina Press, 1989

Welch, Alfred T. "Allah and Other Supernatural Beings: The Emergence of the Qur'ānic Doctrine of *Tawhid*." *Journal of the American Academy of Religion Thematic Issue* 47:4 (1979): 733–757

Welch, Alfred T. "Formulaic Features of the Punishment-Stories." In Issa J. Boullata, ed. *Literary Structures of Religious Meaning in the Qur'ān*. Richmond, Surrey, U.K., Curzon Press, 2000, pp. 77–116.

—— "Muḥammad's Understanding of Himself: The Koranic Data." In Richard G. Hovannisian and Speros Vryonis, Jr., eds. *Islam's Understanding of Itself.* Malibu, C.A., Undena Publications, 1983, pp. 15–52

Wheeler, Brannon M. *Moses in the Qur'ān and Islamic Exegesis*. Richmond, Curzon, 2001

Whittingham, Martin. *Al-Ghazali and the Qur'ān: One Book, Many Meanings*. New York, Routledge, 2007

Wild, Stephan. "Spatial and Temporal Implications of the Qur'ānic Concepts of *Nuzūl, Tanzīl*, and *Inzāl*." In Stephan Wild, ed. *The Qur'ān as Text*. Leiden, Brill, 1996, pp. 137–152

Winkel, Eric. *Mysteries of Purity: Ibn Al-'Arabi's Asrār Al-Tahārah*. Notre Dame, Indiana, Cross Cultural Publications, 1995

Zen, A. Muhaimin. *Tata Cara / Problematika Menghafal Al Qur'an dan Petunjuk-petunjuknya* [*Issues in Memorizing the Qur'an and their Solution*]. Jakarta, Pustaka Alhusna, 1985

VIDEOGRAPHY AND DISCOGRAPHY

Chanting of the Sufi Masters (cassette and CD soundrecording, KAZI Publications), with accompanying musical score, *Remembrance of God Liturgy of the Sufi Naqshbandi Masters* (2nd ed.). Chicago, ABC International Group, 1998

Celebrating the Prophet in the Remembrance of God: Sufi Dhikr in Egypt [videorecording]. Written, narrated, and produced by Valerie J. Hoffman. Urbana, Illinois, University of Illinois at Urbana-Champaign, Office of Instructional Resources, Division of Educational Technologies, 1977

Is the Bible God's Word? (videorecording). Ahmed Deedat and Jimmy Swaggart: Deedat's American Tour. Durban, South Africa, Islamic Propagation Centre International and Elgin, Illinois, Community Productions, ca.1995

The Message: The Story of Islam (videorecording). Transcas International Films.

Recitation of Al Qur'an, Recited by Late Qari Abdul Basit Abdus Samad (videorecording). Recorded live at the Muslim Community Center, Chicago, U.S.A.

LIST OF VERSES CITED

Entries for each *sūrah* are structured by increasing *āyah* number; * indicates that the English meaning, Arabic transliteration, or Arabic rendering of the entire *sūrah* (not partial quote) appears on the designated page; a page number appearing alone indicates the designated *sūrah* is mentioned or discussed on the page with that number; verses are indexed below by *sūrah* according to the format **chapter: verse(s)/page(s)**

1 **Al-Fātiḥah:** *69; *189; *194; 4; 79; 187–9; 206; 209

2 **Al-Baqarah:** 85; **2:8–20**/98; **2:8–15**/79–80; **2:14**/37; **2:23**/166; **2:30–9**/39; **2:30–1**/156; **2:98**/37; **2:115**/92; **2:117**/36; **2:127**/120; **2:136**/79, 175–6; **2:144**/116; **2:148**/29; **2:149–50**/116; **2:163–4**/220–1; **2:177**/33, 114; **2:183–5**/118–19; **2:183–4**/118; **2:185**/61; **2:187**/22, 118; **2:196–203**/120; **2:206**/135; **2:215–20**/132; **2:219**/133, 139; **2:228**/22; **2:255**/93–5, 115, 131, 188, 191, 194; **2:256**/131; **2:285**/33

3 **Āl ʻImrān:** 85; 232; **3:7**/84, 87, 88, 134–5; **3:18**/115; **3:26–7**/79; **3:37**/44; **3:45–6**/232–3; **3:47**/232; **3:63**/101; **3:64**/32; **3:67**/30; **3:84–5**/175–6; **3:86**/115; **3:97**/120; **3:103**/42; **3:113–14**/184; **3:144**/52; **3:159**/112

4 **Al-Nisā':** **4:34**/22, 149, 158–9n.44; **4:41**/239; **4:43**/126, 139; **4:65**/77; **4:135**/ 149, 174–5; **4:163–5**/46–7

5 **Al-Mā'idah:** **5:3**/30; **5:6**/117; **5:8**/174–5; **5:46–50**/232; **5:48**/29; **5:83**/168; **5:90**/126, 139–40; **5:91**/178; **5:116**/34–5; 232, 239

6 **Al-Anʻām:** **6:59**/36; **6:73**/36; **6:74**/30; **6:94**/245; **6:102–3**/35; **6:149**/41

7 **Al-Aʻrāf:** 42; 85; 234; **7:11–25**/39; **7:34–9**/248–9; **7:44**/247; **7:46–9**/242–3; **7:50–1**/247–8; **7:59–102**/234–5; **7:103–72**/235; **7:172**/155, 217–18, 252; **7:180**/204; **7:187**/239; **7:188**/52; **7:200**/38

8 **Al-Anfāl:** **8:1**/78; **8:2**/172; **8:9**/24; **8:17**/24; **8:24**/25, 35; **8:53**/25

9 **Al-Tawbah:** **9:5–6**/26; **9:5**/138; **9:30**/43; **9:100–1**/20; **9:113–14**/26

10 **Yūnus:** **10:38**/166; **10:57**/8; **10:61**/60, 85–6

11 Hūd: 42; 85–6; 234; 238; **11:13**/166; **11:25–95**/235–7; **11:28**/174; **11:37**/92; **11:63**/174; **11:73**/54n.8; **11:98–100**/237; **11:88**/174; **11:121–3**/237

12 Yūsuf: 5; 35; 44–5; 85–6; 88; 185; 231–2; 233; 253; 255; 256; **12:1–2**/8–9; **12:3–4**/231; **12:40**/34; **12:53**/46

13 Al-Ra'd: 85–6

14 Ibrāhīm: 85–6; **14:4**/46, 101; **14:7**/179; **14:24–6**/97–8

15 Al-Ḥijr: 85–6; 234; **15:26–44**/39; **15:26–7**/37; **15:45–99**/238

16 Al-Naḥl: 221; 226; **16:1–18**/222–4; **16:40**/36; **16:49**/221; **16:50–7**/221; **16:64–81**/224–5; **16:67**/139–40; **16:98**/38, 221; **16:101**/135, 136, 221; **16:102**/49; **16:103**/8; **16:110**/221; **16:125**/210

17 Al-Isrā' (Banī Isrā'īl): 206; **17:1**/51; **17:18**/116; **17:61–5**/39; **17:106–9**/168; **17:106**/3, 62; **17:110**/204; **17:174**/137

18 Al-Kahf: 43; 46; 185; 221; 253; 255–6; **18:9–26**/257–62; **18:12**/36; **18:21**/255; **18:23–4**/254; **18:29**/41; **18:30–9**/254; **18:32–4**/98; **18:45–9**/253; **18:45**/255; **18:50**/37, 39; **18:54–9**/255; **18:63**/38; **18:65–82**/262–4; **18:65**/255; **18:83–98**/264–5; **18:109**/265; **18:110**/265

19 Maryam: 85–6; 232–3; **19:23**/46; **19:24–6**/44; **19:27–9**/44; **19:32**/44; **19:35**/232; **19:41–9**/30; **19:58**/168

20 Ṭā Hā: 52; 85, 250; **20:8**/204; **20:115–23**/39

21 Al-Anbiyā': 42; 234; **21:51–7**/30; **21:51–70**/46

22 Al-Ḥajj: **22:17**/241; **22:26–9**/120; **22:33**/88; **22:52**/38,137; **22:78**/218

23 Al-Mu'minūn: **23:12–16**/107n.24; **23:24–5**/52; **23:115**/226

24 Al-Nūr: 134; **24:4**/21; **24:30–1**/146–7; **24:35**/83 ,98–100, 188; **24:39**/107n.43; **24:60**/147

25 Al-Furqān: 52; **25:7–10**/51; **25:32**/62, 185

26 Al-Shu'arā': 41; 85–6; 234; **26:69–191**/238

27 Al-Naml: 52; 85–6; **27:17**/37; **27:22–4**/44; **27:39**/37

28 Al-Qaṣaṣ: 52; 85–6; **28:49**/166

29 Al-'Ankabūt: 52; 85–6; 183; **29:41**/98; **29:50**/51

30 Al-Rūm: 85–6; **30:2–3**/167; **30:20–5**/219–20; **30:21**/22; **30:30**/218

31 Luqmān: 43; 85; 183; **31:27**/63

32 Al-Sajdah: 85

33 Al-Aḥzāb: 25, 28; **33:6**/28; **33:32–3**/145; **33:33**/27; **33:35**/22; **33:40**/23, 43; **33:49**/23; **33:56**/23; **33:59**/146; **33:66**/23; **33:72**/42, 155

34 Ṣabā': 234; **34:12–13**/37

35 Fāṭir: **35:11–17**/226–7

36 **Yā Sīn:** 85; 184; 185; 215n.29; 250; 252; 266; **36:2**/77; **36:29**/251; **36:33–79**/251–2; **36:65**/245; **36:69**/52; **36:71**/92

37 **Al-Ṣāffāt:** **37:35**/115; **37:50–7**/246; **37:96**/161; **37:101–9**/120; **37:130**/267

38 **Ṣād:** 85; **38:1**/77; **38:26**/155; **38:55–64**/249; **38:71–85**/39

39 **Al-Zumar:** **39:21**/247; **39:55–9**/246–7; **39:60**/247

40 **Ghāfir:** 52; 85–6; **40:7**/37; **40:11**/244; **40:16–19**/245; **40:45–6**/249; **40:47–50**/250; **40:52**/240; **40:68**/36

41 **Fuṣṣilat:** 85–6; **41:11**/92; **41:19–22**/245; **41:36**/38; **41:37**/3,186; **41:44**/9; **41:53**/266; **41:54**/161

42 **Al-Shūrā:** **42:38**/112; **42:51**/47

43 **Al-Zukhruf:** 62; 85; **43:1–4**/63; **43:3**/8

44 **Al-Dukhān:** 62; 85–6; **44:1–4**/61; **44:57–8**/237–8

45 **Al-Jāthiyah:** 85–6

46 **Al-Aḥqāf:** 85–6; 234

47 **Muḥammad:** 26

48 **Al-Fatḥ:** 27; **48:10**/92; **48:29**/115

49 **Al-Ḥujurāt:** **49:13**/28, 153; **49:14**/31; **49:18**/28

50 **Qāf:** 85; 240; **50:16**/35; **50:30**/242

51 **Al-Dhāriyāt:** **51:1–6**/76

53 **Al-Najm:** **53:1–18**/50; **53:19**/137

54 **Al-Qamar:** 234; **54:9–55**/238

55 **Al-Raḥmān:** 75; 77–8; 80; 227–9; 243; 250; 266; **55:1–13**/227–8; **55:8**/42; **55:13**/228; **55:15**/37; **55:60**/78,228–9

56 **Al-Wāqi'ah:** **56:1–14**/31–2; **56:7–14**/244; **56:83–94**/243–4; **56:88–94**/32

59 **Al-Ḥashr:** 26; **59:21**/63; **59:22–4**/205–6; **59:21**/205–6; **59:22–4**/208

66 **Al-Taḥrīm:** 21

67 **Al-Mulk:** 156; **67:1–5**/81; **67:6–10**/82; **67:30**/269

68 **Al-Qalam:** 85; **68:17–34**/98; **68:35–7**/80

69 **Al-Ḥāqqah:** **69:40–1**/52

71 **Nūḥ:** 5; 221; 236; 256

72 **Al-Jinn:** **72:1**/37

73 **Al-Muzzammil:** 48–9; **73:1–4**/185–6

74 **Al-Muddathir:** **74:30–1**/37

75 Al-Qiyāmah: 75:16–19/60; **75:22–3**/35; **75:34–5**/78

77 Al-Mursalāt: 76; 78; 229

78 Al-Nabā': 78:1–3/4

79 Al-Nāzi'āt: 77; **79:1–7**/76

81 Al-Takwīr: 81:1–19/241–2; **81:19–29**/49–50

82 Al-Infiṭār: 242; **82:17–18**/78

85 Al-Burūj: 85:21–2/62,136

90 Al-Balad: 2; **90:1–2**/77

91 Al-Shams: 75; 77

94 Al-Sharḥ: *19; 209

96 Iqrā' (Al-'Alaq)**:** 1; **96:1–5**/59; **96:18**/37

97 Al-Qadr: *61; 49; 75; 80–1; 213

99 Al-Zalzalah: *244

100 Al-'Ādiyāt: 75; 76

101 Al-Qāri'ah: 101:4–5/98

103 Al-'Asr: 75

105 Al-Fīl: 75

111 Al-Masad: *18; 79

112 Al-Ikhlāṣ: *32; *75; *196; 68; 188; 195–7; 202; 209; 215n.40

113 Al-Falaq: 79; 184

114 Al-Nās: *38; 79; 184

INDEX

Abd Al-Bāsiṭ 'Abd Al-Ṣamad (Qur'ān reciter) 58, 201
ablutions *see* purity
Abraham (Ibrāhīm), Prophet 16, 30, 43, 46, 52, 54, 79, 120–1, 217, 218, 246
abrogation *see naskh*
Abū Bakr 17, 18, 29, 67–8
Adam (Ādam), Prophet 13, 17, 41, 43, 191
aesthetics *see* moral aesthetics; recitation; visual arts
aging 147, 181, 224–5
ahl al-kahf ("people of the cave") 36, 253, 250, 256, 257–62
ahl al-kitāb see communities
'Ā'ishah (wife of Muḥammad) 21, 146, 149
"Alast," Day of (Q.7:172) 21, 146, 149; *see also* cosmogony; judgment day
alcohol 126–7, 129, 130, 131, 138–40; *see also naskh*
Alexander the Great *see* Dhū'l Qarnain
'Alī b. Abī Ṭālib 17, 18, 68, 96, 99–100, 140
Ali, Kecia, 159n.44
alms *see* charity; *zakāt*; *see also* development; poverty
America *see* United States of America
amulets *see* healing; mathematics; visual arts
angels 24, 34, 37, 51, 52, 170, 213; Jibrīl (Gabriel) 33, 37, 47, 49–50, 59; *see also* faith
Arabic (language) 8–9, 57, 59, 63, 82, 100–2, 162, 185, 191, 193, 195, 200, 207; *see also* inimitability; recitation of Qur'ān; translation
art *see* moral aesthetics; recitation; visual arts
asbāb al-nuzūl ("occasions of revelation") 16, 57, 66, 131–2, 134
Al-Ash'arī (classical scholar) 40, 93–4
al-asmā' al-ḥusnā ("names of God") 32, 34, 203–8, 209; *see also dhikr*; divinity
authority *see fiqh*; *imām*; politics; Qur'ānic sciences; Qur'ānic studies
āyāt ("signs" of God) 3, 51, 63, 155, 168, 219–21, 223–6, 229, 252, 266, 269; *see also* cosmogony; ethics; natural world; Qur'an, text
āyat al-kursi (Q.2:255) *see* throne, verse of the
āyat al-nūr (Q.24:35) *see* light, verse of
āyat al-ṣaif (Q.9:5) *see* sword, verse of the

Bangladesh 152, 155, 161, 212
Basmalah *see* pious expressions

belief *see* communities; divinity; faith; judgment day; knowledge, limits of; theology
Bible (Hebrew and Christian) 5, 97, 210, 230
Bismillāh *see* pious expressions
Bukhārī *see* *ḥadīth*
Butler, Judith 148

calendar 10, 262; *see also* Hijrah
calligraphy *see* visual arts; *see also* Qur'ān, text
cave, people of the *see* *ahl al-kahf*
charity 118; *see also* development; ethics; poverty; *zakāt*
children 44, 121, 149, 171, 180–1, 182, 183, 213, 225, 236, 241–2, 246, 263
Christianity *see* communities; Jesus; Mary; *see also* *ahl al-kahf*; divinity; prophets
climate change *see* environmental crisis
colonialism 143, 151, 154, 161; *see also* politics
communities 23, 26, 30, 32, 42, 104, 112, 148, 152, 172, 218, 233; Christians 16, 18, 34–5, 43, 169, 230, 253; diversity 28–9, 153; Jewish 16, 23, 43, 101, 230, 253; judgment of 31, 234–9, 250–1; polytheistic Arab 16, 34, 137; "people of the book" (*ahl al-kitāb*) 184; race 28, 142, 154; *see also* faith; hypocrites; politics; prophets; judgment day
conversion *see* faith
consumerism 144, 182
cosmogony 35, 217, 226–7; *see also* "*Alast*," Day of; *āyāt*; natural world
creation *see* cosmogony

da'wah (*dakwah*) 153, 160, 172, 210–12, 213
democracy *see* politics
Denny, Frederick 58, 155, 186, 269
development 53, 155, 159n.56; *see also* justice, social; politics; poverty
devil *see* satan
dhikr 7, 173, 177, 184, 203, 210; performance 208–9; and *samā'* (spiritual audition) 199, 203; *see also* *al-asmā' al-ḥusnā*; recitation; Sufism
Dhū'l Qarnain (Alexander the Great) 253, 256, 264–5
dialog *see* rhetoric
diversity *see* communities
divinity 35–6, 92–5, 186, 197, 204, 206–7, 219, 226–7; "God's speech" 9, 77, 222; idols, 28, 30, 34, 46, 164; *tawḥīd* (doctrine) 29, 32–3, 35, 164; *see also* cosmogony; faith; free will and predestination; *al-asmā' al-ḥusnā*; judgment day; knowledge, limits of; Mu'tazilite; theology
divorce *see* marriage and divorce
doctrine *see* faith; *see also* free will and predestination; *imām*; Mu'tazilite; Shi'ism; theology

ecology *see* *āyāt*; environmental crisis; ethics; natural world; oppression
education *see* teaching and learning; *see also* faith; *fiqh*
Egypt 151, 152, 153, 198, 203, 212
emotion 19, 202, 236, 246, 252, 259; reaction to Qur'ān 168–9; weeping, 168, 200, 201
environmental crisis 42, 155–6, 159n.57, 218, 266, 269; *see also* ethics, natural world
Ernst, Carl 193
Esack, Farid 142, 154
eschatology *see* judgment day
esotericism *see* Sufism; Shi'ism
ethics 42, 83, 105–6, 109, 129, 140, 149–50, 154, 155–6, 171, 172, 179, 182, 196, 210, 218, 219, 228, 240, 252, 269; *jihād* 27, 142, 149, 153, 154; *see also* *āyāt*; consumerism; environmental crisis; *fiqh*; gender; *ḥijāb*; hypocrites; intention; judgment day; justice, social; moral

aesthetics; oppression; peace; poverty; slavery; Sufism; war

faith 29, 30–1, 218; conversion 115, 169; "five beliefs" 11, 33–4, 46, 53; *shahādah* 35, 115, 188, 209; *see also* communities; divinity; "five pillars"; free will and predestination; judgment day
Farsi (Persian, language) 82, 101, 105, 151, 160; *see also* Iran; poetry
fashion *see* consumerism; *ḥijāb*
fasting *see* Ramaḍān
Al-Fātiḥah (first chapter of Qur'ān) 4, 69, 101, 187–9, 206, 209
feminism *see* gender; *see also* Ali, Kecia; Butler, Judith; progressive Islam; queer; Wadud, Amina; Wolf, Naomi
fiqh (jurisprudence) 25, 83, 102, 105, 110–12, 121–4, 132–3, 134, 138, 149, 172; *bid'ah* (innovation) 183; *ijtihād* (independent opinion) 149–50; *ijmā'* (consensus) 127; *ikhtilāf* (difference of opinion) 127; jurisprudential "schools" 102, 122–3, 127; legal assessments (*ḥalāl*, *ḥarām*, *sunnah*, etc.) 113, 182, 187; *qiyās* (analogical deduction) 126–7; *uṣūl al-fiqh* (intellectual roots of law) 123, 125–6; *see also* alcohol; *asbāb al-nuzūl*; ethics; faith; "five pillars"; *ḥadīth*; *ḥajj*; *ḥijāb*; knowledge, limits of; marriage and divorce; *naskh*; new media; oppression; politics; prayer; Qur'ānic sciences; Ramaḍān; Al-Shāfi'ī; *sharī'ah*; Shi'ism; slavery; *sunnah*; translation; *zakāt*
fire (*al-nār*) *see* heaven and hell
fitnah see communities; politics; war
"five beliefs" of Islam *see* faith
"five pillars" of Islam 33, 54n.11, 111, 113–21, 127, 143, 187; *see also* faith; Ḥajj; prayer; Ramaḍān; recitation; *zakāt*
free will and predestination 25, 36, 40–1; *see also* divinity; knowledge, limits of; satan; theology

Gabriel (Jibrīl) *see* angels
garden (*al-jannah*) *see* heaven and hell
gender 1, 22, 44, 55n.17, 103, 143–9, 158–9n.44, 169, 181–2, 183, 220, 226, 227; *see also* aging; *āyāt*; children; *ḥijāb*; justice, social; Mary; natural world; oppression; politics; progressive Islam; queer
George, Kenneth 195–6, 215n.33
Al-Ghazālī (classical scholar), 5, 73, 82, 94–95, 98–99, 128, 162–63, 167, 170, 197, 199–200, 202, 206–207
global warming *see* environmental crisis
God *see al-asmā' al-ḥusna*; *āyāt*; divinity; faith; free will and predestination; knowledge, limits of; rhetoric; *sharī'ah*; theology

ḥadīth 5, 6n.2, 15, 48, 71, 87, 89, 104–5, 111, 114, 123, 124–5, 128, 129, 132, 135, 141, 172, 173, 186, 188, 206, 213; *see also fiqh*; interpretation; Muḥammad; *sunnah*; teaching and learning
Ḥajj (pilgrimage) 53, 118, 120–1, 191; lesser pilgrimage 191; *see also* "five pillars"
Hamzah Fansuri *see* poetry
Hasan Basri (Qur'ān reciter) 202
Ḥasan of Baṣra 41, 95
healing 150, 183; "prophetic medicine" 182–3
heaven and hell 37, 53, 81–2, 239, 242–4, 246, 248–50; hell 178, 218; *see also* communities; judgment day; rhetoric
hell *see* heaven and hell
ḥijāb (modest dress) 143–8; *see also* gender
Hijrah (622 C.E.) 12, 19–20, 130; *see also* calendar
homosexual *see* queer
hypocrites (*munāfiqūn*) 21, 79–80, 221; *see also* ethics; oppression

Iblīṣ *see* satan
Ibn Al-ʻArabī (mystic) 93, 118, 136
Ibn Taimiyya (reformer) 150
iʻjāz see inimitability
ijmāʼ see fiqh
ijtihād see fiqh
imām: prayer leader 139, 187; Shiʻite authority 64, 65–6, 99–100, 122, 140; *see also* ʻAlī; Shiʻism
imān see faith
Indonesia 67, 142, 148, 153, 158n.35, 191, 193, 194–5, 201–202, 211, 213, 255–6; *see also* Malay; Southeast Asia
inimitability (*iʻjāz*) 5, 57, 73, 101–2, 163, 166–7, 169–70, 210, 230; *see also* knowledge, limits of; Qur'ān, text; rhetoric; theology; translation
insects *see* natural world
intention (*niyya*) 118, 188; *see also* ethics
internet *see* new media
interpretation 10–11, 12, 81–2, 92–5, 131, 142–3, 149, 154; Isrā'īliyāt 132, 229–30; *tafsīr* (exegesis) 56, 83, 87–91, 105, 151, 152, 153, 200; *ta'wīl* (interpretation) 88, 95, 97–8, 99–100; *see also* knowledge, limits of; "multifaceted"; translation
Iran 25, 95; *see also* Farsi
isrāʼ and *miʻrāj* ("night journey and ascent") *see* Muḥammad; *see also* Sufism
Isrā'īliyāt *see* interpretation; *see also* communities

jahiliyya ("ignorance") 152, 153; *see also* communities
Jesus (ʻIsa), Prophet 34–5, 43, 44, 45, 46, 52, 115, 232–3, 239
jihād see ethics; justice, social; oppression; war
jinn 34, 37, 166
Joseph (Yūsuf), Prophet 5, 34, 43, 36, 231–2, 253, 256
judgment day 31, 53–4, 169–70, 179, 189, 254; and past communities 233–9, 250–1; eschatology 98, 240–3; truth and testimony 35, 239, 244–7; *see also* communities; emotion; *fiqh*; heaven and hell; knowledge, limits of; *sharīʻah*
justice, social 149–50, 153, 154, 175; *see also* colonialism; development; ethics; *fiqh*; gender; oppression; politics; progressive Islam
"*juz' ʻammā*" (last thirtieth of Qur'ān) 3–4, 74, 77, 188

Kaʻbah 16, 120, 191, 192
Kadi Wadad 267n.12
kalām see theology
Kamali, Mohammad Hashim 93, 117, 124, 128–9, 134–5, 141
Khadījah (wife of Muḥammad) 17, 19, 49
Khiḍr (Khāḍir) 55n.14, 255, 262–4
knowledge, limits of 86–7, 94, 97, 99, 140, 207, 223, 231, 253, 355, 257, 161–2, 265
Kugle, Scott 159n.55

lailat al-qadr ("night of power") *see* Ramaḍān
law *see* ethics; *fiqh*; justice, social; new media; politics; *sharīʻah*
light, verse of (Q.24:35) 98–100
Lot (Lūṭ), Prophet 234, 236, 238

madhhab see fiqh
Malay (language) 105, 151, 161–2; *see also* Indonesia; poetry; Southeast Asia
Malcolm X (reformer) 154
marriage and divorce 21, 22–3, 181, 183, 220, 226; *see also* gender; Muḥammad
Mary (Maryam), mother of Jesus 28, 44, 46, 232–3
material culture *see* throne, verse of the; visual arts
mathematics 104, 184, 220, 261; *see also* Qur'ān, text
mawlid (*mulūd*) *see* Muḥammad

"Meccan and Medinan" *see* Qur'an, text; *see also* Muḥammad
medicine *see* ethics; *fiqh*; healing
memorization of Qur'ān 4, 171–82, 211; *see also dhikr*; teaching and learning
miḥnah ("trial" over Qur'ān) 164–5, 198; *see also i'jāz*; Mu'tazilite; politics; theology
modesty *see ḥijāb*
moral aesthetics 160, 162–3, 185, 190, 193, 195–7, 199–202, 211, 213, 217; *see also dhikr*; knowledge, limits of; recitation of Qur'ān; Qur'ānic sciences; Sufism; visual arts
Moses (Mūsā), Prophet 25, 38, 43, 46, 47, 52, 234, 235, 236–7, 255, 256, 262–4; story as political allegory 151, 154
Muḥammad, Prophet 15, 16–17, 19, 22–4, 28–9, 45, 47, 48–52, 78, 101, 131, 133, 169, 173, 182, 185, 188, 233, 250; wives of 21, 22–3, 145–6; veneration of (Mawlid, etc.) 23, 96, 197, 209; *see also* angels; *asbāb al-nuzūl*; emotion; *ḥadīth*; marriage and divorce; politics; Qur'an; *sunnah*
Muhammad 'Abduh (reformer) 151, 154
"multifaceted" Qur'ān 2, 7, 10, 11, 31, 48, 53, 103, 129, 219, 266; *see also* Arabic; interpretation; knowledge, limits of; rhetoric; translation
Mu'tazilite 91–4, 163–6
mysticism *see* Sufism

nabī see Muḥammad; prophets
Names of God *see al-asmā' al-ḥusnā*
naskh ("abrogation") 13, 57, 118, 119, 132–40, 221; *see also asbāb al-nuzūl*; *fiqh*; Qur'ānic sciences
nationalism *see* colonialism; politics
natural world 63, 81, 98, 155, 220–1, 222–5, 228, 241, 244, 269; *see also āyāt*; cosmogony; environmental crisis; judgment day
Nelson, Kristina 198, 199
new media 100, 103–5, 144, 147, 201
New Zealand 213, 268
Newby, Gordon 230–1
niyya see intention
"*nushūz* verse" (Q.4:34) 149, 158–59n.44; *see also* ethics; gender; marriage and divorce; oppression; progressive Islam

"occasions of revelation" *see asbāb al-nuzūl*
oppression, Qur'ānic concept 18–20, 42, 131, 142, 144, 149, 154, 155, 165; violence and preventing 140, 149–50, 158–9n.45; *see also* colonialism; communities; environmental crisis; ethics; gender; hypocrites; justice, social; peace; politics; poverty; progressive Islam; queer; slavery
orientalism *see* colonialism; Qur'ānic studies

Pakistan 152, 161, 212
peace 27, 61, 150; *see also* ethics; faith; justice, social
Persian *see* Farsi; Iran
philosophy *see* ethics; faith; moral aesthetics; Sufism; *see also* divinity; knowledge, limits of; *miḥnah*; prophets; Qur'ānic sciences
pilgrimage *see* Ḥajj
pious expressions 102–3, 184, 187, 203, 206, 208, 209, 254–5; Basmalah 2, 6n.1, 89–91, 97, 189; "*in shā' Allāh*" 103, 213
Pirous, A. D. (artist) 195–7, 202, 208
pluralism *see* communities; progressive Islam
poetry 48, 74–5, 82, 167; Hamzah Fansuri 161–2; Jalāluddīn Rūmī 160; *see also dhikr*; rhetoric
politics 28–9, 44, 112, 149, 151–4, 164–5, 182, 212; Islam and the state 119, 143; *see also*

politics (*cont.*): colonialism; communities; development; environmental crisis; ethics; *fiqh*; gender; *ḥijāb*; interpretation; justice, social; *miḥnah*; Moses; Muḥammad; new media; oppression; peace; poverty; progressive Islam; queer; Qur'anic studies; *salafī*; Sufism; teaching and learning; war
poverty 119, 150, 153, 155; *see also* charity; development; justice, social; *zakāt*
Powers, David 118, 119, 133, 136–7, 138
Powers, Paul R. 124
prayer 79, 116, 179, 189; *ṣalāt* 4, 33, 101–2, 116, 126, 137, 139, 184, 187–8; *see also dhikr*; Ramaḍān; "five pillars"
predestination *see* free will and predestination; *see also* divinity; knowledge, limits of; theology
progressive Islam 153–5; *see also* communities; *fiqh*; gender; oppression; peace; politics
prophets 25, 34, 43, 45, 47, 168, 175, 210, 229, 234–9; and scripture 46, 47, 101; named in Qur'an 42–3, 55n.13; terms for 45; *see also* Abraham; Adam; Bible; communities; faith; gender; Jesus; Joseph; judgment day; Lot; Mary; Moses; Muḥammad
purity 116, 139, 187, 232; ablutions (*wuḍū'*, etc.) 72, 116–18, 157n.4, 179; *see also* Mary; prayer

qiyās see fiqh
queer 154
Qur'ān, text 1, 7, 167; religious history of revelation (Meccan and Medinan) 2, 10, 12, 17, 66; structure 2–3, 3–4, 113, 129, 174–5; style, 9–10, 73–4; transmission and writing, 64, 67–8; *see also* Arabic; *asbāb al-nuzūl*; inimitability; memorization; Muḥammad; "multifaceted"; Qur'ānic sciences; Qur'ānic studies; Ramaḍān; recitation; rhetoric; teaching and learning; visual arts
Qur'anic sciences 56–7, 65–6, 109, 162, 165; categories of 124, 143; "clear and ambiguous", 84–5, 86, 135; "definitive and speculative" 114, 117, 141–2; "general and specific" 84–5, 87, 111, 131–2, 141; *see also fiqh*; interpretation; Qur'ān, text; Qur'ānic studies; recitation; rhetoric; teaching and learning
Qur'ānic studies, non-traditional 13–14, 64–6; orientalism and occidentalism 14–15, 64; *see also* colonialism; *fiqh*; Qur'ānic sciences; Religious Studies

race *see* communities; oppression
Rahman, Fazlur 66–7, 142, 219, 220, 240
Ramaḍān 118–19, 137, 185; *lailat al-qadr* ("night of power", *nuzūl Al-Qur'ān*) 61–2, 80–1, 213; *tarwiḥ* (prayers) 185, 213; *see also* "five pillars"; *naskh*
rasūl see Muḥammad, prophets
recitation of Qur'ān 3, 10, 38, 56, 58–60, 101–2, 134, 164, 169–70, 172, 184–8, 197–202, 211, 212; *qirā'āt* ("readings") 3, 69, 70–3; *see also* Arabic; *dhikr*; memorization; moral aesthetics; teaching and learning
Reinhart, A. Kevin 116–17
Religious Studies 14–15, 65
resurrection *see* judgment day
revelation *see asbāb al-nuzūl*; Qur'an, text; *see also* angels, *i'jāz*; Muḥammad
rhetoric and Qur'ān 73, 110, 167, 174–6, 228–9, 257–2, 269; dialog and address 78–82, 246, 247–9, 258–60; oaths 76–7, 241, 250; parables and similes 80, 97–100, 115, 250, 254; repetition 77–8;

rhymes 75–6, 227; rupture (*iltifāt*) 78, 176; *see also* Arabic; divinity; heaven and hell; inimitability; "multifaceted"; poetry; Qur'ān, text
ritual *see dhikr*; "five pillars"; Ḥajj; intention; Muḥammad; prayer; purity; Ramaḍān; recitation; *sunnah*
Rūmī, Jalāladdīn *see* poetry

Safi, Omid 155
Salafī (reformist) 151, 152
ṣalāt see prayer
satan 38, 121, 221; Iblīṣ 38–40, 256; "satans" 37, 81–2, 170; *see also* cosmogony; free will and predestination; prophets
"satanic verses" 38, 134, 137
ṣawm see Ramaḍān
Sayyid Quṭb (reformer) 152, 167
Sells, Michael 58, 74–5
Al-Shāfi'ī (classical scholar) 122, 123, 124, 125–6
shahādah see faith
shaiṭān see satan
sharī'ah 111, 112; *see also* divinity; ethics; *fiqh*; knowledge, limits of; politics; Qur'ānic sciences
Shi'ism 27–8, 83, 95, 96–100, 112, 122, 165; *see also* 'Alī b. Abī ṭālib; *imām*; interpretation; politics
"signs" of God *see āyāt*
sīrah (biography of Muḥammad) *see ḥadīth*; Muḥammad
slavery 148, 225
South Africa 142, 154, 210
Southeast Asia 148, 161, 197, 211; *see also* Indonesia, Malay
stewardship *see* environmental crisis; ethics; natural world; oppression
Sufism 25, 32, 44–5, 50, 75, 83, 95–6, 118, 136, 162, 166, 170, 191, 193, 203, 208–9, 210, 231, 252, 255, 266; *see also dhikr*; moral aesthetics
sunnah (model of Muḥammad) 48, 114, 117, 121, 124, 138; *see also fiqh*; *ḥadīth*; Muḥammad
sūrah see Qur'an, text
Al-Ṣūyūtī (classical scholar) 57, 138
sword, verse of the (Q.9:5) 138

Al-ṭabarī (classical scholar) 88–91, 94, 127, 135–6
tafsīr see interpretation
tajwīd see recitation
tarwiḥ see Ramaḍān; *see also* prayer
tawḥīd see divinity
teaching and learning 114, 173, 176–82, 186, 211–12; *see also ḥadīth*; memorization; new media
theology (*kalām*) 14, 40–1, 91–5, 165–6; *see also āyāt*; divinity; ethics; faith; free will and predestination; inimitability; knowledge, limits of; *sharī'ah*; Sufism; Mu'tazilite
throne, verse of the (Q.2:255) 33, 93–5, 131, 191, 193, 194
Tibawi, A. L. 101–3
tilāwah see recitation
translation 1, 2, 100, 101–3; *see also* Arabic; inimitability; interpretation; new media

'Umar b. Al-Khaṭṭāb 18, 21, 68, 168–9
Umm Kulthūm (Egyptian singer) 212
Urdu (language) 105, 151
'Uthmān b. 'Affān 68
United States of America 142, 144, 150, 154, 155, 210

veil *see* gender; *ḥijāb*; Sufism
visual arts 190–1; calligraphy 69, 193, 195, 211–12; painting 195–7; *see also* moral aesthetics; Qur'ān, text; throne, verse of the

Wadud, Amina 142, 149, 158–9n.44, 159n.55
war 78, 115, 130, 131, 150, 167; in time of Muḥammad 21, 23, 27; *see also* colonialism;

war (*cont.*):
communities; ethics; oppression; peace; politics
water *see āyāt*; natural world; *see also* environmental crisis; heaven and hell; poverty; purity
wine *see* alcohol
wives of Muḥammad *see* ʻĀ'ishah; Khadījah; *ḥijab*; marriage and divorce; Muḥammad
Wolf, Naomi 144
wuḍū' *see* purity

zakāt (legal alms) 112, 119; *see also* charity; development; ethics; "five pillars"; poverty
Al-Zamakhsharī (classical scholar) 86–7, 91, 93